JEWS AND ISLAMIC LAW IN EARLY 20TH-CENTURY YEMEN

INDIANA SERIES IN SEPHARDI AND MIZRAHI STUDIES

Harvey E. Goldberg and Matthias Lehmann, *editors*

JEWS AND ISLAMIC LAW
IN EARLY 20TH-CENTURY YEMEN

Mark S. Wagner

Indiana University Press
Bloomington & Indianapolis

This book is a publication of

Indiana University Press
Office of Scholarly Publishing
Herman B Wells Library 350
1320 East 10th Street
Bloomington, Indiana 47405 USA

iupress.indiana.edu

Telephone 800-842-6796
Fax 812-855-7931

∞ The paper used in this publication meets the minimum requirements of the American National Standard for Information Sciences—Permanence of Paper for Printed Library Materials, ANSI Z39.48-1992.

Manufactured in the United States of America

Library of Congress Cataloging-in-Publication Data

Wagner, Mark S.
Jews and Islamic law in early 20th-century Yemen / Mark S. Wagner.
pages cm. — (Indiana series in Sephardi and Mizrahi studies)
Includes bibliographical references and index.
ISBN 978-0-253-01482-5 (cloth : alk. paper) — ISBN 978-0-253-01487-0 (pbk. : alk. paper) — ISBN 978-0-253-01492-4 (ebook)
1. Jews—Legal status, laws, etc.—Yemen (Republic) 2. Dhimmis (Islamic law)—Yemen (Republic) 3. Jews—Yemen (Republic)—Social conditions—20th century. 4. Jews—Yemen (Republic)—Politics and government. 5. Jews—Yemen (Republic)—History—20th century. 6. Judaism—Relations—Islam. 7. Islam—Relations—Judaism. 8. Yemen (Republic)—Ethnic relations. I. Title.
DS135.Y4W34 2015
342.53308'5269—dc23

2014014186

1 2 3 4 5 20 19 18 17 16 15

For Eli and Oren

Contents

Acknowledgments *ix*
Note on Transliteration *xi*

Introduction *1*

1 The Islamic Judicial System and the Jews *16*

2 Changing God's Law *38*

3 Muslim Jews and Jewish Muslims *63*

4 Concord and Conflict in Economic Life *96*

5 Intercommunal Violence and the Sharīʿa *124*

Conclusion *151*

Notes *157*
Bibliography *189*
Index *201*

Acknowledgments

I COULD NOT HAVE conceived the ideas explored in this book without Bernard Haykel, with whom I studied as a graduate student at New York University. In a 2002 Arabic paleography tutorial, Bernard led me through Shawkānī's treatise on forcing the Jews of Yemen to collect excrement. Chapter 2 of this book revolves around this work. In October 2002 Princeton University's Woodrow Wilson School convened a workshop that focused on Sālim Saʿīd al-Jamal's relationship to Imām Yaḥyā called "Judaism and Islam in Yemen." There Bernard delivered a paper on Jamal's quest for legal sanction to ride his bicycle, which is also discussed in chapter 2. In this eye-opening paper, Bernard drew attention to the value of Jamal's published collections of documents, which hide in plain sight in the Jewish history section of most research libraries. Haykel's interpretation of the emergence of a branch of Salafism from within the Zaydī school, which he develops in *Revival and Reform in Islam: The Legacy of Muḥammad ʿAlī al-Shawkānī,* is fundamental to this book. Fundamental too is his suggestion of the willingness of Muslim thinkers who represented this intellectual trend to radically change the status quo of the relations between Muslims and non-Muslims.

The historian Menashe ʿAnzi, from the Ben-Zvi Institute in Jerusalem, possesses an encyclopedic knowledge of the literature written in Israel by Jews from Yemen. He has been a wonderful source of advice for me, and I would like to express my gratitude to him. Among other things, he taught me that Sālim Saʿīd al-Jamal's writings belong to a broad and rich world of writing by Jews from Yemen, some of whom acted as intermediaries with Muslim authorities and many of whom did not. I was fortunate to have had the opportunity to read his 2011 Hebrew University doctoral dissertation, "The Jews of Sanaa in an Era of Transition, a Historical Discussion in the Public Sphere: From the Ottoman Conquest until Their ʿAliyah to Israel, 1872–1950" (in Hebrew), but only after this book had been finished. Therefore, I leave it to readers to explore his fascinating work. I thank Sasson Somekh, who inspired me as a teacher and continues to inspire me.

Thanks also to the participants in the workshop "Marginality, Hierarchy, and Ethnicity in Muslim Societies," which met in Berlin in 2005 and Princeton in 2006, for their rigorous discussions of my work and its broader contexts. In this regard I am particularly indebted to Leor Halevi for his thoughtful comments on an early draft of this book. I also thank Gudrun Krämer and Mark Cohen, the conveners of this workshop, as well as Stefan Leder, who attended the Princeton meetings.

When I presented drafts of some material included in the book at meetings of the American Oriental Society, I benefited immensely from the thoughtful and erudite comments I received from scholars who attended. I would especially like to thank David S. Powers. I would also like to thank Lawrence Rosen and Bat-Zion Eraqi Klorman, who reviewed my manuscript for Indiana University Press. Professor Eraqi Klorman was kind enough to share with me her monumental social history of the Jews of Yemen. Professor Rosen, in turn, opened my eyes to the anthropological study of modern Islamic law courts.

I would like to express my deep gratitude to the Office of Research and Economic Development at Louisiana State University (LSU), which supported my writing part of this book with a summer stipend in 2009 and a junior faculty travel grant in 2010. I am grateful to the Louisiana Board of Regents for awarding me its ATLAS (Awards to Louisiana Artists and Scholars) grant and the LSU College of Humanities and Social Sciences for its support of my research during the 2011–2012 academic year. Thanks are due as well to Rabbi Ethan Linden and his wife, Liba Kornfeld, for their help in deciphering some puzzling Hebrew expressions.

Note on Transliteration

In transliterating Arabic, I have used the conventions of the *International Journal of Middle Eastern Studies* with two exceptions: (1) where the initial "a" in the definite article "*al-*" elides, I have written only "*l-*," and (2) "*ah*" indicates a *fatḥa* followed by a *tā marbūṭah.*

When transliterating Hebrew I used the Society for Biblical Literature's "general purpose style," with two further exceptions: I do not indicate the presence of *dagesh forte* in words that follow the definite article or the preposition "*mi-*," and a dot distinguishes the letter "*tet*" from the letter "*tav*" (i.e., "ṭ"). Unless otherwise noted, all translations are mine.

JEWS AND ISLAMIC LAW IN EARLY 20TH-CENTURY YEMEN

Introduction

Imagine a state ruled by a sovereign who enforced Islamic law (*sharī'a*). It was never conquered by a European imperial power, so its legal institutions survived the advent of the modern era more or less intact. The state is home to a sizeable population of non-Muslims. What could these non-Muslims expect from the Islamic legal system? Like any legal system, Islamic law applies to all people, yet it is predicated upon the superiority of the believer over the nonbeliever. Would non-Muslims in this imaginary state be humiliated, or treated fairly, or would they come to expect some combination of the two? Would they be satisfied with the Islamic legal system, or would they seek to change it? If they tried to change it, what might such reform look like in the absence of Enlightenment ideals of citizenship? Such a state would offer us a unique perspective on the thorny issue of the place of non-Muslims in Islamic law.

The idea that Islam is essentially tolerant of non-Muslims except for splinter groups that stray from the consensus constitutes an important trope in scholarship. Those scholars who take up such an approach seek to designate those Muslim traditions that accord with liberal norms of pluralism and human rights as normative.[1] Some scholars accept that both tolerant and intolerant statements concerning non-Muslims abound in Islamic literature and claim that the tolerant statements offer the possibility of saving the tradition from extremists.[2] Yet the practical benefit of reform to Islam's position on non-Muslims is difficult to discern. The sources of sharī'a envision a scenario in which a Muslim ruler and judicial apparatus act as the paternalistic protectors of non-Muslim minorities. Therefore, Yohanan Friedmann, for one, adjudges the application of conclusions drawn from this earlier period to the contemporary world a highly conjectural endeavor.[3]

Some scholars attempt to use a historical approach to explain the contradiction in the Islamic legal tradition between tolerant and intolerant positions toward non-Muslims by positing the hardening of Muslim attitudes toward non-Muslims over time.[4] Yet even those who make this argument concede that the presence of intolerant statements in the early period and tolerant statements in the later period makes theirs ultimately an unsatisfactory solution.[5] Khaled Abou

El-Fadl is surely correct in his description of tolerance in Islam as "fragile" and "contingent."[6] Another scholar, Ze'ev Maghen, speaks of Islam's "multifaceted and pendulating posture vis-à-vis the religio-cultural 'other' that partakes more of dialectic than dogma," or an "eclectic attitude to infidels."[7]

Fortunately we do not need to leave these fascinating questions to the realm of speculation. Yemen's sharīʿa-based legal system survived intact well into the twentieth century. There a sizeable non-Muslim (Jewish) population regularly came into contact with the Islamic courts. Despite Jews' rights to try cases in Jewish courts, Jews in Yemen and elsewhere in the Islamic world routinely brought legal matters, even those only involving Jews, to sharīʿa courts. Muslim jurists, by choice and by necessity, became embroiled in the most intimate details of their Jewish neighbors' lives. Individual Jews, in turn, knew enough about Islam to manipulate the system to their advantage. This book focuses upon attempts by three Jews who served as de facto lawyers within the Islamic judicial system—Sālim Saʿīd al-Jamal (1907–2001), Ṣāliḥ al-Ẓāhirī (1901–1986), and Sālim Manṣūrah (1916–2007)—to draw attention to and capitalize upon the tolerant strands within Islamic law, thus offering us a concrete alternative to speculation.

Yemen is a mountainous country at the southern tip of the Arabian Peninsula. Its rainfall is plentiful compared to the rest of Arabia, and thus it is a predominantly agricultural society. Its geographical isolation made it very difficult for the Ottomans to conquer and keep. With the exception of the port city of Aden and its environs at the southern tip of the country, it was never colonized. Most Muslims in the country belong to the Zaydī sect, a branch of Shiʿite Islam. For a short time there was a Zaydī state in Iran on the shores of the Caspian Sea, but from 897 until the revolution of 1962, Zaydism has been identified with Yemen. With the exception of two periods of Ottoman rule (1517–1636 and 1873–1918), one imām (or several competitors) exercised political power over Yemen. That said, Yemen's strong tribes continuously challenged the centralization of authority.

This book focuses largely upon the reigns of Imām Yaḥyā (1869–1948) and his son Aḥmad (1891–1962). Imām Yaḥyā played an important role in shaping the institutions of modern Yemen, including its legal system. In 1918 he brought Ottoman rule to an end. In 1948 reformist opponents of his regime assassinated him. Their new government lasted only a matter of weeks before Yaḥyā's son Aḥmad took power. Shortly after Aḥmad's death in 1962, a revolutionary regime much like Egypt's Free Officers Movement (and backed by Egyptian military forces) took power in Yemen and has held it ever since.[8]

Yemen was the home to a substantial Jewish community, numbering some 50,000–60,000 out of a total population of 3.5–4 million on the eve of their emigration to Israel in 1949–1950. A combination of economic, religious, and political reasons spurred on this mass emigration. In Yemen the terms "non-Muslim" and "Jew" have virtually one and the same meaning. In this book, where I use the term "non-Muslim" when translating or paraphrasing Arabic sources, the sources themselves use the term "*dhimmī*," which means a follower of a scriptural religion who has entered into an agreement of protection (*'ahd al-dhimmah*) with the Islamic state. Those Muslims in Yemen who especially disliked Jews created an alternative (and false) etymology for the word "dhimmī" by linking it to the Arabic word for "blame" (*dhamm*), thus making "non-Muslim" mean "blameworthy."[9]

Imāms Yaḥyā and Aḥmad were the Zaydī imāms and as such served as both theocratic rulers and chief legal authorities of Yemen (and, in theory at least, of all of Islam). A historian notes that the office of Zaydī imām recognized no separation of powers. It was at once legislative, executive, and judicial in nature.[10] For Zaydī Muslims, who constitute the vast majority of the population of northern Yemen, Imām Yaḥyā was both the Commander of the Faithful, an office that extended back to the earliest years of Islam, and one who could present to his flock the fruits of his independent legal reasoning (called *ijtihād* in Arabic). Insofar as the imām was both ruler and theocrat, Islamic law was, to some extent, what he said it was.

Cases involving Jews in Yemen in the first half of the twentieth century shed light on the broader question of Islamic law's position on non-Muslims. Their broad applicability stems from three factors. First of all, prior to the revolution of 1962 in Yemen, a fully functioning judicial system operated along the lines envisioned by classical Islamic jurisprudence. This system routinely tried cases involving non-Muslims. One would be hard pressed to find a parallel in other parts of the Islamic world with similarly traditional legal systems (in Saudi Arabia, for example). Second, the Muslim jurists in question considered a wide variety of sources from the Islamic legal tradition in making their rulings. "The Zaydī tradition," writes Ahmad Dallal, "is of interest not only because of its continuity, but also because it is informed by all the other Muslim legal traditions."[11] Thus, a given attempt to grapple with an issue brought before their courts by non-Muslims often represented a synopsis of pan-Islamic juristic opinion on the topic. Finally, intellectuals in the broader Arab-Islamic world looked to Yemen as a model for a just society governed by Islamic law. For at least some Muslim reformers, Imām Yaḥyā represented a Muslim ruler who was unsullied by compromise with colonial powers. For example, an influential twentieth-century modernist cleric named Muḥammad Rashīd Riḍā argued that Yemen's theocratic ruler, Imām Yaḥyā, ought to be the caliph—the leader of the Islamic world.[12] 'Abd al-Raḥmān al-Kawākibī and Shakīb Arslān, prominent reformers who had also met the imām, held similarly romantic ideas concerning the leadership potential of the Arabs of the Arabian Peninsula (including both Yemen and Saudi Arabia).[13] Bernard Haykel surmises that the imām "may have toyed with the idea of being caliph."[14] And indeed in 1923 Imām Yaḥyā claimed the mantle of the caliphate for himself, publishing, as "Commander of the Faithful" in Egyptian and Syrian newspapers, a proclamation calling upon Muslims to rally around the sharīʿa and defend against foreign powers.[15]

The romantic idea that Yemen gave birth to reformers free from foreign influence may have led other Arabs to support members of the opposition to the imām. A prominent reformer with a pan-Islamic reputation, Muslim Brotherhood founder Ḥasan al-Bannāʾ, is said to have expressed enthusiasm for the reformist "Free Yemenis Party" that briefly toppled the regime. This, claims historian Abdualaziz Msaodi, stemmed from this particular stereotype about Yemen.[16]

Although it was staunchly Islamic and fiercely independent, the sharīʿa did not represent the only legal system in Yemen. Because Yemen is a tribal society, it is important to note that in the rural villages, where the majority of Jews (perhaps 85 percent) lived, authority figures other than the imām could be more important than him on a day-to-day basis. Moreover, tribal law and custom possessed some autonomy from, and at times conflicted with, the sharīʿa as articulated by urban men of learning. In Yemen the Qurʾanic word "*ṭāghūt*," which might ordinarily mean "idolatry," had the specific connotation of a tribal practice that religious scholars (*ulama*) considered in conflict with Islam.[17]

An undated fatwa that addresses the question of whether tribal law is so objectionable that it makes tribesmen infidels catalogs the ulama's grievances against tribal law and tribesmen: under tribal law, damages imposed on a murderer varied widely according to the status of the deceased.[18] Tribesmen were considered incorrigible robbers.[19] According to the fatwa, women, who, in theory, inherit under sharīʿa, did not inherit under tribal law.[20]

The ulama variously complained that tribal women were alternatively either unduly oppressed or too free. The fatwa writer alleges that tribal women were forced to marry their cousins.[21] Yet a seventeenth-century writer complains that the people of northernmost Yemen allowed a woman to leave her husband and remarry whenever and whomever she wanted.[22] In matters relating to sexual morality, tribal norms differed substantially from sharīʿa norms. Anthropologist Walter Dostal discusses the "phenomenon of socially permitted pre- and extramarital sexual relations practiced by girls and wives in South Arabian tribes."[23] Karl Rathjens, who did research in Yemen in the mid-1930s, wrote in 1951 that among tribes in northern and eastern Yemen, "offering women as sexual hospitality (*Gastfreundschaftsprostitution*) is still common."[24] Rathjens also said that women who owned hostels for male travelers in towns and villages of highland Yemen made prostitutes available to their guests.[25] Two Jewish writers who describe such specialized hostels in Ibb and Laḥj, both run by widows, say that guests were notable Muslims and Jews.[26] One contemporary Yemeni *qadi* (Muslim judge) complains bitterly that tribal *shaykhs* marry off pregnant unmarried women without following the sharīʿa's rules governing fornication. He also decries his colleagues' general acquiescence to the decisions reached by tribal judges and the meddling of shaykhs in Islamic law.[27]

For their part, Jews also tended to exaggerate the conflict between, on one hand, tribal norms and the shaykhs who enforced them and, on the other, the sharīʿa and its functionaries. However, they often portrayed tribal law as having been more just. Where the learned Muslim of the city saw the tribal law as benighted and crude, Jews might portray the shaykh and his code as the embodiment of goodness. If something went as it ought to have gone, a Jew might say, "It is the shaykh's work," and if it went poorly he might say, "It is the jurisprudent's work."[28] One Jewish writer claims that the famous tribal Nuʿmān clan loved the Jews so much that when one son was born they asked a Jewish bibliomancer for a suitable name. He was called "Muqbil" after the last consonants in the names of the Jewish patriarchs: Abraham, Isaac, Jacob, and Israel.[29]

Yet despite the disparity between law and tribal custom and the use of polemical language to characterize it, examples of accord between tribal leadership and men of learning are legion. A judicial clerk in a small village produced an Islamic legal document finalizing the separation of a Jewish couple. The document lists the shaykh and other tribesmen as witnesses, showing the interrelationship of the two sets of norms and authorities.[30] In addition, the sharīʿa enjoyed pan-Islamic legitimacy. Thus it represented the final authority in a way that tribal law did not.

From a literary perspective, memoirs by Jews from Yemen tend to consist of dramatic anecdotes describing conflicts and their resolution. In many of them the audience before the sharīʿa authority (whether that was qadi, provincial governor, or the imām himself) represents the stage for a given anecdote's dramatic denouement. This suggests that for Jews, as well as Muslims, the sharīʿa court, broadly defined, was the place where vindication could be found and finalized. Lawrence Rosen observes that litigants who appear in court often seek an audience for their stories over and above compensatory damages.[31] For both parties the court was the most charged stage for the dramatization of Muslim-Jewish relations.

Thus the idea that early twentieth-century Yemen constituted an ideal laboratory setting for the study of the status of non-Muslims in the sharīʿa requires three major qualifications: (1) tribal law routinely interacted with Islamic law; (2) to some extent, Zaydīs granted carte blanche to their theocratic rulers; and (3) Jews' dramatic courtroom anecdotes might not necessarily mean that legal issues were foremost in their mind. They may have simply made the best stories.

The three prominent Jewish men who worked as intermediaries in Yemen's Islamic legal system left behind a wealth of such anecdotes and documentation. In 1931 a Jew, Rabbi Sālim Saʿīd al-Jamal, bought one of the first bicycles in Sanaa, the capital of Yemen. For the next six years he routinely appeared before sharīʿa court judges, arguing for his right to ride his bicycle outside of the walls of the Jewish Quarter of Sanaa and obtaining official documentation for his progress. Muslim religious legislation that aimed to reinforce the supremacy of Muslims over non-Muslims contained a stipulation forbidding non-Muslims from riding horses or mules. Jamal sought to use his bicycle as a "wedge issue" that would undermine all Muslim sumptuary legislation. He claimed that his struggle to obtain a de facto bicycle license from the sharīʿa courts nearly cost him his life.

In 1939 Rabbi Ṣāliḥ al-Ẓāhirī planned and executed an elaborate plot to avenge his honor and that of the Jews of the city of Radāʿ upon a powerful qadi from Sanaa who had moved there. Despite a prohibition against non-Muslims testifying against Muslims, al-Ẓāhirī succeeded in having the qadi publicly beaten and humiliated by a Jew despite the local sharīʿa court's attention to the affair. Two years later he arranged for Imām Yaḥyā's retinue to be met with a novel display as it passed Radāʿ: a flag of al-Ẓāhirī's design that depicted the local regime's symbols of Islamic legitimacy—namely, the crescent moon, stars, and sword of the caliphs, with a (Zionist) Star of David in the center. Several qadis objected to the flag, but al-Ẓāhirī lobbied the imām for the right to hoist it and won.

By 1949 Imām Yaḥyā had been assassinated and his son Aḥmad had become imām, the State of Israel was established, and most of Yemen's Jews were making preparations to leave Yemen for Israel. Rabbi Sālim Manṣūrah, a Jew from Sanaa, became Imām Aḥmad's Jewish point man in Taʿizz. There he received missives from Jews reporting rampant abuse by Muslims, and he pressed Imām Aḥmad to act. Under the rabbi's influence, the imām acted against the mayor of a small town for having seized the property of the Jews there, fined and jailed another qadi and mayor who had imprisoned the Jews of their town on suspicion of selling alcohol to Muslims, arrested and imprisoned a tribal shaykh who had kidnapped a thirteen-year-old Jewish girl when her family passed through his territory on their way to Israel, and personally whipped a shaykh who had robbed a Jewish family on their way out of his village.

Jamal, Ẓāhirī, and Manṣūrah had much in common. They worked as merchants and their business ventures included catering to the tastes of the Muslim upper class—namely, sales of luxury goods like perfume and alcohol (the latter was illegal). Imām Yaḥyā had the home of Manṣūrah's father, Yaʿīsh, demolished because the father had sold alcohol to Muslims.[32] The three men were independently wealthy. Their families possessed large holdings of property and agricultural land. They enjoyed unusually strong connections with the imāms (either Yaḥyā or Aḥmad). Their knowledge of Islamic law was remarkably good for Jews, so much so that Muslims asked them for their help in drafting petitions and in other legal jobs. They were attorneys in practice, if not in theory.

Although they were learned in the Jewish tradition, none of the three served as chief rabbi, the official position of leadership in the Jewish community of

Yemen. They were unofficial "fixers," "operators," or intermediaries, who were sought out by Jews for their connections with the world of the Muslim learned elite and sought out by Muslims for their lack of entanglement in tribal and other intra-Islamic loyalties, their closeness to the ruling class, and their skills.

During World War II Yemen suffered from severe economic hardship, famine, and epidemics that led to the deaths of a sizeable portion of the country's population, both Muslim and Jewish. Muslim opponents of the regime alleged that the government was at fault, squirreling away (or even selling abroad) needed grain stores.[33] Jews (and some Muslim writers) argued that the opposite was the case.[34] Regardless of government response (or lack thereof), many Yemenis died of disease and starvation during the war. Nissim Gamlieli estimates that a third of the Jewish population perished from disease between 1941 and 1943.[35] A Muslim writer says that in 1943 in the town of Ibb, a local Jew donated burial shrouds for Muslim famine victims to the Muslim leader (*faqīh*) responsible for preparing the bodies for burial. The fact that such meager public services had to be provided by a Jew illustrates the hardheartedness of the regime.[36]

The three Jewish intermediaries left Yemen for Israel at various points in the 1940s. In their old age (1980s-present) they self-published or used obscure Israeli presses to disseminate accounts of their activities in Yemen. Each man seems to have been acutely aware that the world of Muslim-Jewish interaction of their youth had vanished and that each one had an important role to play in preserving its memory for posterity. Nevertheless, these accounts differed substantially in terms of the persona that each man attempted to craft for himself.

From the late 1920s until he left Yemen for Palestine in 1944, Rabbi Sālim Saʿīd al-Jamal served as an advisor, a "point man" on Jewish affairs, and tax collector for Imām Yaḥyā Ḥamīd al-Dīn. Jamal, who was the most prolific of the three intermediaries by a substantial margin, portrayed himself as a civil rights lawyer. His books are peppered with provocations to the sharīʿa courts that he engineered in the 1920s and 1930s. The image of a rabbi hurtling past disapproving Muslims on a bicycle shows us a man who used the Islamic legal tradition to expand the rights of his community and, by extension, non-Muslim minorities in general. For Western audiences the bicycle episode appears to affirm a familiar motif of development theory, whereby Europe's intellectual and technological innovations show Middle Easterners the escape route from their own backwardness.

Jamal was intimately familiar with the practical workings of Muslim law courts, and his attempts to improve the legal situation of Jews in Yemen demonstrate the possibilities for the expansion of minority rights within Islamic law, as well as their structural limitations. Moreover, Jamal understood that the Islamic legal tradition was not monolithic in its treatment of non-Muslims. For him, the fact that some Muslim jurists could be harsh, some lenient, and both firmly backed by authoritative sources was a reality to be embraced and exploited in the quest for expanding legal rights and breaking down the boundaries between Muslim and non-Muslim.

Yet Jamal's work, like that of the two other Jewish intermediaries discussed in this book, betrays a tension between the subject's self-interest and his larger program of philanthropy and political activism. Jamal explains that he sought to provoke the courts with his bicycle "because since my youth I have not been able to tolerate the denial of human freedom."[37] However, it seems that Jamal was the primary beneficiary of his legal stratagems, the vast majority of which did not measurably advance the cause of non-Muslims under sharīʿa, which he claims was their main goal.

Whether one assumes that Jamal had a civil rights program at the time of the events or whether it was a retrospective projection, his project and the documentary evidence he offers give us a valuable and unique window on relations between Muslims and non-Muslims. Although he judged the sharīʿa's limitations upon non-Muslims to be fundamentally unfair, he presented his critique of it from within an acceptance of its enduring value as a legal system for all people. Put another way, when in his eighties he described to an audience of Israeli Jews the provocations to the sharīʿa courts he had undertaken as a young man in Yemen, he maintained that he had merely sought to teach his Muslim interlocutors the fairness implicit within their own legal system.

One series of court documents published by Jamal details an affront to his honor that was perpetrated by Muslim soldiers and Jewish rivals. These men conducted a surprise inspection of Jamal's house and saw his wife's underwear drying on the clothesline.[38] In court Jamal insisted that this viewing of his wife's undergarments harmed his status.[39] This anecdote is a reminder that while his outrage at the "denial of human freedom" may have motivated his provocations, his primary aim was to raise the status of Jewish men in Yemen rather than that of other low-status groups such as women and blacks.

The following pair of anecdotes illustrates the highly defined social hierarchy in Yemen. In the first, Imām Yaḥyā had a bodyguard, a black slave named Ṣumṣām Tawfīq b. ʿAbdallāh. After Ṣumṣām was manumitted, he was unable to find a Muslim woman to marry. Thus he chose a Jewish woman, older and unmarried, who agreed to convert to Islam and marry him.[40] One Jewish writer explains that society comprised three classes, each of which had its own elite: *sayyids*, who descended from the prophet Muḥammad; tribesmen, some of whom were immensely powerful; and those who held low-status professions or were black but who in some cases were rich. A Jewish woman who converted and was not a virgin could only marry a man from the last group.[41] Imām Yaḥyā himself is said to have had a dark complexion, a fact one author points out to explain his legendary antipathy toward photographers.[42]

In the second case, a poor Jewish woman from a small village in the south with the unusual name Ghazāl al-Tayyis ("Gazelle the He-Goat") was known for being exceptionally stubborn and litigious. After a land dispute with two Muslim men, she grabbed her sleeping bag and a torch and traveled to the provincial capital, Yarīm. There she stood out from the crowd of justice seekers at the governor's court by burning the torch, wrapping her sleeping bag around her head in the style of a learned Muslim's turban, and calling loudly for action: "My lord, I will use God and the sharīʿa of Muḥammad b. ʿAbdallāh to squeeze you." The governor was not offended but in fact paid for her food and lodging until her Muslim foes were brought by his soldiers the next day. The Jewish woman and the Muslim men each documented their claims of ownership, and the governor ruled in favor of the woman, offering the men a choice between a fine and a month in jail. At the conclusion of the proceeding the three Muslim men joked that Ghazāl al-Tayyis was both a he-goat, as her name implied, and a "man's man" (*rajjāl*).[43]

Ghazāl also caused problems for the rabbinic authorities. One morning she burned wood in her stove in order to bake bread. The wood gave off a lot of smoke, much of which wafted into the village synagogue next door. The rabbi, with whom she had clashed before, threatened to issue a ban of excommunication against her if she did not put out the fire. The narrator of this anecdote says that when the rabbi made this threat, "she leaped from where she was sitting like a lioness, stood in front of him prepared for battle, and with her sooty face said, 'I am taking you to the [Muslim] judge.'"

She left the bread to burn in the oven, traveled to Yarīm, and convinced the governor to send three soldiers with her back to the village. The rabbi had to feed the soldiers well and pay them for their effort. The next day the woman, the rabbi, and the soldiers traveled to the court in Yarīm. When the woman complained that the rabbi had excommunicated her unjustly, the rabbi countered that the woman was by nature rebellious toward authority. The judge ordered the two Jews to split the fee for the soldiers and advised the woman: "Do what your learned men say and listen to them."[44]

While the rabbi suffered financially for his harsh judgment, the sharīʿa court judge accepted his argument that the woman was a rebel (a "*nāshizah*" in Muslim terms), making her an unworthy candidate on whose behalf the judge might challenge the authority of the Jewish religious establishment. While the woman had reason to believe she would find a fair-minded third party in the Muslim court, this judge conformed to Lawrence Rosen's paradigm for sharīʿa court judges' decisions; he restored the litigants to the social position they occupied before the outbreak of the dispute, "get[ting] people back into working relationships—contentious as they may be—rather than . . . solv[ing] matters in a way that ignores future ties."[45] Indeed, in a similar case involving litigants from the same village, a Jew who had slaughtered a cow without having received the proper certification as a kosher slaughterer protested his excommunication. The governor in Yarīm upheld the rabbis' authority and punished the errant butcher.[46]

These anecdotes show the power the Jewish elders wielded over other Jews, a power that the reformers in question were concerned with upholding. Nevertheless, although they were wealthy and learned men, respect was denied them because of their Jewishness, a fact that continually irritated them.

A Jewish joke revolved around a Muslim superstition, specifically the idea that the prophet Muḥammad guards the gate of paradise. (I have given the story a prosaic translation to emphasize the humor.) A Muslim was perplexed after observing a Jewish funeral, during which seven stops were made for the delivery of eulogies. From a distance it looked as if the Jews were telling the deceased something. When the Muslim brought a shoe to a Jewish cobbler for repair, he asked what it was that the Jews had said. The cobbler decided to play a trick on the Muslim. He warned him that this information was a secret that could not be revealed to outsiders. After the Muslim pleaded with him, offered to pay a hefty sum, and swore to secrecy, the cobbler told him the "secret." Seven times, once for each of the seven days of the week of mourning, the dead man was advised that when he got to the outskirts of paradise he must take a side path that led to the back window. The Muslim asked, "Why do they tell him to take a side path?" The Jew explained that the prophet Muḥammad allowed only Muslims through the gate and sent the rest to hell.

The Muslim was outraged and, despite his promise of discretion, loudly cursed the Jews: "You Jews are the biggest cheats, going in through the back window and taking up all of the space in heaven. I swear that today I will climb to the roof of my house and jump off, so that I may die and tell the prophet Muḥammad: 'Close the back window!'"[47]

The joke summarizes both the Jewish idea that Jewish advancement in a Muslim world required a certain amount of ingenuity, even ruthless trickery, on the part of Jews themselves, an idea that was central to the Jewish intermediaries' quest for social status, and the Muslim idea that there were Jews who were crafty enough to make it happen. Their heaven was the paradise on earth of status, respect, and wealth. It also provides an apt metaphor for the present study of Islamic law using accounts of Jewish intermediaries. Given their relatively high status, this is not the social historian's "view from below," but rather a view through the back window.

Unlike al-Jamal, who portrayed himself as a principled reformer, the intermediary Ṣāliḥ al-Ẓāhirī, who had a qadi beaten up and got away with it and waved an eccentric Zionist flag before Imām Yaḥyā, reveled in the sort of deception on display in the joke about the cobbler. Ẓāhirī (and his son Mordecai, who compiled several of his works) portrays himself as a keen observer of social dynamics who succeeded in shifting power from Muslims to Jews; a staunch Zionist; and a loyalist to Imām Yaḥyā.

There is, however, good reason to count Ẓāhirī among the opponents of the imāms.[48] Mordecai says of his father that the Muslim judges "regarded him as a wise man and a brilliant jurist but also feared him and his involvement in a matter because of the imām's special relationship with him."[49] His knowledge was comprehensive enough that on one occasion, disguised as a qadi, he stopped in a small village while evading pursuit by government soldiers. A Muslim family asked him to resolve an inheritance dispute of theirs, which he did. He produced a fatwa for them and collected his fee.[50]

While knowledgeable in the sharīʿa, Ẓāhirī exhibited a wily character that viewed Islamic law as a game to be mastered in the pursuit of power. However, insofar as many other (Muslim) players habitually cheated through bribery, corruption, and deceit, he did not hold Islamic law in the same regard as Jamal. As with Jamal, the relationship between Ẓāhirī's personal quest for the same level of respectability that learned Muslim men enjoyed and his agenda of empowering the Jews is ambiguous. At the end of the story about his odd flag, Mordecai reports that a saying about his father circulated among Muslims that ran "there is none like Ṣāliḥ among the Jews—in good breeding and manners he is one of the Zaydīs."[51] In his autobiographical books, the elder Ẓāhirī demonstrated the clever stratagems that enabled him to circumvent the stigma of being a Jew in order to be considered "one of the Zaydīs." Ẓāhirī's perspective, which stresses the dark underside of the sharīʿa in relations between Muslims and Jews in Yemen, offers an instructive counterpoint to Jamal's idealistic picture of relations between Muslims and non-Muslims.

The third intermediary, Sālim Manṣūrah, lobbied Imām Aḥmad to crack down on Muslims who took advantage of Jews who sought to leave Yemen. His account of his activities includes a chapter containing documents that Dāwud Ṣubayrī, Imām Aḥmad's tailor, had sent to him "so that they would be published and so that his good name would be remembered forever."[52] This sentiment puts in a nutshell these writers' and other Yemeni Jewish memoirists' appreciation of their own historical significance and their desire to offer a particular portrait of themselves to others. Like Jamal and Ẓāhirī, Manṣūrah was unusually knowledgeable in Islamic law. While incarcerated after the 1948 assassination of Imām Yaḥyā, he was approached by Muslim prisoners who asked him to write petitions to Imām Aḥmad on their behalf.[53]

Paradoxically, Manṣūrah, like Ẓāhirī, portrays himself as both an ardent Zionist, through his activity on behalf of Jews who sought to emigrate to Israel, and a zealous partisan of imāmic rule. Manṣūrah's loyalty and admiration for Imām Aḥmad runs through his work, even as the evidence he compiles points to the imām's hand in impeding Jewish emigration and enriching himself at the expense of Jews. Imām Aḥmad appears as a near-demonic figure in most Muslim sources in Arabic (and in secondary works in European languages). In contrast, Manṣūrah idolizes him as a paragon of justice and a great friend to the Jews. The scholar Tudor Parfitt describes the tendency of Jews from Yemen to venerate the imāms as a species of Stockholm syndrome when he ascribes it to a "psychology of the oppressed which magnified any act of justice and cast a net of oblivion over the persecution, which after all was a banal and permanent feature of day to day life."[54] Thus the intermediary Manṣūrah joins the company of the civil rights lawyer Jamal and the nihilistic Ẓāhirī as a staunch monarchist. Having said this, the "court Jew" paradigm holds some drawbacks. While the imām wielded considerable power, he exercised it within the limits imposed by Zaydī law. Despite their officially theocratic status, Imāms Yaḥyā and Aḥmad faced stiff competition with other local Muslims, including judicial authorities, and often lost.

Where do we find discussions of Jews in the Islamic legal system? While works of Islamic law abound with questions involving non-Muslims, they are often merely hypothetical situations. Yemeni sources in Arabic generally deal with politically significant learned Muslim men; they do not mention the vast majority of Jews and ordinary Muslims who play roles in this book. Thus, in addition to works on Islamic law and autobiographical materials in Arabic, Jewish sources in Hebrew also have been mined extensively. The period between the 1980s and the turn of the twenty-first century witnessed a flurry of autobiographical writing by Jews from Yemen in Israel. I consulted approximately fifty largely self-published books by Jews from Yemen, including works by the three intermediaries. (Although these are not the only books I used, they contribute a significant percentage of the material discussed here, material that has not been discussed elsewhere in English.) These works all contain narratives, and sometimes documents, relating to Jews in Muslim courts. The memoirs pose a unique set of problems. They give verbatim conversations in Arabic and are arbitrarily organized and anecdotal. They emphasize the authors' success and bravery in outwitting villainous Muslims, and although each teems with anecdotes, they seldom corroborate one another.

Sharply dividing factual accounts of life in Yemen from folkloristic material presents difficulties as well. Works that purport to be documentary in nature include storytelling motifs. For example, the sudden death of the wicked (including a number of qadis) is a stock theme in Gil'ad Tsadoq's (folkloristic) *Memory of Yemen.*[55] The non-Jew's miraculous inability to harm a Jew crops up in Ṣāliḥ al-Ẓāhirī's *Stormy Life,* among other sources. More broadly, both Muslim and Jewish Yemeni folktales disseminate the idea that the righteous are rewarded and the wicked punished in this world. One Jew remarks of such tales, "A person is swept up by the tension and adventure, but at the end he is relieved at seeing what is reflected of 'sin and punishment' and the victory of justice over injustice."[56] Arabist Stefan Leder finds the same problem in classical Arabic literature, which did not sharply delineate serious, instructive, and truth-centered narratives from nonfactual, entertaining narration and where even the latter category involved real people rather than invented characters. His observation that learned texts oscillate between factual and fictional bears repeating with reference to the material at hand.[57]

One particular case illustrates the problem. An event that Sālim Saʿīd al-Jamal described as factual is certainly fictive. Ṣāliḥ al-Ẓāhirī's son Mordecai says that Jamal had delusions of grandeur.[58] Less pointedly, scholar Kerstin Hünefeld aptly dubbed the quality of Jamal's account of his activities in Yemen as "egocentric."[59] In 2000 Jamal produced "The Scroll of Salvation," a lurid account of a meeting he had with the Palestinian hajj Amīn al-Husseini in Yemen in 1936, but it is doubtful that this meeting took place.[60] There is no easy solution to the fact that Sālim Saʿīd's works are at once the most demonstrably fictive and the most abundantly factual (in their reproduction of original Arabic documents) from among the autobiographical works by Jews from Yemen.

The authors are predominantly working-class men and women who did not enter the ranks of the Israeli cultural elite. The authors' awareness of their marginality lends the works a measure of defensiveness. Some of this defensiveness stems from the difficulty of claiming their place in the Israeli national narrative, whether out of the late date of their arrival or Israeli Eurocentrism. Moreover, the motives for their emigration seem to have been a mixture of economics and ideology, two qualities that are difficult or impossible to extricate from each other.[61] Nissim Gamlieli, writing of years of poor harvests in Yemen, argues for a link between poverty and messianism that transcended religious identity:

> The hard life, paucity of rain, drought, diseases, epidemics, and plagues made Yemen "a land which is cut off" (Lev. 16:22) and a bitter Exile not only for Jews but for all of the non-Jewish population. Anxiety over physical subsistence, bread to eat, supporting oneself honorably and without degradation pursued a person until the day he died.[62]

Referring to the challenge of eking out a living and the sharp social stratification that excluded Jews and most Muslims from authority, Jewish writer Ratson Halevi commented, "The non-Jews in Yemen were badly in need of a messiah—no less than the Jews."[63] (Muslims, particularly Shafiʿis, also emigrated from Yemen in large numbers.[64])

Autobiographical works by Jews from Yemen tend to be sharply divided between life in Yemen and life in Israel. The authors of these books are thus faced with the challenge of harmonizing the two lives they have lived. The cover of Halevi's memoir, *From One World to Another*, illustrates this dilemma.

What was the process or processes through which the Jewish lawyers were able to manipulate the sharīʿa-based legal system? Though each of the three men examined here portrays himself as a maverick, this book will show that in their efforts they manipulated ambiguities within the law and within wider nonlegal

The cover of Ratson Halevi's (d. 2006) *From One World to Another* juxtaposes Sanaa's Old City with Tel Aviv skyscrapers.

codes that helped define the relationship between Muslim majority and Jewish minority. Insofar as other Muslims and Jews alternatively maintained and transgressed these borders between Jew and Muslim, they were not unique, but represented particularly skillful players in a game whose rules encompassed substantive law, political struggles, and social and economic relationships.

The book sets legal ideals and practice within their wider cultural context. "Just below the surface of judicial decision making," writes Lawrence Rosen, lie "a host of assumptions, attitudes, beliefs, and modes of thought that call for closer inspection."[65]

1 The Islamic Judicial System and the Jews

According to a Syrian who visited Yemen in the mid-1930s, Imām Yaḥyā, then in his late sixties, used to sit each morning under a pepper tree in the courtyard of one of his palaces, with his qadis, issuing legal rulings to a line of impoverished supplicants.[1] For Muslim and Jewish Yemenis who look back nostalgically to the prerevolutionary period, this image evokes the imām's learning, compassion, and personal touch. It calls to mind Justice Felix Frankfurter's hyperbolic contrast between rule-bound U.S. law and the arbitrariness of law in Islamic societies. "We do not sit like a kadi under a tree," he wrote in 1949, "dispensing justice according to considerations of individual expediency." It also reminds us of Max Weber's more subtle notion of *kadijustiz*—the informality and practicality of the Muslim judge.[2]

However, there was much more to what was going on under the pepper tree than met the eye. Imām Yaḥyā thoroughly overhauled the justice system, purging it of Ottoman innovations and training and dispatching judges throughout Yemen in a bid to centralize political power and shut out his rivals. A Jew from Sanaa, Yeḥiel Ḥibshūsh, returned to the same courtyard late in life and contemplated its significance. To him the appearance of equanimity was misleading. "The courtyard was the place of justice but at the same time it was the place of an injustice that manifested itself in the form of bribery," he writes. The imām paid his bodyguards very little (his miserliness and concomitant squeezing of the populace for funds were legendary).[3] They accepted "gifts" in exchange for expediting their presenters' petitions ahead of the line. Even those who stood in line for an audience with the sovereign brought with them a quarter-*riyāl* for the gatekeepers.[4] A given qadi's staff might be on the take as well, Ḥibshūsh explains. A reluctant defendant might bribe a judge's personal messenger to tell his employer that he was unable to find and summon him to stand trial.[5]

In their autobiographical writing, Muslims and Jews offer a richly detailed portrait of the legal system under Imām Yaḥyā, warts and all. They describe the practices and procedures of the courts; the practical workings of Jews' appeal to them, as well as "trouble cases" that arose where Islamic and Jewish law conflicted; the coercion and violence at a judge's disposal; along with bribery, perjury, and forgery.[6] Such accounts also hint at the political reasons why Imām Yaḥyā tolerated and exploited corruption within the judiciary.

Imām Yaḥyā and the Justice System: Reform and Continuity

At first blush, characterizing the justice system in Yemen in the early twentieth century seems a fairly simple task: a Muslim theocratic ruler enforced the sharīʿa in his independent realm. On closer inspection, however, such description proves exceedingly complex. The Ottomans had ruled Yemen since 1873, capitulating to Arab rebels in northern Yemen only in the 1911 Treaty of Daʿʿān. It was not until 1918 that Imām Yaḥyā Ḥamīd al-Dīn, the head of the Arab opposition to their rule, took control of the capital city of Sanaa. Two historians have qualified the extent of the imām's power after Daʿʿān. Thomas Kühn argued that while the Ottomans allowed him autonomy for their own reasons, his sovereignty was nominal in nature.[7] Isa Blumi goes further, stressing the tenuousness of the imām's power even within the Zaydī-majority region.[8]

As a Zaydī imām, Yaḥyā was both a blood descendant of the prophet Muḥammad and a legal scholar (a *mujtahid*). His claim that he would return Yemen to a sharīʿa that the Turks had neglected was central to his campaign for support. One Jew who acted as the imām's agent in a rural area in the north was asked to convince a Bedouin tribe that rejected all outside authority to accept the rule of the new imām. He argued that the imām, unlike the Ottomans, would rule according to the Qur'an. The tribe accepted this, despite its dubious source.[9]

The Ottomans had instituted a variety of changes to the status quo of relations between Muslims and non-Muslims. Some of them were aimed to ease restrictions on Jews in Sanaa. Yet these reforms met with opposition from many local Muslims, leading the Ottomans to back away from the more radical challenges to the sumptuary laws that they were willing to mount in other parts of the empire.[10] Moreover, the Ottomans, who saw in the Jews a loyal labor base, made novel demands of them, including the mandatory grinding of flour for the army and transporting wounded soldiers to the port city of Hodeida upon stretchers.

When Imām Yaḥyā took Sanaa, he summoned the heads of the Jewish community and made it clear to them that they were to be ruled according to Islamic norms of relations between Muslims and non-Muslims. This included a renewed commitment to the Zaydī Yemeni version of the "Pact of ʿUmar."[11] The Pact of ʿUmar, which is a document outlining the sumptuary laws that would ensure the subservient status of the "People of the Book" (Christians, Jews, Zoroastrians, and later Hindus) in the Islamic state, was alleged to have been written by the Christians of Edessa to the third caliph ʿUmar b. al-Khaṭṭāb (r. 634–644).[12] Shiʿi

Muslims, including many Zaydīs, did not like ʿUmar. Nevertheless, the pact is found in the Zaydī legal manuals without his name attached to it.[13]

The imām also renewed the laws developed in Yemen that called for the strict regulation of the sale of alcohol, Jewish collection of excrement, and Muslim custodianship of Jewish orphans (see chapter 2). Imām Yaḥyā told the Jewish leaders that while their religious courts were free to try cases involving Jews, Jews could make recourse to sharīʿa courts as well. Yaḥyā was paraphrasing Qur'an 5:42, the proof text for legal pluralism in Islam: "If they come to you for judgment, either judge between them or turn aside from them."

A doctrinal difference between the Ḥanafī legal school, which the Turks followed, and the Zaydī school, which Muslims in highland Yemen followed, allowed some Zaydīs to "renegotiate" the status of the Jewish Quarter of Sanaa after Imām Yaḥyā took over. Jews claimed that the land was their private property. Some Muslims claimed it was *waqf* land (land belonging to a pious trust) upon which Jews had neglected to pay rent. Ḥanafī law recognizes possession as proof of ownership, even of waqf property, whereas Zaydī law requires documentation of possession and does not allow private ownership of waqf property.[14] A legal maxim summed up the privilege granted documentary evidence in Zaydī Islam: "that which is left behind is the main thing" (*al-aṣl al-baqā'*).[15]

This interscholastic Muslim dispute affected the judicial system more broadly. According to Sālim Saʿīd al-Jamal, the Zaydī recognition of documentary claims to ownership over and against possession created a litigious atmosphere in the wake of the transfer of power from the Turks to the imām. Individuals pursued cases against tribal shaykhs, many of whom had no documentation for their estates. The imām's government, in turn, used the promise of resolving such protracted court battles as a way to gain the allegiance of individual shaykhs who might otherwise rebel against him.[16]

The general fondness among Jewish writers from Yemen for Imām Yaḥyā makes it difficult to gauge the strictness of his policies toward the Jews. Those who argue for his status as a great benefactor of the Jews tend to see his renewal of the various sumptuary laws as halfhearted and sporadically enforced attempts to assuage his rivals among the religiously conservative elite. Jamal makes the far-fetched claim that Imām Yaḥyā restored the sumptuary laws in order to systematically dismantle them, "empty[ing them] of content—in his wisdom!—one by one."[17] Yet this perceived leniency could have been structural in nature. While the Pact of ʿUmar possessed enduring power in Islamic history, its strict enforcement seems to have been exceedingly rare. Mark Cohen has pointed out that Muslims in Fatimid and Ayyubid Egypt often did not implement the "ʿUmaride Statutes."[18] In the same vein, a Jewish writer from Yemen, Aharon Ben David, says of the Pact of ʿUmar: "the rulers applied its ordinances strictly in the cities, less so in the villages, and ignored them almost entirely in the tribal areas of the north, east, and south."[19]

Ordinary social interactions between Muslims and Jews contributed to undermining the sumptuary laws in Yemen. A given imām had to choose between cracking down on the Jews to demonstrate zeal in defense of Islamic norms and encouraging the flourishing of the Jewish community insofar as their poll tax revenue (*jizya*) and other gifts went straight to his discretionary fund. (If it is true that Jewish merchants like Jamal were taxed more lightly than were Muslim merchants, as both Jewish and Muslim sources describe, this practice would have provided the aristocracy with "duty-free" shopping as well.[20]) Yosef Atsṭah, a Jew from Dhamār, tells of when the Turks wanted to collect the jizya from that town's Jews around the turn of the century, the Jewish intermediary would advise those who could not pay to go on the lam until the tax collection was finished. According to him, collecting from every taxpayer on the registry required a military raid on the Jewish Quarter.[21]

Imām Yaḥyā's renegotiation of terms with the Jewish community was part and parcel of a simultaneous expansion and reform of the judiciary. A new corps of trained Zaydī judges who could be sent throughout highland Yemen was needed. The creation of this sector, in turn, was closely tied to the internal politics of the Yemeni elite. According to Zaydī jurisprudence, members of the sayyid class who traced their descent to the prophet Muḥammad could claim the office of imām (though there were other prerequisites as well), even when the office was occupied by another. Due to the threat that they posed, Imām Yaḥyā relied heavily in his administration upon the *qadi* ("judge") class, who possessed the legitimating qualities of religious scholarship but were banned from seeking the office of imām. Although "qadi" means "judge," members of qadi families in Yemen were not necessarily judges by profession. Many were quite poor.[22] To muddy the waters further, sayyids could be judges as well. Regional governors, who were invariably sayyids, also acted as judges.

A Yemeni historian describes the rise of "obscure" qadi families in the early 1920s as a result of the imām's attempts to keep the sayyids in check.[23] Nevertheless, in doing this, which the Jewish lawyer Jamal characterized as "divide and conquer," Imām Yaḥyā continued an Ottoman practice.[24] Similarly, his use of Jewish leaders, among them the "chief rabbi" (*hākhām bāshī*), an office invented by the Ottomans, from whom he expected unswerving loyalty, may be a holdover from the Turks. The imām employed both qadis and Jews as tax collectors from farmers, as had the Ottomans.[25]

In his perceptive 1965 study of factionalism in Yemeni politics, Aḥmad Muḥammad Nuʿmān argued that members of the qadi class played a balancing act of their own, undermining the sayyids by stoking the resentment of them among the (majority non-sayyid) populace and blaming sayyid leaders for the country's woes while avoiding the wrath of the imām by remaining publicly loyal to him.[26] Nuʿmān argues further that the prime minister, Qadi ʿAbdallāh al-ʿAmrī, and his allies encouraged the imām to replace sayyid governors with the princes in the late 1930s. One historian dubbed this policy an "administrative purge" of sayyids in government.[27] ('Amrī was the de facto prime minister.) Qadi Ismā'īl al-Akwa' explains that the terms "ministers" and "ministries" with reference to Imām Yaḥyā's government can be misleading. Each "ministry" consisted of a room, or two rooms at most, in or near the palace, Dār al-Sa'ādah. The ministers were mainly the imām's sons.[28]

By attempting to centralize power within the royal family, the imām earned the opposition of powerful sayyid clans. Moreover, Imām Yaḥyā's sons' designs on the imāmate—real or perceived—caused great controversy among Zaydīs, since the imāmate was not a hereditary office.[29] (Yaḥyā's own accession to the imāmate had been contested in 1904 due to the fact that his father had also been an imām, albeit a weak one by comparison.[30])

In Yemen both sayyids and qadis sported beards, white turbans, and bell-bottom sleeves (sometimes tied behind the back) that indicated their high status. Nevertheless, subtle distinctions separated the two groups. Sayyids might dye their beards red with henna.[31] The qadis' turbans were larger and more rounded, perhaps to accomodate pens and veritable archives of small legal documents.[32] Social tensions between sayyids and qadis flared up in court. A sayyid became incensed when a panel of eminent qadis referred to him in a legal document as "brother."[33]

Both sayyids and qadis enjoyed higher status than did tribesmen. Though Jews held a position well beneath all three groups, Moshe Tsadoq writes of "a weird relationship of mutual scorn between Zaydīs and [prominent] Jews against the tribesman of the village." This shared interest led some judges to rule in favor of Jews in cases involving Jews and tribesmen even when the Jewish litigant was in the wrong.[34]

Three sharī'a courts were established in Sanaa, as well as a court at the imām's residence that was overseen by a judge. Muslims were able to choose the judge before whom they wished to present their case. One of the judges was responsible for cases involving Jews, in addition to his regular duties. Above these four courts sat a court of appeals (*maḥkamat al-isti'nāf*). Highest of all was the high council (*majlis al-'ālī*), consisting of seven judges.[35] The court of appeals met in a wing of a government building built by the Ottomans, the remainder of which was occupied by the Ṣanā'i prison.[36] Imām Yaḥyā, in theory at least, was the ultimate legal authority. His critics saw his insistence on personally reviewing his judges' decisions to be part and parcel of his micromanagement of affairs in Yemen.[37]

The term "courts" can be a bit misleading insofar as judges did not necessarily have their own chambers. They met plaintiffs, along with witnesses, friends, and passers-by, all of whom contributed verbally to the proceedings, in their homes or in mosques. Weekly markets also featured courts where disputes that arose in the course of buying and selling could be resolved.[38] Writing of the courts in the 1970s, a historian makes an observation that likely applied to the prerevolutionary period as well. On the informal setting of judicial proceedings A. Z. al-Abdin notes that "litigants seek the judge anywhere, in his house, in the street, or in the market."[39] And Yosef Qāfiḥ notes that some cases were heard and decided "in the street, [with] a large crowd gathered around [the judge]: soldiers, servants, litigants, and curious passers-by," or in a qadi's home. Others were heard in a court. Qāfiḥ describes the scene:

> The courthouse is a simple unfurnished hall. At its edge a simple mattress was made up, where the judge sits. An upside-down box rests before the judge, where he sets his pen and inkwell. The rest of the room is made up with carpet remnants where the litigants lie down. Sometimes the judge sits in his "courtyard" and as each litigant comes, they spread their garment upon the ground (or, in the case of a Jew, their prayer shawl) and sit on it. . . . When judgment is issued, the judge sits with his legs folded underneath him. The litigants enter and sit before him without any order; the sides make their claims, and the judge, or his secretary (who is usually his son), writes down the basics of the claims and the [sides'] responses.[40]

While there were no "lawyers" per se in the sharīʿa system, a litigant might hire a "trusted man" (*amīn*) or "trustee of the law" (*wakīl al-sharʿ*) who, according to Abdin, ought to "have some knowledge about the sharīʿa, the loop-holes in the law, and the judicial procedure." Some of the suspicion of lawyers familiar to Westerners circulated in Yemen as well.[41] Qāfiḥ, describing the sharīʿa system in early twentieth-century Yemen, writes that "anyone with a sharp tongue was able to be a lawyer. He had no need for formal study of the laws, certification, or permission to appear [before a judge]."[42] Others are more gracious. Aharon Ben David describes the lawyers who congregated around the courthouse in a northern Yemeni town, saying, "They were knowledgeable *in* sharīʿa law and provided services to any who asked—including Jews."[43]

Jews in the Sharīʿa Courts

If the imām explicitly permitted Jews to use Jewish courts, what do his reforms to the Islamic legal system have to do with the Jews? In fact, Jews in Yemen (and elsewhere in the Islamic world) used the sharīʿa courts frequently. In 1920 two groups of Jews from Yemen became embroiled in a dispute over a plot of land in Shaʿarayim, a Jewish settlement in Palestine. To the chagrin of the official Zionist institutions, they took their case to the sharīʿa court in nearby Ramlah.[44] This anecdote shows that even when given the option to turn to other legal forums, at least some Yemeni Jews believed that the sharīʿa courts were the proper venue for tricky cases.

Jews' appearance as claimants in sharīʿa courts predated these twentieth-century developments. In the eighteenth and nineteenth centuries, Yemeni rabbis railed against Jews who took recourse to Muslim courts, because it undermined their own authority (and presumably deprived them of income). They also regarded it as a sin.[45] Ironically, it was precisely the Muslim government's involvement in the activities of the Jewish courts that gave these courts their power. The government collected a portion of all fines that the Jewish courts levied, and therefore it had a financial incentive for upholding the rabbis' decisions.[46] Nevertheless, Yemeni Jews brought many of their disputes to Muslim courts, even those involving only Jews.[47] Jews who bought property from Muslims preferred that these transactions be recorded by a sharīʿa court. Should a dispute arise, the Muslim court document would give them firmer footing than would the Jewish court (*bet din*). The sharīʿa court's more extensive investigation into the ownership history of a given property would provide additional security.[48] Other Jews engaged in "forum shopping," bringing their disputes to the courts that offered the highest likelihood of success. For example, Jewish women with brothers, faced with inheriting nothing from their dead fathers under Jewish law, turned to Muslim courts, where they inherited half as much as men.[49]

Some Muslims were aware of this discrepancy between Jewish and Muslim laws of inheritance for women and sought to exploit it themselves. A Jew in Damt who owned a number of fields died, leaving behind a son and two daughters. Under Islamic law his two daughters were entitled to a share of the inheritance, but this was not so under Jewish law. His son rented some of the fields to his father-in-law and sold part of them to him outright in 1901. Twenty-two years later one of the daughters hired a Muslim attorney (*wakīl*) and claimed her rights as a co-owner of the land in the sharīʿa court. In order to make this claim, the woman would have needed enough money to refund the purchaser of the land. The brother claimed "that the plaintiff's bequest was measly—she owns nothing and those who are putting her up to claiming rights of co-ownership are [the defendants'] rivals."[50] Thus, the brother suggested to the qadi that the Jewish woman was acting as a straw buyer for one or more Muslim landowners with whom the brother competed. They had put up the money she would need and presumably promised her additional money.

The qadi rejected the woman's claim, arguing that her ownership extended only to the portion of the field she had inherited, which had not been designated at the time of the sale, and that a co-owner's objection to a sale must be made at the time of sale. However, he ordered the defendants to pay the woman for her share of the back rent on the land and to have an experienced arbitrator divide the land between the successors.[51]

Jewish divorce cases in Yemen routinely involved both Muslim and Jewish courts, because one or both parties perceived an advantage in involving a Muslim court in their case. Sometimes one or both Jewish parties turned to Muslim courts to "adjust" the divorce settlement. In other cases the Muslim court drew up a document finalizing the spouses' financial obligations to one another and the bet din provided a Jewish document of divorce (a *get*). Sometimes the Jewish court adjusted the settlement that had been reached by the Muslim court.[52]

Not all interactions between Muslim and Jewish family law proceeded harmoniously. In some cases making them work together required drastic measures. In 1933 in a village in the south, a poor Jewish woman named Saʿīdah worked as a housekeeper in the home of a wealthy Jew. After she became her family's primary breadwinner, she and her husband drifted apart and eventually divorced. Her employer wanted to make her his second wife. The narrator of this anecdote wryly observes that this marriage would have served as a stone that killed three birds for the employer: satisfying the lust he had conceived for his maid, irritating his existing wife, and freeing him from having to pay the woman for her housework.

Saʿīdah's ex-husband complained to the governor that he wanted her to be his wife again and that five Jews, including his ex-wife's employer, were preventing this from happening. The three-month waiting period, after which a divorce is finalized, had not yet expired, and Islamic law did not require the woman's consent to reconcile. After being summoned to the courthouse, the Jewish men responded that voiding a divorce in Jewish law required the woman's consent. The governor issued a ruling validating the ex-husband's position and had the men jailed.

When the wealthy Jew's first wife appeared at the prison and the Muslim prisoners saw her beauty, they castigated the Jew for his greed in marrying Saʿīdah as well. He bribed the jailer and escaped to Sanaa with Saʿīdah and married her in a rushed ceremony. It was evening, and in his haste to consummate the marriage he followed her to the river where she was bathing. In the darkness he groped the wrong woman and a great hue and cry ensued. A rabbi in Yarīm eventually sorted out the situation between Saʿīdah, her ex-husband, and the wealthy Jew: the Muslim governor's ruling would be destroyed, Saʿīdah would stay married to her new husband, and the ex-husband would receive a large payment for damages.[53]

In this unusual case the rabbi bent Islamic law in order to make it fit within the strictures of Jewish law. In another case a couple divorced under Islamic law and married according to Jewish law found themselves in a much worse predicament. In the early 1920s a Jewish man in Yarīm, apparently infuriated by his meddlesome father-in-law, divorced his wife according to Islamic law by declaring three times that he divorced her. The couple wanted to be reconciled, but in order to do so the woman would have to marry a *muḥallil.* Under Islamic law a woman must be married to another before she can be reconciled to her husband. Due to this fact, a muḥallil (literally "one who renders licit") would provide an expedient short-term marriage partner in a given region. Nissim Gamlieli described the old man in his village who filled this position as "the community's stud he-goat."[54]

Such a marriage would transgress Jewish law, according to which the woman was still married. The local rabbis also could not arrange a Jewish divorce. Thus, according to both Islamic and Jewish laws, the couple could neither divorce nor could they remarry. Under the advice of the imām, the governor overruled the local qadi, who seems to have been averse to ignoring the letter of the law.[55]

Other problematic cases revolved around the peculiarities of Jewish matrimonial law. Three of four Jewish brothers from a small village in the south converted to Islam. When the sole Jewish brother died, his younger brother was obligated to marry his widow. (Jews in Yemen practiced levirate marriage [a widow's remarriage to her dead husband's brother].) Though the younger brother was a Muslim, and thus out of halakhic jurisdiction, he nonetheless wrote to the bet din in Aden recusing himself of this duty and apologizing for his conversion.[56] In his study of the records of rabbinical court of Sanaa, Amnon Ḥever found a perplexing phenomenon: in many cases Jewish converts to Islam divorced in Jewish courts. He surmises that a financial incentive brought the Muslim husband to the Jewish court in order to produce a Jewish document of divorce that would allow the woman to remarry.[57] As in the case of the would-be levirate marriage, it is also possible that the Jewish courts continued to exercise some moral authority over former Jews.

Jews came to the sharīʿa court with clear disadvantages. Testimony was foremost among these. Islamic law holds the testimony of a non-Muslim (or a woman) to count for half of the testimony of a Muslim man. Thus, in cases that involved a Muslim's word against a Jew, the Muslim should always have won. Jews complained that judicial personnel were especially solicitous of bribes when it came to them. Insofar as graft was widely decried by Muslims as well, some level of hyperbole is possible. Yet Nissim Gamlieli says that sharīʿa court judges liked judging cases involving Jews and Muslims because for the Jews bribery was the only way to improve their odds of success as opposed to strategies such as the appeal to one's kinship group or the leveraging of land holdings of which Muslims might avail themselves.[58] On the other hand, the fact that Jews were simultaneously under the protection of the imām and the tribal shaykh could affect the outcomes of cases in unpredictable ways.

Moreover, the fact that a Jew's testimony held little weight could be skirted in various ways by the rich or enterprising. Nissim Gamlieli says that Jews who came into contact with the sharīʿa courts as plaintiffs or defendants "usually had a fair trial in spite of the constitutional-religious discrimination in favor of the Muslims in the law of witnessing." Why was this the case? "When a Jew needed Muslim witnesses he 'bought' them—even from the market. Give the most respected tribesman a coin and he will be a witness, swearing for your benefit, even on matters that he neither saw nor heard."[59]

Jewish communities beyond Yemen used Muslim courts, even in cases involving only Jews. In his study of the court records of Ottoman Jerusalem, Amnon Cohen describes the great frequency with which this happened and concludes that "the oft-repeated warnings in Jewish sources not to make use of 'gentile courts' therefore were not given out of a halakhic-theoretical narrow-mindedness, but were a result of daily reality."[60]

However unlikely it seems, in practice Muslim courts in Yemen occasionally used the personnel or techniques of the Jewish courts. (These are scenarios at which the prescriptive sources of Islamic law do not even hint.) The fact that the Jewish courts issued their rulings in Judeo-Arabic (Arabic in Hebrew characters) generally ruled out their use by Muslims. However, in small villages, where a rabbi might be handier than a Muslim man of learning, such instances occurred. Occasionally a Muslim needed a legal document that would reflect the moral authority of the bet din, as happened in 1888 when a Muslim stranger (and a sayyid to boot) bought a house in the Jewish Quarter of Damt.[61]

Shalom Medinah reports seeing two shaykhs ask a rabbi of Yarīm for a legal ruling to settle a dispute between them.[62] Ṣāliḥ al-Ẓāhirī, whose knowledge of Arabic and Islamic law was unusually good, issued a legal ruling on a dispute between two Jews with an Arabic translation and asked one of the claimants to have a Muslim judge sign the Arabic version. The judge refused, claiming that a legal ruling could not be written by a Jew. Ẓāhirī lodged a complaint with Imām Yaḥyā and soldiers brought the errant judge to Sanaa from Radā', a five-day journey. The imām signed the legal ruling and sentenced the judge to eight days in the Ṣanā'i prison.[63] The judge may not have provided sufficient argumentation for his refusal to sign, and the fact that the case in question involved only Jews meant it had low stakes. Yet by writing a document that was essentially an unsigned fatwa, Ẓāhirī transgressed the prevailing jurisdictional divisions between Jewish and Muslim courts, and the imām backed him.

In at least one instance, Imām Yaḥyā forced a Muslim to face Jewish justice. The Jews of Sanaa possessed an elaborate ceremony for extracting judicial oaths, based on Geonic precedent.[64] The ceremony took place at the al-Dhamārī Synagogue in front of the "Torah of the Ages" (*tawrāt al-dahārī*), a scroll believed to have been written by Moses himself.[65] Funerary preparations were made on behalf of the man who swore falsely, for he would surely die. Water for washing a corpse was brought, as well as a bier, a shroud, a pickax to dig the grave, a hoe, a basket for the displaced earth, and frankincense. Burning the frankincense would help disguise the putrid odor emitted by the false witness immediately after death. Ten rams' horns would be blown ten times each, and the oath would be made before the assembled audience.[66] Imām Yaḥyā was so impressed by the persuasive power of this ceremony that he once ordered a Muslim whom he believed to be committing perjury to submit to it. The Muslim in question, a wealthy merchant, fled the scene before swearing, thereby forfeiting his claim.[67]

A similar element of theater surrounded the Muslim procedure for the extraction of judicial oaths. A Muslim merchant believed he had paid a Jewish merchant 500 riyāls, the Jew's son reports. The Jew demanded that the Muslim swear to it. The Jew asked Qadi Luṭf al-Zubayrī, the judge responsible for Jewish cases in Sanaa, to bring the Muslim to the Great Mosque, one of the oldest and most esteemed mosques in the Islamic world, and have him swear on "'*al-Mūrah wa l-manqūrah*,' books holy to Islam."[68] (The Jewish narrator has garbled the story. "*Al-Masmūrah*" and "*al-manqūrah*" ("the nailed" and "the bored") are the names of the two pillars on either side of the Great Mosque's prayer niche (*qiblah*). On the way to the mosque along with Qadi Luṭf, the Jew, and a crowd of merchants who supported one of the two disputants, the Muslim relented out of apprehension. "The belief among the Muslims," writes the Jew's son, "was that he who swears [falsely] and cheats a Jew will never be able to repent of his sin. . . . The swindled Jew will leave hell, snatch the Muslim who cheated him on his way to paradise, and drag him [back] to hell to face justice."[69]

Aharon Ben David, from the northernmost part of Yemen, explains that Muslim judges expected Jews to take oaths in Hebrew. A Jewish man of learning (*mori*) was often summoned to court for this purpose. Yet many of these oaths, though they were in Hebrew, were nonsensical or meant the opposite of what they ought to have meant. Through them, Jews quietly mocked Islam. In one instance a qadi dispensed with the need for the mori who would administer the oath and proudly ordered a Jewish defendant in the theft of a copper pot repeat after him a nonsense Hebrew oath word for word: "may *fat and honey* run in your belly if you saw or stole the pot." (The words "fat and honey" are Hebrew and the rest is Arabic.)[70] In a case from Dhamār, the governor was suspicious of a Jewish witness's Hebrew oath. When he made him swear in Arabic, the Jew relented from his planned perjury.[71]

How often this happened is not clear. Yet the idea that interacting with the Islamic legal system might demand a certain loosening of ethical standards was not limited to oath taking. Ṣāliḥ al-Ẓāhirī tells of a Jewish *qāt* (a mild stimulant) chew in Dhamār where the participants debated whether or not the biblical commandment to report what one has witnessed (Lev. 5:1) was canceled by the fact that the testimony of Jews counted for very little in Muslim courts.[72]

Coercion and Punishment in the Justice System

As one would expect, in executing their judicial duties and solving contemporary problems, members of the Islamic judicial apparatus often engaged with the tradition of legal scholarship; therefore, some of their work possessed a scholarly quality. Yet cases in which they offered no reference to authoritative sources were not uncommon. Moreover, since they had various types of coercive violence at their disposal, they were able to influence the facts of a given case themselves.

At least some ordinary Yemenis, Muslim and Jewish, believed in the efficacy of authorities' use of coercive tactics. A Jewish yarn tells the story of a cow, illegally sold to three different people by a single man, who had absconded. A judge gave the strange order that the cow be imprisoned in a dark place until it revealed the identity of its owner. After three days in a dark cell without food, the cow was released and returned to its home village, leading one of the qadi's soldiers straight to the guilty man.[73]

A person might be imprisoned as a punishment, as a preventive step, or as a measure that might spur the prisoner to cooperate with the authorities. While the imāms' prisons varied considerably in the harshness with which prisoners were treated, stints in them tended to be very unpleasant. Food needed to be provided prisoners by family members. Those who had no family to bring food sometimes starved to death.[74] Bedbugs, lice, and other insects flourished.[75]

According to the Jewish intermediary Ṣāliḥ al-Ẓāhirī, Muslim prisoners were occasionally able to wash themselves at a nearby mosque, but for Jews bathing was nearly impossible. During his own imprisonment Ẓāhirī jumped into the prison well in a desperate attempt at bathing and was punished with "curving" (*'aṭf*), a procedure in which his hands and feet were bound to one another with short, heavy chains for a long period of time.[76] Later capitalizing on Imām Yaḥyā's piety, which extended to ensuring the observance of Judaism, Ẓāhirī wrote to the imām that he had "seen a nocturnal emission," which required him to visit the Jewish ritual bath before being able to pray again. The imām gave him special dispensation to leave prison to bathe in the Jewish Quarter under such exigent circumstances. Subsequently Ẓāhirī claims to have had such dreams with great frequency. He did, however, have to pay the soldier who accompanied him and bribe the prison staff.[77] By paying bribes he enjoyed lengthy visits from friends and even acquired wine for his Sabbath observance.[78] Similar arrangements were made for other Jewish prisoners.[79] As this anecdote shows, in a seemingly paradoxical manner, laxity pervaded this system in addition to severity, a topic that is expanded upon in chapter 5.

Upon arrival in jail, a prisoner's feet were often chained. Both closing and opening the shackles required heavy blows with a hammer, so the danger of breaking a prisoner's ankles was always great.[80] A bribe guaranteed the new prisoner's ankles gentler treatment.[81] Nissim Gamlieli explains that the shackler was a fixed position in the judicial retinue, and one always accompanied a qadi to his appearances on market day.[82]

A Muslim imprisoned for participation in the coup against Imām Yaḥyā describes conditions of informal brutality in his prison memoir. Heavy fetters, sometimes multiple sets, were attached to prisoners as a punitive measure. (He blames the Jewish blacksmiths of Sanaa for fashioning these painful devices.)[83] The worst of all such punishments was called "heaviness" (*thaqālah*), which consisted of "an iron coat that covered the head, back, and shoulders" and was so dangerous that it was applied only for short periods of time.[84] Cells varied in size. One prison in Maḥwīt used an extremely small cell (about 5 feet by 5 feet) for punishment.[85] Yosef Qāfiḥ says that the Ṣanā'ī prison in Sanaa often held eight to ten prisoners in a cell measuring 13 by 13 feet.[86]

The Ḥajjah prison, which is remembered in postrevolutionary Yemen as the worst one, was overcrowded, dark, filthy, and infested with pests. The little outdoor space reserved for prisoners was made available only after sustained protest. Prisoners' staple food consisted of so-called country rice that contained many stones and had to be purchased from the prison. They suffered from malnutrition, wounds caused by heavy fetters, and other ailments. Medicine was difficult to get. Imām Aḥmad sent penicillin to two prisoners who had complained of their suffering, along with a bill for it. Being imprisoned could become quite expensive for other reasons as well. Prisoners had to pay a daily rental rate for their "accommodations."

A bribe could lead to a visit with a loved one. Prisoners who could not afford to buy multiple changes of clothing were especially miserable. Some prisoners' young children stayed with them in prison.[87] Yosef Qāfiḥ reports that poor prisoners often stayed in prison for months longer than their stipulated term because they were unable to pay the bill for the various fees they had accrued while serving their sentences.[88]

In Yemen a person who was arrested was expected to pay a set fee to the police or soldiers who were sent by a qadi or other authority to apprehend them for their trouble. Harsher still was the practice anthropologist Shelagh Weir calls "forcible billeting."[89] Sālim Sa'īd al-Jamal explains how this worked. Soldiers who were sent to someone's home were entitled to a "right of lodging." The homeowner had to pay them a daily rate, along with any charges that resulted from hardships they encountered on their journey to his home or reimbursements for expenses they incurred. He also had to house them and give them his best food, drink, qāt to chew, and tobacco. Since this was often one of the best meals a hungry soldier in the imām's army would get, he would eat with gusto. Billeting soldiers, who required a great deal of food and qāt, in private homes was one of the imām's discretionary punishments.[90] Yet some soldiers took the "right of lodging" from people to whose homes they had not even been sent.[91] Opponents of the imām demanded an end to the practice.[92] In addition, Jamal says that anyone who resisted arrest and forced the policeman to fire his gun in the air had to pay an additional fine, plus an exhorbitant fee for the bullet.

The Seedy Side of the Islamic Legal System

The focus in scholarship on sources that describe what ought to happen in the law as opposed to what actually happened has obscured some of the less savory aspects of the functioning of Islamic courts. Paraphrasing the contents of the "comportment of the qadi" literature, Wael Hallaq says that arbitration was always preferable to adjudication and that "protracted adjudication and postponements in the judicial process were . . . abhorred."[93] He writes that the idea that witnesses must possess integrity guarded against perjury "just as their counterparts, the court's legal experts (*ahl al-'ilm*), ensured the soundness of the application of the law."[94] Court functionaries worked either "free of charge or nearly so" or, alternatively, could "charge the litigants . . . an appropriate fee," but were forbidden to take bribes.[95]

In Yemen judicial bribery was rampant.[96] Bribery was not limited to judges, but permeated the entire system of law enforcement. According to Yosef Qāfiḥ, even judges who were principled enough to refuse bribes still accepted "gifts," which he says were legally permissible.[97] A Jewish boy was beaten and robbed. His mother, who was a renowned cook, had carefully cultivated a warm relationship with the provincial governor and local sharī'a court officials by sending them fine pastries. She pursued a case against the Muslim who harmed her son and won.[98]

Much earlier, Zaydī jurists had reached two different conclusions as to how a qadi's need to make a living ought to be weighed against the potential abuse of litigants. The *Sharḥ al-azhār* (*Commentary [on the Book of] Flowers*) preserves this heated debate. All agreed that a qadi, whose benefit to the Muslims was beyond question, ought to earn a salary, perhaps a good one. But could he accept additional payment from a litigant? The pro-payment camp argued that a person who serves as a qadi does so as a gratuity on behalf of the community and thus deserves a gratuity beyond a set salary. The qadi's secretarial duties (reading and writing) could be separated from judgment. Since others were paid for secretarial work, a qadi could be paid for such work as well. Those who were against payment rejected this putative division of labor, insisting, in the words of an anti-payment writer, that "the [written] ruling makes him responsible for its implementation and for safeguarding the wealth of another. This does not occur without him writing his name on the document that obliges him do this." The pro-payment Imām al-Murtaḍā (d. 1437) countered that the qadi's ethical responsibilities to the litigant are limited to pronouncing a ruling, not acting to prevent hypothetical future wrongdoing.[99] In general, both sides in the debate focus upon the appropriateness of the payment and the judge's entitlement rather than delving into the possible effects of the practice upon the payer or upon the judicial process.[100]

Another Jewish source describes "a phase of bargaining and competition over the pay of the judge" during which "each side adds more and raises the amount of the payment in order to pressure his opponent to pay the same amount, which was all praiseworthy and good in the eyes of the judge."[101] Through this tactic the litigant with the most money to spend gained an automatic advantage at trial. In Dhamār, probably during World War I, two Jewish brothers beat another Jew.[102] The Jew who was beaten up sued for damages. The sole Muslim witness, who had business ties with many Jews, offered his services as mediator. He asked both sides for a cash payment in advance. The plaintiff balked, offering to pay only from a successful damage award. The defendants agreed not only to his fee, but gave him an additional riyāl "to testify well." And so he did. He said:

> Your honor, there was a little skirmish in the shop . . . but I did not see anyone strike the plaintiff or touch him, even with his little finger. I also saw—and this is God's honest truth—that after the plaintiff left the store he raked his own back across a stone wall until it was covered with blood.[103]

Ṣāliḥ al-Ẓāhirī, one of the Jewish intermediaries, paints a sorry picture of the life of Muslim judges in Yemen. Married men neglected their wives and children in order to study the *Commentary [on the Book of] Flowers* in Sanaa for years in the hopes of receiving one of a few judicial posts in the provincial cities. Those who came from notable or wealthy families could support themselves on their family fortunes.[104] Ẓāhirī says he once found a high court judge (unnamed) signing an appeal on a prior judgment that he himself had issued. The Jew confronted him.

This was not technically a case of bribery, but of deliberate prolongation (*taṭwīl*). Under Imāms Yaḥyā and Aḥmad, official appointment documents (*taʿyīnāt*) exhorted a qadi "to treat the two parties with equity, to demand justice for the wronged, and to organize the affairs of the court in a way that prevents the [further] entanglement of the dispute, preventing the lassitude and prolongation that delay a solution."[105]

This was (and is) a charge levied against sharīʿa court judges, and those who make it rely upon the actual size of the documentation produced in a given case. One Yemeni qadi laments that decisions issuing from judges who resort to this odious practice "can be ten or more meters long—and these are words without benefit."[106] Jamal says that one of the legal reforms Imām Yaḥyā introduced when he came to power was to encourage brevity and speed. Claim, rebuttal, rebuttal of the rebuttal, and so on, all needed to fit on one small (10 cm by 13 cm) piece of paper. Yet this reform mainly affected government proceedings, while the courts themselves still took their time and produced lengthy documents.[107] The fact that scribes generally wrote on long scrolls of paper, which could be unfurled as the need arose, allowed all materials relating to a particular case, including witness statements and appeals, to be centralized but did not require the level of concision demanded by the small sheets of paper that Imām Yaḥyā favored. In addition, some judges wrote in an elaborate, flowery style and not necessarily out of a desire to prolong matters.[108]

Despite these measures, some identified prolongation as a defining evil of the imāms' judicial system.[109] One qadi says that early in Yaḥyā's rule, judges had no source of income other than bribes and "fees." This improved after the imām

Photo of Qadi Zayd al-Daylamī (d. 1947) from Aḥmad Muḥammad al-Shāmī, *Riyāḥ al-taghyīr fī l-yaman* (Winds of Change in Yemen).

began paying monthly salaries.[110] However, many others deemed these salaries unsufficient. The judge who admitted to having deliberately prolonged a case by overruling himself defended his actions as a logical consequence of imāmic rule. This was likely Zayd al-Daylamī (1867–1947), whom the Jew Ẓāhirī had befriended. Daylamī was an early supporter of the reformist Free Yemenis Party (*Ḥizb al-aḥrār al-yamaniyīn*), which aimed to replace the government of Imām Yaḥyā and his sons. "There are those who use power and there are those who use their minds," the qadi said. "The imām rules over all of those who live in Yemen and uses all of the resources for his own benefit through the use of force. I and many like me, who do not rule with the aid of military force, use spiritual force."

The judge explained that he received a "starvation salary" and that he had been paid the equivalent of a year's pay to overrule himself. The clients in question were litigious and wealthy tribal shaykhs who oppressed others and took bribes themselves. The judge sought to reassure Ẓāhirī that the trust between the two of them would prevent the judge from doing the same with the cases he undertook. Ẓāhirī says this was indeed the case. The two men had a long and productive friendship and socialized with one another.[111] Similarly, a judge in Radāʿ, hoping to receive a bribe, told Ẓāhirī he did not have enough money to make preparations for a Muslim festival because "we [judges] have difficulties getting by on the imām's salary."[112]

Arabic sources also attest to Daylamī's bribe taking. "He did not refrain from taking payment from those who pursued suits before him," writes Qadi Ismāʿīl al-Akwaʿ, "especially from a plaintiff." Another qadi sent Imām Yaḥyā a poem that contained the lines: "my lord, this Zayd al-Daylamī is selling God's judgment for money / despite his learning God is leading him astray / would that he did not know he was erring when he did so."[113] Already in 1918 Qāsim al-ʿIzzī, the trustee of Sanaa's waqfs, wrote a long letter to Daylamī chastising him for his greed. (The modern historian who reproduced it in full did so, he says, "as an admonition to the rulers and qadis who stretch out their hands for money from those who bring disputes to them.") According to ʿIzzī's letter, Daylamī had justified his actions by pointing to the high pay of regional governors as well as substantial withholdings from his monthly salary.[114] A 1940 judicial appointment letter from the imām for a chief judge in Hodeida that Bernard Haykel translated includes the admonishment that "he is not to take anything from the adversaries in the name of wages, and this holds for all judges of districts and sub-districts; we have provided them with enough [wages] to suffice them."[115]

Shamāḥī describes how Daylamī and ʿAbdallāh al-Wazīr, who became imām after Yaḥyā was assassinated, torpedoed an attempt by Imām Yaḥyā and his supporters among the religious scholars (*ulama*) to condemn two agitators against the government.[116] Daylamī had been appointed to lead a council of ulama that audited the imām and tried to investigate his misappropriation of funds.[117]

Among other things, this council admonished the imām to "improve the circumstances of those in charge of government departments without exception by raising salaries to defend against its use as a pretext for bribery and taking from the weak."[118] Considering Daylamī's considerable expertise in taking bribes, a better man for the job could not have been found.

Ḥayyim Tsadoq recalls receiving permission from the imām to travel to Eritrea. Giving Jews permission to seek work abroad was a legal fiction through which the imām avoided contravening his own ban on Jewish emigration to Palestine.[119] When he brought his "exit visa" to a qadi who was close to the imām, the qadi requested twelve riyāls, an amount the Jew claimed could support a six-person household for six months. Seven weeks later, while the imām was conducting one of his routine Friday visits to a mosque at the edge of the Jewish Quarter, he got the sovereign's attention just as he was being driven off in his black sedan and handed him a written complaint. (This had been written by another Jew who knew Arabic well.) "When the king heard about the bribe he became angry, drew a pen from his turban, and wrote to the qadi, quickly and furiously 'do not delay even a moment.'" The qadi relented and signed the "visa."[120]

It is worth noting that in the semiofficial historiography of the Yemeni revolution against the imāms, both Yemeni historians and some Jews who relocated to Israel accept the qadis' rationalization that their ostensible corruption stemmed directly from the low salaries the imām paid. Indeed, the centrality of unhappy qadis like Daylamī to the opposition meant that the raising of judicial salaries became a central demand of the revolutionary movement.[121]

In contrast, one contemporary writer who interviewed members of the imāms' judicial apparatus says a qadi could make a good living under the imāms. A qadi in a high position like the court of appeals received 150 Maria Theresa thalers (called riyāls) and five measures of grain (including wheat, barley, and sorghum) per month.[122] Qadis with less prestigious positions received about half the salary and three measures of grain (usually without the variety). The imāms showed favor to some of the latter, giving them salaries as high as 100 riyāls. Both grades of judges also received a servant, a muleteer, a mule, and the fodder and gear necessary to maintain and ride the beast.[123] "Avarice was one of the characteristics of the judges of the lower stratum who served in rural towns," writes Sālim Sa'īd al-Jamal. The low salary the imām paid them created this situation, he explains. The fees they charged and bribes they received served as their main source of income.[124]

Aharon Ḥamdi explains that ordinary people appealed to Imām Yaḥyā against judges who took bribes during his morning "office hours" when he opened the doors of his palace to the public.[125] This suggests as well the political dimension of judicial bribery in the imāms' Yemen. While the imām may have created a situation in which bribery was almost inevitable, charges of corruption could be used as ammunition against lower-level functionaries if the need arose.

Of course, litigants tried to "game" the legal system as well. A poor sayyid in Damt specialized in forging land deeds for Muslims and IOUs for Jews. For land deeds he wrote the document, inserted the names of witnesses long deceased, allowed it to yellow in the sun, then claimed to have found it among the papers of his dead father, who was venerated as a saint in the community.[126] Litigants hired false witnesses, scripted testimony for codefendants, and manipulated damage assessors, phenomena that will be discussed in chapter 5.

In 1918 Yaḥyā b. Muḥammad al-Iryānī, an eminent qadi who would later become the head of the court of appeals in Sanaa and a clandestine opponent of the imāms, lamented the state of the law in Yemen in a poem he wrote to his nephew, also a qadi and a member of the opposition:

> It is a pity we cannot apologize to the Turks, for we promised to apply the sharīʿa absolutely.
> We told them: you have demolished its edifice, when the palace of the truth had been taller even than Khawarnaq [a palace in Baghdad],
> That when we had our chance we would dig a trench between truth and injustice.
> But once we owned it from hoof to hump we missed our chance and concocted an excuse.
> Indeed, you will think I am speaking of a curiosity, even though you are fully aware that I speak the truth
> [Concerning] the circumstances and affair of the rulers of this age. They have offered to the greedy a cup of aged wine.
> They have been avaricious with God's law, complaining of the statutes of the Almighty. They limited [them] until a vast open space became a stricture.
> They put off judging between two parties for months, meanwhile complaining that the West had become the East,
> Punishing them with grievous torment while speaking of how their ruling would show meticulous thought.
> But a precise ruling is rare—the one in the right has got nothing but harm and misery.
> After this there is no hope for the one in the right to find a supporter in order to pin down an opponent—though the justice of his cause shines forth.
> The one in the wrong is given free rein, with no control, looking for that which allows the highest profit in the sharīʿa.
> He may seek to appeal a ruling, his intention being the debasement of an opponent who has impoverished himself in the dispute.
> Then Truth calls out: "You cannot grasp me for I have gone to hang at the edge of the Pleiades."[127]

Qadi ʿAbd al-Karīm Muṭahhar, a loyal member of Imām Yaḥyā's administration, got hold of a number of scathing letters that a member of the then powerful

Wazīr sayyid clan, Muḥammad b. ʿAlī al-Wazīr, who led a small rebellion in 1922, had written about the imām. He argued forcefully against them in his official biography of the imām, *Katībat al-ḥikmah min sīrat imam al-ummah* (The Record of Wisdom Concerning the Life of the Imām of the Muslims).

Qadi Ismāʿīl al-Akwaʿ, an opponent of the imām's regime and the author of a monumental study that offers, among other things, a history of twentieth-century Yemen, reproduced Muḥammad b. ʿAlī al-Wazīr's handwritten letters, which were in bad shape. However, he did not type them and discuss them the way he usually did with handwritten documents he reproduced in his book. Historian Muḥammad b. ʿĪsā al-Ṣāliḥiyyah, whose work provides a rare pro-imāmic slant, deciphered the part of the letters that offered specific criticisms of the imām. Thus in this exchange we see the overlap of two distinct debates over the legacy of the imāmate in Yemen: one between a rebel sayyid and a loyal sayyid in the early 1920s, and a second between two historians in the late 1990s.

In one of his letters Muḥammad b. ʿAlī al-Wazīr remarks bluntly that under Imām Yaḥyā Yemen witnessed "the disappearance of the sharīʿa and its having been made an instrument for taking money from the people unjustly. If one of the weak or oppressed complained, he was sent back to his oppressor. He who had a just case did not pursue it, because he knew he would never win." Ṣāliḥiyyah strives to refute these charges. He comments that dissatisfaction with those among the imāms' employees who had already been entrenched in government since Ottoman rule, and who had origins in "middling" families, already fueled the nascent opposition in the 1920s. Against the charge of callousness toward the marginalized, Ṣāliḥiyyah points to the imām having personally attended to the plight of the poor each morning in his own palace courtyard.[128]

Such characterization of the prerevolutionary judicial system as a "golden age" is rare but not unique. Imāms Yaḥyā and Aḥmad conducted oral interviews with applicants to the judiciary and investigated their ethical comportment (e.g., commanding the good and forbidding the bad, prayer habits).[129] Imām Yaḥyā is reported to have said of his hiring practices, "We are looking for men for jobs, not jobs for men." Nevertheless, despite his involvement in the opposition to the imām's despotism, Qadi Muḥammad al-Akwaʿ strains credulity when he claims that not only were all of the imām's judicial hires intellectually distinguished, but "I never knew or heard that he had appointed a qadi . . . who disturbed the peace, got drunk, was an ignoramus, or had bad morals, or was a crude boor."[130]

Jews (and, one might speculate, many Muslims as well) held much lower expectations of Muslim judges. In one Jewish folktale, a veritable legion of Jews and Muslims pursued a poor Jew to a qadi's house. The Jew had harmed each of them. He charged one a princely sum in exchange for a chicken, killed a donkey belonging to another, accidentally suffocated an infant while asleep, and afterward killed an old man when he tried to commit suicide by jumping from a third-story roof. After growing tired of waiting for an audience with the judge, the Jew dashed inside, avoided the qadi's bodyguards, and slipped up the stairs to the private quarters. There he caught the qadi drinking brandy (*'araq*). The qadi rendered judgment against all of the poor Jew's accusers and netted him sizeable damages, asking only that the Jew become his regular brandy connection.[131]

Moving from the realm of storytelling back to reality, Jamal says that Qadi Luṭf al-Zubayrī, the Sanaa judge who was largely responsible for disputes involving Jews, disgraced himself. He was on his yearly vacation at his second home in the resort town of al-Rawḍah when a girl wandered into his garden. He plied her with grapes in hopes of seducing her. When she resisted his advances he raped her, and his crime was observed by witnesses. One of Imām Yaḥyā's wives interviewed the girl, and then she was sent away to live in the all-sayyid town of Ḥūth. Zubayrī died in prison, and when he died no one would accompany his body to the cemetery.[132] This information is related only by Jamal. It is no wonder that Muḥammad Zabārah's biographical dictionary, which accounts for the intellectual pedigrees of Yemen's Muslim elite, did not discuss it.

Why did Imām Yaḥyā put up with qadis who took bribes, committed crimes, and organized against his rule? Many of them served him as useful intermediaries between political factions. Some, like Chief Minister 'Abdallāh al-'Amrī, maintained channels of communication with sayyid clans whose members were credible competitors for the imāmate. 'Amrī also maintained contact with the opposition, which included his son Muḥammad.[133] While Zayd al-Daylamī, Qāsim al-'Izzī, Luṭf al-Zubayrī, Ḥusayn al-'Amrī, and Aḥmad al-Jīrāfī were all critics of Imām Yaḥyā, they issued a 1924 statement in favor of designating Prince Aḥmad the "heir apparent," thereby flouting the Zaydī school's disagreement with dynastic succession.[134]

Early in Yaḥyā's reign, Luṭf al-Zubayrī headed the committee that built the imām's army. As such he was partly responsible for investigating newly conscripted officers.[135] In the 1930s he sent a younger man who, according to one Muslim writer, was like an adopted son to him to infiltrate an opposition circle in Sanaa.[136] Qadi Luṭf was either the great-uncle or the uncle of Muḥammad Maḥmūd al-Zubayrī, one of the most prominent opponents of the imām and a former high court qadi. In 1941 the latter Zubayrī trusted him enough to ask him for his opinion on an unpublished work of his. Soon thereafter, his (great?)-uncle searched his house, confiscated his papers, and turned them over to the imām.[137]

As for judges' political affiliations and their impact upon their decision making, a central line of research that legal realism opened, the Yemeni case provides instructive examples. The Jewish intermediary Jamal saw the qadis who opposed him as the backbone of the opposition to Imām Yaḥyā and suggested further that his struggle for Jewish advancement hastened the end of the imāmate in Yemen. While this reading of a critical turning point in the history of modern Yemen cannot be confirmed with the evidence at hand alone, Jewish sources provide rare insights into the internal dynamics of the troubled relationship between the imām and the Muslim intelligentsia who played a major role in precipitating revolution.

2 Changing God's Law

The ways in which Muslims and Jews in Yemen distinguished themselves from one another could be interpreted in two contradictory yet perfectly plausible ways. They represented either fairly arbitrary traditions accrued over a long period of time or norms derived from a general principle or principles. For example, the fact that Jewish men in urban areas wore sidelocks, dark-colored robes that exposed their calves, and black caps likely predated attempts to legislate their dress. Moreover, since Jews themselves had their own reasons to promote self-segregation, they may have had their own reasons for these specificities as well.

The laws applying to non-Muslims as they are recounted in prescriptive legal works strongly suggest that Jews' public behavior emphasizes their social inferiority to Muslims, not merely their difference from them. However, this principle informed other realms of social contact between the majority and the minority that were not legislated. According to Jews from one village in lower Yemen, Jewish humility extended to poverty, and Jews with wealth made great efforts to hide their financial state.[1] Similarly, a Syrian traveler contrasts the cleanliness of the interior of Jewish homes in Sanaa with the filthy streets of the Jewish Quarter.[2] Newly available imports offered previously undiscovered opportunities for non-Muslim ostentatiousness. One writer describes how a handful of Jewish notables in Radāʿ who did business in Aden owned wristwatches, which were extremely rare.[3] One Jewish author mentions a ban on Jews wearing showy eyeglasses.[4] According to the *Roiling Sea* (*Baḥr al-zakhkhār*), a Zaydī law manual, they were not to wear silver or gold signet rings.[5] In 1930 Sālim Saʿīd al-Jamal ordered two fancy copper kerosene lamps from Egypt. For a short time his house became the brightest in Sanaa, next to the imām's two palaces, which were the only electrified buildings in Yemen. However, the imām diplomatically suggested that Jamal sell him the lamps for their use in mosques.[6]

By appealing to the socio-legal principle of humiliating the non-Muslim, Muslim "reformers" sought to expand the scope of the original set of laws set out in the legal manuals of Zaydī jurisprudence. As will be shown in this chapter, some Muslims and Jews set the very arbitrariness of the laws, as relatively innocuous elements of inherited tradition, against the principles of humiliation that some of their contemporaries derived from the laws.

The Greatest Humiliation

In May 1940 Sālim Saʿīd al-Jamal received an urgent message from a Muslim scholar in a village in north Yemen. A group of Jews who were charged with collecting human and animal excrement and the bodies of dead animals had complained to the provincial governor that their coreligionists ought to either share equally in their demeaning work or share equally the profits of their more lucrative trades. (Most Jews in the village were carpenters or blacksmiths who repaired Muslims' farming tools.) The local governor accepted the complaint and jailed the Jewish blacksmiths and carpenters pending their agreement to one of these options.

The Muslim scholar wrote the jailed men's request in appropriate legal language and sent it by courier to Jamal, who then brought it to Imām Yaḥyā. The men asked for their liberty and also asked for "a decisive ruling that [would affirm that] each Jew ought to practice his fixed profession and [would] prevent the dung-collecting non-Muslims from disturbing us."[7] The imām obliged, ordering the governor to free the men and affirming the division of labor between Jewish craftsmen and dung collectors.

This conflict was not limited to the tribal hinterlands of Yemen. Jamal was responsible for collecting the *jizya* (a poll tax levied upon non-Muslims) of the Jews of Sanaa, and his handwritten tax registry lists the Jewish dung collectors. The 1935 registry lists twenty-two men as *muṭayyibīn* (sanitation workers) and indicates that their tax burden is to be shouldered by the community. He also obliterated their surnames to prevent the shame attached to this profession from being passed on to their descendants.[8]

The Jewish dung collectors formed an endogamous caste. The larger Jewish community excluded them from weddings, religious education, certain acts of communal worship, and marriage outside of their own group.[9] In turn the dung collectors occasionally went into hiding. This led to the arrest of some of the more prominent members of the community, who were thereby forced to offer the dung collectors better pay before they would return to work. In addition to effacing their surnames from the tax registry, Jamal issued a legal ruling publicizing the work of the dung collectors and stressing their merit for relieving the rest of the community of this duty.[10] However, these were halting steps in a career otherwise marked by audacious challenges to the status quo of Muslim-Jewish relations.

It is possible that in the 1940 case Imām Yaḥyā might have aimed to find the easiest way to free the imprisoned craftsmen, upbraid an overly independent governor, or please a Jewish aide. Yet by affirming dung collection as a Jewish profession, the imām also affirmed that the legal reasoning that led to its creation in the late eighteenth century still possessed validity. Indeed, when he took Sanaa from the Turks in 1918, Imām Yaḥyā renewed the "Latrines Decree," which mandated that Jews collect human excrement.[11] In 1928 the imām's son Aḥmad got wind of the fact that the dung collectors in the city of Ṣaʿdah, in the far north of Yemen, were sayyids. He jailed members of the Jewish community until an end to this scandal could be found. A local Muslim and a low-status Jew from another town, along with his wife and son, were found to do the job. This Jewish family eventually converted to Islam.[12]

Much earlier, in 1874, the Ottoman governor of Yemen had tried to lift the decree but faced opposition from both conservative Muslims and Jewish dung collectors who stood to lose their livelihood.[13] Ottoman (and later Turkish republican) administrators in Yemen objected to decrees such as these but, faced with Arab uprisings, rarely wanted to pay the political price of opposing them. Although these administrators were unsympathetic to attempts to humiliate the Jews on religious grounds, their tenuous grip on Yemen led them to devise new ways of making use of the Jewish community, which was in no position to argue. Under Turkish rule Jews had to grind flour for the army and transport badly wounded soldiers upon stretchers to the port of Hodeida, from whence they would be transported to Istanbul.[14]

The Ottomans in Yemen failed to live up to ideals of breaking down the distinctions between Muslim and Jew that had been disseminated in edicts from 1839 and 1856, and especially after the Young Turk revolution of 1908. Nevertheless, Jews in Yemen became acutely aware of these changes that affected non-Muslims elsewhere in the empire. This awareness, in turn, led them to reassess what was possible in Yemen. In 1910 Jewish leaders in Yemen wrote to Ottoman chief rabbi Ḥayyim Naḥum demanding an end to discrimination in the courts, which dismissed Jewish testimony in cases involving Muslims. After the Treaty of Daʿʿān, prominent Jews wrote letters to colleagues in Palestine complaining of harsh treatment in the Zaydī courts.[15]

As mentioned above, the Ottomans also made the Jews responsible for grinding flour for the army, a task that devolved upon Jewish women equipped with grinding querns. According to ʿAmram Qoraḥ, this duty, which brought with it very modest payment, initially benefited poor and widowed Jewish women. However, when the number of soldiers grew and the number of Jews fell through emigration, families had to hire women to enable them to fill their quotas of flour.[16] In the time of Imāms Yaḥyā and Aḥmad, Jews in some parts of Yemen still performed this task. According to a Jew from Manākhah, mills had begun to be imported toward the end of Ottoman rule. However, they broke down during the imām's rule, and since no one had the expertise to repair them, the old system was reintroduced. Jews ground flour for the army for low wages.[17] Muslim writers Ismāʿīl and Muḥammad al-Akwaʿ list forcing (unspecified) people to grind flour for the army without payment among the evils perpetrated by Imām Yaḥyā's son Ḥasan during his tenure as provincial governor of Ibb.[18]

Ṣāliḥ al-Ẓāhirī says he asked the imām to agree to pay the Jews for this work and the imām agreed. Nissim Ṭayri, from Radāʿ, confirms that this happened, and that the imām agreed to pay one-half riyāl per 55 kilos of flour. He adds that once the possibility of payment became a reality, Muslims wanted to grind flour as well. The imām refused, arguing that the Jews were entitled to the task and to payment by virtue of having done it for free for so many years.[19]

Local Muslims tried to pressure Ẓāhirī to relent in his quest to turn the production of flour for the army into paid work and hired mercenaries to stop him. On the eve of the Sabbath they found him in the synagogue, where he was repairing a Torah scroll. Ẓāhirī says the mercenaries were shocked to find themselves unable to raise their hands against him. (The miraculous protection of the pious is not an uncommon theme in such anecdotage.) Afterward, three men who had hired the first two thugs sat in wait for Ẓāhirī in a copse of trees. Ẓāhirī, having been warned of their presence, fetched a pistol and confronted them. Though the law did not permit Jews in this part of Yemen to bear arms, he says that Muslims had given guns to him and to many other Jewish merchants.[20] He convinced the Muslims that their grudge was with the imām, for whom, they said, "we are only for the good of his tribe."[21] This did not end the affair. In July and August 1949 Jews from Manākhah wrote to Sālim Manṣūrah, Imām Aḥmad's "court Jew" in Taʿizz, complaining of a "grinding edict," upon which the town's mayor would not allow them to renege, and asking "to be freed of the duty of grinding the grain that we are obliged to perform."[22]

The assumption that the harm in allowing Jews to live unmolested among Muslims needed to be periodically balanced out through humiliating labor seems to lie behind an incident described by Nissim Gamlieli. Sometime in the 1930s the governor of Damt was expecting a small group of foreign visitors. Soldiers rounded up the town's Jews and put them to work widening the main road and clearing it of stones.[23] He also requisitioned carpets and water pipes from the homes of wealthier Jews for his palace and for tents erected for the occasion. He had five Jews he considered wealthy imprisoned in the palace and held them responsible for paying the expenses of the visit. Some of the Muslims who gathered to watch the Jews work disapproved. They were also shocked to see that when the visitors arrived, they walked on foot like peasants rather than riding horses.[24]

Shalom Bene Moshe, a Jew from a fertile river valley in lower Yemen, reports that some provincial governors were charged in the mid-1940s with trapping some of the area's baboons for sale abroad. (In contrast, other sources report that locals were ordered to kill the baboons.) The governors, in turn, hired local Jews, Muslims, and enlisted men to undertake this task. The soldiers had some success, although they killed many more baboons than they captured, and the local Muslims balked at the task. Eventually the task devolved upon the Jews alone.[25]

Ratson Halevi comments that although baboons harmed crops, "the farmers avoided shooting them out of the belief that the baboon was a quarter human."[26] Nissim Gamlieli, another Jew from the same region, explained that local Muslims upheld the "Qur'anic tradition" that the bands of baboons descended from the Children of Israel, who had angered God through the construction of the Golden Calf.[27] In the *Commentary [on the Book of] Flowers,* the foundational text of Zaydī jurisprudence, one jurist argues that Jews ought to wear dark-colored clothing "so that they would look like monkeys."[28]

Corvee labor like grinding flour, clearing roads, and killing baboons paled in comparison to the so-called Latrines Decree. The idea that Jews ought to collect excrement was the brainchild of Muḥammad 'Alī al-Shawkānī (1760–1834), a figure often hailed as the renewer of the thirteenth Islamic century. He is the most famous Muslim thinker Yemen has produced and is widely regarded as a crucial intellectual predecessor of Islamic modernism. Shawkānī's writings on this question need to be taken into account in order to form a balanced picture of his thought. Examining these writings may also point to some of the pitfalls in the version of reforming Islam from within which he is identified. Moreover, the story of the Latrines Decree illustrates a rather spectacular failure of what Sherman Jackson identifies as Islamic law's "safety net principles," as well as a successful attempt by the custodians and interpreters of the law to ensure that the weak remain weak.[29]

In the first of a series of eight short treatises from the 1790s on the legality of forcing Jews to collect excrement, Shawkānī mounted a defense of the proposal in response to a questioner who is identified elsewhere as the emir of the Yemeni town of Kawkabān, 'Īsā b. Muḥammad (d. 1793).[30] The remaining treatises consist of arguments against the proposal written by three scholars, one of whom was the son of the emir of Kawkabān, as well as Shawkānī's rebuttals of each of them.[31]

It is not clear whether the debate between Muslims in the 1790s over the legality of forcing Jews to collect excrement was merely hypothetical. Were Jews ordered to collect excrement before, during, or after this exchange? The nineteenth-century writer Ḥayyim Ḥibshūsh sheds some light on this issue. The author explains that a relative of the reigning imām owned a bathhouse. The bathhouse owner had a rival who taunted him by saying that he "emptied Jewish bathrooms of excrement." This was said in the presence of the chief qadi, Yaḥyā [b. Ṣāliḥ] al-Saḥūlī.[32]

The mud-brick tower houses that define Yemeni urban architecture usually have a bathroom on the top floor. Urine flows down a pipe that is designed to dry it quickly. Excrement falls down a separate chute to a small room on the ground floor. This room has a hatch that can be opened from the outside.[33] Because wood was scarce, human and animal feces was shaped into cakes and then dried and used as kindling to light cooking fires or as fuel to heat the bathhouses.[34] (Animal bones were used as well.) Dung was also used as fertilizer. Jewish writers describe how families threw ashes from cooking fires down the chute to absorb moisture and contain bad smells. Farmers periodically emptied the waste from the hatch at street level and used it as fertilizer in their fields.[35] They used the ashes from these fires as fertilizer as well. In ʿAmrān, north of Sanaa, Jews spread the ashes from bathhouse fires over the fields.[36] Despite these Yemeni particularities, it was not unheard of for non-Muslims elsewhere in the Islamic world to perform sewer work. This occurred in Muslim Spain, Morocco, and Central Asia.[37]

The imām was embarrassed by the charge that his kinsman trafficked in Jewish feces. The chief qadi, Saḥūlī, suggested to him that allowing Muslims to collect excrement, especially from the houses of Jews, was bad for Islam.[38] In addition to lifting this shame from Muslims, forcing the Jews to collect excrement would offer corporate welfare to the bathhouse industry, giving owners a captive workforce to supply their fuel as well as very few reasons to pay them. It would also defray the costs they incurred in offering free baths to prominent Muslims.[39] Thus it seemed to be a "win-win" proposition for the qadi.

Saḥūlī served as chief qadi during the debate over whether or not the Jews should collect excrement. When he died in 1795, Shawkānī assumed his post.[40] Saḥūlī and Shawkānī had other common interests as well. Saḥūlī wrote a work that may or may not be extant titled "On Taking Custody of Non-Muslim Children When Their Parents Die," a cause that was taken up by Shawkānī. [41] Shawkānī's short work on the same subject, a "discussion of the children of the infidels" revolves around the theological question of whether one may be admitted to heaven on the basis of works alone. Like Shawkānī, Saḥūlī stood out from other Zaydī scholars for his intense interest in Sunni *ḥadīth* collections.[42] This is worth bearing in mind, because the idea of seizing Jewish orphans and converting them to Islam revolves around one particular hadith: "Every boy is born with '*fiṭrah*'—his parents make him a Jew or a Christian."[43] For philosophically minded Muslims, this hadith offered a sociological view of the acquisition of religious belief. Every person is born with a predisposition toward metaphysical reasoning (*fiṭrah*), and their parents steer them toward a particular religion. Other, more traditionally minded Muslims stressed the hadith's specification of Judaism and Christianity. For them it meant that every person possesses an innate disposition toward Islam, but non-Muslim parents lead their children astray. The latter interpretation lay behind the "Orphans Decree," which Imām Yaḥyā renewed in 1919 or 1921.[44]

Anecdotes contained in the memoirs of Jews from Yemen often involve the protagonists becoming separated from their families and pressured to convert to Islam. These suggest that the official policy of converting orphans drew from a wider cultural norm where vulnerable Jews were to be absorbed into the larger Muslim society, even if some persuasion, even force, was required. For example, a Jewish boy who worked as a servant in the imām's palace recalls the imām and his wives gently pressuring him to convert. He allayed the imām's fears for his soul by citing a local proverb: "No tribesman has ever returned from heaven crowned with a garland nor has a Jew returned from hell burned to a crisp."[45]

Saḥūlī must have issued what later became known as the Latrines Decree after the year 1775, when he resumed his post of chief qadi after a fall from grace, and long enough before 1791 that Shawkānī could defend the ruling of his senior colleague by saying: "Now the Jews of Sanaa . . . have begun to envy each other over the profits [of dung collecting], vying with one another over them and exulting in them with great joy."[46] Thus, Saḥūlī probably thought of forcing Jews to collect excrement, but Shawkānī became the primary advocate for the law.

Shawkānī makes three basic points: (1) God recommends humiliating non-Muslims as a general principle, and their humiliation is perpetual; (2) non-Muslims ought to provide a broader interest (*maṣlaḥah*) in exchange for living in most places; and (3) Muslim collection of excrement is a legal impossibility. Shawkānī's first main argument revolves around the last two words of the Qur'ān's "jizya verse" (9:29): "until they give the poll tax submissively while they are humiliated."[47] Most Qur'ānic commentators understand "while they are humiliated" as a circumstantial clause describing the act of paying the jizya, which is either humiliating in and of itself or ought to be accompanied by a ritual slap or some other symbolic act. Shawkānī interprets the humiliation as extending beyond the moment of tax collection. Thus his understanding of the verse would lead to the translation: "until they give the poll tax submissively—[for] they are *continually* humiliated." For him, non-Muslim humiliation is ongoing and Muslims must enforce it.

The idea that the ritual humiliation of non-Muslims ought to be limited to the act of collecting the jizya conflicted with the sumptuary regulations (such as the prohibition against non-Muslims riding horses or mules) that emphasize the superiority of Muslims over non-Muslims. These are not limited to a specific moment. Furthermore, if Muslims are obligated to enforce such minor humiliations, few of which find precedent in the Qur'an or hadith, then the Jews ought to take responsibility for collecting excrement, which Shawkānī describes as "the greatest and most important type of humiliation, especially given its necessity due to the fact that this destructive shame adheres to the distinctive emblems of the Muslims." Here it is important to note that Shawkānī singles out Jews for humiliation, a fact that differentiates him from most scholars, who use discursive categories like "People of the Pact" (dhimmīs) to discuss non-Muslims. To give one example, he argues that the Jews' poverty is part of a divine plan: "Misfortune always visits them and mishaps befall them one after the other as time passes."

Shawkānī also argues for the utility of collecting excrement. He emphasizes that Jews' residence in territories "other than their lands" depends upon their offering a benefit that outweighs the benefit of expelling them. (The Zaydī definition of "their lands" is discussed elsewhere in this book.) Shawkānī says, "If attentiveness to benefit makes forcing them [to leave] permissible, how can it be forbidden to force them to do something that is of a lesser level of harm to those who are forced but many degrees greater in utility?"

Finally, Shawkānī argues that the burden of proof is on those who would justify Muslim collection of dung, not the opposite. Forcing the Jews to collect excrement is not an innovation. The innovation had already occurred when Muslims began collecting excrement from Jewish houses, but Muslim scholars did not respond to this properly at the time. As far as forcing Jews to collect excrement is concerned, "this type of humiliation is permitted us by [humiliation's] adherence to them unless there is a legal reason to prevent it.[48] Shawkānī utilizes a type of inductive reasoning called "suitability" (*munāsaba*) in order to cope with the lack of scriptural sources that deal with the collection of dung. He argues that Muslim collection of dung has been ruled out as "suitable" because it conflicts with one of the five "constraints" of Muslim legal theory—namely, the "preservation of religion."[49] It conflicts with this principle insofar as honor is intrinsic to Islam, a point Shawkānī makes with reference to the hadith: "Islam is lofty and none are made lofty above it." After taking into account textual indicators such as those he sees at work in the jizya verse, or the hadith I just quoted, ordering the Jews to collect dung becomes "unimplemented [by the prophet Muḥammad] but suitable."[50] Therefore, Jackson is correct in asserting that the "constraints" of Islamic legal theory could provide a remedy for novel situations faced by the community, but only if one takes for granted, as Shawkānī did, that the community a priori excluded non-Muslims.

Shawkānī's critics repeatedly stress the novelty of the law, a tactic that made sense in the context of his avowed literalism in interpreting scripture. For example, in his treatise refuting Shawkānī, ʿAlī b. ʿAbdallāh al Jalāl (1756–1810 or 1825), a Sanaa scholar, asks: "Was no one at the time of the Messenger of God aware of the meaning of [the jizya] verse, [instead needing to wait] until recent times when someone thought to heat bathhouses by burning excrement? This is truly amazing!"[51] Jalāl argues that something seems amiss when the putative generality of humiliating the Jews is contrasted with the minutiae of collecting human excrement and selling it to city bathhouses. He implies that giving people a general license to humiliate represents depravity and that Muslims are certainly capable of thinking of more cruel things they might do with or to non-Muslims if they had the license to do so. He questions as well the severity of this specific humiliation, noting that worse has been done to non-Muslims by better people (i.e., at the birth of Islam the finest generation of Muslims conquered the infidels' cities, killed, and plundered). He also argues that explicit prohibitions against theft and murder annul whatever prescriptions for the treatment of non-Muslims might be inferred from these cataclysmic events.[52]

Jalāl accuses Shawkānī of finding divine commandments in anecdotal scriptural material and then, making matters worse, using them for the sole purpose of arguing for permissibility (*jawāz*) when obligation (*wujūb*) is the purpose of divine commands. He challenges the logic behind Shawkānī's claim that *not* forcing Jews to collect excrement obligates Muslims to do it. Three times he suggests that the issue could be resolved if the bathhouses burned expensive firewood rather than free excrement. Thus he implies that Shawkānī is a shill for the bathhouse industry who hides his equation of public and business interests behind faulty legal arguments. He describes Shawkānī's arguments against Muslims' collecting excrement as being little more than overheated rhetoric: "affected and rhythmic language that excites wonder in the listener and seizes hearts by the legion."

Another critic of Shawkānī, 'Abdallāh b. 'Īsā al-Kawkabānī, attacks the idea that the Jews' humiliation is perpetual. If, as Shawkānī argues, they must be humiliated at every moment and not only when paying the jizya, the Islamic state's truce with them would become null and void every time a Jew fell asleep or ate a meal, to say nothing of perfectly legal interactions between Muslims and Jews where humiliation is either absent or very subtle indeed (i.e., business partnerships or friendships, even where conversion is the ultimate aim). Kawkabānī argues that if the benefit to Muslims of Jews living in their midst is predicated upon the Jews providing this benefit of their own free will, as is the case with paying the jizya, then they cannot be forced to collect excrement, and if they are hired to do it, they must be paid. This objection implies that Kawkabānī knew that in at least some cases they were not being paid for this work.[53] He also points out that the interests of the public and those of bathhouse owners are not identical, because a bathhouse "is a permitted thing that provides access to forbidden things"—namely, the vices that stem from women bathing there.[54]

Kawkabānī challenges Shawkānī's idea that touching feces is forbidden to Muslims for the damage it causes to their pride by noting that using feces as fertilizer has been deemed permissible by a wide range of scholars.[55] In addition, these scholars exempted the use of dung to light ovens from the general ban on making use of forbidden things.[56] For him, excrement is ecumenical. "That which lights a stove is not Jewish and is not Christian," he writes. It is simply an unfortunate byproduct of being human, and therefore nobody is above touching it. He tells the story of a man from Basra, Ibn al-Shikhkhīr, who saw a man dressed in fine clothing and walking with haughtiness. Ibn al-Shikhkhīr chastised the rich man, who asked, "Do I know you?" He said, "I know *you*. Your beginning is a putrid drop, your end is a stinking corpse, and in the meantime you find yourself between urine and feces."[57]

The implication of 'Abdallāh b. 'Īsā's position is that Shawkānī's argument would rule out Muslims doing any undesirable work when there are non-Muslims who can be made to do it. He argues instead that a Muslim who performs menial labor has been assigned this work by God for being vile or stupid. Islam is not hurt by it, and a poor Muslim who collects excrement to sell does not thereby become an infidel.

It is important to note that traditional Zaydīs are more punctilious than other Muslims in the avoidance of ritual impurity, a fact to which their elaborate ablutions attest. Many Zaydīs will leave their underwear outside a mosque for fear that it contains traces of impure matter. (Sunnis and those Zaydīs who lean toward Sunnism ridicule this practice.)[58] Some Zaydīs (but not Shawkānī) believe that non-Muslims convey ritual impurity (see below).[59] Thus it is ironic that the traditional Zaydī participants in this debate, who believed that both feces and non-Muslims were impure, rejected the proposal that Jews be forced to collect excrement.

Shawkānī concedes to ʿAbdallāh b. ʿĪsā that his initial argument in favor of coercion contradicted the principle that Jews ought to provide benefit of their own free will. Even though the title of his initial treatise in favor of Jewish dung collection contained the phrase "forcing the Jews," he tries to dodge this criticism by arguing that he did not really mean coercion by this. "I am not saying force the Jews to do this in spite of their hatred for it and lack of assent to it," writes Shawkānī. "I say instead: present them with it, and if they accept it and agree to do it, then it is fine, but if they refuse, order them to leave [Yemen]."[60]

In responding to his critics on the benefit of forcing Jews to collect excrement, Shawkānī shifts his ground measurably. The benefit is no longer protecting Muslims from shame as it was in Shawkānī's initial treatise. In subsequent treatises he presents the law as a solution to the harm suffered by people who live in cities that stems from the buildup of excrement. He chooses another of the five basic constraints of legal theory: the avoidance of harm. "Defending the people of cities from harm is the most important goal [of the law]."[61] He states that the fact that the ability to heat baths is made possible by collecting excrement is irrelevant.

So why are Muslims unable to alleviate this public health problem on their own? First, Shawkānī judges the admonitions against Muslims becoming ritually impure through contact with feces to outweigh the permissibility of using it. Second, he concludes that the fecal matter whose use his scholarly predecessors had approved must have been dry and therefore not terribly disgusting, whereas that collected from the collection rooms in the houses of Sanaa was moist and therefore forbidden for Muslims to touch. Finally, he notes a tradition in which sinners are punished in hell by being doused in their own urine. If God judges urine to be awful, it stands to reason that feces would be worse.

Shawkānī's successful attempts to force Jews to collect excrement and surrender their orphans to be raised by Muslim families were innovations to Muslim-Jewish relations that were specific to Yemen. Ironically, the Muslim sect that predominated in Yemen—and only in Yemen—the Zaydīs, was not the source of these innovations. Scholars who saw themselves as returning to the original sources of Islam and turning away from the authority of the Zaydī (Shiʿi) imāms championed the new policies. Many of the judges who Imām Yaḥyā empowered through his expansion of the judiciary would have considered themselves the direct intellectual heirs of Shawkānī's legacy. Through his primary teachers in Islamic studies, Imām Yaḥyā traced his own intellectual genealogy back to Shawkānī.[62] The imām was also viewed as something of an expert on Shawkānī in the wider world of Islamic learning. In 1925 a shaykh of al-Azhar, a preeminent center of Sunnism in Cairo, asked the imām for permission to transmit a work by Shawkānī, among others, and the imām granted it.[63]

Today the so-called servants (*akhdām*), clothed in distinctive orange overalls, perform sanitation work in Yemen. One Jew explained the transition from Jewish to black labor in a 1949 letter to Sālim Manṣūrah in Taʿizz. In it he detailed attempts by authorities to force Jewish tradesmen who practiced trades that were exclusively Jewish and who wanted to leave Yemen to teach their skills to Muslims. These included silversmiths, soap makers, tobacconists, dyers, potters, carpenters, bakers, metalworkers, and garbage collectors.[64] The last of these jobs, however, was not to be given to ordinary Muslims. "The [Jewish] sanitation workers will teach the blacks," wrote Qoraḥ.[65]

Muḥammad ʿAlī al-Shawkānī is a hero of Salafism in its many manifestations in that he is seen to represent a third way between orthodoxy (*taqlīd*) and those reformers who capitulated to European ideas. Even some scholars who have written on Shawkānī, such as Wael Hallaq and Ahmad Dallal, seem to view him in much the same way: as an advocate of independent legal reasoning (*ijtihād*), a foe of unquestioning allegiance to legal orthodoxy, and a staunch defender of scriptural purity against outside interests.[66] Dallal contrasts Shawkānī with those who rely upon "the loose application of the principle of *maṣlaḥah* [public benefit]."[67] Yet in this controversy he did just that, and we are able to listen to his orthodox Zaydī critics who seem to say: if this is what happens when the gate of independent reasoning (ijtihād) is opened, it would have been better had it remained shut. This debate also underscores the hard reality underlying the putative flexibility of the sharīʿa.

The Rabbi's Bicycle

If traditional Zaydīs defended the status quo of Muslim-Jewish relations against radical and cruel agendas, Jews themselves tried to make the law more permissive. Non-Muslims in Yemen were forbidden from riding horses and from riding saddles in the ordinary manner. This was due to a specific stipulation in the sumptuary laws concerning the transportation used by non-Muslims living under the protection of the Islamic state. One Zaydī jurist opined that since non-Muslims were not allowed to carry weapons, the law followed from the fact that a horse was the deadliest weapon.[68] This seems to be a case of drawing the bull's-eye around the arrow.

In the popular imagination, horses were thought to be noble animals, and this nobility conflicted with their (or even their offspring by donkeys) being ridden by lowly Jews. Legally, non-Muslims could only ride sidesaddle. (The Arabic word for "sidesaddle" itself already sounded archaic to medieval Muslim commentators.) Jamal explains that this qualification made it easier to tip them over if the necessity to do so arose. One Zaydī Muslim commentator adds that the obligation to ride sidesaddle applies only when an actual saddle is present.[69] That is, a Jew could ride a donkey bareback in the ordinary fashion.

Jews in Sanaa were forbidden from riding donkeys outside of the Jewish Quarter due to an additional stipulation of the sumptuary laws: a non-Muslim ought to dismount in the presence of a Muslim.[70] Thus, a non-Muslim riding through a busy Muslim neighborhood would have been a practical impossibility.

A Jew from the Shafi'i south, Yosef Riḍā, recalls that the laws regulating Jewish transportation and requiring Jews to dismount in the presence of Muslims were applied only when Zaydīs arrived as a consequence of the imām's defeat of the Turks. A local Sunni shaykh was mystified by the law when a newly arrived Zaydī sayyid insisted a local Jew be pulled off his donkey. It is said that when the carpetbagger pressed the issue, the shaykh threatened to kill him.[71]

The riding issue constituted a particularly tense arena for interactions between Muslims and Jews in Yemen. One Jew recalls how his parents hired an Arab camel driver to take him from Sanaa to his family's village. On the way a turbaned sayyid chastised the Arab for seating an impure Jew atop "the holy camel." (Camels are addressed in the sumptuary laws only insofar as they might bear a saddle, and if a camel is saddled, a non-Muslim must ride it sideways.) The Arab defended his passenger.[72] Mordecai al-Ẓāhirī, the son of Ṣāliḥ al-Ẓāhirī, a Jewish intermediary with Muslim officialdom, tells of an incident in his youth when he and his father were traveling through the crossroads town of Ma'bar, south of Sanaa, in the company of an eccentric Jewish convert to Islam named Nissim. Father and son rode a mule while Nissim, who wore his military uniform and carried weapons, walked.

Nissim, who by all appearances was a Muslim, allegedly asked a passing Muslim peasant who was driving a donkey if he would rent him the animal. The Muslim seems to have irritated Nissim by indicating to him that he was to be addressed as "hajj." The hajj rented him the donkey and followed behind. Nissim seated the boy Mordecai with him on the donkey, which occasioned protests from the Muslim. "I rented my donkey to the captain and not a Jewish dog like you," he exclaimed. Unbeknownst to the Muslim, Nissim struck the donkey in the head with his rifle butt. When it lay down, he complained bitterly to its owner. "If it happens again," the donkey's owner said, "saddle me up and ride me." After they resumed their journey, Nissim hit the donkey again, this time causing it to lose consciousness. Nissim climbed on the hapless hajj's back, beating him with a stick until it broke. Then he demanded to be paid for his trouble.[73]

Mordecai al-Ẓāhirī recalls an encounter he had when he was in prison in his late teens with a wealthy Sanaa merchant named Qadi Muhammad al-Thawr.

(Not everyone from a qadi family was a religious judge.) According to Ẓāhirī, al-Thawr's family was quietly supportive of the rebellion against Imām Yaḥyā, and al-Thawr had been sent to the prison because he had loaned a sum of money to the leader of the rebellion, 'Abdallāh al-Wazīr, who seized power after the assassination of the imām in 1948 and claimed the imāmate.

While in prison, Qadi al-Thawr asked Mordecai about his father, Ṣāliḥ, with whom he had a troubled relationship. After the prodding of another Muslim inmate and upon receiving Qadi al-Thawr's permission, Mordecai told the assembled company what had transpired between his father and the new prisoner. One very hot and dry summer day at noon, Sanaa's merchants were rushing home for their afternoon qāt chews. Chewing qāt, a mild mood-altering drug, is a popular pastime in Yemen and parts of East Africa. The merchants preferred to travel on foot, Ẓāhirī explains, in order to be especially thirsty for the chew, which amplified the effects of the drug.

Qadi Muḥammad al-Thawr had encountered Ṣāliḥ al-Ẓāhirī riding down a Muslim street on a white donkey. Horses and white donkeys pointed to the high status of their riders. While horses were forbidden to Jews, white donkeys were provocative in that their ostentatious color (a color that was associated with Islam) violated the spirit, if not the letter, of the law that differentiated Muslims from Jews by means of riding animals. Moreover, Ẓāhirī did not ride sidesaddle—his legs were on either side of his mount—nor did he utter the standard words "whatever you wish" when he passed the Muslim. The Jew rode in comfort while the qadi dripped with sweat.

Qadi al-Thawr angrily demanded that the Jew dismount. At the same moment that the Muslim reached up to push him off the donkey, Ẓāhirī dismounted on the other side of the animal and insulted the Muslim by momentarily pointing the sole of his foot at the Muslim's face. A crowd of onlookers gathered. Ẓāhirī accused the qadi of highway robbery and announced his intention to pursue legal action, while the Muslim audience lamented the man's contravention of the protection that was vouchsafed the Jews by both God and the imām. In order to teach Qadi al-Thawr the magnitude of his mistake, Ẓāhirī shuttled between his most powerful Muslim contacts, complaining to the chief judge, to the imām's son, Ismā'īl, and to the chief of the imām's bodyguards.

Qadi al-Thawr's afternoon qāt chew was interrupted by a series of men, each of whom came to apprehend him. (Sālim Sa'īd al-Jamal recalls that having soldiers arrest a rival during the afternoon qāt chew in front of his friends was especially humiliating and required a special bribe.[74]) Ẓāhirī had arranged for the men to arrive at intervals. The police came to bring him to the courthouse, and then came Prince Ismā'īl's men, and finally the imām's bodyguards. Each group of law enforcement officials received larger payments than the previous group. Ṣāliḥ al-Ẓāhirī was present and made it seem to Qadi al-Thawr that he tried to convince the three groups of soldiers to lower their prices when in fact he ensured that they were amply compensated. Qadi al-Thawr told Ẓāhirī's son Mordecai and the other listeners in the jail, "I know the Jews as people who bow their heads before any Muslim." However, he confessed to having underestimated Ṣāliḥ al-Ẓāhirī, a man with connections. He also said that his story demonstrated the truth of the proverb "men are dogs and crows [i.e., mortal enemies] until they get to know one another." Ṣāliḥ al-Ẓāhirī and Qadi Muḥammad al-Thawr became friends, and in prison the Jew's son strenghtened the Qadi's relationship to the family. Before he was released from prison, Qadi al-Thawr left Mordecai al-Ẓāhirī sufficient money to pursue his appeal.[75]

Ṣāliḥ al-Ẓāhirī spent a month and a half evading Imām Aḥmad's troops after the beheading of 'Abdallāh al-Wazīr and the overthrow of his regime. He once fell asleep outside a village near Sanaa and was awoken by a Jew riding his donkey to work in another village. The local shaykh had warned both Muslims and Jews against harboring the fugitive. In order to allay the Jew's suspicions as to his identity, he spoke to him "in plain Arabic, the language of the crude among the Arabs, who cast opprobrium on the Jews," and ordered him to dismount from his donkey and give the "sayyid" a ride.[76]

In some cases a Jew's riding an (impure) animal seems to have exacerbated anxieties concerning the Jews' putative ritual impurity. It is claimed that five Muslims accosted a Jewish merchant who was traveling through a town in Lower Yemen. They accused him of riding through a Muslim cemetery on his donkey, forced him to dismount, and confiscated the animal. He protested that if the town road itself cut through the cemetery, he could hardly avoid riding on it. The local shaykh complained to the governor on the Jew's behalf. The governor sent soldiers to fetch the would-be donkey rustlers and questioned them. After they admitted that they often drove their livestock along the selfsame road, he asked, rhetorically, "What differentiates the Jew's donkey from your donkeys?" The men were jailed and the Jew got his donkey back.[77] The Muslim men's objection may have been only a pretext to steal his donkey. However, it is also possible that the presence of the Jew together with the large animal led them to start thinking about the impurity of each in a way that a Muslim with his animal would not.

In other cases low-status Muslims were present when a high-status Muslim tried to correct a hierarchical infraction involving a riding animal. Rather than closing ranks with the Muslim, they would side with the Jew. As one story goes, a Jewish cloth merchant once traveled with a Muslim camel driver near Yemen's Red Sea coast. In this very hot region the Muslim wore only a wrap around his loins; his upper body was exposed. On the road the two men encountered a sayyid from Sanaa, who upbraided the Muslim for being half naked and walking on foot while the Jew, fully clothed, rode a donkey. "His speech was not the way a human being speaks—it possessed eloquence from above the stratosphere," says the Jewish narrator of the anecdote. The camel driver, who disliked sayyids and was perhaps a bit off himself, knocked the learned man off his donkey.[78]

In Sanaa in the early 1930s a Muslim on horseback ordered a Jew riding a donkey with his young nephew to dismount. Immediately afterward a flying projectile struck the Muslim's horse, causing it to rear. The horse threw its rider. His foot caught in a stirrup on his way down, and his robe bunched up around his head, leaving "his bottom bare before the eyes of the sun and the sky." A Muslim shepherd boy who nursed a pathological hatred for sayyids had thrown the projectile, a chunk of wood. The shepherd was a marksman of sorts when it came to throwing chunks of wood. The two boys, Jew and Muslim, became close friends and blood brothers. The Muslim boy even grew heavy sidelocks in solidarity with his new "twin."[79]

In the 1920s an encounter with a sayyid who demanded he dismount led "Blackjack Cohen," a Jewish tanner from Lower Yemen, into a career of highway robbery. A haughty sayyid from Sanaa, who did not know that "the Jews of Shar'ab did not take [that] law seriously," demanded he dismount. The tanner made himself a blackjack and tracked down the sayyid and his manservant. Then he said, "How dare you, bastard son of a bastard, curse my grandfather?," knocked the two of them out, and robbed them. (Thenceforth, Blackjack Cohen repeated this "cold-blooded" line each time he prepared to mug a Muslim.)[80]

Not all such anecdotes of interfaith tension surrounding transportation end in violence. In Sanaa itself, the ostensible renewer of Zaydism, Imām Yaḥyā, seems to have ignored rules governing Jewish transportation.[81] In one case he is said to have pardoned a Jew who beat one of the princes in a feat of horsemanship. In another, a Jew hired to crack a safe for the imām insisted upon being chauffeured to the palace atop a mule.[82]

Nissim Gamlieli tells a story about his mother and her twin sister during a time when locust swarms descended upon Damt and the surrounding region. Local Muslims and Jews hurriedly collected the insects at night during their inactive phase. (Eating locusts is permissible under both Muslim and Jewish dietary laws.) A sayyid from one of the villages in the area offered cold water to the weary locust hunters. When he saw two Jewish girls straining under their burdens, he halted a camel caravan and ordered the owner to bind the girls' burdens to these noble animals.[83]

The law against Jews riding in the presence of Muslims was enforced in patchwork fashion. A black sayyid (the son of an Arab father and his black maid) riding a donkey in a village near Sanaa confronted a Jewish merchant from the south when the merchant did not dismount from his donkey. The Jew, who had been drinking some excellent 'araq, protested that no such rule existed where he was from and that even in Ta'izz he could ride unmolested in the presence of a prince. The sayyid dismissed the Shafi'i Muslims of the south and the royal family itself as "sons of donkeys." The Jew, emboldened by drink, pressed further. If Jews shared low status with some Muslims, yet God only cared about their treatment, did this not prove their chosenness? The Muslim then asked how the Jews viewed them, and the Jew explained that they were obligated to follow the Noahide commandments (the minimal commandments given to Noah and incumbent upon non-Jews). The sayyid asked if his demanding that the Jew dismount contravened these rules.

Just then two princes raced up on fine horses. "Four brothers, two on top of the other," one quipped when he saw the Jew and the black man on their respective donkeys. The Jew was offended but he appreciated the joke. He pulled out his bottle and took a swig, eliciting peals of laughter. One of the princes stuck his hand into the Jew's bag and grabbed a bottle of ʿaraq for himself, and then they raced off. The Jew later caught up with the princes, was paid, and sold them more alcohol.[84]

A Muslim stopped a Jew from said southeastern hinterlands in the market of Ma'rib and demanded he dismount from his donkey. The Jew protested that in his home town, Bayḥān, no such rules were applied to Jews. He took two witnesses and lodged a case against the Muslim with the local qadi. The qadi accepted the Jew's argument, imprisoned the Muslim for three days, and ordered him to pay damages.[85] Some Jewish writers from northernmost Yemen say that most Muslims in their region did not observe the taboos surrounding Jews' choice of riding animals. In one instance a group of sayyids on foot physically prevented a Jew from dismounting his donkey. However, he admits that encounters between mounted and solitary Jews and Muslims sometimes led to violence. In such instances the Jew might strike the Muslim and the Muslim would be too embarrassed to complain.[86]

In 1927, when Sālim Saʿīd al-Jamal had just started his career as a merchant, he set out to the market to buy a "Ḍubyānī" donkey, a donkey bred especially for riding, which was more expensive than an ordinary load-bearing donkey. Such donkeys were very large, white, and had loud voices. They were raised in only one part of Yemen. Jamal bought the donkey, as well as a saddlecloth, "like the Muslims had," on which he sat.[87] The Ḍubyānī donkey "was a donkey that was suitable for the Messiah," wrote Shalom Medinah.[88] Rather than dismounting upon leaving the Jewish Quarter, Jamal resolved to ride his donkey the three kilometers to his place of business in the market every day.

On his first day riding the donkey, two Muslims stopped Jamal on his way home.[89] One was a customer of Jamal's and owed him money. The other served as supervisor of public morality (*muḥtasib*), a fact that presumably added to the gravity of Jamal's charges. They demanded he dismount but he refused. They pulled him down by force and said, "This Jew is drunk—smell him."[90] They told him that he would soon have to appear before the chief judge, Zayd al-Daylamī,

נא   הרב רבי אברהם בדיחי

הרב רבי אברהם ב"ר יהודה בדיחי

הגאון סבי מארי אברהם בדיחי, שמעתי עליו מפי רבים כשהוא עוד היה בחיים, שהוא היה בלימודים יד ימינו של הרה"ג יחיא קאפח, והחזן הראשי בבית מדרשו במשך כמה שנים, עד שבאו רבני בתי כנסת רבים עם ראשי קהל בית הכנסת מהרי"ץ, חילו את פניו ושיכנעו אותו ואת הגר"י קאפח, שהוא צריך להיות ראש בית הכנסת הגדול של מהרי"ץ הנקרא כניס בית צאלח.

האדמו"ר אברהם בדיחי
ותלמידו המחבר הגר"ש גמליאל

וכך היה, עמד בראש בית הכנסת הזה שנים רבות עד שהתחיל להזדקן בשנת התרע"ט. ואז הקדיש את החדר הכי גדול שבביתו השני, לעסק התורה ולתפילה כפי שיתבאר להלן. מיום שעמד בראש בית הכנסת הזה, קבע את ישיבתו שם. והיו באים רבני בתי הכנסת ואחרים המקדימים לקום בחצות הלילה ללמוד אצלו, אני התחלתי בשנת התרע"ד לישון בחדרו, כדי לקום וללכת יחד אתו לבית מדרשו בבית כנסת מהרי"ץ. ראיתי שהיו באים בזה אחר זה. ובשעה אחת אחר חצות, כבר היו כולם יושבים לפניו כחצי גורן עגולה גדולה כפולה, כחמישים איש בערך. ולומדים גמרא בבלית עד שעה שלוש בערך ונפטרים. ונכנסים אחריהם אנשי המשמר השני כפי שיתבאר להלן. כל אחד ואחד מהרבנים של המשמר הראשון, הלך לבית הכנסת שהוא עומד בראשו ולימד את צאן מרעיתו בספרי הפוסקים. מי בהרמב"ם ומי בשולחן ערוך, עד זמן הברכות של הציצית והתפילין, מתפללים שחרית, ואחריה לומדים כשעה את השילוש לגירסה בלי פירוש.

סדר הלימוד אצלו כך היה, בתחילה לגרוס אינש והדר ליסבר, כיצד? הרב התחיל להם את המשנה, וכולם קראו אותה במנגינה הצבורית קריאה ראשונה ביחד, חזר וקרא אותה לפניהם במנגינת היחיד, והסביר אותה גם עם פירוש רבינו עובדיה ופירוש הרמב"ם למשניות, ולאחר שענה לתלמידים על כל השאלות, חזרו וקראו את המשנה קריאה שניה ביחד, ואז התחיל הרב להם את הסוגיה בגמרא במנגינה הצבורית, וכולם קראו אותה קריאה ראשונה ביחד אם היא סוגיה קטנה, או עד הפיסקה של המתניתין אם היא גדולה, חזר וקרא אותה במנגינת היחיד , והסביר
כל

Sālim Saʿīd al-Jamal (d. 2001) with his grandfather, R. Avraham Badīḥī (d. 1939), circa 1935. From Shalom Ṣeʿadyah Gamliel (Sālim Saʿīd al-Jamal), *Ḥakhme ha-yehudim be-teman be-dorenu ve-ʿad samukh litqufat ha-tana'im.*

but Jamal did not believe them. By charging him with drunkenness, which carried a stiff penalty, his opponents attached criminal consequences to Jamal's effrontery.

The next morning two soldiers arrested Jamal and brought him to a courtroom that was already full of Muslim and Jewish spectators. Instead of hiring a lawyer, Jamal argued before Daylamī that he would defend himself.[91] The *muḥtasib* testified that Jamal was out riding a donkey after the sunset curfew and cursing the Muslims. "Make way, pricks; move it, assholes," he was alleged to have said according to the record of the proceedings.[92] After forcing him to dismount, the *muḥtasib* and his companion said they found that Jamal was drunk. Two other Muslims bore witness to his drunkenness.[93] Non-Muslims were allowed to drink, but they were not allowed to get drunk. One Zaydī jurist resolves the seemingly difficult case of bibulous dhimmīs with a terse: "Drunkenness is not permitted in any of the religious laws."[94] Since the evidence of drunkenness no longer existed at the time of trial, the four Muslims had devised a clever way of using the sharīʿa to punish the Jew for his contravention of a nonlegal norm. The Jewish intermediaries Jamal and Ẓāhirī both complained that Muslims tried to silence them by accusing them of serious crimes that relied mainly on the testimony of (false) witnesses.

Jamal had crafted a subtle legal provocation when he left for work on his new donkey. If the rationale behind the sumptuary laws' ban on non-Muslims riding horses stemmed from a horse's intrinsic honor, the same principle applied to his high-end donkey. Whether the animal was wearing a saddle is not clear (as was mentioned, he describes the saddlecloth alone). If so, he had no legal basis to ride through a Muslim neighborhood with his legs on either side of the animal. If not, his gambit showed a knowledge of an opinion in the *Commentary [on the Book of] Flowers* whereby riding sidesaddle applies only to riding actual saddles. His Muslim opponents did not take the bait; instead they accused him of drunkenness.

In court Jamal argued that he rode the donkey because he was ill. He had shifted his ground, backing away from his initial provocation. The four Muslims' charge of public intoxication still stood at the center of the proceeding. He parried this more serious charge by suggesting that the only way his Muslim interlocutors could know the smell of wine was if they themselves were wine drinkers. This comment elicited a rebuke from the judge and angry outbursts from Muslim onlookers. However, it was quite a good point. The legal manuals fail to explain how a Muslim would know the smell of alcohol, much less why two adult male Muslims would be witnesses to another person's utter inebriation without having had a hand in it.

The *muḥtasib* testified that he knew the smell of alcohol because it was used in the manufacture of bullets, a trade he used to practice for the government.[95] One witness, who had been responsible for collecting a tithe from Jews' grain and butter under Turkish rule, said he knew the smell from the vessels that Jews from the country used to transport their grain to the city for tithing. Such vessels were occasionally recycled wine jars. The second witness said he had smelled a "foul smell" from Jamal but did not know that it was alcohol.[96] (Given that the Jew ran a perfume shop, one would assume that his default aroma was fairly pleasant.) These were reasonable answers and Jamal was forced to take a different approach.

After receiving the judge's permission to ask a question, Jamal asked whether the Muslim witnesses had kissed his impure mouth in order to detect the telltale odor emanating from the depths of his belly. The courtroom was momentarily filled with laughter.[97] The rabbi's question was humorous because the idea that the Muslim men got that close to him was embarrassing to them. Zaydīs were split on the issue of whether non-Muslims conveyed ritual impurity. Some doctrinal authorities noted that the prophet Muḥammad had brought nonbelievers into the mosque of Medinah, performed ablutions with them (which remove ritual impurity), and cooked in their vessels. Others argued that nonbelievers, even Sunni Muslims, conveyed ritual impurity.[98] Ritual impurity was thought to be transmitted through contact with an impure person or with fluids that had come into contact with him. In practice some Yemenis drew water from wells that Jews also used and ate food that Jews had cooked.

In contrast, other authorities insisted that all nonbelievers, even "nonbelievers by [incorrect] interpretation" (i.e., Sunnis), were impure. Calling a Jew "impure" or "dog" (an impure animal) were fairly common insults.[99] Bathing proved a common demarcation line, with Jews and Muslims using separate bathhouses. In areas where people bathed in rivers and streams, the two communities might bathe in different places within the same river or stream.[100] In the village of al-Saddah the Muslims bathed upstream from the Jews, lest the latter's impurity pollute Muslim bathers.[101] Some Muslims also objected to Jews drawing water from their wells, lest they pollute them.[102]

The legal category of ritual impurity, which was conveyed by contact and could be lifted, albeit inconveniently, through full body washing, often shaded into broader nonlegal conceptions of the Jew as dirty and smelly. The impurity that Muslims attributed to Jews was not limited to physical contact or contact with fluids, nor was it shared equally between all nonbelievers. A Yemeni revolutionary tells the story of Imām Yaḥyā hosting a French naval delegation in one of his homes. In order to one-up the imām for his improper intimacy with infidels, a shaykh invited a group of Jews from his homeland in eastern Yemen to stay in one of his houses. The imām summoned the shaykh and asked him about this. The shaykh explained that he housed the Jews in the top floor of his house, which prevented their filth and characteristically bad smell from ruining the rest of the house.[103]

Jews held negative stereotypes of Muslims as well, regarding them as unrefined, simple, and foul-mouthed.[104] One writer remarks of a particularly wild

Muslim boy who was blissfully ignorant of the pain of his impending circumcision: "for this boy who knew neither a teacher nor shame there was only one word to define him: a goy—Ishmael in every way."[105] Jews regarded some Muslim practices, such as the circumcision of adolescents (and adults) and *taḥlīl* marriage, as particularly shocking.[106] Some Jewish sources go so far as to allege that Muslims sometimes used the blood of Jewish children to treat leprosy, a kind of blood libel in reverse.[107]

Since a Muslim would have to touch an impurity or a liquid emanating from it in order to become impure, the law establishing smelling the breath as proof of drunkenness would not have served as a good argument (unless Jamal tended to spit a lot). Thus Jamal brought out into open court the nonlegal penumbra around the issue of ritual impurity, which both Muslims and Jews in the court recognized. (Perhaps a measure of homophobia operated as well.) By doing so he used the legal norm (avoidance of physical contact) against the nonlegal norm (avoidance of close proximity), reasoning that the Muslims' embarrassment at having transgressed the latter norm would trump their desire to have him sentenced for public drunkenness.

This time they walked into his trap. They said they had smelled the alcohol "on his person" (*fī dhātihi*), but not from his mouth. This fact absolved him of the crime. Smelling alcohol on his breath, according to the ruling that resulted from the case, "is the rule for the noble [Zaydī] rite in testifying to a smell. Therefore there is no mandatory punishment to be imposed other than his imprisonment for ten days."[108] He was held in the Ṣanā'i jail, which, like the other jail in Sanaa, had a special cell for Jews across from the guards' station.[109]

Jamal claims that at the time he did not know of this evidentiary technicality in cases of suspected wine drinking and attributed his success instead to divine providence.[110] Disputes in the Zaydī school existed over the testimony that proved intoxication. One of the interpreters of the *Commentary [on the Book of] Flowers* concluded that if two male witnesses testified that the smell of alcohol came from a man's body (*jawf*) and not from his mouth, he was not guilty of the crime.[111] A qadi who was a member of the opposition (and thus a confederate of the presiding judge) solved the dispute in a legal manual published twenty years after this incident. There the qadi concluded that smelling wine on someone's person proved that person's guilt of the crime of wine drinking.[112] It is certainly tempting to think he may have had this case in mind when he closed this legal loophole. Jamal's successful attempt to maneuver his opponents into having to testify to smelling his breath was noteworthy in another way. A Muslim accused of public intoxication would not have been able to make use of it. In this instance the Jew's weakness under the law and nonlegal social norms was transformed into a strength.

In 1931 a new opportunity arose for a provocation in the riding arena. Jamal says that bicycles arrived in Yemen that year, and he bought one from a Muslim.[113] (A French traveler reports Turkish officers riding bicycles around Sanaa in 1899.[114]) Needless to say, the sumptuary laws, which already struck late medieval writers as archaic, did not say anything about non-Muslims riding bicycles. Yet "even riding a bicycle led to a negative result," writes Mordecai al-Ẓāhirī. This author explains that "those who used human-powered vehicles, either youths or people who spent time outside of Yemen who adopted the strange habit of riding bicycles, were thought of as belonging to the intermediate category [between riding a horse and riding a donkey]."[115] Speaking of his boyhood in the late 1930s and 1940s, a sayyid from a powerful family told anthropologist Gabriele vom Bruck that "[the children] were not allowed to ride a bicycle—an activity considered to be both vulgar and one which displays a lack of self-restraint."[116]

"My arguments," Jamal writes, "needed to be convincing and to show that I did not intend to cast from myself the yoke of humiliation that lay upon the Jews and [to] carefully preserve the honor of the Muslims." If these arguments did not succeed, they "could cultivate land that would be useful in any other matter."[117] In other words, the bicycle offered a wedge issue that could render the law void by separating its arbitrariness from the legal principle of preserving the social hierarchy.

Jamal sent Qadi Muḥammad b. ʿAbdallāh Muṭahhar a request to ride his bicycle to Yarīm, a town near Sanaa. He also sent him a gift. Qadi Muṭahhar consulted Qadi ʿAbdallāh al-ʿAmrī, Imām Yaḥyā's chief minister, who advised Muṭahhar to speak with the imām. The imām granted Jamal permission to ride his bicycle on June 5, 1931, writing, "May God guide you. It is preferable to travel by riding a donkey, but if you wish to ride on a bicycle there is nothing to prevent it."[118] The imām's statement in favor of Jewish donkey riding had no precedent in law. It affirmed either (or both) the hierarchical assumptions of the sumptuary laws and their arbitrariness as received tradition. The license he gave Jamal to ride his bicycle might represent a one-time dispensation—a remedy for the extenuating circumstances of travel between the two cities—or a general license.

Jamal interpreted it as representing the latter. He may or may not have ridden his bicycle out of Sanaa. Yet he began riding it everywhere over the next several years, even in Muslim neighborhoods of Sanaa. Jamal says he did this "in order to get them used to it."[119] The tension that Jamal's bike rides generated among some Muslims led him to renew his court battle in early 1934. Again he contacted Qadi Muṭahhar. The qadi again consulted colleagues among the jurists. Jamal says he was warned by Muslim friends that if their more pious coreligionists saw a Jew riding a bicycle, "the world darkened for them" and that such riding was seen as an attack against Islam.[120]

He asked a second time for written permission to ride his bicycle, again mentioning putative long-distance travel. He said he needed something in writing to show those who stopped him along the way to Maʿbar, a crossroads town two days' journey from Sanaa, as well as a "license (*tarkhīṣ*) to ride a car in any direction." At that time automobiles and trucks were being imported to Yemen. At some point before the debate at hand, the imām had granted Jews permission to ride in cars.[121] Here we see Jamal again trying to use the bicycle issue to initiate a broader conversation.

This time the imām took a slightly different stance than he had in 1931. He must have realized now that Jamal's requests to travel to other towns served as pretexts for travel within Sanaa. He replied in the following manner: "If it is for journeying, there is nothing wrong with it, but in Sanaa there is a fear for non-Muslims from youths and the like."[122] Jewish writers note that young Muslims in Sanaa threw rocks at the Jews, particularly those who contravened norms of dress (by wearing Turkish or European clothing, for example). Naturally, the young people acted at the behest of adults. Therefore, Jamal's interpretation of the imām's reference to "youths" as a euphemism for those adult Muslims who strenuously opposed his bike riding was logical.[123] In making this statement, the imām diplomatically sidestepped Jamal's attempt to force him to take an unpopular position by making reference to those who, by nature, would not be swayed with logical proofs.

The imām had already admitted in 1931 that no law prevented a Jew from riding a bicycle; therefore, Jamal pressed the issue of legality. He wrote to the imām again, this time asking about "the matter of the People of the Pact riding bicycles, seeing as there is neither lengthy discussion of it nor does it refer back to earlier precedent (*wa-lam taʿud ifādah*).[124] On January 25, 1934, the imām concluded there was no harm in riding a bike but specified that such activities were to be confined to the Jewish Quarter alone. This response offers an illustration of the imām's diplomacy. He offered a compromise that would both placate loyal Jews by allowing bicycle riding and appease elite Muslims by limiting said riding to the Jewish Quarter.

If the imām was unwilling at this point to confront conservative Muslims, Jamal decided to use the courts to soften the opposition to Jewish bike riding himself. He brought his "license" (the document he received from Imām Yaḥyā) to the judge Luṭf al-Zubayrī, asking him to affirm the imām's ruling in exchange for cash and gifts. This well-respected scholar's affirmation of the ruling, Jamal hoped, would vitiate the opposition of other Muslim men of learning. Zubayrī was also notoriously corrupt; thus any principled opposition to the Jew's plan could be overcome with money. The imām made explicit reference to this fact in a 1939 ruling concerning a Jewish woman's property claim. There he pointedly advised Zubayrī to "refrain from [taking] an unjust fine."[125] Zubayrī was closely connected to the cadre of qadis who formed the core of the opposition to the imām. He was, nonetheless, loyal to the imām, and his close ties to the imām's opponents made him a valuable ally.

Thus Jamal seems to have hoped that lucre would accomplish what legal arguments could not. Zubayrī obliged, writing on the back of Jamal's "license" on June 21, 1934: "There is nothing wrong with it, but the action is to be in accordance with the noble license, and this should not be spoken of any longer." By stating that the matter should not be spoken of, Zubayrī may have sought to conceal his own involvement, thus denying Jamal the opportunity he sought to widen the conflict. Jamal says that Zubayrī, who hoped to receive another bribe, claimed he had foiled a plot to kill Jamal as he rode his bicycle.

Several years later, in the late 1930s, Jamal attempted to leave the Jewish Quarter on his bicycle and was stopped by the police captain, Aḥmad Jābir. The gates to the Quarter were manned by policemen who conducted searches for contraband alcohol. Jamal's paid informants told him that the Muslim scholars who opposed his bike riding had exerted pressure on Aḥmad Jābir.[126] This suggests that Jamal had been riding his bicycle outside of the Quarter during the intervening years without any objections from the police. Jamal filed a complaint against the officer with his superior, the governor of Sanaa, Ḥusayn b. 'Abd al-Qādir. Jamal says that, like Zubayrī, 'Abd al-Qādir was a secret opponent of the imām's rule. This is confirmed by a Muslim source that says of the governor, "His body was with the imām, but his heart was with the people."[127] Mordecai Yitshari also says the governor took bribes.[128] The governor summoned the officer, who declined to answer questions in front of Jamal. His silence may suggest that he was protecting his employer from embarrassment.

Jamal went to the imām again, this time asking for "an extension of the noble license." Winter had arrived and the time had come for the well-heeled Muslims and Jews of Sanaa to visit their vineyards in outlying towns. The imām ordered the governor to order the police captain to allow Jamal to travel outside the Jewish Quarter. It is possible that the imām knew the governor was an opponent of his and thus reversed himself on Jewish bicycle riding as a way of gaining an advantage in his rivalry with him. Jamal made efforts to befriend the officer and later learned from him that three of his opponents had made overtures to the heir apparent, Imām Yaḥyā's son Aḥmad.[129]

Even after a further overture to the imām, Jamal was unable to ride his bicycle past the guards. He says that his father, who did not support his provocations, overheard threats against Jamal's life. Jamal identifies his enemies as Zayd al-Daylamī, the chief judge of the court of appeals; Qadi Luṭf al-Zubayrī; head of waqfs, Qāsim al-'Izzī; and the *muḥtasib* who pulled Jamal from his donkey in 1927. The imām's son 'Alī sought to allay Jamal's fears, describing the governor as a figurehead and his opponents as ineffectual as "dogs barking at the moon."[130]

In 1937 Jamal turned to the imām a seventh time, this time focusing exclusively on the guards of the gates to the Jewish Quarter. The imām approved Jamal's request and sent him to Qadi 'Abdallāh al-'Amrī along with one of his slave bodyguards, Ṣumṣām. Ṣumṣām delivered the imām's written opinion—"It is no problem, God willing" (*lā ba'sa in shā allāh*)—to the qadi. Qadi al-'Amrī told Jamal to deliver the imām's orders to the governor of Sanaa in his name. He also affirmed that the Jews of Yemen could make use of any form of transportation and advised Jamal not to bring the matter to the imām again. Jamal delivered the document to Governor 'Abd al-Qādir.

Jamal recounts learning from the imām's sons that the imām's underlings understood that when their employer added the pious formula "God willing" (*in shā allāh*) to his ordinary "there is no problem" (*lā ba'sa*), he meant to threaten them.[131] He had used this formula in his last ruling concerning Jamal and his bicycle. This development suggests that Jamal's dogged (and probably irritating) persistence had led the imām to abandon his attempts at compromise and use more coercive tactics on behalf of his Jewish underling. It may also suggest that whereas in 1931 the imām tried to pacify conservative opponents of his rule, by 1937 he had despaired of such tactics and was prepared to act against them.

For Europeans the bicycle represented a host of progressive ideals, among them technology's capacity to facilitate capitalism, the rejuvenation of the body through exercise, and social mobility through competitive sports.[132] While Jamal justified his bike riding with reference to its positive effect on his work schedule, it is clear that he was uninterested in a broad agenda of increasing Yemen's economic productivity by means of bicycles. Nor did he express any interest in the health benefits of routine exercise.

Insofar as the design of the bicycle necessitates putting one's legs on either side of it and moving one's clothing away from the chain, and in its vague resemblance to a riding animal, the bicycle offered a unique provocation against Muslim sumptuary laws governing non-Muslim locomotion. It is clear from the persistent Muslim opposition to his riding that Jamal succeeded in his self-appointed role as gadfly. His many legal challenges mounted in defense of his bike riding likely cost him a small fortune.

Jamal maneuvered Muslim jurists into an uncomfortable position. Riding through Muslim neighborhoods, faster and higher in the air than his betters, bare legs splayed about his contraption, Jamal may have seemed the quintessence of insolence. Indeed, the main objection that Muslims raised to his riding the bicycle was that it constituted incitement. This helps explain the long duration of Jamal's bicycle campaign. Perhaps larger groups of Jewish bicyclists would have resulted in conservative Muslims becoming inured to this spectacle. Nevertheless, Jamal's ideal of cycling differs from the struggles over the ideals embodied by the bicycle in Europe—its solitary quality: Jamal rode alone. His rides through Sanaa in the mid-1930s embody both the promise of a transformation in Muslim-Jewish relations and a sense of the likelihood of failure of his solitary struggle with the sharī'a.

Jamal had another agenda as well. He made his bicycle campaign a bone of contention between Imām Yaḥyā, his rivals among the Muslim elite, and his son Aḥmad. It seems he was able to earn the imām's backing (and thus the legitimation of the sharīʿa of the prophet Muḥammad) by emphasizing to Imām Yaḥyā the extent to which his agenda irked the imām's enemies. At the same time, he tried to neutralize said enemies through bribery and paid informants. He also tried to "flip" lower-level functionaries (like the police officer) by cementing personal relationships.

These patterns recur in both the wrangling over the Latrines Decree in the 1790s and the debate over Jewish bicycle riding in the 1930s. The reigning imām faced an internal political challenge from his rivals, and the Jews were caught (or placed themselves) in the middle. Both Muslims and Jews could (and did) make the point that the sumptuary laws were holdovers from a bygone age and thus might be maintained for the sake of upholding tradition, but not for a loftier goal. Both cases represent changes at opposite ends of a system that was resistant to change. In the first, a group of Muslim scholars distilled a principle from the sumptuary laws in order to expand their scope. In the second, a Jew found allies among Muslim authorities living and dead in order to annul one specific sumptuary law and then use its annulment as a wedge to destroy the rest.

3 Muslim Jews and Jewish Muslims

The sharīʿa imposed explicit handicaps upon non-Muslim litigants. Since the system was hierarchical in nature, those suppositions did not require justification. Nonlegal codes that were operative in the context of social relations also pointed to a person's Muslimness or Jewishness. These were no less relevant to participants in legal proceedings than those described (or legislated) by substantive law.

A stipulation of the sumptuary laws asks that non-Muslims pray quietly. In practice this specific use of the human voice had a more general application as well; thus, Jews were expected to keep their voices down in the presence of Muslims.[1] They were also expected to be obsequious to Muslims. "Despite their learning and good breeding," Mordecai Yitshari writes of the Jewish male elite of Sanaa who were hauled into jail on trumped-up charges, "they were very cowardly."[2] A Muslim saying reflects Jews' perceived reluctance to get involved in intra-Muslim disputes due to their weakness: "Even if you have a hundred Jews [on your side], do not appeal to them, saying 'save me!'"[3]

Such meekness, which was identified as a Jewish trait, may have led listeners to dismiss a Jewish speaker in a legal setting. Relevant here is a study of courtrooms in North Carolina in which anthropologist William M. O'Barr noted that jurors found the testimony of those who spoke in a "powerful" style, marked by formality, apparent certainty, and narrative, more credible than those who spoke in a "powerless" style, marked by hesitancy and hypercorrection. The "powerless" style was more common to women and minorities.[4]

A humorous tale told by both Nissim Gamlieli and Ṣāliḥ al-Ẓāhirī encapsulates the idea that the Jew has already lost the battle the moment he opens his mouth. A poor Jewish simpleton found a silver riyāl. He exclaimed, "Seeing that You have given me one, give me something even greater." Just then the funeral procession of a Muslim notable passed by and a Muslim overheard the Jew. Thinking that the Jew was referring to the deceased and hoping that an even more important Muslim would die, he beat the man. He ordered the Jew to say instead, "O God, have mercy on the offspring of the believers." The poor man began repeating this phrase in a loud voice. A sanitation worker passed by, dragging a rotting dog carcass. He came upon the poor man and said, "Oh? From the bad smell?" Afterward, the imām's womenfolk walked by smelling strongly of perfume. Their guards, hearing the same sentence, thought he was impugning their ladies' honor, so they beat him too. He asked them what he should say instead. They told him to say, "How beautiful! How pleasant!" He saw two Muslim hooligans arguing and striking each other. He used his new sentence. A bystander beat him up and said, "Hey, Jew, you sound satisfied and enjoy the fists hitting the jaws of the Muslims, but no longer. . . . From now on say, 'May God cause love and peace to dwell among the offspring of the believers.'" The poor man passed by the meat market and came across some dogs fighting. He kept his distance and said his new sentence. A Muslim butcher thought that by "the offspring of the believers" he meant the dogs, so he beat him. He told him that in the future he should say (to dogs), "Get lost." Just then he passed the cobblers' market and a cobbler, hearing his new expression, thought the Jew intended him and stabbed him in the arm with his awl. Rather than taking him to court, the cobbler took the silver coin as recompense for the abuse he had endured from the Jew.[5]

Although Jews spoke colloquial Arabic, the fact that their spoken language was exceptionally chaste differentiated them from the Muslims. Avraham Madhalah describes how the word "look down" (*istakhī*) in the Aramaic translation of the biblical verse "Look down from Your lofty abode in Heaven" (Deut. 26:15) sounded so much like the Arabic expression "my brother's asshole" (*ist akhī*) that Jews from the south modified it. In contrast, Jews from the north did not recognize "asshole" (*ist*) as a bad word. A hungry northern Jewish tobacco seller wanted to trade tobacco for corn with a farmer in the south. The farmer wanted to make him convert, so he offered him a big basket of corn if he would only say two words, "*ist al-nasm*," which to the northerner meant "the cat's behind" and to the southerner meant "the cat's asshole." In the south a Jew's cursing was akin to conversion to Islam. The farmer announced to the local rabbi that the Jew had converted to Islam. At an impromptu rabbinical court hearing concerning the man's case, it was determined that he had not intentionally used foul language, and his "conversion" was voided.[6]

While all Jews in Yemen spoke vernacular Arabic, few were literate in Arabic. Since literary Arabic is the formal register of the language, most did not speak the decorous Arabic appropriate to the courtroom. (Reports of the literacy rate among Muslims in the early twentieth century diverge dramatically. A member of an Iraqi military delegation in the early 1940s judged illiteracy to have been eliminated among men through the good efforts of the imām. Another report preserved in the Central Zionist Archives estimates that just 10 percent of Muslims were literate.[7]) When the Jews of one neighborhood were asked to sign a document in the 1930s, many were unable even to sign their names in Arabic and had to find someone else to do it for them.[8] One Jew recalls his elementary school teacher striking a classmate for asking the meaning of the classical Arabic word "*ṣanādīd*" (chiefs of an army) in Se'adya Gaon's translation of Genesis 36:15: "these were the chiefs among Esau's descendants." The teacher understood neither the Hebrew nor the Arabic words.[9]

Formal legal language was suffused with Qur'anic idioms and expressions. A Jew remarked that learning Arabic was intrinsically connected to learning about the Qur'an and Islam, realms of knowledge that represented a "dangerous border" that Jews ought not approach. Jews were not permitted to touch the holy text, let alone read it.[10] Two Jewish writers describe learning Arabic by studying Se'adya Gaon's Arabic translation of the Torah.[11] One, Ratson Halevi, says that such studies allowed him to help his Muslim peers, who could read but lacked comprehension, while he stood outside of their school window.[12] The wealthy merchant Sulaymān Ḥibshūsh owned a Hebrew translation of the Qur'an (presumably Hermann Reckendorf's 1857 version), among other hard-to-get books.[13] Sālim Sa'īd al-Jamal reports hearing that Luṭf al-Zubayrī, the qadi who was a bitter foe of his, had complained to Imām Yaḥyā about the Jew's use of Qur'anic idioms. Jamal protested that he was attempting to use legal language rather than Qur'anic expressions and says the imām accepted his argument.[14]

A Jewish purveyor of spices and tobacco was arrested for wrapping a Muslim customer's purchase in paper that contained Qur'anic text. Neither the Jew nor the Muslim who had sold him the paper knew how to read Arabic, and both were exonerated by Imām Yaḥyā.[15] Some Jews were accused by individual Muslims of Qur'an desecration or blasphemy. Yet when a Muslim madrasah student accused a Jewish boy of knocking a Qur'an out of his hands, Imām Yaḥyā punished the Muslim.[16]

Some Muslims leveled the serious charge of blasphemy (*sabb*) against Jewish opponents. In 1924 a Jew who had learned literary Arabic in Yaḥyā Qāfiḥ's modern school and worked as a clock repairman got into a conversation about religion with one of his Muslim customers, a sayyid. The conversation turned ugly when they began discussing Lot. The Muslim insisted that Lot was a prophet, while the Jew described him as a debased man who slept with his own daughters, unions that produced the bastard nations of Moab and Ammon. The sayyid slapped the Jew and summoned witnesses. The Jew was jailed for ten months while a qadi deliberated his fate. A fatwa ordering his execution was drafted. Prominent Jews, including Chief Rabbi Yaḥyā al-Abyaḍ and Ṣāliḥ al-Ẓāhirī, lobbied the imām in defense of the Jew. One of them, Yosef Shemen, who wrote in the mid-1930s, says he was also prosecuted for maligning Lot while defending the man.[17]

Abyaḍ and another Jew took a printed "Tāj" (which included the Pentateuch in Se'adya Gaon's Arabic translation) and sought an audience with the imām. When it was granted, the men insisted that the ostensibly offensive statements that the clock repairman had made were, in fact, contained in the Torah. They read him the story of Lot in Genesis in Arabic. A wealthy Muslim wholesaler, who was a friend of the imprisoned Jew, lobbied on behalf of him as well. The Jew was freed, but was to receive forty lashes. The Muslim placed his sheepskin coat under his Jewish friend's robe and told the soldiers who were to deliver the punishment that the man was too weak to endure flogging. So they gave the Jew thirty-seven light blows and three hard blows, which must have been mitigated by his "body armor."[18]

Mordecai al-Ẓāhirī, who was jailed following the assassination of Imām Yaḥyā, recalls issuing the following warning to another Jewish prisoner, whose statements concerning religion he found unacceptable:

> You are not aware that you are exposing yourself to serious danger. If, God forbid, some slanderer tried to claim that you insulted "the prophets of the nations" (*nevi'e ha-'amim*) [i.e., Muḥammad], and brought another man with him who would testify that he heard everything that you said, they would immediately sentence you to death.[19]

Jamal, one of the three Jewish lawyers, claims to have been charged with insulting the prophet in 1938. A Muslim claimed that on the morning of March 5, he, the muḥtasib from the 1927 donkey incident, a kinsman of one of the "witnesses" in the same case, a soldier who worked for Qadi Luṭf al-Zubayrī,[20] and a Muslim snuff merchant who had a lot of dealings with Jews were on a street near the Jewish Quarter when Jamal passed by on his bicycle. According to the man who lodged the complaint, Jamal dismounted in order to engage the men in conversation.

According to the Muslims' testimony, one of the Muslims said to Jamal that a man as smart as Jamal would do well to convert to Islam, since Islam is better than Judaism. They alleged that Jamal then denied this, arguing instead that Islam had no basis, that Muḥammad wrote the Qur'an in imitation of the Torah, that the Qur'an's admonition "do not engage in disputation with the People of the Book" was intended to prevent Muslims from learning this truth about their false prophet and false scripture from the Jews, and that the Zionists would win. Each of the five Muslims affirmed that Jamal had said this.

Although he denied having made this blasphemous speech to these men, Jamal concedes that he believed the conspiracy theory about the Qur'an according to which two Jewish renegades, Yefet ben Ovadiah (Muḥammad b. 'Abdallāh) and Ovadiah ben Shalom ('Abdallāh b. Salām), forged the Qur'an. Even more intriguing is Jamal's statement that he shared this theory with one of the imām's sons. This (unnamed) prince, he claimed, had a Jewish mother and had doubts about the Qur'an.[21]

Rumors circulated among Jews in Yemen revolving around the Jewish roots of prominent Muslims. Some Jews claim that Qadi 'Abd al-Raḥmān al-Iryānī (d. 1974), a leader of the opposition to Imām Yaḥyā and future president of Yemen, was a Jewish orphan who had been forcibly converted by Muslims.[22] One of the imām's sons was said to have had a Jewish mother, making him Jewish according to halakhah. The most common candidate was Aḥmad.[23] Jamal's relationship with Aḥmad suddenly turned from friendly to tense, so perhaps Aḥmad divulged the contents of this controversial conversation with al-Jamal to the Jew's opponents. A more likely possibility is that Jewish converts to Islam informed Muslims of this forged Qur'an theory. If Jews who were discreet believed this, perhaps this particularly shameless Jew would voice it publicly.

Both Jamal and the Jew who maligned Lot got into trouble for saying things that Jews believed but should not have voiced in the presence of non-Jews. This problem with translation dogged Jews in less dangerous situations as well. Some Jews found it difficult to stem the flow of Hebrew words into their own vernacular Arabic. A Jew who cut off his sidelocks, dressed as a Muslim, and took the name "Aḥmad" in order to make the overland journey to Aden (and Palestine) gave himself away by using the Hebrew word "*dat*" (religion) in his oaths.[24] In Hodeida in 1951, a Jewish woman who was undertaking the journey to Palestine swore that she would apostatize if she had to ride in a truck with her husband any longer. A Muslim overheard her say "*itshammad*"—a word that combines the Hebrew "apostasy (*shmad*) with an Arabic verb form—and insisted she be brought before the governor to convert. However, once the Muslim truck driver was bribed to say he had not overheard any such expression, the matter was dropped.[25]

Problematic encounters between Jews and the Arabic language could sometimes simply be misunderstandings of the high register of the language. In May 1949 Rabbi Hārūn Ḥamdī wrote a letter to Ṣālim Manṣūrah, Imām Aḥmad's Jewish "point man" in Ta'izz, describing some of the difficulties experienced by Jews who were trying to make arrangements to leave Yemen for Israel. In it he says he heard a radio news item on negotiations between the United States and Great Britain in which the British representative denied that his government opposed Jewish emigration and insisted that it had established various collection points for Jews who intended to leave. The report called such a place a "*marsā*," Arabic for "anchorage" or "disembarking point," and said the American had written to the imām, requesting that he set up a marsā in Sanaa. A Jew who was trying to leave Yemen did not understand this word from the radio news and wrote to Ḥamdī asking if the imām had, in fact, opened the way for Jewish emigration. Ḥamdī asked Manṣūrah to send a telegram to the man that included the following language: "What you have said is correct. After you asked about the meaning of the word 'marsā,' which the radio uses, and which is what they are demanding of the imām, I consulted the Arabic dictionary and it said that a 'marsā' of the sea is an opening for anchoring ships."[26]

Some Jews, like Jamal, Ẓāhirī, and Manṣūrah, succeeded in learning the literary Arabic that would allow them entrance into the world of the Muslim elite. This development only occurred around the turn of the twentieth century.[27] One of the first Jews to learn formal Arabic, Ḥayyim Ḥibshūsh, was asked by other Jews why he brought Arabic books with him to the Torah service at his synagogue. He responded by saying that reading the Torah reminded him of verses from the Qur'an and its associated literature.[28] Imām Yaḥyā's grandfather used to discuss early Islam and the ancient Arab tribes with Ḥayyim Ḥibshūsh, and the young Yaḥyā often picked up the essence of these conversations.[29] Ḥibshūsh was a member of a movement within Yemenite Judaism called "*Dor De'ah*" ("the Enlightened Generation"), which mounted fierce opposition to Jewish mysticism (kabbalah), the use of magical amulets, and the Jewish educational system. On the last of these fronts, R. Yaḥyā Qāfiḥ, the chief ideologue of Dor De'ah, tried to introduce the study of Arabic and Turkish into the Jewish curriculum.[30] Qāfiḥ placed ideological primacy upon medieval Judeo-Arabic philosophy (works by writers like Se'adya Gaon and Maimonides), which necessitated a good working knowledge of formal Arabic.[31] Moreover, Qāfiḥ was said to have had such a thorough knowledge of Arabic literature and calligraphy that Muslims brought him old manuscripts to identify.[32]

Other Jews learned Arabic through situations requiring close contact with Muslims that were not of their choosing. Aḥmad al-Shāmī, a Muslim who was a member of the short-lived government that took over after Imām Yaḥyā's assassination, recalls his conversations with an erudite Jew who had already been in the fearsome Nāfi' prison for twenty years after being convicted of killing his cousin. The jailed revolutionaries (who called themselves "the Free Yemenis"—*al-Aḥrār al-yamaniyūn*), who were mainly men of learning, "used to laugh when he corrected errors in the recitation of the Qur'an by some of the Aḥrār who were not careful in their reading of God's book and only improved in Nāfi'."[33]

Ṣāliḥ al-Ẓāhirī's Arabic was much better than that of most Jews. He was asked by Jewish workers in Radā' to write in Arabic the receipts they would need in order to pick up their weekly pay while working on government projects.[34] As a boy, Ẓāhirī had been taken to a prison as a hostage against a debt his father owed. As the story goes, while Ẓāhirī was in prison in Radā', a Muslim lawyer, himself imprisoned on suspicion of suborning perjury, taught him Arabic while the lawyer chewed qāt. A teacher taught the Qur'an, poetry, and belletristic essays to the imprisoned boys, all of whom were Muslim except for Ẓāhirī. One day a conservative sayyid (a descendant of the prophet Muḥammad) who had been jailed witnessed the Muslim lawyer teaching him Arabic and objected, "How can you teach the pure letters to an impure Jew"? Ẓāhirī's father, who was present, made a retort and the sayyid slapped him. The lawyer then upbraided the sayyid for having contravened the unwritten taboo against harming Jews. Sometime later the younger Ẓāhirī, accompanied by his burly cousin, encountered the same sayyid outside of town. Ẓāhirī's cousin mounted his donkey to aggravate the man. When the sayyid demanded that the Jew dismount in his presence, he jumped on the sayyid's back and beat him until he defecated. The incident was not spoken of again.[35]

Ṣāliḥ al-Ẓāhirī acquired a knowledge of Islamic law in a similarly circuitous manner. His mother made clothing for the family of Muḥsin al-Darwīsh (d. 1955), a wealthy sayyid of Radāʿ. Another Jewish writer, Nissim Gamlieli, says that this sayyid, who served as a judge, constantly squeezed the Jewish community with bogus fines and solicited bribes, especially from wealthy Jews. Imām Yaḥyā eventually removed him from his post.[36] Before festivals Ẓāhirī's mother worked in their home and her children played with Darwīsh's children. One of Muḥsin al-Darwīsh's sisters married Imām Yaḥyā.[37] Ṣāliḥ al-Ẓāhirī's childhood friendship with the sister led to his invitations to the imām's palace in Sanaa on a weekly basis. There he brought coffee to the imām's sons during their lessons. They allowed him to listen and shared their books and notebooks with him on subjects like Arabic literature, geography, and the *Commentary [on the Book of] Flowers.*[38] Later in his life, Ẓāhirī's mother would try to persuade the Darwīshes' daughter to intercede with the imām in order to have her son released from prison.[39]

Ṣāliḥ al-Ẓāhirī's son Mordecai, who was in prison in the late 1940s, knew Arabic well enough that Muslim prisoners and prison staff paid him to write petitions and correspondence on their behalf. The prisoners did not receive set "sentences" but were incarcerated at the discretion of an authority figure. Therefore, such informal appeals could hasten their release. Arabic poetry, however, represented a stumbling block for Mordecai. He participated in literary gatherings with his fellow prisoners during which they composed poems or songs from the semi-vernacular "*ḥumaynī*" repertoire and told stories from *The 1001 Nights.*[40] After Mordecai's attempts at poetry fell flat, a Muslim politely reminded him that "when a man dies he is still learning."[41]

Jews not only gave themselves away through their faulty Arabic. Clothing and hairstyle distinguished them from Muslims; therefore, they could not rely upon whatever equalizing effects conservative courtroom attire might offer. A turban and white garments would instantly identify a man as a Muslim, whereas sidelocks, a black cap, a dark-colored robe, and bare calves signified a Jewish man.[42] Since no physiognomic distinction between Muslims and Jews existed, Jews (and Muslims in exceptionally rare cases) found that transgressing the sartorial signposts marking these social boundaries could serve their interests.

Turkish rule offered new opportunities for Yemenis to dispense with the visual markers that distinguished different groups within society. Writing of his travels in Yemen in 1911–1912, Shmuel Yavnieli wrote:

> Hats—*tarbushes* in every color—have little by little replaced the local head coverings, especially among the Jews, in the big mercantile cities in the course of their dealings with Turkish government clerks. (From Ibb to Sanaa and ʿAmrān we encounter the tarbush on the heads of the Jews of the city.)[43]

The Turks forced the new style of dress on the Muslims. In 1895 the Turkish government ordered all Yemenis who worked for the government, including tribal shaykhs, to wear Turkish dress: "exchanging turbans, the crowns of Islam, for red Turkish tarbushes and clothing," writes Zabārah. The decree remained in effect for seven years.[44] Though many Jews embraced the new form of dress, some within the traditional elite found it threatening. One sayyid who attended the Turkish military college in Sanaa sent Imām Yaḥyā a complaint in verse about his having to wear pants, coat, and tarbush.[45] In the south a Muslim who wore a fancy tarbush under the Turks' orders simply wrapped white cloth around it when a clan loyal to the imām monopolized power.[46] Elsewhere, a tasseled tarbush that a Jew acquired in Aden became a bone of contention between two powerful Muslims. The sayyid Muḥsin al-Darwīsh, Imām Yaḥyā's brother-in-law, objected so strongly that he knocked it off the Jew's head. The local shaykh insisted he wear it. Nevertheless, the Jew deferred to the sayyid.[47]

Jews also opposed changes to their own traditional modes of dress. Jewish opponents of Yaḥyā Qāfiḥ's school accused students of tucking their sidelocks under their tarbushes or even cutting them off altogether. According to Jewish sources, the qadis objected to individual Jews' changes to their dress and even rallied young people to throw stones at those who did so.[48] Imām Yaḥyā also took a firm stand against such radical haircuts for Jews.[49] The seventh-century Pact of ʿUmar mandated that non-Muslims wear a type of belt called a "*zunnār*." In Yemen the word "zunnār" referred to the sidelocks that Jewish men grew.

Ṣāliḥ al-Ẓāhirī went "undercover" as a Muslim several times. Once he was sent on a mission to a village in the tribal lands east of Radāʿ to supervise the construction of a government building, thereby extending the central government's sphere of influence. Accompanied by a group of the imām's soldiers, he was ordered to wear an army uniform. He was supposed to employ Jewish builders from the area but not to identify himself as a Jew to the tribesmen. Ẓāhirī faced a number of unexpected challenges. The vast majority of Jews did not know how to take care of horses. A Muslim soldier was sent on the mission solely to take care of his horse. While he maintained his disguise as a Muslim, Ẓāhirī ordered the builders to construct a synagogue for the town as well.[50]

Years later Ẓāhirī evaded capture by Imām Aḥmad (Yaḥyā's son) by dressing as a Muslim. At a mosque one Friday his Muslim companion (who knew he was a Jew) identified him to the flock as a famous Muslim scholar from a patrician family who was a close relative of the imām. The congregation asked Ẓāhirī to lead them in their prayers and he did so. Ẓāhirī said that after the people left, they were heard swearing, "By God, we have never heard a prayer with such pure diction and melancholy like the prayer of this honorable man."[51]

Some Jews left the imāms' Yemen for Aden (and thence to Palestine) by cutting off their sidelocks and dressing like Muslims.[52] A Jew who masqueraded as a Muslim on this journey performed Muslim prayers with his Arab traveling companions. Once he arrived in Aden he had to prove his Jewishness to skeptical soldiers and Jews.[53] "With [a] belt around my waist and [a] turban on my head, I looked like a 'strictly kosher' tribesman," remarks another.[54]

Muslims sometimes dressed (or were made to dress) like Jews, usually as a form of humiliation. A Muslim who accompanied Imām Yaḥyā on an outing beyond the city walls complained that the sharp appearance of the Jewish children who followed the imām's retinue constituted an incitement against the Muslims. The imām ordered the man to buy a skullcap and sidelocks from the Jews and to wear them in order to assuage his jealousy.[55] Another Yemeni source describes a learned Muslim who, faced with an imām's openness toward Jews who wanted to convert to Islam as well as a lack of interest in Muslims, infiltrated his court dressed as a Jew.[56] Since the making and sharpening of knives was generally a Jewish profession, Muslims in small villages sought out Jews for haircuts. Aharon Ben David tells two anecdotes of Jews who played practical jokes on tribesmen by "accidentally" leaving them sidelocks.[57]

Not all instances of Muslims dressing as Jews were jokes. During the rebellion against the Turks at the turn of the twentieth century, Muslim villagers in the south of Yemen sent their families into the mountains to hide when they saw Turkish troops approach. Old women who were too frail to flee dressed as Jews and hid in Jewish homes. Although the soldiers asked about the remarkable profusion of elderly women in the Jews' home, no harm came to them.[58]

Because legal proceedings in Yemen were not restricted to a formal courtroom setting, much was accomplished during meetings at private homes, where participants would eat, chew qāt, or smoke. Among tribesmen, sharing a meal created a temporary cease-fire in a feud, and the slaughter of animals offered restitution for a variety of misdeeds.[59] Jews were not excluded from the commensal aspect of the legal culture. However, Muslim and Jewish dietary laws represented another set of codes to differentiate Jew from Muslim.

The traveling Jewish craftsman, writes Shlomo Dov Goitein, "carr[ied] with him the indispensable coffee cup in a little basket fastened by a strap of leather to his bag of tools."[60] It allowed Muslims to give him coffee without going so far as to allow him to drink out of their cups. It also allowed the Jew to avoid making use of a Muslims' cups, which may have contained nonkosher broth. This cup on a strap thus becomes a fitting symbol for the problematic relationships of commensality between Jews and Muslims as well as Jews' own self-segregation. Novelist Shim'on Ballas describes an identical taboo as the red line in interreligious social relationships beyond which only converts to Islam would tread among the Jews of Iraq.[61]

Such taboos would have been more stringently observed in urban areas or by high-status Muslims (sayyids and qadis). In rural areas Muslim-Jewish commensality was the norm. The Bedouin, whose hospitality was the stuff of legend, might hire a kosher butcher just to be able to honor a Jewish guest with a meal of mutton.[62] One Jew says that for Jews who plied their trades for Muslim clients, good (and kosher) food "constitute[d] an essential condition of work."[63] The norms of hospitality were such that Yemenis invited travelers of both religions into their homes for meals.[64] Some Muslims who hosted Jews who passed through their villages prepared dairy meals for them, using cooking vessels devoted to this purpose alone.[65] Other Jews describe being offered dairy meals by Muslims but do not discuss how (or in what vessels) they were prepared.[66] A Jew who worked as a tailor for the royal family in Taʿizz ate only from copper vessels, which the family did not use in the preparation of meat, "in order to avoid opprobrium."[67]

Muslims could prepare meals for Jews that were quite rich but nonetheless kosher. When it came to dairy products, Jews were permitted to eat clarified butter that had been made by Muslims, although there was some question as to whether non-Jewish butter might contain camel's milk (camels are not kosher).[68] According to Ratson Halevi, rabbis allowed Jews to eat Muslim cheese, despite the possibility that its production might have involved the prohibited mixing of milk and meat. Moreover, one Jewish ascetic who found this ruling insufficiently punctilious enlisted two Muslim women to make kosher cheese for him, using fig sap rather than sheep's rennet to curdle the milk.[69]

Halevi also describes Muslim zeal for a spongy sourdough sorghum flatbread (much like the Ethiopian *injera*) that only Jews made, called "*laḥūḥ*."[70] "The *goyim* were crazy about it," he writes, "and one of their notable men even admitted 'if one day we decide to convert to Judaism it will be on account of laḥūḥ." A Jew who converted to Islam for a woman and performed the pilgrimage to Mecca maintained two links to Judaism, the same author writes: weekly meals of "laḥūḥ and *lasīs*" (laḥūḥ with bean stew).[71]

While restrictions on intra-religious dining varied considerably, eating meat represented a "red line" in relations between Jews and Muslims. A proverb runs, "Nothing differentiates us [Jews from Muslims] other than butchering and marriage [to our coreligionists]."[72] Jews who flouted the imām's ban on emigration attempted to infiltrate the British colony of Aden dressed as Arabs. Since Jews and Muslims were so difficult to tell apart, Muslims in al-Milāḥ village, a way station near the border, used nonkosher meat as a de facto Jew detector.[73] In the mid-1940s a Jewish boy who converted to Islam cut his sidelocks, dressed, and prayed as a Muslim but still refused to eat meat slaughtered by Muslims. This made his shaykh suspect his motives. He related what the shaykh said: "Eating meat is the test and the evidence of whether he is a Muslim or a Jew."[74]

For Jewish families who lived in small villages, buying kosher meat or finding a kosher slaughterer represented a great challenge. A healer prescribed bed rest, the application of mustard oil, and infusions of chicken broth to a woman who had been stricken with influenza. Since the village's kosher slaughterer had gone to a wedding in another village, her young son, accompanied by an armed Muslim, brought a hen on the two-hour trek through the wolf- and hyena-infested wilderness to the next village to have it butchered.[75] The boy grew up and moved to another village, where he served as butcher.[76] Immediately following the family's move, the wives of the local shaykh gave his eight-year-old daughter cuts of fresh lamb, which she brought home to her father wrapped in the folds of her dress. He was put in the delicate situation of having to refuse his new patron's generosity. By telling his daughter to return the meat, he taught her that intra-Jewish cohesion trumps even the crucial relationship to the tribe.[77] On one occasion the same butcher was approached by a twelve-year-old girl with a rooster. She was a member of the only Jewish family in their village. Since no kosher slaughterer lived near her village, eating meat required half a day's journey in each direction to a large market. The rabbi slaughtered her rooster on the condition that this stubborn and beautiful "real mountain girl," who faced the perils of travel alone, marry his son.[78]

In Yemen if a Jew wanted to convert to Islam, he had to eat soup made with an animal slaughtered by a Muslim in addition to the requirement for conversion to Islam that was common among all Muslims (the recitation of the profession of faith in the presence of witnesses). Jews on the verge of conversion were often poor, desperate, and therefore hungry. Some desperate Jews were "born again" two, three, or even four times in a series of remote mountain villages in order to enjoy the food and camaraderie they received from Muslim strangers during the "honeymoon." But if the culprit was caught, his temples would be seared with hot irons to prevent him from sprouting another set of sidelocks with which to mislead the Muslims into thinking he was a potential convert.[79]

The questions of if and when such an amoral Jew would eat nonkosher food formed the basis for popular proverbs among Muslims and Jews covering a variety of situations. Yemenis used the expression "force a Jew to eat soup" for attempts to convince a stubborn person of something or to cajole a guest into eating his host's food.[80] Among Jews the saying "he apostatized for tripe soup" referred to someone who gave up something valuable in exchange for a measly thing (tripe soup being considered a rather unappealing nonkosher dish). In contrast, "if he has already apostatized, at least he should eat chicken breasts" has the opposite meaning, along the lines of "if you are going to sell out, at least do it for something worthwhile."[81]

Eating nonkosher meat was thought to make a Jew into a Muslim, even if the Jew had not intended to eat it, much less convert. In the late nineteenth century a plague struck a traveling Jewish salesman. A Muslim family took him in and nursed him back to health with regular infusions of broth. When he returned to his community and asked how this inadvertent sin might be expiated, they informed him that by eating the soup he had already become a Muslim. His ensuing conversion to Islam was a mere formality.[82]

For the "ape man," who Ratson Halevi describes as a Jew who raised himself in the wilderness from the age of ten until age seventeen, "the word meat represented his urge to exist."[83] With only his father's butcher knife and some matches, he survived on a veritable cornucopia of forbidden meats: trapped birds, rabbits, ravens, and a wild pig. When he encountered a human settlement in his teens, a Muslim informed this Jewish Tarzan that by eating rabbit he had already become a Muslim.[84]

Some Muslims were less cautious in observing the taboo against eating Jewish meat. One Jew recalls a visit to his home by his employer, a powerful tribal shaykh, during Sukkot. The shaykh not only ate the meat dishes the Jew's family prepared for him, but he also said that Muslims who would not eat meat slaughtered by Jews were in error. However, when the Jew worked in the shaykh's home, he was served only dairy dishes.[85] (Muslims sometimes ate meat that Jews had ruled nonkosher, but it was a source of controversy.[86]) Another Jew recalls a generous shaykh bringing to the rabbi a sheep to slaughter and cut it in two. The shaykh kept half for himself. He invited Jews, who brought their own kitchenware, to his home to feast on the other half.[87] Lebanese American traveler Ameen Rihani reports that in Sanaa Muslims had to give Jews they had insulted or harmed part of a slaughtered cow.[88] Given that Jews were forbidden from eating meat butchered by Muslims and vice versa, it is not at all clear how this could have been the case.

A Muslim named Ḥusayn al-Maqbalī, imprisoned for his opposition to Imām Yaḥyā, recalls sharing a prison cell with three Jews who had been jailed because "they cultivated their knowledge and inclined toward emancipation (*taḥarrur*)." Since prisoners were responsible for feeding themselves at their own expense, the Muslim suggested that the cellmates all dine together. The Jews refused, since the meat was not kosher. The Muslim said to one of the Jews, Yūsuf al-Jamal, "You call for emancipation, yet a reactionary idea grips you. We are the sons of one homeland and we both call for freedom." The Jew replied, "Yes, that is correct. We will eat everything equally except for meat." "Not at all," said Maqbalī. "We will eat everything as equals, including meat." "Agreed," said the Jew. When the food was procured, said Maqbalī, "we ate equally after mixing their food with our food." Maqbalī's radical act of interreligious eating earned him a threat from the warden, who was unmoved by his quotation of a Qur'anic verse that seems to support his stance. Moreover, a leader in the opposition movement, a Sanaa merchant, reproached him as well.[89]

While interreligious generosity was the ideal, hard times did not always allow for it. Muslim clients often socialized with Jews in their shops, which were often part of the Jews' homes. Jews spoke in a special cant language that drew

Der Silberschmied El Abjad in seiner Werkstatt.
(Aufnahme aus Sana'a von Hermann Burchardt.)

DER FRÜHERE ZUSTAND DER JUDEN IN YEMEN. [1])

Von Hermann Burchardt.

Im äußersten Süden Arabiens, in der jetzt türkischen Provinz Yemen, gibt es eine sehr große Anzahl Juden, jedoch nicht, wie man vermuten würde, in den Handelshäfen des Roten Meeres, sondern vorwiegend in den Städten und Dörfern des Hochplateaus, in den schwer zugänglichen Gebirgen des Yemen und des nördlich daran grenzenden Asir. In der Hafenstadt Hodeida sah ich gar keine Juden, ebensowenig in den größeren Städten des Küstenlandes. Von Hodeida nach Sana'a reisend, traf ich die ersten in großer Zahl ansässigen Juden in Menàha, einer kleinen Gebirgsstadt von ungefähr 6000 Einwohnern. Hier sind die meisten Läden des Sùk (Basars) in ihrem Besitz. Man erkennt sie sofort an den langen Schläfenlocken, wie auch an ihrer Kleidung. Ackerbau scheinen sie auch im Yemen nicht viel zu treiben, denn auf dem Wege nach Sana'a zeigte man mir Felder, die von Juden bebaut wurden, als Merkwürdigkeit.

[1]) Geschrieben 1901. — Hermann Burchardt (ein bedeutender jüdischer Forschungsreisender, der hauptsächlich die Länder des Islam bereiste) wurde Ende 1909 im Yemen von aufrührerischen Arabern ermordet. — Sämtliche Abbildungen aus dem Yemen sind nach den photographischen Aufnahmen des Verfassers. — (S. a. Bemerkung zu den Abbildungen im Inhaltsverzeichnis.)

— 9 —

Photo taken by Hermann Burckhardt (d. 1932) of Yaḥyā al-Abyaḍ (d. 1932) in his silversmith's shop with a Muslim who may be Muḥammad al-Maḥalwī (d. 1936). Published in Hilfskomitee für die Juden in Jemen, *Von den Juden des Jemens* Berlin: Orient Verlag, 1913.

وليس فيها فراش ولا سبورة ولا مقاعد بل يقعدون على التراب والمعلم على دكة بين يديه جملة عصي والسوط والفلكة، والأولاد يكتبون دروسهم على الألواح الخشبية، والمداد عبارة عن حجارة بيضاء لينة يبلونها في الماء ويستعملونها كمداد أبيض على اللوح الذي صبغ بمادة سوداء، وهكذا لا يكمل الأولاد القرآن إلا وقد قاسوا أنواع العذاب.

ولم يتطور التعليم إلا بعد دخول الأتراك وفتحهم للمدارس وكانوا يسمونها (المكتب) وهي تعد بالأصابع وقد شنت ضدها

١٢

Photo of Muḥammad al-Maḥalwī (d. 1936) from Ṣāliḥ al-Sunaydār, *al-Ṭarīq ilā l-ḥurriyyah.*

from both Hebrew and Arabic to allow secret communication between, for example, a man and his wife. In such cases the shopkeeper would use code words to tell his wife that he wanted her to prepare him food or coffee but did not want to offer it to his guests.[90]

Of course, insofar as Islam had a proselytizing mission, Muslims routinely encouraged Jews to join their ranks through conversion. Nevertheless, in Yemen converts to Islam from Judaism were still held at arm's length by many Muslims. Popular expressions like "A Jewish convert to Islam is more polluting than a Muslim," or "If a Jew converts to Islam, his sidelocks are on his belly," or "A Jew is a Jew, even if he converts to Islam" all capture this idea.[91] In a folktale, villagers in an exclusively Jewish village were chagrined to find that not one of the cows they slaughtered was kosher. When they converted to Islam to spite Judaism, God had the last laugh. They became the lowest-status Muslims of all: black "*dawāshīn*," who lived in tents and could not intermarry with other tribesmen.[92]

The candy maker and leader of a revolutionary cell Muḥammad al-Maḥalwī engaged in far-ranging discussions of religion with Chief Rabbi (and Dor De'ah partisan) Yaḥyā al-Abyaḍ. They discussed the Hebrew Bible and New Testament (which Maḥalwī had consulted in Arabic translation). After reading a refutation of Christianity by an Indian Muslim, a book on which the Muslim and the Jew had no trouble agreeing, they reached more fraught territory. Maḥalwī asked why Abyaḍ did not convert to Islam, given his extensive background in Islamic texts. According to one of Maḥalwī's Muslim disciples, Abyaḍ said to him, "I possess status and position among the Jews, even among the Muslims—especially those in the government. If I converted to Islam how would they regard me? I would either clean up filth or roughen grindstones. . . . Who among them would marry me to his sister or his daughter?"[93]

Despite this sociological dimension of Jewishness, Muslims in Yemen did not view Jews as merely a rank in the social system. The Muslim majority accepted the myth of the impermeability of identity by encouraging Jewish observance. In a document claiming to represent the prophet Muḥammad's rules for the Jews of Islam, as opposed to the inauthentic stipulations of the Muslim sumptuary laws, the prophet commands, "[The Jews] are not to forsake their religion for another. Nor or they to desecrate their Sabbath or do any work on it."[94] This document was forged by Jews from Yemen for internal circulation and thus represents a Jewish ideal of Muslim protection of Judaism. Although exaggerated, it is no mere fantasy, because Muslims in Yemen accepted the role of defenders of Jewish practice and ritual.

Salim Manṣūrah, Imām Aḥmad's Jewish intermediary, records a 1949 conversation in which he tried to convince the imām to allow the Jews to leave Yemen for Israel. The imām advised him, "You know that the laws of Palestine are like those of America—not a single Jew will remain Jewish [there]. Islam and

Judaism only remain in Yemen. Do not fear. We will protect you."[95] Imām Yaḥyā is said to have jailed one of his messengers for seven days for making a demand of a Jew that would have caused the Jew to violate the Sabbath.[96] Imām Yaḥyā "forced us to observe our Judaism by avoiding the profanation of Sabbaths and holidays," writes Shalom Qoraḥ.[97] After emigrating, Sālim Saʿīd al-Jamal and Ṣāliḥ al-Ẓāhirī decried the militant secularism of the Israeli state. Ẓāhirī wrote a letter to David Ben Gurion unfavorably comparing the state of religion in Israel with the imām's Yemen.[98]

Some anecdotes suggest that Muslims viewed Judaism not simply as a set of practices that might keep the Jews separate but as a source of fascination. Early in his reign the imām visited a synagogue that housed a Torah scroll that was thought to bring miracles. This visit is said to have left a great impression upon him. He is also said to have asked a Jewish mattress maker who worked for a time in his palace to translate passages to him from Tractate *Avot* (the "Sayings of the Fathers") and the *Shulkhan Arukh* for several hours on Sunday mornings.[99]

Yosef Atsṭah, a Jew from Dhamār, recalls that some of the most observant Muslim notables held Judaism in such esteem that they attended the house of study (which was in a synagogue) every Thursday, where they listened intently to the recitation of Seʿadya Gaon's Arabic translation of that week's portion from the Pentateuch. "When it was over," he writes, "they kissed the study book like we did and, before our teacher, emphasized 'your Torah is the real thing.'"[100] On his way to Friday prayers in Taʿizz, the regional governor used to stop at the synagogue at the tomb of the wonder-working kabbalist R. Sālim al-Shabazi. In doing so he killed two birds with one stone, showing respect for a central figure in Yemeni Judaism and collecting some costly gifts left behind by Jewish pilgrims, such as carpets and perfume.[101]

Ṣāliḥ al-Ẓāhirī says he taught the Hebrew language and the Hebrew Bible, the Mishnah, and the *Shulkhan Arukh* to a scholarly kinsman of the imām's.[102] The same man once sent Rabbi al-Ẓāhirī a poem in Arabic that contained Hebrew expressions rendered in Hebrew characters (an extraordinary example of Muslim Judeo-Arabic). In it he meditated on the ongoing exodus of Yemeni Jews to Palestine and alluded to the ingathering of the exiles as depicted in specific verses in the books of the prophets.[103]

Nor were the Muslim veneration of Jewish spiritual powers and insistence upon the zealous observance of Jewish ritual quirks of the imāms or the Zaydīs. A Jew, Yosef Riḍā, recalls Muslims in the villages in the (Shafiʿi) south who wrapped Jewish phylacteries around their heads to cure headaches, and others who stole fringes from prayer shawls, burned them, and inhaled the smoke. The same writer sought to call to mind the dulcet voice of a cantor in a synagogue by recounting the tale of a Muslim who rented a shop in the Jewish part of town and obtained special permission from the local rabbinical court to listen to the prayer service. Though he had to stand outside, the performance brought tears to his eyes, and he kissed the head and feet of the cantor.[104]

Among villagers, having Jewish mourners at the funeral of a Muslim notable testified to the importance of the deceased. Once, when a stingy shaykh drove off Jews who had traveled to a funeral, the Jews prosecuted him in a court consisting of the local governor and other shaykhs for his disgraceful breach of the (tribal) norms of hospitality, and the shaykh was forced to pay them or risk a bad reputation.[105]

One Jew who lived outside of Sanaa risked expulsion, imprisonment, the confiscation of property, and execution by tribesmen for violating the Sabbath, Ḥayyim Ḥibshūsh reported.[106] Reuven Shar'abi, whose family were the only Jews in their village in southern Yemen, describes being accosted by his (Shafi'i) shaykh for having arrived home from an errand having left very little time to prepare for the Sabbath. "In Yemen, especially in the villages," he explains, "[Muslims] believed that if Jews sinned they brought a curse and suffering upon the entire land. For this reason they usually demanded that the Jews be strict in the observance of the Sabbath and the other commandments that were public. The system was: *either* Judaism *or* Islam."[107]

While the Sabbath perhaps represented the most visible expression of Jewish observance, some Muslims seem to have known a fair amount about the observance of less famous Jewish rituals. A Muslim customer confronted a Jew who was conducting business in the market of a village in the south on the evening before the festival of Shavuot. Reasoning that the Jew had erred by not allowing himself enough time to return home to his own village before the festival began, the Muslim forced him to spend the holiday at his house. The bet din later investigated the Jew's putative desecration of the festival and found him not guilty.[108]

In Bayḥān a group of young Jewish men decided to play a trick on their rabbi. One of them borrowed women's clothing and jewelry from an aunt and impersonated a Muslim *sharīfah* (a notable tribeswoman). The "sharīfah" knocked on the rabbi's door and asked for an amulet that would win back her errant husband. The trick was soon discovered and the young men were admonished against dressing like women. The town's rumor mill soon expanded upon the incident. A Muslim complained to a local judge that he had overheard local women complaining that a man dressed as a woman had kissed them and that it was no longer safe to go out at night. The judge rejected this story as baseless but reminded the Jews that the Torah forbids transvestitism.[109]

In Yemen intra-Muslim sectarianism complicated attitudes toward the Jews. When Imām Yaḥyā took power, members of his administration, Zaydīs from the north, fanned out across the (Shafi'i) south and became newly assertive.[110] In addition to taxation, the most fraught arena of inter-sectarian interaction, the proper treatment of the Jewish minority became an issue. A rabbi in Ibb told a

Syrian traveler that the local Shafi'is were hostile to Jews and that he had heard that the Zaydīs were better. He said that while complaints of ill treatment would earn prison and fines from the governor, they avoided lodging such complaints against the tribesmen.[111] Other Jews judge the Zaydīs to have been more harsh than Shafi'is in their dealings with Jews because of their punctiliousness in religious matters, among other reasons.[112] Yosef Riḍā, who was from the south, attributes drought and bad crops in the latter part of Imām Yaḥyā's reign to the idea that "the Zaydīs polluted the land."[113] He also recalls a group of Zaydīs upbraiding his shaykh for greeting him by his first name, Yūsuf, which is the name of a prophet.[114] The Shafi'is of southern Yemen, Avraham Madhalah says, called the northern Jews "the Zaydīs' Jews" and hated them with both the hatred they reserved for the Zaydīs and that held for Jews.[115] Even Jewish women in a town at the border between Imām Yaḥyā's realm and the British Protectorate in Aden refused to allow a group of northern Jews stranded there to draw water from the well in order "to magnify the hatred of the Zaydīs and the Jews among them." It took the intervention of a Muslim soldier from the north before they were allowed to drink.[116]

Occasionally Jews became embroiled in intra-Muslim disputes of a sectarian nature. In 1918 the powerful Shafi'i shaykhs of Lower Yemen pledged their allegiance to Imām Yaḥyā. However, they had engaged in a serious discussion of founding their own independent polity shortly beforehand, and some still nurtured dreams of secession long afterward. Some even made overtures to the British in Aden.[117] In 1922 a Jewish leader approached the governor of Ta'izz, a Zaydī sayyid, warning him of a conspiracy among local shaykhs to establish a Sunni (Shafi'i) state independent of the imāms' Yemen. The governor "did not attribute importance to this, nor did this information attain the level of truth and certainty," writes Aḥmad b. Muḥammad al-Wazīr, "for it came from a Jew and perhaps he intended to foment a dispute between the Muslims and trick them."[118]

Mordecai al-Ẓāhirī, who was in prison as surety for his father after the assassination of Imām Yaḥyā in 1948, describes one of his fellow prisoners as "the Messiah," a penniless Jew of uncertain origins who wandered Yemen proclaiming the impending redemption. He spoke Italian, smoked heavily, played cards with the foreign prisoners (among them Palestinian Arabs who fought for the revolutionaries), and undertook small magical feats in exchange for cigarette money. (This may or may not have been Ezra Ḥazzī, a former convert to Islam who announced his messianic mission in 1949.[119]) He routinely uttered blasphemies against Judaism that were bad enough, reasoned Ẓāhirī and a coreligionist convicted of selling alcohol to a Muslim, that they might "cause rain to stop."[120] ("It was widely believed [among Yemeni Muslims] that Jewish prayer, both communal and individual, can affect rainfall," writes historian Bat-Zion Eraqi Klorman.[121])

Yosef Riḍā comments that ordinary Muslims routinely asked for Jews to perform their prayer of healing (*mi she-berakh*) upon them and were even willing to pay for the service.[122] Ẓāhirī tried to convince his fellow prisoner not to violate the Sabbath in front of the Muslim prisoners, "who tried not to hurt the feelings of the Jews on the Sabbath. If they saw a Jew passing by on an Arab street by chance on the Sabbath the jokesters among them would have rebuked him: 'Hey Jew, don't desecrate the Sabbath!'"[123]

Muslim judges could recuse themselves from cases involving non-Muslims. Yet one finds them ruling even on parochially Jewish matters. The eighteenth-century jurist Muḥammad 'Alī al-Shawkānī, who was discussed in chapter 2, wrote a treatise condemning Maimonides's allegorical interpretation of bodily resurrection, likely relying on testimony as to its contents from Jewish informants.[124] In 1913–1914 Imām Yaḥyā ruled on whether Jews could read the Zohar (see below), and in 1935 he ruled on the tricky issue of the status of synagogues as property in Jewish law.[125]

Some Muslims used their familiarity with Judaism to cement friendships with Jews. "He loved to make the acquaintance of Jews," Ṣāliḥ al-Ẓāhirī recalled of a sayyid in Radā', "to converse with them and even to learn a smattering of Hebrew words from them. Whenever he met a Jew in the market he let loose a few of those Hebrew words of his."[126] One Muslim merchant who was a fixture in the Jewish Quarter of Sanaa, making his living selling firewood and fodder to Jews, learned Jewish songs, wedding melodies, and biblical passages.[127] Muslims in Sanaa used to visit their Jewish friends on Fridays, where eating the roasted snacks and baked goods that Jews prepared before the Sabbath served as a form of entertainment.[128]

Such familiarity with Judaism might be acquired at a young age. Qadi Muḥammad al-Akwa' lists "annoying the Jews" in his catalog of games that the Muslim children of Dhamār used to play. Groups of roving youths descended upon the Jewish Quarter every Friday, entered Jews' homes, and demanded snacks. Then they went into the synagogues to watch them pray.[129]

Economically based intimacy had its limits. In Radā' Muslim women worked for Jews by chopping wood, grinding flour, tending their livestock, and performing other services. However, they returned home at night. A Jew who took in a Muslim orphan was accused of trying to convert her to Judaism. A qadi questioned the Muslim girl, who revealed that she knew about rules governing the observance of the Sabbath and the Jewish dietary laws. Of course, the other Muslim girls who worked in Jewish homes probably knew as much through observation, but the fact that this particular girl lived with the Jewish family cast her knowledge in a sinister light. The Jew who took her in was subjected to "donkeying."[130]

Both Muslims and Jews in Yemen had reasons to argue that the boundaries between them were self-evident and impermeable. Nevertheless, autobiographical works by Jews feature numerous picaresque characters who transgress these boundaries as often as the need to reinvent themselves arises. These figures are often regarded as bad Jews and worse Muslims. Mordecai Yitshari describes a

Jewish *jinn* charmer/con artist who impersonated a Muslim sayyid, married a *sayyidah,* was caught and converted to Islam, became an army officer, reverted to Judaism, and emigrated to Palestine.[131] Ratson Halevi tells of the previously mentioned "ape man," a Jewish orphan who grew up in the company of baboons, taught himself to survive in the wild, became a de facto Muslim, reverted to Judaism, and emigrated to Palestine.[132] Such evident delight in the human capacity to make a home in the alleyways between identities finds expression as well in stories of Jewish converts to Islam who were insincere not merely in their conversion but as a matter of course; for example, a man who studied at the Azhar in Cairo, relished strong drink, and became a powerful politician in Aden, and a highwayman whose Jewish partner in crime informed him that praying a few *rakʿahs* would not be the end of the world.[133]

In 1931 a Jewish girl from a village near Bayḥān married another Jew from Bayḥān and moved into his house, which abutted the homes of two Muslim families. (Jews in that town did not live in a separate quarter.) She befriended the neighbors and in the eighth month of her pregnancy decided to convert to Islam. Her husband, who had been married twice before and had lost several children, was distraught, and demanded in vain to be given his newborn son. The convert was married to the son of her Muslim neighbor, and the Jew remarried and raised another family. After the signing of the Oslo Accords in the mid-1990s, a son from this second family succeeded in making telephone contact with his Muslim half brother in Yemen.[134]

On its face the story revolves around the classic romance theme of sibling recognition and reunification. Yet the contact between the Israeli Jew, Shalom, and his Yemeni Muslim brother, ʿAbd al-Qādir, fails to offer the anticipated happy ending. Though the two men share a genetic link, they remain utterly alienated from one another. Their conversation offered each man a mirror that distorted his own life. Rather than romance, the story of one brother becoming a Muslim Yemeni and the other a Jewish Israeli seems to represent a particularly astonishing gnomic demonstration of fate's capricious ability to dispense with such seemingly concrete categories as religious and national identity.

Although the Jewish intermediaries upheld the separation of Muslim and Jew, at least when it was expedient, their agenda required them to blur the borders between Arabic and Hebrew, Islam and Judaism. Unlike such amoral, yet enthralling, figures who skulk in the borderlands, their subterfuge paradoxically needed to be performed in the light of day. Imām Yaḥyā suffered from arthritis in his legs. On the advice of his Italian physician, he set out in 1941 for a six-month stay at Ḥammām Damt, an area of hot springs. In preparation for his convalescence, a new road had been paved to the springs, new buildings erected, and a modest marketplace emerged, all in a short period of time. The new road passed by Radāʿ. For days the Jews of Radāʿ drilled for their reception of the imām in the main synagogue of the town. They composed a pair of songs in Hebrew and in Arabic praising Imām Yaḥyā and offering wishes for his speedy recovery. Ṣāliḥ al-Ẓāhirī, along with a calligrapher and a silversmith, made an unusual white flag, a hybrid of imāmic-Islamic symbols and Zionist motifs. The flag of imāmic Yemen was emblazoned with a white saber—which may have represented ʿAlī b. Abī Ṭālib's sword, Dhū l-fiqar—as well as stars and the Muslim creed.[135] Ẓāhirī's flag featured a Star of David in the center, the saber to its right, and a crescent and star to its left. Verses in Hebrew and Arabic praising the Commander of the Faithful marked the borders.

The town gathered to greet the imām's motorcade, but he had been detained at the house of a shaykh who insisted the imām stay with him. Meanwhile the mayor of Radāʿ noticed the Jews' flag and ordered soldiers bring Ẓāhirī to the governor. The judge who was with the governor insisted that the flag was forbidden, since "Jews do not have a flag," and the governor confiscated it. Ẓāhirī protested that to all intents and purposes his was the Yemeni flag. Ẓāhirī went to the shaykh's house, where the imām was staying, and sought his intervention. Imām Yaḥyā ordered the Jew's flag returned to him.[136]

Even unambiguous Muslims with no particular interest in Judaism were drawn (often against their will) into the inner sanctum of their Jewish neighbors' theology. In 1913–1914, in Muslim courtrooms in Yemen, two groups of Jewish scholars debated the legality of studying the Zohar, a central text in Jewish mysticism. The question of the legitimacy of the kabbalistic tradition had generated a schism within Yemenite Judaism that split its leadership. Imām Yaḥyā, his son (the future Imām Aḥmad), and various Muslim scholars weighed in on the issue of the Zohar's legality. In thirteenth-century Cairo, Jews appealed to the Muslim authorities to protest innovations to the synagogue service undertaken by their leader. Though these innovations were consciously Islamicizing, the Muslims sided with the offended congregants.[137] The 1913–1914 legal discussions offer a similarly rare example of Muslim courts adjudicating a substantive issue within Judaism.

The Jewish parties to the court proceedings imagined Islam in making their arguments, and the Muslim authorities imagined their own ideal Judaism when judging the schism among the Jews. One of the Jewish parties to the court proceedings depicted Islam as the de jure (and perhaps de facto) defender of monotheism. The other appealed to an Islam that defended society from change. The Muslim authorities, in turn, saw the schism within Judaism as an extension of Muslim sectarianism in Yemen. These creative misunderstandings of sectarian differences informed a wide range of interactions between Jews and the sharīʿa courts in the 1930s and 1940s.

Kabbalistic traditions suffused Judaism in Yemen. These included the study of the Zohar, a mystical commentary on the Torah written in thirteenth-century

Spain (to its adherents the text is much older and was set down in writing only in the thirteenth century); the singing of erotic paraliturgical poetry; and the belief in amulets and other magical practices. The Yemenite Jewish movement called Dor De'ah, which arose in the early twentieth century, sought to purge Judaism of such practices. With the rise of this movement, an elaborate series of litmus tests differentiated pro-kabbalah Jews from anti-kabbalah Jews. Naturally, whether or not one studied the Zohar served as a clear indication of factional affiliation. One zealous anti-kabbalist is said to have planned to use a copy of the Zohar to make a stepladder that he would use to reach his library.[138] Others threatened to burn the Zohar and the *Shulkhan Arukh,* a legal code containing some kabbalistic content.[139]

The two factions tended to differ on the issue of prayer rite (see below). Pro-kabbalah Jews repeated congregational prayers after the precentor (*shaliaḥ tsibor*) had recited them. Anti-kabbalah Jews did not repeat them.[140] The two sides disagreed violently over whether a word from a verse of the Psalms (118:25) that was part of the liturgy should be repeated three times (kabbalists) or just once (Dor De'ah).[141] Pro-kabbalah Jews kissed the fringes on their prayer shawls during the recitation of the *Shema'* (the profession of faith) and brought a chair for the prophet Elijah to a circumcision ceremony. Anti-kabbalah Jews did neither of these things.[142]

Ṣāliḥ al-Ẓāhirī describes how the issue of "honoring the table" (*kibud ha-shulkhan*) became a litmus test for factional affiliation that divided the participants in festive gatherings in Sanaa in the early twentieth century. After the meal was finished, the kabbalist faction took the table (essentially a large tray) away, then returned it and set a small piece of bread upon it before performing the grace after meals. Rabbis from both factions convened a meeting on the issue. There Rabbi Yaḥyā Qāfiḥ denounced the practice as polytheistic (the table should not be returned at all, in his view). In 1932 the merchant (and pro-kabbalist) Hārūn Ḥibshūsh pursued a case against three Dor De'ah partisans in a Muslim court, alleging that they had violently removed the table after a meal and beat him up. The qadi concluded that there were no actionable issues in the case that would justify a fatwa, but since each side wanted the incident recorded in detail, his staff would oblige them.[143]

The reasons for the outbreak of the schism are unclear. Explanations include a clash between the personalities (and generations) of the rabbis representing each faction, the provocative tone of the younger anti-kabbalists, and a dispute over the proceeds of kosher slaughter.[144] Historian Menashe 'Anzi suggests that one faction adhered to the progressive values of the (Muslim) Young Turk bureaucracy, while their competitors, bending with the winds of change brought about by the ascendance of the conservative imām Yaḥyā, became similarly traditionalist.[145] Whatever the causes, by the end of the summer of 1913 the kabbalists had won their bid to maintain control of communal institutions and had marginalized their critics.

In time the two factions regarded one another as non-Jews. They would not intermarry, nor would they eat meat slaughtered by butchers from the opposing faction.[146] In 1944 refugees at a transit camp in the Aden Protectorate petitioned the American Jewish Joint Distribution Committee to refrain from allowing the anti-kabbalists to emigrate to the Land of Israel because they were not, in fact, Jews.[147] The division within Yemenite Judaism persists today.

Scholarship on the schism over the kabbalah in Yemenite Judaism tends to follow three main approaches. The first, a conciliatory tendency aimed by Yemenite Jewish writers at an audience of Yemenite Jews, details the history of the controversy in order to minimize and smooth over the rift in the community.[148] The second tendency, a modernist interpretation aimed at the Israeli general public and an academic Hebrew readership, describes the rift as a Middle Eastern interlude in the paradigmatic modernization of Judaism. This approach emphasizes the European roots of the Yemenite Jewish reform movement and uses terms borrowed from the experience of European Jewry (like *haskalah*, Hasidim, and *mitnagdim*) to describe the conflict in Yemen.[149]

One or more "enlightened" European scholars who visited Yemen may indeed have planted the seed for the controversy over the kabbalah. The Austrian Jewish archaeologist Eduard Glaser (1855–1908), who spent several years in Yemen in the 1880s, provided R. Yaḥyā Qāfiḥ, who later became the central figure in the reform movement, with scientific instruments and Hebrew books printed in Europe. He shared an interest in astronomy with Qāfiḥ, and the two apparently were friends. Glaser was already the focus of factional strife in an anonymously authored Hebrew book from 1937 where the author states that Glaser was a non-Jew, a fact allegedly confirmed by a Jew who followed him into a bathhouse and took note of his foreskin.[150] Another candidate most often cited for this dubious honor is the French archaeologist Joseph Halévy, who came to Yemen to investigate Sabaic antiquities in 1869–1870 on behalf of the Académie Française and railed against the kabbalah.[151]

The third tendency in interpreting Jewish sectarianism in Yemen, which can be designated "Arabist," takes into account the Arabic-Islamic context. R. B. Serjeant, an eminent scholar of South Arabia, briefly discussed the imām's involvement in the Jews' dispute over the kabbalah, describing it as "a very instructive case of co-operation between Muslims and Jews in defence of the traditional way of life in Sanaa."[152] The Syrian writer Camīlia Abū Jabal mentioned the case in her 1999 *The Jews of Yemen*. To her, the case reflected the complete freedom of religious expression that Muslim authorities granted the Jews of Yemen.[153] These readings share a certain superficiality. Perhaps the fact that Jews turned to Muslim courts to pursue this dispute reflected a broader spirit of cooperation. On the other hand, the paralysis of the Jewish leadership created an obvious practical motive to turn to the Muslim courts. Moreover, the litigants presented specific and contending interpretations of Judaism and Islam. In other words, the roles played by Muslim views of Judaism and Jewish views of Islam also played important roles within the controversy over the kabbalah.

The most important document of this interaction is a 1914 fatwa. A book on Yemenite Jewry printed in Tel Aviv in 1945 included a rather poor reproduction of it, along with a Hebrew translation of its contents.[154] I published an edition and translation of the document based upon that reproduction.[155] The fatwa designates the first of the two parties to the court proceedings the "Qāfiḥ faction," after their spiritual leader, Rabbi Yaḥyā al-Qāfiḥ (1849–1932). Qāfiḥ, a former chief rabbi, astronomer, and reformer, led a vigorous campaign against the kabbalistic tradition and in favor of a Judaism that he believed to be authentic. He designed and directed a modernizing Jewish school in Sanaa that taught natural science and the Turkish and Arabic languages, as well as a religious curriculum.[156] (His school was intended to replace the traditional "*maktab*," where texts were memorized by rote.) The second camp, which the fatwa designates the "Isḥāq faction," was led by Yaḥyā Isḥāq, the sitting chief rabbi, who defended the kabbalah. Leading rabbis affiliated with each faction appeared in court before the Muslim judge, Yaḥyā b. Muḥammad b. ʿAbbās al-Ḥūthī, and later before Imām Yaḥyā.

An eyewitness to the events of 1913 is the sole source for important background information to the courtroom drama of 1914. According to this writer, who wrote a report on events in Yemen for a Hebrew newspaper under the pseudonym "Sālim al-Jahrāzī," R. Qāfiḥ and his students sought the backing of the shaykh and ruler of al-Sirr province, north of Sanaa.[157] They also sought the intervention of Imām Yaḥyā's son Aḥmad, then resident in Qiryat al-Qābil, a village also to the north of the city. Aḥmad sent one of his brothers to Sanaa to investigate. He also asked R. Yaḥyā Isḥāq for a translation of the Zohar into Arabic. The rabbi insisted that the work should not be translated.

The kabbalists, in turn, appealed to the Ottoman governor. (Though the Turks had ceded much power to the imām in 1911, they still ruled Sanaa.) The governor backed the (kabbalist) chief rabbi, Yaḥyā Isḥāq, and had the anti-kabbalists jailed. This represented the first of many thirty-day jail terms for the group's leadership. Aḥmad influenced the governor to secure the men's release, but they were soon arrested again. In a move that reflected the tense and delicate relationship between the Turkish governor, the Zaydī Muslim majority, and the Jewish minority, the Ottoman governor presented the kabbalists' case to the Zaydī court of appeals. Onlookers included prominent Muslims like Prince Aḥmad and about fifty Jews.

The anti-kabbalists emphasized that the proliferation of divine attributes that characterizes the kabbalah constituted polytheism, displaying for the assembled Muslim scholars depictions of the "sephirotic tree" that depicts the emanatory system of the Godhead. They argued that its ten circles represented ten gods. An anti-kabbalist, Riḍā al-Ṣārūm, demanded the Zohar be brought and passages translated into Arabic for the audience, but this did not happen. About a month later the anti-kabbalists complained to Imām Yaḥyā. He asked Qadi al-ʿAmrī to interview rabbis who led the two factions, and his deliberations became a part of the fatwa that was written in 1914.[158]

Although Jahrāzī's 1913 letter describes the anti-kabbalists as having broken ranks and approached the Muslim authorities first, each side would later accuse the other of having brought the case to a non-Jewish court, something Yemenite Jews routinely did but seldom admitted.[159] A member of the anti-kabbalah faction writes in his memoir that Imām Yaḥyā heard about the strife within the Jewish community and asked each side to send two representatives to his residence in al-Qaflah in the territory north of Sanaa. Each camp sent two representatives, and the four Jews spent several days with the imām, during which they informed him of the nature of the dispute. They asked him to appoint a trustworthy judge who could resolve the dispute once and for all. The imām appointed Yaḥyā b. Muḥammad b. ʿAbbās al-Ḥūthī to the task.[160] Hūthī held a court proceeding in the imām's residence in Sanaa. According to a Jewish source, two Muslim merchants who had a lot of business dealings with Jews also attended but are not mentioned in the fatwa.[161]

According to the fatwa, the goal of the arbitration was to produce a document expressing the consensus of both sides. Roughly its first half contains the comments of the ruling judge. He exhorts the Jews to adhere to established customs in the observance of festivals, prayer, and books to be studied. He also emphasizes the need to avoid both coercion and verbal abuse by one faction or the other. He then discusses the issue of the Zohar. The second half contains Imām Yaḥyā's comments. Imām Yaḥyā had a reputation for "micromanaging" the legal system. In addition to addressing the legality of the Zohar and the question of what works Jews may study, the imām seems to have seen the proceedings as an opportunity to settle a number of outstanding, and not necessarily connected, issues with the Jewish community: five synagogues whose construction was of dubious legality, the problem of Jewish women who dressed immodestly, and whether Rabbi Qāfiḥ's modern school should be allowed to operate.

On the last point, a qadi who knew Imām Yaḥyā said the imām possessed an intense intellectual curiosity that extended to natural science, philosophy, and contemporary thought. Nevertheless, he opposed the dissemination of nonreligious knowledge in his realm.[162] In the late 1930s the imām cracked down on a Muslim school in Dhubḥān that had introduced modern subjects into its curriculum and sent a scholar as an emissary "to teach the Zaydī rite in the school of Dhubḥān and to spread among its students the love of the people of the prophet [i.e., the sayyids]."[163] Just as opponents had accused Yaḥyā al-Qāfiḥ's Jewish school of foreign meddling, the provincial governor in Taʿizz described "Christian" influences in Dhubḥān.[164] (In Yemen, Christianity served as the rhetorical equivalent of infidelity. "The Imām [Yaḥyā] used the word 'Christians'," writes Aḥmad Jābir ʿAfīf, "to take a stand against any modernizing project."[165] ʿOvadiah Zandani recalls Muslim neighbors cautioning him that the positive letters from Jews who had settled in Palestine had been forged by Christians who had really killed them and stolen their women.[166])

Whether or not they initiated the legal proceedings, each Jewish faction sought to use them to their advantage. The anti-kabbalist faction sought to use the court proceedings to capitalize on what they reasonably believed would be a strong distaste for the kabbalah on the part of the Muslim jurists. The kabbalist faction sought to use the court proceedings to portray their opponents as threats to the existing social order.

The text of the fatwa makes clear that the kabbalists had the upper hand. The fatwa repeatedly asserts the kabbalist Rabbi Yaḥyā Isḥāq's authority. After appearing in court, leading members of the anti-kabbalah faction, including Rabbi Qāfiḥ himself, were again imprisoned. However, the fatwa shows a concerted attempt on behalf of both the presiding judge and Imām Yaḥyā to placate each of the two Jewish factions, often at the risk of clarity. This overly inclusive tendency manifests itself most clearly in the fatwa's emphasis on preserving the status quo in ritual observance and social practice; while permitting those who disagreed with it to follow their instincts, it stipulated that neither those preserving the status quo nor those diverging from it attack the other—verbally or otherwise.

The overriding concern of the Muslim jurists was preserving the social order and reducing strife between the two factions. The kabbalist camp denounced the anti-kabbalists to the Muslim authorities as agents of foreign powers and adherents of the Greek philosophers.[167] They made the incendiary charge that the pupils in Rabbi Qāfiḥ's modern school tucked their sidelocks under their tarbushes, or even cut them off altogether, in imitation of their Turkish instructor. The fatwa inveighs against "the removal of sidelocks, shaving of beards, or such things as would change [the Jews'] normal appearance."[168] The kabbalists also accused the anti-kabbalists of being revolutionaries intent on overturning Muslim hegemony and agents of European powers.[169]

Both the judge Yaḥyā b. Muḥammad b. ʿAbbās and Imām Yaḥyā gave considerable leeway to individual Jewish scholars' beliefs about what was "firmly established" (*thābit*) in Judaism and what part of it was "innovation" (*muḥdath*). Along these lines they emphasized the inappropriateness of coercion as a means of settling the dispute between the two parties, as the judge proclaimed: "None of them is to be coerced into being present or participating in something which they do not believe to be a fixed part of their religion." Imām Yaḥyā made his opposition to religious coercion abundantly clear to an unnamed Jew who challenged his ruling during a later phase of the dispute, in the mid-1930s. According to Sālim Saʿīd al-Jamal, Imām Yaḥyā asked this man: "Do you want me to coerce you in your beliefs? Coercion is never acceptable. If I were to coerce someone, I would coerce all of you into [following] the law of Muḥammad."[170]

The anti-kabbalist camp portrayed their opponents as men who dabbled in polytheism, a position that Rabbi Qāfiḥ took in his written polemics against anthropomorphic language in the Zohar.[171] Unnamed anti-kabbalists claimed in the Muslim court that the Zohar "negates God's unicity and His attributes." Already in November 1913 Yaḥyā Isḥāq wrote to the Ottoman chief rabbi in Istanbul, complaining that this charge threatened the lives and property of all the Jews.[172] Given that the Islamic state's tolerance for Jews was contingent upon their monotheistic beliefs, this was a loaded accusation. It is unlikely that those who made it were unaware of either its gravity or the potential impact it might have in a Muslim legal setting. Indeed, some Zaydī scholars held Sunni Muslims to be infidels because they practiced anthropomorphism (called *tashbīh* or *tajsīm*), among other things.

The fatwa, however, shows that the judge was relatively unconcerned with the directions taken by the two Jewish factions in arguments over the Zohar. This was because both sides agreed that no Jew needed to study it. In his written comments, Imām Yaḥyā affirmed the judge's ruling and went even further in defending the Zohar. He said that the Zohar's contradiction of the Torah "did not appear to be central, as we explained to those present, and as they themselves admitted." Imām Yaḥyā ruled that "what should be studied in their synagogues and academies is that which Yaḥyā Isḥaq studies of that which is not new."[173] By saying this, Imām Yaḥyā attempted to placate both camps. Yaḥyā Isḥāq, the head of the kabbalist camp, studied the Zohar; therefore, providing that it was not an innovation, the Jews should study it. The question of whether the Zohar constitutes an innovation is left ambiguous. However, considering the fatwa's syntactic linkage between the books Yaḥyā Isḥāq studied and the need to preserve the sartorial customs that distinguished Jews from Muslims, one can make a strong case on the basis of the text of the fatwa alone that the imām wanted the study of the Zohar, as a time-honored practice in Yemenite Judaism, to continue. Similarly, the imām asked that Rabbi Qāfiḥ's modern school be closed but added, "If one of them wished to study an area of knowledge that was unconnected to their religion, like speaking and writing Arabic or Turkish, arithmetic, and the like, there would be nothing to prevent them."[174]

Ironically, the dynasty to which Imām Yaḥyā belonged, the house of Ḥamīd al-Dīn, took an exceptionally dim view of Islamic mysticism, a position that was rooted in Zaydī tradition. Imām Aḥmad, Yaḥyā's son, demolished a number of tombs that common people venerated, as had several of his predecessors among the imāms.[175] One source says this campaign of destruction included the tomb of the kabbalist R. Sālim al-Shabazi, which was venerated by both Jews and Muslims. (It was rebuilt in 1935 with Aḥmad's blessing.[176]) In the fatwa on the Zohar, the Zaydī judge defends Jewish mysticism in order to preserve the status quo. Thus, it is an example of the ends (the preservation of the traditional order from change) justifying the means (the defense of mystical texts).[177]

As was mentioned, the case seems to have been a qualified victory for the kabbalist faction. The fatwa affirmed the authority of their leader, Rabbi Yaḥyā Isḥāq, and reiterated his role in preserving the status quo of relations between Jews and Muslims. Yet the emphasis on a Jewish scholar's individual belief as to whether or not a given aspect of Judaism was fixed in tradition or an innovation, and on the rejection of coercion in matters of belief, supported the anti-kabbalah faction. In fact, when the dispute between the two factions flared up again in 1935, it was the anti-kabbalist faction that routinely demanded that the imām's ruling in the "fatwa of al-Qaflah" be upheld.

This case was probably the first in which Imām Yaḥyā emphasized the importance of an individual's own beliefs in choosing one of two religious options: the need to avoid coercion, and the need to avoid all recriminations based upon such matters. It was not, however, the last. In 1919 he promulgated a nearly identical ruling to manage the differences in rite between Zaydīs and Shafi'is. He ordered that they must pray together in the mosques without disturbing one another.[178]

In the early 1940s visitors from Iraq witnessed the imām's coerced ecumenicism in action. Some Shafi'is had complained that a Zaydī sayyid discounted their prayers, since they were not performed according to the norms of the Zaydī rite. Imām Yaḥyā summoned them all to his audience chamber in Sanaa. After they arrived, they all sat silently in the imām's presence. When the muezzin announced the noonday prayer, the assembly prayed behind the imām according to the Zaydī rite. The zealous sayyid relished his apparent triumph. After the group had eaten lunch, the muezzin announced the evening prayer. Now the imām led prayers according to the Sunni rite, turned to the zealous sayyid, and said to him, "May you perish! I am the imām of the Muslims, not only the Zaydīs." Then he had the sayyid sent to prison.[179] Similarly, a scholar interviewed by Gabriele vom Bruck described how Imām Yaḥyā rebuked a preacher who commemorated (Shi'i) 'Ashura for breaking the country apart at the seams.[180]

The episode showed a strikingly permissive attitude toward Sunni Islam on the part of Imām Yaḥyā. A mid-twentieth-century Zaydī legal manual, *The Golden Crown on the Laws of the Rite,* provides a convenient summary of Zaydī attitudes toward Sunnis under the rubric of "judging the apostate." Some held that Sunnis, as believers in determinism and anthropomorphism, and therefore "infidels by [their incorrect] interpretation" (*kuffār al-ta'wīl*), should be offered a choice between conversion to Zaydī Shiʿism or death. Others thought that as believers in a sacred book (the Qur'an), Sunnis should be offered the status of protected non-Muslims and made to pay the poll tax. Others held that Sunnis could be buried in (Zaydī) Muslim cemeteries, that one could pray behind them in the mosque, and that their testimony in court could be offered equal weight to that of a Zaydī—their punishment for infidelity (*kufr*) would be exacted in the afterlife. Some imāms rejected the concept of "infidels by [their incorrect] interpretation" altogether, holding that Sunnis should only be held to "the laws governing Muslim transgressors—[theirs] is a transgression whose adjudication requires neither abasement nor elevation."[181]

Imām Yaḥyā's attempts to assuage both conservative Zaydīs and Zaydīs who leaned toward Sunnism ultimately failed. To the former he seemed soft on Sunnis, as well as being willing to bend the rules when it came to the issue of succession. The pro-Sunni faction within the opposition (for whom Shawkānī represented the ideal) saw the imām as the persecutor of any who questioned the principle of rule by Hashemite. One such revolutionary tells of how another narrowly escaped being jailed when investigators missed an anti-Shiʿi work while searching his library for objectionable books.[182] Imām Yaḥyā also gave considerable leeway in determining religious policy to his underlings, some of whom were hard on Sunnis. Yaḥyā b. Muḥammad ʿAbbās, the judge who initially ruled on the Zohar, would alienate many Sunnis when he pushed Zaydism on the population of al-Ḍāliʿ, where he was posted as governor.[183] Another governor who was known for being a strict Zaydī forced muezzins in (Shafiʿi) Ibb to add a Shiʿi clause to the call to prayer.[184] A Shafiʿi sent the imām a poem complaining bitterly of the governor of Taʿizz. In it he bitterly mocked this governor, putting these words in his mouth: "O Shiʿi haters, yours is the party of perdition, so pay the poll tax, you wannabe Jews."[185]

Looking back on the controversy over the kabbalah some sixty years later, Jamal astutely observed that Imām Yaḥyā's policy toward Jewish sectarianism was exactly his policy toward Muslim sectarianism.[186] Ultimately the fatwa failed to resolve the dispute over the kabbalah. Its excessive inclusiveness, however, was not its fatal flaw. It faltered because of a misunderstanding of the practicalities of Jewish prayer on the part of the Muslims who drafted the fatwa. In general the kabbalists followed one distinct prayer rite, the anti-kabbalists another. The issue of rite in Yemeni Judaism has its own complex history. The Sephardi rite, called "Levantine" (*shāmī*) in Yemen, was associated with the kabbalists. Most members of the Qāfiḥ faction prayed in the "local" (*baladī*) rite. This rite was believed to reflect the state of the Yemeni liturgy prior to the dissemination of kabbalistic ideas in Yemen in the late Middle Ages. There were, however, kabbalistically inclined rabbis who followed the "local" rite, among them Yaḥyā Isḥāq.[187] Therefore, by demanding that Jews pray according to the kabbalist Yaḥyā Isḥāq's rite, as the imām once did in the 1930s, the Muslim authorities unwittingly strengthened the hand of the anti-kabbalist faction while perhaps thinking they were ruling in favor of the first faction.[188]

In the fatwa Imām Yaḥyā ruled that each Jew pray according to his own rite, a solution later adopted for doctrinal disputes between Zaydīs and Shafi'is. This solution, however, possessed a problem in its application to the Jewish community. Zaydīs and Shafi'is differed substantially in their theological ideas and in their views of the Islamic past. Yet if the difference between how they prayed, which revolved around the placement of the hands on the thighs (Zaydīs) or on the chest (Sunnis) while standing, caused a lot of strife, it was not an issue that would actively disrupt the other group's prayers. In contrast, if every member of a Jewish prayer quorum did not follow the rite of the precentor, the service would lose its order. When the controversy over the kabbalah reemerged in 1935, the imām's unwillingness to address this discrepancy between Islam and Judaism would become a bone of contention.

In fact, Jamal may have deliberately misled the imām on this issue in the 1930s. Jamal suggested that a prayer precentor who belonged to the anti-kabbalah faction in a synagogue whose leadership was hotly contested between the two factions be allowed to pray according to his rite and that anyone who complained should be fined.[189] Jamal neglected to mention that the rite of a precentor would trump any other congregant's rite by virtue of his duties. In a similar instance, Jamal reported telling the leaders of the anti-kabbalah faction that it was best to keep the imām in the dark about the inapplicability of the individual rite solution to Judaism, for fear that it might strengthen the hand of the opposing faction.[190] Jamal says he told a Zaydī judge on two occasions that a solution involving adherents of each of the two rites praying together was unworkable. The second time he told the judge this, he added that the suggestion was a very good one for Muslims, explained the differences between the two Jewish rites in Yemen, and described the differences between the two factions over the Zohar.[191] It is possible that the judge in question never relayed this information to Imām Yaḥyā.

Perhaps the view of Jewish sectarianism as an extension of Muslim sectarianism colored Imām Yaḥyā's and other Zaydī jurists' outlook to the point that they preferred to ignore this contradictory information. The loaded charge that the anti-kabbalah faction made in court—namely, that the kabbalist faction's fondness for anthropomorphisms made their monotheism suspect—reared its head several times during a later stage of the controversy in the mid-1930s. In a letter to Imām Yaḥyā dated September 12, 1935, representatives of the anti-kabbalah camp wrote, "We are those who affirm exalted God's unicity, and the Isḥāq faction [that is, the pro-kabbalah camp] does the opposite."[192] Almost a year later, the heads of the anti-kabbalah camp decided to charge their rivals with polytheism (*ishrāk*) once again. Jamal says this move was aimed to discourage prominent Muslims from taking their side.[193]

Already in the first phase of the dispute (1913–1914), a Jew affiliated with the pro-kabbalah camp, Saʿīd al-Naddāf, who had recently arrived in Palestine, spelled out the implications of the charge of polytheism for an audience of Yemenite Jews in Jerusalem. In Naddāf's colorful account of the events of 1914 Imām Yaḥyā holds the following exchange with Riḍā al-Ṣārum, one of the two anti-kabbalah scholars who traveled to al-Qaflah to meet him:

> [The imām] asked, "Do you study the Zohar?" Riḍā al-Ṣārum replied, "No, I cannot study it, because it makes a number of anthropomorphic statements concerning the Creator." The imām replied, "What you say may be true, but doesn't the entire Torah speak in anthropomorphic language? Does it not say, 'Israel is my first-born son' (Ex. 4:22) and 'we shall make man in our image' (Gen. 1:26)? Also, in the Prophets and the Writings there are similar matters, as in what King David says in Psalm 45—what is the meaning of these [statements]?" [The anti-kabbalah scholar] answered, "What is said in that Psalm is said concerning the groom and the bride in order to increase their joy." The imām replied, "Nay—these are all spiritual matters, not corporeal anthropomorphisms, and they are all 'esoteric matters' (Deut. 29:28) that are spoken of here. If you persist in asking such thickheaded questions like an uneducated man (God forbid!), it all becomes vanity and emptiness, your religion becomes nothing but vanity, your blood becomes permissible to us, and every person who is called a Hebrew will, God forbid, disappear. Know that if the words of the Zohar are not accepted, then the Torah must follow and, God forbid, everything will be negated. From this day forth, understand and return from your [errant] path. Go in the footsteps of your forefathers and do not change a thing."[194]

In Saʿīd al-Naddāf 's letter, Imām Yaḥyā defends the Zohar, quoting Hebrew scripture in the process! The imām here is made to push the anti-kabbalah camp's argument ad absurdum: if anthropomorphic language is in itself a sign of polytheism, Jews who follow the Torah are not Jews, but polytheists and thus outside of the protection afforded to "Peoples of the Pact" by the Islamic state.[195] Were anthropomorphisms actually to transgress monotheism, the Jews would be offered the choice between conversion to Islam and death.

If Zaydī jurists strove mightily to fit the two Jewish rites into the local paradigm of Zaydī- Shafiʿi sectarianism—a realm of intersecting legal and nonlegal codes whose relevance is not immediately apparent—how did the Jewish factions view Islam? Islamic law was the law of the land. Therefore, trying to win in a Muslim court by presenting arguments with a Muslim cast, one might argue, had little to do with Islam per se, but merely showed pragmatism on the part of the litigants.

Here it should be remembered that the preceding letter was written in Hebrew for a Jewish audience in Jerusalem. Its depiction of Imām Yaḥyā as an authority for Judaism transcends power politics in the Jewish community of Yemen. Members of the kabbalist faction, in turn, seem to have viewed Imām Yaḥyā as the paternalistic preserver of the social order—and, by extension, Jewish tradition—from the encroachments of foreign cultures and misguided would-be reformers. In accusing their enemies of polytheism, members of the anti-kabbalah faction were not only seeking to weaken their opponents in the eyes of their enemies. It is quite possible that they also genuinely believed that Imām Yaḥyā, and Zaydī jurists in general, would lend a sympathetic ear to their grievances against kabbalistic texts and their teeming anthropomorphisms. Imām Yaḥyā's opposition to superstitions, which were among the targets of the anti-kabbalists' ire, is mentioned in several Jewish sources.[196]

The plot thickens insofar as the Dor De'ah movement may have had Islam, rather than a European Jewish archaeologist, as its inspiration. Historian Bat-Zion Eraqi Klorman made the intriguing suggestion that Dor De'ah's vision of the reform of Judaism drew from the reformist Islam of intellectuals like Jamāl al-Dīn al-Afghānī and Muḥammad 'Abduh.[197] Much of the Zaydī elite in Yemen showed hostility to these reformers.[198] As the preceding discussion has shown, Jewish reformers made attempts to appeal to this elite using terminology with which they could identify. Nevertheless, works of Islamic reform inspired many of the pro-Sunni opponents of the regime. These included *Tafsīr al-manār,* a modernistic commentary on the Qur'an; treatises by Arslān and Kawākibī; works by Ṭāha Ḥusayn and 'Abbās Maḥmūd al-'Aqqād; and books critical of Shi'ism like Nashāshibī's *al-Islām al-ṣaḥīḥ* and Alūsī's *Kitāb al-tuḥfah al-ithnā' 'ashariyyah.*[199] Following a roundup of such regime opponents, one Muslim recalls the group being derided by the jailer and by ordinary Muslims as "*darādi*'" (partisans of Dor De'ah) and says the imām accused them of wanting to bring Christianity to Yemen.[200] This comparison may have represented more than just rhetorical bluster. Muḥammad b. 'Abdallāh al-Maḥalwī (d. 1936), a leader of the group that would eventually overthrow Imām Yaḥyā, engaged in frequent discussions about Judaism and Islam with Chief Rabbi Yaḥyā al-Abyaḍ, a member of Dor De'ah.[201]

Aside from the issue of a direct genetic link between Islamic reform and Dor De'ah, the anti-kabbalists kept a certain image of Islam in mind, with Imām Yaḥyā as the zealous guardian of a pure monotheism that they admired in Islam and sought to instill in Judaism. In his account of the controversy between the two factions, Jamal made a comment worthy of discussion. Jamal, it is to be remembered, became a prominent representative of the anti-kabbalah faction in the mid-1930s. Despite his closeness to Imām Yaḥyā and other prominent Muslims, and being a person well-versed in the practical application of Zaydī law, Jamal occasionally indulged in polemics against Islam and its founder. He rounded out one such polemical discussion on a conciliatory note, conceding that Maimonides was correct in his positive assessment of Islam in the *Mishneh Torah.*[202] The prophet Muḥammad, according to Jamal, "had done a great thing in affirming Exalted God's unity."[203] The anti-kabbalah faction likely saw Imām Yaḥyā as fulfilling a similar role: that of a militant and uncompromising defender of the monotheistic ideal.

Nissim Ṭayri recalls an animated argument he had with a rabbi in Radāʿ in the 1930s over the nature and meaning of Muslim prayer. The two men were patronizing a stall that sold stone cooking vessels across from a large mosque during noon prayers. From that vantage point they surreptitiously observed the worshippers. Their solemnity, careful choreography, and polite silence despite crowding amazed the two Jews, especially when they compared it to the cacophony of the synagogue. For one of the Jews, this in some sense justified Muslim hegemony and Jewish exile (although he was also under the impression that the Muslims were worshipping Muhammad).[204] Such ambivalent attitudes toward Islam represented the norm among Jews in Yemen.

To sum up, the difficulty of maintaining distinctions between Muslims and Jews, which was often in the interest of both communities, generated great anxiety among Yemenis. Since the two groups of people were physically indistinguishable, the weight of tradition and the imprimatur of divine law could (and sometimes were) cast aside with a wardrobe change and a few motions of a pair of scissors. This intermediary physical and conceptual space spawned such strange hybrids as shape-shifting Jewish-Muslim tricksters, a sayyid who wrote Judeo-Arabic poetry, and a flag emblazoned with the sword of the Shiʿite Imams and the Zionist Star of David. The danger of admixture grew at the turn of the century when some Jews publicly lobbied to abandon such distinctions, ceased speaking Arabic softly and solecistically, and learned to present themselves with the eloquence (and sometimes the practical lawyering skills) of Muslim men of learning. In taking stock of the Jewish community in the fatwa on the Zohar from 1913–1914, the Muslim elite appears pulled in opposite directions. They stress the importance of maintaining all traditional distinguishing marks, but when they imagine Jewish sectarianism their frame of reference is thoroughly Islamic. Thus even the realm of theology and ritual, which one might assume was kept untouched throughout such interreligious contacts, betrays the same problematic impossibility of keeping the two groups separate.

4 Concord and Conflict in Economic Life

Liminality and the Traditional Economic Order

In Yemen entire industries and trades were dominated by Jews. Architects, builders, carpenters, masons, metalworkers, plasterers, whitewashers, cotton carders, mattress makers, dyers, weavers, gunsmiths, gunpowder makers, tar makers, recyclers of used cartridges, sieve makers, tobacconists, snuff grinders, cigarette rollers, makers of water-pipe parts, well diggers, and forgers of antiquities were generally Jews.[1] (Some Muslim religious conservatives had trouble with the idea of Jewish builders building mosques.[2])

The tribal ethos of the Yemeni Muslim privileged agricultural work. The religious elite avoided (or made efforts to appear to avoid) all commerce.[3] Therefore the trades were generally denigrated by Muslims. Pinḥas Qafarah explains that after Jews began leaving Yemen in large numbers and Muslims took their jobs, "many of their [Muslim] brothers looked down upon them and there were those who accused them, saying that if they practiced these professions there was no doubt that their grandfathers were Jews who converted to Islam." Jews also believed this to be true of Muslim tradesmen in villages.[4] Put differently, the tribesman viewed the cities as filled with weak people who could not protect themselves and so relied upon the political authorities. In addition, selling or failing to cultivate his land was shameful.[5]

The division of labor, and resulting mutual dependency, between individual Muslim agriculturalists and Jewish craftsmen could be formalized in an "*umlah*" agreement; such agreements were sometimes recorded and enforced by sharīʿa courts, which prosecuted violators.[6] In rural areas these agreements between a shaykh and his Jews might include Jewish work that ought to be kept "off the books": casting spells and distilling alcohol.[7]

Considering Jewish dominance as craftsmen, tribesmen in rural areas who ranked the Jew low in the social order fawned and groveled when they needed something made or repaired. Jews often extended them credit until a harvest.[8]

Such role reversals must have generated tension for both parties. They did (and do) so in the case of butchers, Muslims of low rank, who were considered weak and effeminate yet nevertheless possessed the power to embarrass a man by apportioning him a tough cut of meat.[9]

Notwithstanding a provision in the sumptuary laws that forbade Jews from working for the Muslim government, it could hardly avoid hiring Jews. "Most government building projects fell on Jewish shoulders first," writes builder Nissim Ṭayri.[10] Imām Yaḥyā himself hired Jews to adorn the walls and ceilings of one of his palaces with plaster ornaments and to furnish it with beds.[11] Both the imām and his chief minister hired a Jewish painter to work on their homes.[12] A Jew built the arches and installed imported porcelain tile in a governor's palace in Taʿizz.[13] Interreligious tensions sometimes entered the construction site. Ṭayri recalls that while expanding the Radāʿ jail, he ordered some trees chopped down for lumber. The trees were dear to a Muslim who hated Jews, although he did not own the trees. When the man attacked the Jewish workers who did the chopping, he was apprehended and fettered.[14] In the late 1920s Imām Yaḥyā decided to have at least part of his army's uniforms produced locally, and for twelve years a small army of Jewish weavers brought their work to a large tent at a government compound in Sanaa, to be paid by the weight of their handiwork.[15]

Jews worked for well-to-do Muslims as servants, nannies, launderers, and clothing ironers.[16] Due to their less strict standards of modesty, Jewish women could work as servants.[17] An Iraqi visitor says that Muslims had no difficulty employing Jewish servants and that they also hired Jews to cook their meals.[18] Jews were prominently represented among candy makers.[19] They also roughened millstones and repaired broken pottery with iron, made jewelry, wove fabric and carpets, and embroidered the cuffs of women's trousers and other garments. The son of a woman who embroidered clothing says the only time he saw his mother chew qāt was before the Muslim festivals, when she was so busy she needed to keep herself awake and alert.[20] Industrialization and cheap imports resulted in the disappearance of many of these professions, an important fact in explaining the economic malaise that led most Jews to leave Yemen for Israel.[21]

Jews also performed jobs that were considered polluting for their relationship to dirt, animals, and feces. They were potters, oven makers, tanners, leather workers, shoemakers, makers of saddles and sheepskin coats, and silversmiths.[22] The link between pottery and impurity requires some explanation. Much of a potter's time was spent gathering flammable materials other than wood, including dried animal dung, to fire their kilns. Despite this ostensible explanation, the disgust incurred by this activity was for some a matter of taste. Nissim Gamlieli avers that "there are people to whose noses the smell of burning cow manure is as sweet as the smoke of the water pipe or incense, and there are others for whom such smoke brings to their noses the smell of the kitchen and the steam from pots of coffee."[23]

In addition to disposing of feces, Jews had to remove animal carcasses. In Dhamār this job fell upon one man. He supported himself by selling the hides and milk of dead livestock, the latter to (Jewish) soap makers. Local soap was made at night because of the bad smell involved.[24] Prominent Muslims complained to the governor that the commercial relationship between the carcass mover and the soap makers was defiling them. Therefore, the governor instituted a system whereby the owners of deceased livestock would pay set fees for the sanitation service, which varied according to the size of the animal. Those who attempted to dispose of dead animals themselves would face a steep fine.[25] Other professions bore a connection with latrine work. Shmuel Yavnieli listed four Jews as makers of dried cow-manure cakes (*mikhabbī*) in Dhamār in 1911, a practice in which Muslims also engaged.[26] In addition to the aforementioned *ṣaḥḥāb* ("dragger" [of animal carcasses]), the *maṣṣār,* who cleaned wells and houses' urine sumps, and the *mijaḥḥif,* a lavatory cleaner, represent similar professions that may not have been limited to Jews.[27]

The connection between silver work and impurity is difficult to establish. It may relate to the (Muslim) belief that the proceeds from the trade are usurious in nature.[28] It may, like pottery, relate to the unpleasant fuel used to build fires, or a connection with dentistry, and thus bodily pollution. Chief Rabbi Yaḥyā Abyaḍ (d. 1935) ran the royal mint, and the workers there were all Jews. "Not even the prime minister," writes Sālim Saʿīd al-Jamal, who worked briefly as an apprentice silversmith, "had the right to enter that part of the royal court, because the king had decided that entrance was forbidden without the permission of the rabbi."[29] Jews had run the mint in Sanaa since at least the nineteenth century. Minting coins involved smelting silver with copper, and individual Jews were charged, rightly and wrongly, of adulterating the currency in order to enrich themselves.[30]

Soon after Imām Yaḥyā took over, he set about changing the currency. Banking, however, was considered un-Islamic.[31] Gold coins and silver thalers (riyāls) remained the same, but in place of the Turkish copper "quarter" (*rubʿiyyah*) he had the copper *buqshah* (worth one-fortieth of a riyāl) and half-*buqshah* pieces minted.[32] Jewish silversmiths and others whose business suffered during World War I set about collecting scrap copper and minting the new coins. Yosef Ḥubarah, who engaged in this business, says that competitors from the pro-kabbalah faction in 1920 complained to the imām that the Dor Deʿah Jews were adulterating the currency. The governor of Sanaa got a list of all of the silversmiths in the city (approximately eighty in all), had them rounded up by the police, and sent them to jail. The men were released when it became clear that the affair was an intra-Jewish squabble.[33]

Making silver jewelry could be a risky profession. A Muslim scholar claimed that the Jewish silversmiths of Sanaa plotted to make the Muslims' children illegitimate by adulterating silver jewelry. Since marriage agreements stipulated certain weights of silver, alloying the metal rendered the marriages void.[34] In a similar case, the silversmiths were jailed by Imām Aḥmad on suspicion of adulterating their products.[35]

Aharon Ben David, from the far north of Yemen, says that sometimes when a tribesman brought a Jewish silversmith silver riyāls to make jewelry, the Jew would steal some of the silver. If the worker or his assistant needed to talk about the need to add some copper (up to 25 percent would not be detected) to compensate for the missing metal, one would say in Aramaic "mix in 'under its burden,'" deliberately avoiding the word "copper," which sounded similar in both Arabic and Hebrew. This was a reference to the Aramaic translation of a portion of Exodus 23:5 that runs "resting under its burden." The missing word "resting" sounds much like "quarter."[36] Such graft might have unintended consequences. A silversmith in Yarīm who was (correctly) suspected for this type of heist had to convert to Islam to escape punishment.[37] Adulterating the currency stemmed from reasons other than greed as well. Already under the Turks, silversmiths began importing machines that produced silver filigree, forcing many older smiths out of the profession. However, once the imām consolidated control, replacement parts for the machines became unavailable and younger silversmiths had to teach themselves to do the work entirely by hand. They used alloy because they did not know how to do without it. The arrival and then withdrawal of mechanization, along with new taxes, charges for rent, and a new quality control apparatus led to what Aviva Klein-Francke called a "crisis of silversmithing," which left very few practitioners of the trade active by the early 1930s.[38]

Silversmiths sometimes moonlighted as dentists because their delicate pliers worked well for pulling teeth. Bene Moshe tells of an incident in the 1930s of a Jewish silversmith in a small village in the south of Yemen who passed a Muslim in the market on the right. The Muslim was offended by this breach of decorum and slapped the Jew in the face. He later approached the Jew, imploring him to pull a decayed tooth. The Jew put him off until the following day, by which time the man's jaws had swollen. He then thrust his pliers into the man's mouth and pulled the diseased tooth along with the healthy tooth that abutted it. The Jew walked away from the transaction satisfied at having exacted revenge. The Muslim happily noted that he had two teeth pulled for the price of one.[39]

Ottoman rule over Yemen brought new economic opportunity. A new mercantile elite who supplied the military arose in this period, many of whom came from the lower ranks of the traditional social order.[40] Some Jews were able to join this elite as well. Yemenis enjoyed greater freedom of movement, and long-distance transportation became less perilous.[41] Most important, Sultan ʿAbd al-Ḥamīd II (1876–1909) opened Yemen to foreign trade.[42]

However, the new economic environment also led to the slow demise of professions long identified with the Jews. Bat-Zion Eraqi Klorman points out that while some Jews (among them the intermediaries featured in this book) became wealthy through imports and exports, the availability of manufactured goods harmed Jewish artisans.[43] Around the turn of the century a Jewish blacksmith who specialized in making scales for use in the market struggled to contend with this change by teaching himself how to make facsimiles of the large scales that were beginning to be imported from Europe.[44] A silversmith in a small town, whose business consisted mainly in decorating Muslims' weapons, remarks that the new European rifles left no room for ornamentation.[45] Jews were cognizant of both this changed environment and the new skills that might enable them to weather it. In 1903 rabbis wrote to the Alliance Israelite Universelle in Paris, asking that they build a new "school for languages and trade (*malakhah*)" because "most of the people of our community roam around, searching for food for themselves and their babies by employing the trades they used to employ, but they cannot find it, for the spirit of the age will not give them a path to tread any longer."[46]

In 1913 R. Yaḥyā Qāfiḥ and a sizeable roster of Yemeni rabbis wrote to the Ottoman government in Istanbul asking for the establishment of a "preparatory and professional" (*iʿdādī miktsoʿi*) school for Jews in Sanaa.[47] A modern school was established and Qāfiḥ led it for the two years of its existence. An Alliance official, Yom-Ṭov Tsemaḥ, whose objection to the school's emphasis on Turkish may have stemmed in part from French chauvinism, nevertheless offered an insightful analysis of the role language learning might play in improving Yemeni Jewry's economic prospects. He observed that the small-scale Jewish merchants in Sanaa who began operating during Turkish rule used middlemen in Hodeida. This sapped their potential profits. He said, "The Jews who currently work in commerce need to be able to free themselves from the guardianship of the Greek traders in Hodeida, to send correspondence to the trading houses of Europe, and to buy the commercial goods they need from the source itself."[48]

Jewish merchants, like the Ḥibshūsh brothers of Sanaa and Hārūn Shiḥb in Manākhah, dominated the sale of coffee beans for export and husks for internal consumption (in a hot drink called *qishr* (husk).[49] Other merchants, including Sālim Saʿīd al-Jamal, Ṣāliḥ al-Ẓāhirī, and Mordecai al-Ẓāhirī, provided the Muslim aristocracy with perfume. Jamal designed his own cologne, which he sold to Muslim notables.[50] "The Arabs loved strong cologne a great deal and used its unadulterated form on their clothing," writes Mordecai al-Ẓāhirī.[51] The Muslim elite's taste in perfume, in turn, set the aromatic standards that upwardly mobile Jews strove toward. Yosef ʿAtsṭah describes the ineffable aroma of perfume made from the *kādī* plant, a scent "designated for the wealthy Muslims." Jews who had mercantile relationships with wealthy Muslims were able to buy this rare perfume for their wives.[52]

Sālim Saʿīd al-Jamal ordered unusual items from an agent in Alexandria.[53] At least one imām felt that he paid lower prices to Jewish merchants than to Muslims.[54] (Some of the wealthy shaykhs who were stuck in Sanaa tending to their court cases, and some of the tribal "hostages" of the imām who enjoyed unusually permissive treatment, were also customers of Jews who sold luxury goods.[55]) The primary tax that Jews paid went directly to the imāms, in the form of the poll tax. This would have given the rulers additional incentive to patronize Jewish businesses.[56] Yosef Tobi argues that in the 1920s and 1930s the regime pursued a policy of nationalizing commerce that harmed the economic status of the Jews. While some Jewish merchants, who enjoyed special ties with the aristocracy or were able to import machinery from Europe to mechanize their crafts, benefited from this policy, the majority, particularly small-scale craftsmen, faced new competition with Muslims that had not previously existed.[57]

This conclusion requires further research, especially in light of the common assertion among Muslim writers that the imām relied heavily upon Jews in implementing his economic policies. The imām's sons and ministers controlled numerous quasi-monopolies, which earned them the enmity of small traders in large cities who were unable to compete with them.[58] The Yemeni historian Abdulaziz Msaodi argues that Imām Yaḥyā used taxes and customs fees to punish (Shafiʿi) merchants who had backed the losing side during his bid for power.[59] A council of ulama led by Qadi Zayd al-Daylamī warned government officials against meddling in trade.[60] Muslim merchants perceived a special relationship between Jewish merchants and the imām. Indeed, it is not surprising that members of the administration would rely upon Jewish merchants, who were loyal and small-scale (and thus nonthreatening) in pursuing their business interests.

Yemeni historian Muḥammad ʿAlī al-Shahārī writes that the monopolistic trade that developed between the imām and Jewish merchants exacerbated the already widespread hatred for Jews among Muslims. (However, he does not distinguish between Jewish dominance in the trades and the new class of importers.)[61] "Imām Yaḥyā put no restrictions upon Jewish mercantile activity," writes another Yemeni historian. "Indeed, we find a monopolistic trinity between them, the most powerful administrators, and him."[62] In the early 1940s a visitor from Iraq noted that a handful of Jews, acting in tandem with Jews in Aden, "controlled the rudder of trade."[63]

The Sunaydārs, one of Sanaa's most prominent Zaydī merchant families, produced a number of opponents to Imām Yaḥyā. Al-ʿIzzī Ṣāliḥ al-Sunaydār lists among the evils of imāmic rule their "granting the Jews free rein in trade," making them compete with Muslim merchants, and allowing them to use their homes to store goods, whereas Muslim merchants had to pay for storehouses and various attendant costs. Muslim merchants were selectively taxed. All of these factors led Muslim merchants of Sanaa to support the opposition, he argues.[64]

During Ramadan in the summer of 1920 the chief broker (*ʿĀqil al-dallālīn*) of Sanaa's market attempted an "end run" around a Jewish merchant with good ties to Imām Yaḥyā. He brought a complaint to the governor of the city against the Jew Sulaymān Ḥibshūsh and his sons Hārūn and Nissim. The complaint, which Yeḥiel Ḥibshūsh says was "signed by hundreds of merchants," alleged that Ḥibshūsh and his sons sold them ordinary goods while hiding sought-after goods in storehouses in the Jewish Quarter (in defiance of the established practice of storing goods in two large storehouses in central [Muslim] Sanaa), that they extended credit to Muslims capriciously but to Jews reliably, and that they sold goods to the Muslim merchants at retail rather than wholesale prices.

Yeḥiel Ḥibshūsh claims that Nissim Ḥibshūsh turned to Imām Yaḥyā and the very next day the Imām had a long fatwa drawn up that protected him.[65] Yeḥiel Ḥibshūsh describes this complaint as an anti-Jewish conspiracy by a Jew hater aimed at agitating Muslims against ordinary Jews. While this certainly sounds like an exaggeration, his claims that the imām saw the complaint as an unacceptable challenge to his authority and that the defeated merchants spoke bitterly of "the imām of the Jews" sound plausible.[66] (The tension between the imām and Governor ʿAbd al-Qādir was discussed in chapter 2.)

Another instructive example of the putative imāmic-Jewish mercantile alliance revolves around the same Jewish family. Imām Yaḥyā took a tithe from each coffee harvest and it was sold at auction. One year the crop was of a particularly good quality, and the imām's agent invited three prosperous Muslim coffee merchants to bid on it. The men engaged in insider trading, agreeing before the auction that each would suggest a different price and that the one who succeeded would divide the purchased coffee with the others. The imām wanted a Ḥibshūsh representative at the auction. Lest he be seen as confronting the Muslim merchants, Hārūn Ḥibshūsh sent his young son Yeḥiel to the auction. His bid, which was a little higher than the prices offered by the other merchants, was accepted. The Muslim merchants demanded and received financial compensation from Hārūn, who became the sole seller of the coffee tithe. "The imām was satisfied by the higher price, which was just. My father was satisfied with the stand that he had taken and the compromise that had been reached," writes Yeḥiel Ḥibshūsh.[67]

Resentment against the new Jewish mercantile class was limited to neither their Muslim competitors nor Muslim religious conservatives. Ḥayyim Tsadoq, a Jew from Sanaa who emigrated to Palestine, then returned to Yemen as a representative of the Jewish Agency, writes about their status during the lean years of World War II:

> These "important" Jews . . . never worked, yet had their bread (and sometimes a lot of it). With their work they mainly supported those who worked for the government, but what was left over sustained and supported their families. "Their hands were in everything and everybody's hands were in them" as the verse [Gen. 16:12] says. Their morality was dubious, and usually most were counted among those whose fear of God was lacking, so much so that if a Jew was jailed it did not disturb their repose. Indeed, this happened. As for this

> class of people who were close to the government, a saying circulated widely among the Jews: "He who values his own life should steer clear of them" [Prov. 22:5].
>
> Their closeness to government ministers did not merely obligate them to fill [the ministers'] pockets, but also to take care of several more matters, chief among them supplying brandy, which Muslims were prohibited in the strictest terms from drinking and enjoying. This duty forced these people to arrange the production of "private" liquor in their own houses—making the forbidden drink there. Their recompense was exponential, and this source of income was used to grease the wheels of their business.[68]

Tsadoq's resentful broadside illuminates several interconnected issues. He suggests that the wealthy Jewish intermediaries were primarily enriching the Muslim elite and that alcohol did not represent one among many luxury goods, but was central to this relationship.

According to Ṣāliḥ al-Ẓāhirī, who hated Jamal, the latter was an expert winemaker and sold his product to Muslims, among them the imām's sons ʿAlī and al-Qāsim. He was rounded up and jailed in a 1932 crackdown on the Jewish alcohol industry. Jamal's father also made wine.[69] (Jamal claims that he did not make alcohol and was, moreover, a teetotaler.[70])

Tsadoq's paraphrase from Genesis is interesting insofar as it comes from an unflattering description of Ishmael, who Jews (and Muslims) consider the patriarch of the Arabs. According to its ordinary exegesis, the verse points to Ishmael's warlike character. Here, given the context of insider financial dealings, Tsadoq seems to suggest in his choice of Bible verse that these Jews have become Arabs through their shady business practices.

The dominance of Jews in professions like making jewelry, weaving, tailoring, embroidering, selling fabric, and selling sewing goods brought Jews in close contact with Muslim women and reinforced popular stereotypes that they constituted a kind of "third sex."[71] Muslim women went shopping in the Jewish Quarter because they found a good selection of fabric there. These shopping trips were also a social activity. The Ṣubayrī brothers opened a big women's clothing store on a road separating the Jewish Quarter from a Muslim neighborhood. A Syrian traveler describes the orderly stacks of colorful silks from Syria and France, cotton cloth, and English wool in the store, all shipped by caravan from Aden.[72] The popularity of the store created tension with Muslim merchants, and they or others asked Qadi ʿAbdallāh al-ʿAmrī to investigate. The qadi found men and women crowding the doors of the shop flirting with one another. Yeḥiel Ḥibshūsh, who relates this anecdote, explains that such activity could only have taken place in the Jewish Quarter, where the authorities already turned a blind eye to various morally dubious activities.[73]

Qadi al-ʿAmrī ordered the Ṣubayrī brothers not to allow Muslim women into their shop, an order that was, needless to say, disastrous to their business. One of the Ṣubayrīs appealed to Imām Yaḥyā, who devised a solution: designate separate doors for men and women. However, after the opening of the second door, some men and women still gravitated toward the opposite sex, claiming they had no way to distinguish between the two doors. Eventually a policeman needed to be posted at door to the shop to solve the problem.[74]

The showiness of women's clothing related, at least in part, to popular superstition and the world of magic, another area where Jews were thought to play an important mediating role. According to Yosef 'Atsṭah, a Jew in Dhamār whose children had all died in infancy, finally had a healthy son. His mother, a healer, advised him to pierce the child's ears and dress him in girls' clothing: a striped robe adorned with seashells and mother-of-pearl. ' Atsṭah explains that pretty girls wore such garments to draw the attention of passers-by away from their beauty, thus averting the evil eye.[75]

Jewish men, who could not bear arms and were protected by others, in a sense occupied an intermediate space between male and female. The Jews of Turbah, a town in Lower Yemen where the Nu'mān clan was based, repaired jewelry for Muslim women. Unlike Muslim men, they were allowed to ascend to the women's quarters on the top floors of their homes.[76] Nissim Ṭayri recalls that Muslim men did not protest when male Jewish workers interacted socially with the women of their families. In addition, Muslim families with many children allowed their sons and daughters to act as the manual laborers under the direction of a Jewish artisan, a license they would not permit Muslim artisans.[77] "One ought to trust neither a Jew nor a woman," a shaykh said in prefacing his arbitration of a dispute between a Jew and a Muslim woman. He continued: "Women and Jews make mountains out of molehills. How much you weaklings have in common."[78]

In the popular imagination of both Muslims and Jews, at least some Jews were considered particularly effective intermediaries between the mundane and the supernatural.[79] Therefore Jews were amply represented in professions related to magic. Ṣāliḥ al-Ẓāhirī was neither a believer in amulets nor a monogamist. Nevertheless, he was approached by a wealthy Muslim woman who wanted an amulet that would keep her husband from marrying a second woman.[80] A Muslim guard was imprisoned with Mordecai al-Ẓāhirī for having been derelict in his duties. He had allowed the assassins of two of Imām Yaḥyā's sons to escape without firing his gun.[81] The guard had fallen in love with one of the imām's daughters after having watched her come and go to the palace regularly. He asked the Jew to obtain a "bill of love" (*waraqat ḥubb*) for him to ensure the success of his unlikely love affair. The younger Ẓāhirī began to make preparations to comply with the strange request but was relieved not to have to furnish the item in question. The soldier was transferred to another prison before the promised liaison with the princess could be realized.[82]

Nissim Gamlieli tells the story of a married Muslim woman in Damt who went insane as a result of a love spell that a male admirer ordered from a Jewish miracle worker. Her husband divorced her while she was pregnant, and she became homeless. Her strange habit of bringing her infant daughter to the town cemetery and burying the child up to her neck led a Muslim family to take in the baby. The authorities bound the woman and suspended her inside a well for hours on end in order to try to exorcise her demon. When that was unsuccessful, a sayyid with a promising future in magic tried to exorcise her demon. Magic required that one be able to "gather [jinn] and dismiss them." Unfortunately, the sayyid had mastered only the first art. (Tribesmen called upon sayyids, like Jews, to interact with the supernatural world.[83]) After summoning the jinn, he became possessed himself and fell in love with the woman. Eventually the same Jewish magician who had inadvertently bewitched her was able to cure the woman and exorcise the sayyid of both his demon and his love for her.[84]

In addition to inhabiting the liminal space between male and female, earthly and supernatural, Jews also had a reputation for facilitating the transgression of conventional morality. This had an impact on their financial dealings with Muslims. Under Ottoman rule, some Jews helped homesick Turkish soldiers ease their sorrows by opening their homes to them as taverns. Jews sold alcohol and hashish in one of Sanaa's markets.[85] Some even smuggled in opium from India.[86] Shalom ʿUzayrī, who left his work as a silversmith to make wine and ʿaraq to sell to Turks, had one of the largest wineries in Sanaa in his home.[87] The Ḥamdī family amassed its fortune by selling wine made from grapes grown in a vineyard outside the city and enjoyed the protection of two shaykhs from al-Sirr, a grape-growing region.[88]

Imām Yaḥyā cracked down on such activity as soon as he entered Sanaa in 1918. Muslims caught drinking (along with magicians, adulterers, and an unfortunate Jewish photographer) were subjected to a ritual humiliation called "donkeying" (*ḥawmarah*), in which the accused was bound and forced to march (or ride a donkey backward) with a drum affixed to his or her back or belly for passers-by to beat or to pelt with rocks and garbage.[89]

The imām allowed Jews to make alcoholic beverages for their own consumption. ʿAraq was made from raisins, honey, dates, and figs, in that order of preference.[90] In the north, raisins constituted the raw material of choice. Grapes grow well in Yemen, and since many Jews needed them, they were among the most lucrative crops. One rather desperate effort by Muslim opponents of wine drinking skirted the winemakers entirely, aiming instead to prevent fruit sellers from selling in the Jewish Quarter.[91] In the south, alcohol was generally made from honey, which Jews either produced themselves or bought from Muslim beekeepers.

The government allowed Jews to distill alcohol because wine was required for the observance of the Sabbath, festivals, and life cycle events. (However, they were asked to be discreet in their consumption.) Though selling it to Muslims was illegal, the high prices that such bootlegging could garner made it worth the risk for some Jews.[92] Chewing qāt caused insomnia, and many Muslims could blame their contravention of Islam's ban on alcohol on sleep deprivation.[93] Two anecdotes describe Muslims making spurious arguments to the effect that only wine made by Christians was forbidden to Muslims.[94] (A Jewish family monopolized the sale of alcohol to the British in the Aden Protectorate, but since the British were largely Christian, this did not raise objections.[95]) In 1932 Imām Yaḥyā cracked down on the Jewish alcohol industry. According to Goitein, this was because Jews had sold wine to an important aide of his.[96] Sālim Sa'īd al-Jamal says the imām cracked down again on Jewish alcohol sales in 1936.[97]

A 1931 document written by Chief Rabbi Yaḥyā al-Abyaḍ and preserved in the Yemeni National Archives stipulates the process through which the liquor industry would be supervised. It was presumably the result of a dialogue between the chief rabbi and Prince Aḥmad, who is mentioned in it. Abyaḍ's frustration with the seeming inevitability of the collective punishment of Jewish wine sellers is palpable. It divides responsibility between representatives of the two factions (pro- and anti-kabbalist) and each neighborhood within the Jewish Quarter, noting that neither faction ought to be allowed to supervise the other "given the serious dispute and the intense hostility among them on matters of rite (*madhhab*)."[98] Any movement of wine or spirits beyond the walls of the Jewish Quarter would require written permission. If a Muslim with alcohol was found outside of the Jewish Quarter, which would lead to the humiliation and punishment of the Muslim and the demolition of the house of the Jew who sold it, the two Jewish factions would investigate.[99] Despite mandatory searches at the gates of the Quarter, Abyaḍ says merchants sometimes received permission to sell alcohol to foreigners or to Muslims, and Muslims went to the Jewish Quarter after dark, two factors that made tight control over the alcohol supply challenging.

Since the financial incentive to sell alcohol to Muslims was so appealing, Jewish leaders seem to have felt that the Jews of Sanaa were doomed to incur this punishment. (According to Ṣāliḥ al-Ẓāhirī, the wall around the Quarter was built as the result of a push by Yaḥyā Abyaḍ to prevent poor Jews from selling alcohol to Muslims, among other reasons.[100]) Ya'īsh Manṣūrah, who is listed as one of the supervisors of the wine industry in the 1931 document and was the father of Imām Aḥmad's Jewish intermediary, was convicted of selling alcohol to Muslims and saw his home demolished on orders from Qadi Luṭf al-Zubayrī. (This qadi complained to Imām Yaḥyā in the mid-1930s that he was frightened of entering the Jewish Quarter for fear of being accosted by drunken Jews.[101])

The 1931 document contained twelve rules. It insisted that the alcohol be made and stored in secure locations, that a small number of Jews be responsible for selling it, that careful records be kept correlating sales to amounts of alcohol, that it be sold only to upstanding individuals (a reprobate "should drink his portion in the winery"), and that profits needed to be regulated. (Jamal explains that the last rule aimed to prevent the five wealthiest vintners from monopolizing the trade.[102]) Several rules dealt with the quality of the product: the raisins should be clean and could be sugared only once with a specified amount of sugar, "because sugar wine—even a little—is harmful to some people." (Refined sugar was imported, and people in rural parts of Yemen rarely saw it.) Adding sugar to wine, a process called chaptalization, can increase the alcohol content without necessarily making the wine sweet. Jamal explains that some winemakers cut corners by using as much inexpensive sugar as they could as opposed to expensive raisins.[103]

The rules further stipulate that the dregs should be discarded and "that the percentage of alcohol should not be lower than the sixteen percent that is customary for wine." (There is, of course, some irony in a teetotaling Islamic theocracy mandating that only such powerful wine be sold.)[104] One Jewish writer reports that while staying in a lodging house in southern Yemen, he encountered Ṣāliḥ al-Ẓāhirī, who was in the region collecting the jizya for the imām. He shared the bottle of choice ʿaraq that he always carried with him with the Jew's father. His father dipped in his pinky and lit it with a match, demonstrating its potency to his sons.[105] The wife of a French physician who worked in Sanaa in 1947 reports buying "high alcohol wine" in the Jewish Quarter.[106]

A group of Jews from a northern town stopped in Dhamār in 1950 on their way to Aden, and thence to Palestine. According to Shalom Bene Moshe, the governor took special interest in one of them, a poor man named Shimʿon al-Khamrī. The Muslim assumed from his name (*khamr* means wine) that the man knew the vintner's art and invited him to his residence to talk. In fact, the Jew's ancestors had migrated from a Yemeni village called Khamr, but he knew a bit about making ʿaraq. To the governor's detailed questions the Jew explained that making it was expensive. Each good bottle required about a pound and a quarter (a *raṭl*) of "fine black raisins of the Bashārī variety." The governor gave him five riyāls to make alcohol. The Jew was frightened, but his wife reassured him with the Talmudic precept "the law of the land is the law." (He was, in fact, breaking the law.) He bought raisins, soaked them, and let them ferment in large pots. On the third and fourth day he crushed them. At the end of the seventh day, when white foam had risen, he cooked the mash and then, when it was potent enough to catch fire, bottled it. The governor pronounced its taste to be that of paradise. During his stay in Dhamār the Jew amassed a fortune as the governor's private vintner.[107]

One wealthy Jew in the south had Muslim workers make ʿaraq behind his house, and he sold it to Muslim soldiers and to the governor himself. In his case his close relationship to the governor (and perhaps the secret they shared) allowed him freedom he might not have otherwise enjoyed.[108]

The threat of turning other Jews in to the Muslim authorities on these charges served as a powerful tool for stifling dissent within the Jewish community. The division of authority over wine production between pro-kabbalah and anti-kabbalah factions was aimed to combat this threat. In addition, for Muslims, accusing a Jew of such crimes could tarnish the reputation and credibility of Muslims with whom the Jew had a relationship, making them guilty by association. According to Jamal, conservative opponents of the regime suspected some of Imām Yaḥyā's sons of being wine drinkers (which they evidently were).[109] Their friendly relationship with Jamal, they may have reasoned, must have been cemented with the cup.

According to Yeḥiel Ḥibshūsh, the young men and women of the Muslim aristocracy held clandestine parties, one of which was raided by the chief of police. The imām's son ʿAlī, who a Muslim source describes as an alcoholic, was in attendance.[110] He shot the police chief in the hand with his pistol rather than face the embarrassment of discovery.[111] Mordecai al-Ẓāhirī used to deliver alcohol to a close aide to Imām Yaḥyā's son Ismāʿīl, who delivered it to both his employer and his brother, Prince Yaḥyā.[112] When Shalom Bene Moshe was a boy, he made frequent deliveries of ʿaraq to the residence of Prince ʿAbbās. There he was apprehended by a sayyid and whipped daily over a period of four days. Despite this, the profits of bootlegging were substantial, and less than a year later Bene Moshe delivered ʿaraq to a judge in a small town, carefully circumventing his suspicious aides.[113] A lurid 1962 book by an opponent of the regime alleges that a fatwa was issued permitting members of the royal family forty-five pounds of raisins each for the production of alcohol.[114] Aḥmad Jābir, the officer in charge of the Jewish Quarter (and thus liquor inspections), who was pious in his outward comportment, was also a drinker. He used to procure a bottle of alcohol from the al-Ẓāhirī family each Friday before prayers. Mordecai al-Ẓāhirī's mother used to smuggle goods out of the Jewish Quarter, including weapons and ammunition for a tribal leader who was close to her husband, by bribing the guards with alcohol so that they would not search her baskets.[115]

In 1933 Qadi Luṭf al-Zubayrī, who was principally responsible for cases involving Jews, demanded a surprise alcohol inspection of Jamal's residence. Before the inspection Jamal bribed the qadi's son, Aḥmad (who Imām Aḥmad would appoint to a judicial post in 1958), to discover the names on a list of Jewish homes to be raided. The qadi's son also told Jamal that Jamal's Jewish rivals had bribed his father in order to have Jamal's name added to the list.[116] Al-Jamal's wife and children were the only ones home at the time of the inspection, and the police were accompanied by the chief rabbi, Yaḥyā al-Abyaḍ, and two Jewish rivals of Jamal's. These men saw Jamal's wife's underwear hanging on the clothesline, which, Jamal explains, was very shameful. Jamal protested to the imām's aide, ʿAbdallāh al-Wazīr (who would claim the imāmate fifteen years later when Imam Yaḥyā was assassinated). Jamal also sought monetary damages from the two Jews he believed to have instigated the investigation.

Jamal took an assertive, even impudent, tone in his written complaints to ʿAbdallāh al-Wazīr, Qadi ʿAbdallāh al-ʿAmrī, and Prince ʿAlī. "This matter is your responsibility and you will be held accountable on the day on which you will stand before God," he wrote.[117] "God will hold you accountable if I am not treated fairly."[118] However, Imām Yaḥyā did not punish Jamal for his impudence. The documents show that he issued a stern rebuke to Luṭf al-Zubayrī, writing: "Qadi Luṭf, let us cease troubling the Jews over every dispute that is solved according to God's sharīʿa. We have work to do that would make the mountains weary."[119]

Three years later, in June 1936, the imām's son and the future imām, Aḥmad, spearheaded a new campaign against the problem of Jews selling alcohol to Muslims. Jamal recommended that the Jewish community protest. He got into an argument with Prince Aḥmad that led to enduring bad blood between the two men.[120] Soon after he submitted the complaint he had written on behalf of the Jewish community, Zayd al-Daylamī ordered Jamal arrested, chained, and brought to the Ṣanāʿi prison. In exchange for a bribe, Jamal received shackles that were loose enough that he could slip out of them and sleep at home. He spent twenty-one days in prison.[121] Collective punishment of Jews when a Muslim was found drinking continued. In Maḥwīt in 1946, heads of prominent Jewish families were jailed after a sayyid was found drunk. (Jews alleged that he sneaked into a home when the owners were away and drank their liquor.)[122]

Accusations of Jewish bootlegging continued until the mass exodus of 1949–1950. In 1949 a Jew in Yemen wrote a letter to Yisrael Yeshayahu, an Israeli politician of Yemenite origin who served as a bridge between the would-be immigrants from Yemen and the Israeli government, saying that the Jews of the village of Rimmah had been accused of trying to intoxicate two Muslim girls with wine in order to rape them.[123] In Ḍawrān a qadi had sixteen Jews imprisoned on the charge of selling alcohol to Muslims. Imām Aḥmad had the qadi jailed and ordered him to pay the Jews eight hundred riyāls in damages.[124] Given the imām's involvement in the imprisonment of prominent Jews of Sanaa in 1949 (to be discussed in chapter 5), by punishing the qadi the imām seems to have been announcing that such actions were his prerogative and his alone.

The increasing availability of imports also harmed the Jewish distillers, even though they practiced the one profession within the Jewish community that seemed "recession-proof." A Jew from Raydah told the Yemeni writer ʿAbd al-Karīm al-Rāziḥī, "Before the Jews left for Israel they made liquor and the Muslims drank it. For us, that work is all dried up now. Some [Muslims] got really rich and do not like 'country' [liquor]. . . . All they want is whiskey from the Christians."[125]

In Yemen interreligious tensions found expression in other financial dealings whose illegality was more clear-cut than in the realm of alcohol sales. Describing the tense atmosphere of commercial transactions between Muslims and

Jews in Damt, Nissim Gamlieli claims that Muslims lionized thieves and that Jewish merchants were especially vulnerable both to them and to unscrupulous customers. One sayyid who impudently ate a Jewish salesman's valuable peaches without paying for them justified his actions by saying, "We are your fathers and you are our children." Even the qadis at the gate of the market frowned upon complaints against thieves.[126] If one lends credence to Gamlieli's analysis, we find a cultural dimension to the resentment against wealthy Jewish merchants. Not only were their business practices unfair, but also their very success constituted insolence inappropriate to their low status.

However, Gamlieli is overly categorical in his judgment. A Jew from Lower Yemen, Reuven Shar'abi, recalls having been swindled at a village market and seeking justice in the sharīʿa courts. He had brought coffee to a weekly market but had not succeeded in selling it, so he paid for it to be stored until the next market day. The following week an unfamiliar Muslim offered to buy it and offered the qadi of the market as his bond. The Jew's eagerness to sell outweighed his suspicion. The qadi weighed out and priced the coffee, and the man promised to return to pay the following week. However, he did not return. After waiting three weeks, the qadi furnished the Jew with a letter formalizing the debt and a Muslim guide who knew the man's whereabouts.

After two days' journey to the Muslim man's village, Sharʿabi and the guide visited the market. There they sold all of their goods except for six and a half pounds of coffee. The Jew found the man, showed him the letter, and, believing him to be negotiating in good faith, agreed to add the coffee to his bill. The man would not pay either debt, nor would he return the letter. The Jew then approached the market's qadi and told him the story. The qadi broke off a sprig from the qāt he was chewing and told the Jew to deliver it to the man. The man received this "subpoena" but refused to appear. The judge then sent the Jew with two soldiers to fetch the man, which they did. The man presented his dagger (*janbiyyah*) to the qadi with much histrionics, promising to pay fifty riyāls should it be true that he intended to flout the judge's orders.

The judge read the letter from the first market judge and ordered the man to pay. Since he could not pay, the judge paid the Jew the twenty riyāls he was owed. The man could not produce the coffee either. The judge ordered him to buy another six and a half pounds of coffee in the market (which he evidently had enough money to buy) and to give it to the Jew. The Jew then divided the coffee among the qadi's soldiers. The qadi ruled that the unscrupulous merchant would need to pay him the fifty riyāls he swore to pay in order to get his dagger back. The Jew took his money and went into hiding for three weeks in fear of the merchant's revenge.[127]

The preceding story contradicts the idea that Muslim thieves were applauded. The first market qadi was willing to act as bond for a Jewish seller, a transaction that must have been necessary to the large transactions that enabled the market to function. The Muslim man's failure to pay his debt reflected poorly on his creditor. The second qadi, who was based in the town where the swindler lived, found an ingenious way to uphold principles that were central to ethics and finance and still make a significant amount of money by forcing the crook to adhere to the terms of his gratuitous oath. Whether the Jew's hiding at the story's denouement was necessary is impossible to judge. However, it suggests that a Jew's success in business at the expense of a Muslim was viewed by some as an affront to the honor of Islam.

Of course, Jews stole from Muslims as well, as was noted of silversmiths. Tales of poor Jews who successfully "lift" foodstuffs from Muslims play a part in the trickster literature of the minority. One such tale concerns an itinerant Jewish tradesmen who was paid by the local farmers only at harvest time, a common feature of agreements between Jews and tribesmen in rural areas. One tribesman would not give him his share. The Jew enlisted a group of dawāshīn who were then engaged in a form of harvest-time "trick or treating." (A farmer who did not offer them donations of grain would become the subject of invective song.) The Jew and the blacks stole the tribesman's harvest, illustrating the proverb that "all thieves are brothers" (*al-sirq ihkhwah*).[128] Jews shared the prejudices of the majority toward low-status Muslims like *muzayyinūn* and *akhdām*.[129] (To Jews their own humiliation stemmed from a divine plan.) Nevertheless, the idea that Jews might find natural allies in low-status Muslims and could together make common cause against the elite finds expression in other sectors of Jewish culture. For example, a Jewish storyteller relates a number of wondrous tales containing no Jewish themes or characters whatsoever about "ʿAlī the Weeder," a Muslim from the bottom of the social ladder who gets the best of the sayyids, qadis, and the rich, usually with the help of his clever wife.[130]

Real Estate Crises

Petitions to Sālim Manṣūrah, who served as the point man on Jewish affairs for Imām Aḥmad in Taʿizz, extensively detail the economic hardships occasioned by the ongoing migration of Jews from Yemen to Israel: Muslims refused to repay debts to Jewish creditors; local governors stymied attempts to sell property, and when it was sold it went for a pittance; Jews were fleeced by "coyotes" who owned cars and trucks; and they were charged various ad hoc "taxes" in cash and jewelry at crossings into the port of Hodeida, or from one of the emirates of the Aden Protectorate to another.[131] Highway robbery, violence, and kidnapping also occurred, say the reports, sometimes at the hands of Muslims who had previously been good neighbors.[132] Sometimes the truck drivers and highway robbers were in cahoots.[133]

The wave of Jewish emigration imperiled debts between Muslims and Jews as well. A Jew from Lower Yemen, David David, says that some Muslims exploited the opportunity by avoiding repaying debts to Jews or, alternatively, "discovering" debts that had not previously existed.[134] Some Jews attempted to leave Yemen without settling their real debts. In one story a rabbi who was preparing to leave his village had his box of valuables stolen by a Muslim. These included silver, six hundred riyāls, and a stack of pledges (*mashkonot*) belonging to Muslims. When a sympathetic Muslim gave him information on the thief's identity, the rabbi located and confronted the thief. After offering to pay the rabbi for "watching" his property, the thief attacked him with his dagger. The rabbi raised a hue and cry, and a crowd of onlookers assembled, including the owners of his pledges. He paid the thief, retrieved his box, opened it in front of the crowd, and found the pledges but not the money. The thief, apparently in cahoots with the rabbi's pledge holders, had successfully carried out a "sting" operation.

The pledge owners, who felt (correctly, it seems) that the rabbi intended to leave the country without paying them, headed for Damt with the rabbi, where the governor of Radāʿ province was visiting. The rabbi asked that the thief be punished and said he wanted his money back. The pledge holders wanted to be paid. The governor quickly discerned that the rabbi would not be willing to wait for the thief to be brought to Imām Aḥmad in Taʿizz and tried (and for whatever reason was not willing to imprison him), so he suggested an unorthodox solution. He offered to give the rabbi one hundred riyāls from the royal treasury, with another five hundred going to charity. The funds recovered from the thief, who was now in jail, would also go to charity. The pledge owners got their pledges back, but they were not able to force the rabbi to redeem them. Unbeknownst to the rabbi, his wife had found the missing six hundred riyāls among their belongings. In a nod to the governor's wisdom, the rabbi dedicated the money to charity.[135] Here the governor seems to have seen in the men's heavy-handed scheme to collect on a Jew's debts to them a challenge to the state's authority that needed to be punished severely even if it meant a de facto abetment of Zionism.

In a similar situation in a village, six hours' journey south of Bayḥān, a Muslim creditor offered to forgive a Jewish shopkeeper's debt in order to allow him to emigrate to Palestine. In exchange the Jew would transfer to the Muslim a list of smaller sums he was owed by others (presumably Muslims). The Jew, a widower, stubbornly refused the Muslim's largesse and remained in Yemen with his young son. A few months after the mass emigration of Jews from the region, the Jew died and his son converted to Islam. In 1995, following a chain of improbable developments including the signing of the Oslo Accords, the Muslim was reunited with his Jewish family at the Amman airport.[136]

Situations in which a minority, faced with imminent mass departure from a country, descended into a financial crisis arose frequently in the twentieth century. The Jews of Iraq make an instructive comparison. From 1949 to 1951 the Jews, who made up a sizeable percentage of Iraq's mercantile class, underwent the traumatic loss of their property as a result of government efforts to prevent those who planned to emigrate to Israel from taking their wealth with them. The Iraqi government's ban on the sale of Jewish property and foreign exchange transactions by Jews, which stemmed at least in part from the hope of deterring Zionism, had the reverse of its intended effect. It created a pervasive atmosphere of uncertainty as the once-affluent community shunned mercantile activities and rushed to sell its assets for a fraction of their market value, receiving cash that most were unable to take out of Iraq.[137] While Jewish emigration may have led to an excess of real estate stock, the seeming inevitability of the Jews' departure led to a "land grab" by some non-Jews, especially in rural areas, who sought to coerce Jews into giving up desirable property.[138]

The State of Israel explored the possibility of setting up a sham holding company to safeguard these assets, but this strategy was never implemented.[139] Palestinian intellectual Abbas Shiblak ironically contrasts Israel's interest in the nationalization of Iraqi Jews' property with its neglect of the property of the Jews of Yemen, who had been the victims of similar policies of the government of Yemen.[140]

While the merchant class in Yemen was significantly smaller than that of Iraq, Yemen's Jews underwent a similar process. Bat-Zion Eraqi Klorman notes that the voluminous body of letters and memoirs by Jews from Yemen rarely mention the large financial losses that Jews, particularly urban merchants, suffered.[141] Perhaps these writers saw a contradiction in demonstrating both their ideological and religious commitments to Zionism and their status as economic refugees. Jews in Yemen often sold their property for a fraction of its market value, faced coercion to sell from neighbors, and converted assets into cash that they were unable to take out of the country.[142] In the absence of sustained interest from foreign governments and organizations, some Jews attempted to devise solutions of their own.

In the realm of financial transactions, the Zaydī school's emphasis on documentary evidence, summed up in the legal maxim "That which is left behind is the main thing" (*al-aṣl al-baqā'*), could trump the sharī'a's privileging of Muslim testimony. A conflict between Sālim Saʿīd al-Jamal and a Muslim who he claims owed him a small sum of money put this principle to the test in the realm of interfaith relations. The Muslim claimed that a Jew's general lack of trustworthiness (*amānah*), which gainsaid the acceptance of Jewish testimony against Muslims, also included documentary evidence. Jamal claims that Imām Yaḥyā not only repeated the maxim concerning the primacy of documents but also argued for the trustworthiness of the Jews of Yemen.[143] This contention finds partial corroboration in an imāmic ruling that was promulgated in 1949 or 1950 that either goes against Zaydī scholarly consensus or answers a question that never came up in the legal literature.[144] The ruling stated that the account book of a reputable and trustworthy merchant must be accepted as evidence "without distinction between Muslim and dhimmī."[145] The timing of this ruling, which coincides with the mass emigration of Jews from Yemen, suggests that Imām Aḥmad sought to facilitate rather than stymie Jews' collection of outstanding debts. The ruling also offers limited substantiation for the claims made by members of the Jewish mercantile elite that they enjoyed a special relationship with the imāms.

Jews claimed that the paucity of documentation for their claims of private ownership of the Jewish Quarter of Sanaa stemmed from the periodic looting of the city by tribesmen. A court determined that waqf land was "mixed" (*multabis*) with land privately owned by Jews. A onetime payment of 7,500 riyāls (the figure is 8,000 in another account) from the Jewish community to the waqf was negotiated in 1918.[146] The chief rabbi was made responsible for allotting the payment to community members. In August 1949, while many Jews were leaving Yemen for Israel, Sālim Manṣūrah received a letter in Taʿizz from a Jew in Sanaa. The letter informed him that Ḥasan, the brother of Imām Aḥmad who served as governor of Sanaa, had devised a new plan for disposing of the property of the emigrants. Since the land of the Jewish Quarter was "mixed" and had been bought from the waqf for a fixed sum, Jews who wanted to sell their homes had to document their ownership and would be paid for them out of the original 8,000-riyāl payment that had been made to the waqf (with no adjustment for inflation). This was no act of largesse toward the emigrants. Muslim buyers who had already bought houses at higher prices wanted their money back, Jews who had not yet left stood to receive a very small sum for their houses, and property that had already been vacated would revert to the waqf, since the owners were not present and probably could not document it even if they were still in Yemen.[147]

The deterioration in the economic status of the Jews of Yemen predated the 1949–1950 exodus. In Yemen in the early 1920s a law was passed that made the property of Jews who left Yemen "to live under another government" the property of the state.[148] Its most alarming provision stipulated that Muslims who bought property from Jews would keep it only as long as the Jewish seller remained in Yemen.[149] The law was intended to dissuade Jews from leaving Yemen for Palestine, but it harmed the economic situation of all Jews, irrespective of their desire to emigrate, in that it generated reluctance among Muslims to buy property from Jews. The crown also rented many properties that it had seized back to Jews.[150]

The harm caused by the law was mitigated by the fact that the Yemeni government did not possess sophisticated methods of monitoring the population. Therefore, the difficulty of keeping track of individual Jews made the nationalization order hard to implement. Jews from the imām's Yemen who spent lengthy periods of time in the British colony of Aden engaged in trade or making unsuccessful arrangements to leave Yemen for Palestine returned home expecting to have maintained ownership of their property. Others traveled abroad on business, and the government lacked (or was unwilling to assert) the power to determine whether they were in Eritrea, for example, or whether they had, in fact, emigrated to Palestine. According to a Yemeni historian, Imām Yaḥyā was forced to clarify such issues in a communiqué he issued to his administration in July 1943. In it he said that those who needed to travel abroad to make a living needed to apply for a de facto exit visa that would last for a finite period of time. He asked his governors to seek clarification from applicants for the reasons for their travel and to assemble documentation of their assets. The document forbade leaving Yemen as an emigrant and made clear that Yemenis who did so would lose both their immovable property and their citizenship. Its specification of Palestine clarifies as well that he was concerned with Jewish emigration.[151]

A 1937 case revolves around the very rapid changes in the legal status of Jewish property in the decade or so between the end of Turkish rule and the law seizing emigrant property. A Jewish woman claimed ownership of a house in a town north of Sanaa where another Jew lived. Under the Ḥanafī law of the Turks, the right of possession trumps documentation. However, after 1918, when Zaydī law was reintroduced, the Jewish woman took the squatter to court. He was ordered to pay back rent. He then countered that the house had belonged to her and her brothers. Since her brothers had emigrated to Palestine, the house should belong to the state. (Unless the state was charging less rent than his landlady, his only motive would have been spite.) At the highest court in Sanaa the woman claimed that her brothers had left in 1899 or 1900, well in advance of the nationalization law. The imām accepted her interpretation of the law as non-retroactive.[152]

This Jewish real estate crisis entered a new and more intensive phase after the assassination of Imām Yaḥyā and the establishment of the State of Israel in 1948.[153] It should be borne in mind that there was no "land grab" of Jewish property between the promulgation of the nationalization order of circa 1920 and Imām Aḥmad's 1949 order that all Jews who left Yemen must sell their property. After 1949 Sālim Manṣūrah responded to the real estate crisis by trying to convince the imām to order the state treasury to purchase Jewish property or to assign a trustee who would oversee their property until a time when they could be sold at fair market prices.[154]

While Imām Aḥmad seems to have tried to facilitate the sale of Jewish property and appointed an agent, he did not try to ensure that Jews would receive fair market prices. [155] One Jewish source says the imām ordered regional governors to dispatch soldiers to assess the property of Jews throughout Yemen, charging them a fee for this "service," and looted the Jews of Dhamār outright.[156] Another source says that Imām Aḥmad dispatched soldiers to protect Jews in one village when he got wind of a plot to rob them.[157]

Imām Aḥmad's constituency also included Muslims who, through wealth or connections, were able to purchase Jewish property at very low prices. These included a number of his brothers. 'Alī, Yaḥyā, and Muṭahhar moved into vacant houses in the Jewish Quarter of Sanaa.[158] ʿAlī Zabārah, from a prominent sayyid clan, moved into the grand Ḥibshūsh house.[159] Finally, Aḥmad Jābir, the hard-drinking police officer in charge of the Jewish Quarter, became the chief intermediary for property transactions involving the Jews of Sanaa and likely became very wealthy in the process.[160]

In 1925 a Jew who wanted to leave Yemen approached Sālim Saʿīd al-Jamal. He owed Jamal money. The man wanted to give him a grain field he owned to satisfy his debt but realized that it would soon be expropriated. After the man left, Jamal wrote a letter petitioning Imām Yaḥyā. In his letter he emphasized the man's debt, as well as the idea that he had gone missing abroad. He wrote, "The debtor disappeared in the inside lands [i.e., outside Yemen]."[161] He does not refer to him as an émigré and does not mention Palestine. By calling the man "the missing debtor," Jamal tried to shift the focus from the man himself to the problem of the unpaid debt and, by implication, the rights of the debtor. He also implicitly argued that all that could be reasonably concluded about the man was that he was missing. No evidence testified to his living "under another government" as the nationalization order put it. If Imām Yaḥyā accepted this, the nationalization law would become moot and the man's debt to him would be repaid. The imām did not accept this argument. He wrote: "There is no doubt that a debt must be settled out of the indebted's wealth, and it is the judge's responsibility to stand in for one who is missing. However, it is clear from the question that the indebted was a non-Muslim. His disappearance places him outside the Pact [of ʿUmar] and his wealth belongs to the Muslims' treasury."[162]

The imām's son al-Qāsim, who owned land adjacent to the field, bought it, and with the proceeds of the sale he paid Jamal the money he was owed. Because the imām satisfied his debt, Jamal claimed this as a partial victory.[163] Yet there is no evidence that would indicate that in doing so the imām had enacted a general policy rather than a onetime dispensation for a confidante.

A similar case arose concerning a cow. A Muslim took care of a cow that belonged to a Jew. He brought the Jew's family a quota of the cow's butter and calves and kept some of the milk. This was a common feature of cow ownership in Yemen.[164] The cow's owner moved to Palestine. After he left, the Muslim stopped bringing butter to the family and claimed ownership of the cow. Eventually he petitioned the imām's son ʿAlī, saying, "Your Excellency knows that the non-Muslim in question is in Jerusalem (*al-bayt al-maqdis*)."[165] Rather than give the cow to the Muslim, the crown confiscated it.[166]

In 1934 two shoemakers who wanted to leave Yemen approached Jamal. They had to sell their houses to cover the costs of the journey. As it was well known that mass-produced imports made it difficult for shoemakers to sell their wares, Jamal tried a new tactic. He wrote the imām a letter in which he argued that the availability of "cheap rubber shoes and the like from abroad" made it impossible for the men to earn a living in Yemen. Because of this economic hardship, they had to go elsewhere—anywhere.[167] The argument for financial exigency separated the issue of Jewish emigration from the Palestine issue. Surely the imām could not argue in good faith that leaving Yemen would cause the men financial ruin when staying in Yemen was doing just that. But that is exactly what he did. He wrote at the top of the petition, "Permission [of this] is impossible. Staying is better for you than going."[168]

The nationalization order conflicted directly with sharīʿa principles of property ownership. Mordecai al-Ẓāhirī relates that his father, Ṣāliḥ, who owned a lot of property, had half of a house in a village near Sanaa. When the co-owner left Yemen for Israel, the state became the owner of the entire house. Ṣāliḥ al-Ẓāhirī pursued legal action against the imām by means of Luṭf al-Zubayrī, claiming he had bought the co-owner's half before his departure. The imām's laconic comment on his petition, "this is legally binding" (*bihi sharīʿah*) meant Ẓāhirī had succeeded.[169]

Pursuing a similar strategy, on May 10, 1937, Jamal wrote a petition he labeled "a query for the ulama." It reads:

> May a non-Muslim claim abutters' rights (*shufʿah*) against another non-Muslim in Islamic law, seeing that it is legal in Mosaic law? And if one claims abutters' rights against another according to Jewish law but the one against whom abutters' rights is claimed refuses, choosing Islamic law instead, would the claimant be forced into this, or would the one against whom the claim is lodged be forced to return to the law of his religion, seeing that the right goes to the claimant?[170]

Shufʿah normally refers to a co-owner's exercise of a privileged option to buy his partner's share in an immovable, indivisible property. Among Sunnis of the Ḥanafī rite and among Zaydīs, however, the right to preemption extends not only to co-owners but also to neighbors. (The Ḥanafī rite was the school of legal interpretation in the Ottoman Empire and in South Asia.) For these two schools, preemption protects two different constituencies: it safeguards a business partner's interests from harm by his partner, and it preserves a link between kinship and housing by preventing the encroachment of strangers. Here it is important to note that abutters' rights are primarily an urban issue. "Shufʿah," writes Saudi architect Saleh al-Hathloul, "should have helped the quarters within the [Arab-Islamic] city preserve their own character."[171]

Neighbors' rights to preemption can be found in pre-Islamic Arab, Jewish, and Hindu law as well.[172] Halakhic works discuss the right of preemption for neighbors (called "*din bar metsra*" or "*matsranut*"), as well as the denial of this right to heathen (Babylonian Talmud, Baba Metsia 108b).[173] During an 1884 case that went before a Jewish court in Yemen, a man who bought a home only to have the sale suspended by another Jew's claim of abutters' rights claimed he had bought the house only to prevent it from having been sold or rented to a non-Jew.[174]

A neighbor's potential to meddle with a contract for the sale of property led to the creation of a number of legal fictions (*ḥiyal*) intended to prevent neighbors from lodging claims of abutters' rights: the buyer and seller exchange a house and money not as a sale but as mutual gift giving; the buyer pays much more than the person claiming abutters' rights only to receive a substantial sum back from the seller as payment for a paltry thing; a strip of land between the property for sale and the neighbor is left unsold; or a small portion of the building is made into a pious endowment (a waqf).[175] The eighteenth-century Yemeni jurist Muḥammad b. ʿAlī al-Shawkānī sought to place limitations upon abutters' rights for neighbors.[176] (In postrevolutionary Yemen the state abolished abutters' rights for neighbors, basing their decision upon Shawkānī's dissenting view.[177])

The last Zaydī imams, Yaḥyā and Aḥmad, also issued rulings aimed at curtailing the use of these legal fictions.[178] Yet they affirmed abutters' rights for neighbors.[179] In one famous case, Imām Yaḥyā claimed ownership of a house in Sanaa belonging to a tribal shaykh through abutters' rights, and a qadi rejected his claim.[180] It is possible that when Jamal crafted his "query for the ulama," he sought to appeal either to Imām Yaḥyā's desire to reform this area of the law or the imām's sympathy with the use of the law in pursuit of self-interest.

As the 1884 case before the Jewish court showed, abutters' rights for neighbors served as a bone of contention in property disputes between Muslims and Jews in Yemen. Thus, Sālim Saʿīd's question about abutters' rights represented his most audacious attempt to render the nationalization order null and void. He knew enough not to ask if non-Muslims could claim abutters' rights against Muslims. However, if non-Muslims had abutters' rights against one another, Jews who left Yemen could sell their homes to other Jews, concentrating property and wealth within the group in the spirit of the law. Unless one is to assume that potential Jewish property buyers like Jamal intended to pay pre-exodus market prices out of love for their coreligionists instead of the low prices that Jewish property actually commanded, wealthy Jews like him stood to make a lot of money as well. If they stayed in Yemen, they would have amassed large valuable urban properties.

Whether his claims to altruism can be given credence or not, Jamal crafted his provocation in terms of rights due non-Muslims under Islamic law. He wanted to know whether Islamic law allowed non-Muslims to own property in the same way it allowed Muslims to own property. Did the purchase price paid by a Jew for property represent a true sale, or was it "key money"?[181]

The issue of Jewish abutters' rights affected sales of agricultural land as well. Among the Yemeni tribes, fellow tribesmen are entitled to bid first on agricultural lands.[182] For farmers, abutters' rights facilitated their acquisition of contiguous fields.[183] While Jews in Yemen generally did not work as farmers, some Jews acquired large land holdings and either hired Muslim workers or worked the fields themselves.[184] For the residents of a Jewish village in the south, these fields were usually much closer to the neighboring Muslim villages than to the home village. This indicated that they had probably been acquired from Muslims in the past. However, the local shaykh often had the last word in the assignment of land rights. Ratson Halevi, a Jew from Lower Yemen, describes a Jew asking of a shaykh, and receiving, the right to cultivate a neglected plot of land.[185] Muslims who challenged Jewish land ownership and could document their competing claims had a distinct advantage. Halevi writes, echoing Jamal, "Jews had no land rights."[186] The existence of Jewish agricultural lands presented a problem when it came to taxation, because the tithe on crops represented the canonical tax upon Muslims (*zakāh*). There is contradictory evidence that indicates that either the authorities collected the zakāh from Jews, they made due with taxing Muslim tenant farmers of Jewish-owned lands, or they did not charge Jews this tax.[187]

Muslim writer ʿAbdallāh Juzaylān tells of a Muslim farmer who converted to Judaism for its lighter tax burden in the 1940s. Even the threat of execution, the canonical penalty for apostasy from Islam, did not dissuade him, and in the end the future Imām Aḥmad was forced to absolve the farmer of one year's tax in order to coax him back into the fold of the believers.[188]

The Zaydī prohibition against Jews exercising abutters' rights against Muslims was either ignored or irrelevant (in that the Muslim seller's volition was unchallenged, competing Muslim buyers did not exist, or situations in which a Muslim could claim this right in addition to a Jew were extremely rare). A trove of legal documents belonging to a wealthy Jewish family from Damt includes documentation of Muslims' sale of lands to the family in exchange for cash for large expenses (e.g., a daughter's wedding, the hajj).

Since territory played such an essential role in the tribesman's self-definition, such sales of land to Jews were not always ordinary sales. Instead a Muslim seller might retain the option of rescinding the sale (an agreement called "*iqālah*"). This rescission might occur years after the original sale, and when the seller invoked it he had the option to either return the money or goods used to make the purchase or to finalize the sale.[189] A "sale with the option of withdrawal" (*bayʿ al-khiyār*) offered another option for managing the interreligious tensions that accompanied the sale of Muslim land to Jews.[190] With this arrangement the Muslim tenant farmer might pay a tithe in crops to the Jewish landlord that he otherwise would have paid the state.[191] He might also pay rent. It is not clear why Jews in some parts of Yemen seem to have bought land outright and other sales were conditional. Both types of land ownership are described in majority-Shafiʿi regions. Perhaps since Jews who were relatively well-off owned land, other Jews who described the existence of Jewish ownership of such lands were unaware of such subtleties.

Cases in the Damt trove show that qadis supported Jewish claimants in property disputes with Muslims. In one case from 1885–1886 in which a prominent shaykh tried to avoid having to pay rent on property he had provisionally sold to a Jew, a qadi granted the Jew the right to unilaterally terminate the contract. He concluded by citing the hadith "the [default] position is that of the buyer" (*al-qawl qawl al-mushtarī*). His ruling was soon overturned by another qadi, who objected to the unilateral renegotiation of a contract but still allowed the Jew a small victory.[192]

Jamal's second question in his "query to the ulama" about the two parties choosing different legal systems represented a contingency plan: even if Imām Yaḥyā rejected the abutters' rights of non-Muslims against non-Muslims, the option of sending cases where each party chose a different legal forum to the Jewish courts, which would enforce a Jew's right to preemption against a Jewish neighbor, would present him with an elegant and discreet remedy.

While it is not an issue he discusses in his recollection of his thought process, other cases in which Jamal used the Islamic legal system indicate he had a good working knowledge of Zaydī law concerning property. He describes a statement of the prophet Muḥammad (hadith) that runs "an unbeliever cannot establish a waqf, and there are no abutters' rights for the People of the Pact" as being contained in the *Commentary [on the Book of] Flowers*.[193] But this is not a hadith; its two parts are not found together, the two statements are paraphrased, and they are not in that particular book. A comparable hadith, "There are no abutters' rights for a Jew or a Christian," is found in one of its marginal commentaries.[194] In any case, Jamal was clearly aware that the hypothetical issue of abutters' rights for non-Muslims would provoke controversy among the Muslim scholars.

Jamal may also have known that the Zaydī law manuals preserve a disagreement on the question of a non-Muslim exercising abutters' rights against another non-Muslim. By drawing attention to this disagreement he furnished the imām with a Zaydī argument for overturning the nationalization order. The *Book of Flowers* describes four situations under which abutters' rights may be exercised (in descending order): one who shares ownership of a property, one who shares a common water source, one who shares the same dead-end street, or one who is an abutting neighbor.[195] It excludes the abutters' rights "of an unbeliever over a Muslim absolutely or of an unbeliever in our lands."[196] The last sentence is ambiguous. If non-Muslims "absolutely" do not have abutters' rights, why does it mention two groups? How do the two groups of non-Muslims differ?

The precedence in Islamic abutters' rights of those who share a dead-end street over next-door neighbors can be explained in the following manner: In the context of Islamic urban architecture, the dead-end street, in the words of

François-Auguste de Montequin, "serves the mass of a determined number of dwellings in whose core it penetrates in order to give them access." Therefore, the inhabitants of the homes that shared such a street were more likely to be members of the same group than those of an abutting house, separated by a wall, which would have had its own dead-end street.[197]

Zaydī writers after the *Book of Flowers* upheld the prohibition against a non-Muslim buyer exercising abutters' rights against a Muslim seller.[198] Most quote hadiths in defense of this position. But why might a non-Muslim sell to a Muslim while being unable to exercise abutters' rights? In the fifteenth-century *Commentary [on the Book of] Flowers,* Imām al-Murtaḍā (d. 1437) explains that "a sale price is extracted by mutual agreement and abutters' rights are taken by force."[199] According to this imām, the non-Muslims' rights are limited to residence and possession.[200] A contemporary of Jamal, Qadi Aḥmad b. al-Qāsim al-ʿAnsī (d. 1970), made the same argument in his manual of Zaydī law, *The Golden Crown on the Laws of the Rite.*[201]

A contrasting view is found in the earlier (fourteenth-century) opinion of Imām al-Muʾayyad (Yaḥyā b. Ḥamzah [d. 1348]), who follows the Ḥanafī and Shafiʿi schools in arguing that non-Muslims possess abutters' rights "due to the preponderance of textual proofs and because it is a right that is intended to repel harm and in this unbeliever and Muslim are equals."[202] Muʾayyad also rejects the *Book of Flowers'* exclusion of non-Muslim abutters' rights "in our lands."[203]

Shawkānī takes a similar route, stating that non-Muslims possess abutters' rights "because they have what Muslims have concerning that which the law necessitates regarding the prevention of corrupting influences."[204] However, Shawkānī, as was mentioned, argued against the idea of abutters' rights for neighbors. He also advocated making life unpleasant for Jews. Neither fact would have made his work a means for advancing Jamal's cause.

Both sides in the disagreement among Zaydīs recognized a double-edged quality to abutters' rights for neighbors. While it may be a God-given right (and a natural human urge) to amass property for one's family, the exercise of this right would inevitably lead to conflict with other groups, since urban property is finite. For the proponents of abutters' rights for non-Muslims, the benefit of the right outweighs its cost. By reasserting the religious hierarchy, the opponents of preemption for non-Muslims sought to deny its capacity to undermine the Islamic social order. In this vein, Wael Hallaq describes preemption as a law that "would ultimately have led to Muslims being deprived of the right to purchase houses in the predominantly non-Muslim cities and towns that had been conquered."[205]

The same problem arises in the work of Dutch architect John Habraken, a prominent representative of the Open Housing movement. Habraken challenges various dogmas of modernist architecture. He dismisses as self-serving illusion the modernist preference for the design of public spaces and breaking down physical boundaries (or at least making them out of glass) in the interest of breaking down traditional hierarchies. For Habraken, modernist housing provides the illusion of openness, but the suburban home's security system and neighborhood watch serve the same human inclination toward territorial control and expansion that is embodied in the essentially open-ended urban housing of a medieval Middle Eastern city.[206] Open Housing advocates similarly open-ended public housing as a means of allowing the urban poor the greatest possible control over their physical environment.[207]

Habraken argues that the control of territory and sense of security that result from one group deciding who comes in and who stays out make a positive impact on a territory's robustness and its likelihood for future improvement.[208] When confronted with the moral problem of excluding another group from an urban area, Habraken concludes that such exclusion is inevitable and pervasive. But it is also conducive to social cohesion and reduces crime.[209] In housing, hierarchical relations cannot be avoided.

Jamal's bid to use abutters' rights to reverse the nationalization order failed. Imām Yaḥyā's reply to his provocative query was "the answer [to your question] is that Jews have no right to preemption in lands other than theirs, because they do not own property."[210] A decade later Jamal was in Jerusalem himself, embroiled in a land dispute with his Palestinian landlord, Ṣalība Qattān. Though a renter in his building in the Ratisbonne neighborhood of Jerusalem (today part of tony Reḥavia), Jamal sought to cement his claim on a two-story house by renting two apartments in it. He describes his 1946 dispute with Qattān as a proxy war between the Arab League and the Jewish Agency. The Arab League, he alleges, tried to evict him. The Jewish Agency advised him not to try to buy the building, as it would be his after the impending war. And so it was.[211] Although not technically an abutters' rights case, this epilogue seems in many ways to justify the Zaydī jurists' fears about the role of the law in exacerbating interreligious conflict. It also offers an echo of the financial crisis in Yemen. By shrewdly acquiring refugee property at minimal expense, as the most prominent Muslim Yemenis had done in the Jewish Quarter of Sanaa, perhaps Jamal finally and belatedly gained admission to the ranks of the Muslim elite, if only in a symbolic sense.

Two grand houses in Sanaa and Jerusalem stand as monuments to the failure on the part of both Muslim Yemenis and Israeli Jews of devising solutions to the moral and legal issues surrounding property discussed here. In a 1989 account of a visit to Yemen, Yeḥiel Ḥibshūsh describes with nostalgia the once-bustling and opulent Ḥibshūsh home in the Jewish Quarter of Sanaa known as "*ha-armon*" ("the palace"). It had been a monument to the hopes of the Jewish elite for participation in Yemen's public life. Having been acquired by a sayyid family, the property had subsequently fallen into disrepair, an otherwise unremarkable building in an exclusively Muslim neighborhood.[212] Ṣalība Qattān's villa in Reḥavia, representative of the same desires on the part of the Palestinian elite, now stands empty and dilapidated in an expensive, almost exclusively Jewish neighborhood while Jamal's heirs sort out their claims to it.

Indeterminacy deeply affected the contours of the economic relationships between Muslims and Jews in Yemen, relationships in which the sharīʿa played an important role. As people who did not generally own and work the land, Jews constituted a service sector along with groups of low-status Muslims. The Jews (and their ethnic quarters) stood betwixt and between male and female, the mundane and the supernatural, sobriety and intoxication. This seeming rootlessness enabled some to seize new opportunities in imports and exports in the twentieth century. However, during the real estate crises that Jewish emigration to Palestine prompted, that same perception of rootlessness led Muslims to deny Jews property ownership.

5 Intercommunal Violence and the Sharīʿa

Violence: Theory versus Practice

In theory, Muslims and Jews in Yemen could not behave violently toward one another. In practice, violence across the hierarchical boundaries between Muslim and Jew seems to have been relatively common. Jewish sources provide contradictory answers to the question of whether Yemen under the imāms was a particularly violent place. Some credit Imām Yaḥyā with the virtual elimination of crime through his focus on law and order. Others (some of the same people) describe numerous violent robberies, particularly attacks by tribesmen on traveling Jewish salesmen in unsettled areas.[1] Such merchants, who were often unarmed, seem to have made easy prey. Jews in the process of emigrating were likely to carry all of their worldly belongings with them. Sālim Manṣūrah tells the story of two Jewish men who, having packed all of their things upon a pair of donkeys and setting off on the journey for Israel, were assaulted and robbed by the shaykh of their small village and some of his male relatives, who were armed with hatchets. The two wounded men headed straight to Imām Aḥmad's palace in Taʿizz, where they loudly demanded justice. The imām ordered soldiers to bring the shaykh and his men. He drew his whip and beat the men within an inch of their lives and then imprisoned them for eight months.[2]

Jews might also find themselves caught in the middle of vendettas between the tribe with whom they were affiliated and a rival tribe, or small-scale rebellions against the central government. They might even exacerbate such vendettas. One writer relates of an epic tragedy touched off when a tribesman's uncle slapped "his" Jew and him. His mother encouraged him to take violent retribution. He killed his uncle, his nephews killed him, and his mother paid the blood price.[3]

As was discussed in chapter 2, breaches in animal-riding etiquette seem to have provoked this type of violence against Jews. Such nonlethal violence across religious boundaries was common, with Muslims beating Jews and, more surprisingly, Jews beating Muslims.

In theory, Jews did not own weapons. In practice, Jews in rural areas of the north and southeast bore arms in public. One Jewish writer tells of an attempt by a Muslim notable in northern Yemen in 1904 or 1905 to impress officers in Imām Yaḥyā's army with the marksmanship of the local Jews by holding a small target in his hand for them to shoot.[4] In Bayḍā' in 1928, armed Jews fought the imām's troops alongside tribesmen.[5] An anecdote describes a Jew from the north discovered with a sword on his way out of the country in 1951 and deemed a "*ḥarbī*"—a warlike non-Muslim not entitled to protection.[6] In other parts of Yemen, Jews kept guns in their homes for protection but did not carry them in public.[7]

In theory, people who occupied the lower rungs of Yemen's social strata expected more powerful Muslims to protect them from violence in exchange for their submission to the status quo. There were several semi-ritualized ways that Jews asked to become the client of a local tribal shaykh and the shaykh formally announced the establishment of such a relationship. In the far north of Yemen a Jew looking for a new patron would hammer a nail into the lintel of a powerful Muslim's door and then say, "This is my nail and I am sticking it in this house," a seemingly cryptic statement whose intent was perfectly clear to all who heard it.[8] One Jewish writer, Yosef Ḥubarah, jailed in Sanaa in 1920, recalls asking for the sponsorship of Muslim notables who were also imprisoned. "I pulled on a bunch of hair from my sidelocks and said, as was customary, 'I am your client, be jealous of me!'"[9]

In theory, it was taboo for Muslim men to use violence against Jews or women. "In Yemen it was a given that a Muslim was forbidden from raising his hand against a Jew or a woman," writes Mordecai Yitshari.[10] Within the realm of tribal norms, violence against a woman, guest, or client represented, in the words of A. Z. al-Abdin, "one of the gravest crimes called *al-'ayb al-aswad* (the black shame)."[11] Anecdotal material suggests that tribesmen indeed saw Jews under their protection as extensions of their honor and avenged attacks on them.[12] The highway robbery of a Jew in the nineteenth century touched off a small war between his shaykh and the tribe of those who had attacked him.[13] One anecdote set in the late nineteenth century tells of a Jewish merchant with good connections to the Bedouin tribes in eastern Yemen. The merchant once traveled there accompanied by a tribesman armed with a spear. During the journey the tribesman tried to kill the Jewish merchant and steal his merchandise and money. He threw his spear, just missing the Jew. Then he laughed, pretending he had not meant any harm. The Jew seized the tribesman and frog-marched him to the nearest Bedouin camp. After delivering him to the shaykh of the tribe, he told him of his guard's treachery. The shaykh took little time to deliberate. He flew into a rage, took the Jew's shoe, and used it to slap the tribesman's cheeks. He then ordered the tribesman to crawl to the Jew, kiss his feet, and beg his forgiveness. The Jew suggested this element of the sentence be foregone, but the shaykh would hear nothing of it. "The criminal grazed on the dust of his feet as he had been ordered," writes the Jew's grandson, "begging for mercy, expiation, and forgiveness."[14]

Such retribution ought not be proportionate. It would ideally cause damage more grievous than the harm initially inflicted. A maxim runs "He who harms you [my Jew] by means of water I [the shaykh] shall harm by means of blood."[15] (Imām Yaḥyā quoted a variant on this saying during Jamal's blasphemy trial). However, such escalation seems to have been the norm only where the offender against the Jew belonged to a rival tribe.

This overweening attention to the Jews' security occasionally led to misunderstandings. In the town of Bayḥān in the 1920s, on Tisha b'av, a fast day commemorating calamities in Jewish history, shaykhs from a local Bedouin tribe observed the weeping and lamentations of the local Jews. They ordered their tribe to take up arms and march on the synagogue. When they arrived, the shaykhs demanded to know the whereabouts of those had so aggrieved the Jews.[16]

Chapter 1 enumerated conflicts between the sharīʿa and tribal law (the so-called *ṭāghūt*). The ulama condemned the tribal practice of tying compensatory damages to the status of the deceased. In this area Jews fared much better under tribal law, which multiplied damages elevenfold because of their status as weak clients of the tribes, than under the sharīʿa law of blood prices.[17] Writing of the murder of a Jewish moneylender by a Muslim, apparently in the mid-1940s, Shalom Bene Moshe explains how this facet of the sharīʿa operated. The family of a Muslim who was murdered was entitled to either blood money or having the murderer executed. When Muslims killed Jews, however, the murderer's execution was gainsaid and the victim's family received a standard blood price of 700 (or 750) riyāls in cash, goods, or property. (The perpetrator was imprisoned as well.) In this case the government imprisoned the murderer indefinitely, transferred some of his belongings to the family of the deceased as part of the payment, and levied a fine upon residents of his and the surrounding villages.[18]

Despite the taboo against beating up Jews, Muslims occasionally did so. But because of the legal disparities relating to witnessing, the victims did not go to the sharīʿa courts.[19] Jews also behaved violently toward Muslims. Shalom Bene Moshe tells of an incident that occurred during the Monday market in a village in Lower Yemen, probably in the late 1930s. A Jewish boy sold some matches and string to a young Muslim. The Muslim did not pay and scuffled with the boy. The boy complained to an adult Jew, who was a wealthy merchant. The adult Jew confronted the Muslim man, who responded by trying to hit him. The Jew slapped him in the face. This outraged Muslim buyers and sellers in the market. A soldier knocked the Jew out with his rifle butt and brought him to the shaykh's house for judgment. The Muslim man who had been slapped and the crowd of witnesses followed. The shaykh advised the Muslim to hide the fact that he had been slapped by the Jew, "for this will be an eternal shame for you and your offspring.

Your children will be a source of mockery and derision among all creatures, and you will never again be able to lift this shame from atop them." While this admonition guaranteed the Muslim's silence, the Jew would still have to make amends for his infraction. He began throwing money at the would-be witnesses to his crime. Once the hefty sum of seventy riyāls had been distributed, the mob who had been clamoring for his punishment began singing his praises. The Jewish boy regained his matches and string as well.[20]

A Jew in Dhamār had a shop. The sayyids of the town, who despised manual labor, had little more to do than chew qāt and attend to their prayers. One such indolent young sayyid loitered around the entrance to the Jewish man's shop, fingered his merchandise, and insulted it and him. The Jew noted that the sayyid was physically weak but armed with rifle and knives. Yet at one point the merchant snapped. He quoted the Yemeni proverb "One who makes himself into feed gets scattered by roosters." He pulled the sayyid into his shop, shut the door, and beat him up. The next morning the sayyid, in tears, was on his way to the bruise assessor in preparation for a lawsuit against the Jew when an older sayyid stopped him. (A notary who assessed bruises was part of the criminal justice system in Yemen.[21]) After the young sayyid told the older sayyid what had happened, the older man counseled him to never tell a soul about it, "for shame and ignominy will be your lot and you will never again be able to show your face in the street." After the young man took his advice, the old man went to the Jew's shop. He told the Jew of the great favor he had done for him, asked only for a riyāl for qāt in payment, and received it.[22]

A Jewish merchant in the same town slapped a Muslim merchant in a fit of rage. Among the Muslims who rushed to the scene was one man who wrote a list of everyone who was present and from which a judge might summon witnesses. (It is not clear whether any of these men actually saw the Jew strike the Muslim.) The Jews of the town stayed in their homes and waited for the denouement to the episode, which they reasoned would only be bad for them. The Jew hired a Muslim attorney and had him deliver a gift to the governor. When the governor made one of his daily rounds, during which villagers sought his judgment, the Muslim who was slapped and the man who wrote the list of potential witnesses flagged him down. The governor apparently regarded the compilation of the list, as well as the fact that the men on the list had volunteered to act as witnesses, as impudent usurpations of a qadi's judicial duties: only the qadi determines the witnesses to summon. He ordered each volunteer witness jailed for ten days and fined and had the list writer jailed for a month and fined for his aggression against the Jew.[23]

In each of these assaults the Jew got away with the crime. Yet each involved a substantial financial loss in legal fees, highest in the case of the Jew who slapped a Muslim in public. That Jew, whose aggression had been witnessed by others, needed to compensate them monetarily. (This phase in the arbitration was neither explicitly advised by the shaykh nor did he object to it.) In each anecdote a Muslim arbitrator (shaykh, sayyid, or governor) successfully avoided a legal proceeding against the Jewish aggressor. In two cases such arbitration revolved around older Muslim men cautioning younger men against the shocking naiveté that led them first into physical confrontations with Jews and then into turning to the criminal justice system when they lost those confrontations. Even where the Muslim victim insisted on pursuing a legal remedy in spite of the shame, as in the second anecdote, the organization that went into gathering the "facts" of an attack, which may or may not have been witnessed, raised the specter of mob justice and a challenge to the authority of the government and its judicial apparatus.

In some cases involving Jewish violence against Muslims, Jews sought to manipulate divisions within the Muslim community. In Bayḥān in 1940 a Jew caused a disturbance in the town synagogue after feeling he had been unfairly denied the honor of distributing sweets for the festival of Simchat Torah. He was apprehended by tribesmen, and in a fit of rage he throttled their shaykh, Ṣāliḥ Aḥmad. He was beaten and imprisoned in the shaykh's house.

During this period two tribes in Bayḥān were locked in a violent and lasting feud. The Jew's wife challenged the shaykh of the enemy tribe, Ṣāliḥ al-Aṣwār, to rescue her husband, "who is under your protection." Aṣwār gathered a group of armed men as well as the shaykh of a third tribe. He then challenged Ṣāliḥ Aḥmad's authority over the local Jews. The latter shaykh explained that since the Jew had caused a disturbance in the synagogue, he was holding him until other Jews paid a surety for his release. Aṣwār replied, "Let me be a surety before all for this Jew who you imprisoned and not only for him but for every Jew from one end of the earth to the other." The Jew was released, but rather than rushing home, he gloated over his victory. The "third-party" shaykh cautioned the Jew to be quiet "lest the place become a cemetery for us all."[24] In this case the feud between the two tribes, each of whom eagerly sought pretexts for conflict, enabled both the Jew's attack on the shaykh and his wife's appeal.

'Ovadiah Zandani explains that during hard times some young tribesmen robbed vulnerable travelers in wild areas far from the watchful eye of their elders.[25] In 1948 a Muslim assaulted and robbed a Jew in a desolate area on the border between the imāms' Yemen and the Aden Protectorate. The Muslim bore the unlikely name "Son of Hunger" (*ibn al-jawʿ*), which suggests that he fell into the category of a luckless tribesman. The Jew complained to the governor of the nearest town, but Imām Yaḥyā had just been assassinated and the governor was gearing up for a full-fledged rebellion. After the new regime headed by ʿAbdallāh al-Wazīr had been defeated and Aḥmad established his position as imām in Taʿizz, the Jew traveled to the city and complained to a shaykh of the Nuʿmān clan. The shaykh referred him to the local governor, Aḥmad al-Jandārī, who ignored his entreaties. The Jew returned to shaykh ʿAlī, who sent a telegram to Imām Aḥmad that read, "Do justice by the Jew [even] without witnesses, even if the complaint involves damages (*qaṣaṣ*). He who opposes this will get his just desserts." This strongly worded order called upon the imām to ignore the sharīʿa's evidentiary rules that ought to have gainsaid a case revolving around a Jew's word against a Muslim without witnesses.

Governor Jandārī then sprang into action, sending soldiers to apprehend the thief, extracting a confession, and levying heavy fines for both assault and robbery. The Jew insisted on "a bruise for a bruise" (Ex. 21:25) and struck the Muslim man in the face in view of those assembled. The Jew who related the anecdote asks how "a Jew could raise his hand against a non-Jew in the palace's courtyard before hundreds of onlookers," an act that would normally get the Jew into trouble, even if done more clandestinely. He suggests that the thief may have had a prior record that justified such humiliation.[26]

Even when one knows little about either the Jew or the thief, political allegiances in Yemen in 1949 nevertheless shed light on the episode. Both the Ottomans and Imām Yaḥyā had trouble ruling the area around Taʿizz due to the strength of local authorities, who were armed with heavy weapons left by the Turks. But since it was populous and extremely fertile and rich in other resources as well, its pacification was necessary.[27] The powerful Sunni Nuʿmān clan had ruled the area since the time of the Ottomans, and ʿAlī al-Wazīr, the governor of Taʿizz from 1919 to 1937, had worked tirelessly to suppress their influence. In 1949, with ʿAlī al-Wazīr's nephew having claimed power after Imām Yaḥyā's assassination and the two men having been executed, the Nuʿmāns seem to have regained some of their status. Thus, Imām Aḥmad would have had a sensible reason to take orders from them, as happened in this case. Thus, if one accepts the Jewish narrator's claim that the Nuʿmāns were extremely solicitous of the local Jews, in this case the imām's remarkably permissive stance toward one Jew derived entirely from the identity of the Muslim who stood behind him. In 1950 Aḥmad Muḥammad Nuʿmān, a major figure in the opposition that had led to the coup, was released from prison and publicly praised Imām Aḥmad.[28]

As David Nirenberg argues in *Communities of Violence*, while the analysis of the potential and actual violence against Jews can be difficult to extricate conceptually from European anti-Semitism and Nazism, such a teleological approach must be avoided in favor of a "more integrated approach."[29] The conflict over Palestine complicates matters further. If tensions between Muslims and Jews that occasionally erupted violently possessed a context in Yemeni politics, they interacted as well with world politics.

Supporting evidence from Yemen can be adduced to each of the major rationales that are ordinarily provided to explain anti-Semitism in Europe, yet none are satisfactory in isolation. The violent riots and looting of the Jewish Quarter of

Sanaa following the assassination of Imām Yaḥyā in 1948, during which a number of Jews were killed, support the idea that the majority population viewed the Jews as vassals of a monarchical estate that, once removed, rendered their protected status moot.[30] Yet the "church" in this "church and state" equation could hardly be separated from the theocratic imām and his family, and the tribesmen who descended upon the entire city—in the words of ʿAbdallāh b. ʿAbd al-Wahhāb al-Shamāḥī, "as if ravenous locusts had been scattered about, their mouths slavering for all of the treasure, riches, and money Sanaa possessed"—had received Aḥmad's blessing.[31] Aharon Ḥamdi tells of how the tribesmen simply hated Sanaa and were happy to loot its neighborhoods, be they Muslim or Jewish, whenever the opportunity arose.[32]

Mordecai al-Ẓāhirī explained Muslim violence against Jews in terms that assume the (Marxist) alienated consciousness of the proletariat. "Muslims in the cities of Yemen arranged pogroms against Jews not out of extreme Muslim religious zeal," writes Ẓāhirī, "but out of an ignorance and boorishness that drew them to every word of propaganda and incitement that was uttered by the mouths of those who wore the Zaydī religious robes."[33] Ẓāhirī's references to "propaganda" suggest as well that in his time it was already too late to attempt to isolate the Arab-Zionist conflict from preexisting prejudices.

In 1932 Avraham Ṭabīb made an intriguing contrast between European anti-Semitism and the oppression of Jews in Yemen. In Europe Jew haters occasionally organized pogroms "and afterward their anger abated for decades." In Yemen mass violence against Jews was very rare but daily harassment was worse. The European anti-Semite, argues Ṭabīb, was like a fox in a henhouse, content to kill a hen now and then while the other hens went about their business. In Yemen "the whip was always stretched over their backs and they had no rest."[34] Leaving aside the political context of Ṭabīb's argument (he sought to move the plight of the Jews of Yemen to the forefront of the Zionist agenda), his argument remains thought-provoking, suggesting that the sumptuary laws and other near-ritualized forms of nonlethal violence made massacres unnecessary.[35]

Some Jewish writers make the intriguing suggestion that a subsection of the sayyid class served as the source of antagonism toward Jews. That is, those holding this hereditary office who lived in relative squalor were likely to take great umbrage at even minor infringements of sumptuary restrictions by Jews.[36] An anecdote illustrates this point. A Jewish woman sent her young son to the fields where Muslim farmers were harvesting grain. Her friend's husband owned one of the fields, and the friend had promised the Jewish woman a portion for her family. The husband was a sayyid named Muḥammad, and he toiled along with the other laborers. The Jewish boy asked one of the workers, who happened to be the sayyid himself, for the location of "so-and-so's field." The sayyid, embarrassed at the Jew's having omitted his title, "*Sīdī* Muḥammad," in front of the other laborers, denied that the boy was in the right place, sending him off to another field. Eventually his mother's friend, who he hadn't recognized because she was stooped over the grain, convinced her husband to relent. The boy remained confused. How was one supposed to discern a person's prophetic lineage if some sayyids wore turbans and others were bareheaded and barefoot? His mother explained that Jews ought to avoid this problem by addressing every Muslim as "sīdī."[37] All non-sayyids, Jew or Muslim, were expected to use this form of address, which Muḥammad Qā'id al-Ṣā'idī says, "expressed the distinctive condition of a class of people who enjoyed the rights of political and social leadership at a time when others only had the right to listen and obey."[38]

Non-sayyids were expected to kiss the hands of sayyids upon greeting them and, for the hoi polloi, to kiss their knees as well. "If the Hashemite [i.e., the sayyid] wanted to reply to this greeting," wrote Yemeni revolutionary Muḥammad Aḥmad Nuʿmān, "it was not more than placing his hand on the shoulder of the citizen whose back was bent as he kissed his knees."[39]

In addition to matters of heredity, the close quarters of cities also intensified attentiveness to social boundaries between Muslims and Jews. (This could also be said for the social boundaries between men and women.) The same writer remarks, far too categorically, that in the village Jews did not address Muslims as "sīdī," both Muslim and Jew were "sons" of the merciful shaykh, and "relationships of mutual respect and friendship prevailed." The shaykh of his village always sided with the weak, even when the imām took the opposite view.[40] The city turned such ideals on their heads. Any Muslim could humiliate or steal from a Jew while the Jew abased himself and groveled.[41] A Jew from Sharʿab recalls admonishing a shaykh's son who was sent to Sanaa to study "not to learn the hatred of Jews from them."[42]

A Jew from the far north of Yemen, ʿOvadiah Zandani, says that when he traveled to Sanaa in 1936 for a business trip, he doffed the dagger and turban he wore at home, put on a *jalabiyyah,* and tucked his long hair under a cap, leaving a lock exposed on each side. "I looked at myself and saw that I was a different creature," he writes. While he was on his trip, non-Jews went out of their way to curse, raise their staves as if to strike, throw rocks at, and pull the Jew off of his donkey. When he was ready to leave and a guard at the gate of the Jewish Quarter demanded he wait to have his bags checked for alcohol, he could take it no longer. He changed back into his clothing, girded his dagger, let his long hair flow, put on his magnificent turban, and mounted his donkey. Then he went to another gate, rapped on it with his staff, and demanded to be let out "in the manner of a free man."[43]

Nissim Gamlieli, who generally describes the shaykhs with great admiration, says that a subsection of poor shaykhs (like the poor sayyids described above) caused trouble for Jews. Shaykhs who had lost everything with Imām Yaḥyā's rise to power were concentrated in one village in the south where the governor of Damt (a ninety-minute journey from the village by foot) tried unsuccessfully to keep them powerless and contained. When he was assassinated they wanted revenge, and the Jews, says Gamlieli, were both vulnerable and supportive of the monarchy. They took the wealthy Jewish merchants of Damt as prisoners and looted their homes. Those who paid large ransoms were released. Other, more obstinate Jews remained in prison for the short lifespan of the revolutionary regime.[44]

The descriptions of Yemeni Muslims' reactions to Zionism contained in the self-published accounts by Jews from Yemen ought to be taken with more than the usual degree of skepticism. They are often keen to demonstrate sympathy for the Zionist movement among the Muslim elite. For example, Yeḥiel Ḥibshūsh tells of a conversation with one of Imām Yaḥyā's top aides on the day the King David Hotel was bombed. The sayyid explained that the Zionists in Palestine would defeat the armies of the neighboring Arab countries "because they [the Arabs] have lands and cities of their own. In contrast, you Jews act out of understandable motives. The Jews do not have any place other than Palestine."[45] In contrast, Ṣāliḥ al-Ẓāhirī and others observed that the animosity of Muslim Yemenis toward Jews increased after the establishment of the State of Israel.[46]

On occasion competing stances on the Palestine question led to intra-Muslim disputes. A Jewish writer explains how a grassroots boycott of Jewish merchants in one village market was publicly denounced by the local sharīʿa court judge.[47] Arabic sources attest to strong opposition to Zionism, as well as empathy for the Jews in Yemen and abroad, among the Yemeni elite. Already in 1925 Yemenite Jews in Jerusalem had complained that opposition to Yemenite Jewish immigration to Palestine from the Jerusalemite mufti Amīn al-Husseini had led the imām to curtail their freedoms in Yemen. However, Israeli politician Yisrael Yeshayahu disputed this claim, arguing that foreigners, even those of the pious Muslim variety, held little sway over the imām and (more improbably) that he upheld the Jews' stake on Israel much like an evangelical Christian.[48] Husseini had earned a reputation as a pan-Islamic leader for his opposition to Zionism. Imām Yaḥyā sent an emissary, Muḥammad Zabārah, to the general Islamic conference in Jerusalem in 1931, where Zabārah initiated a long relationship with the mufti.[49] In 1934 Husseini visited Yemen in order to assist in mediating a cease-fire in a conflict with Saudi Arabia.[50] According to Tudor Parfitt, the mufti impressed upon Imām Yaḥyā his opposition to Jewish immigration to Palestine from Yemen, and the imām restricted Jewish emigration after this visit.

Sālim Manṣūrah says the mufti met with Chief Rabbi Yaḥyā al-Abyaḍ. During his meeting with the rabbi, Husseini is said to have asked for a written account of the Jews' satisfaction with life under the imāms. For the rabbi, having to write such an account constituted a "lose-lose" situation: his expression of contentment with life in Yemen would bolster the case against allowing emigration to Palestine, and his expression of discontent might signal a rising tide of rebelliousness among the Jewish population that the imām would need to address forcefully. According to Manṣūrah, Imām Yaḥyā's son ʿAlī was present at a meeting between the imām and the mufti and told him that the mufti had presented the imām with Rabbi Abyaḍ's letter, the contents of which are a mystery, and that the imām agreed to curtail the movement of Jews from Yemen.[51] Shortly after the United Nations vote to partition Palestine in 1947, British officials complained that one of the mufti's emissaries had worsened tensions between Muslims and Jews in Aden, where eighty-two Jews had been killed in riots.[52] The riots in Aden frightened the Jews of nearby Bayḥān, who were reassured when the town's governor had the following message broadcast from the minarets:

> Citizens are forbidden from committing any act against the Jews who live with us. From one who takes clay from them we shall take blood. To all who want to go and wage *jihād* with the Muslims of Palestine we give permission—let him go. But the Jews who live with us are our responsibility (*akwālinā*).[53]

Three years after the mufti's visit, Imām Yaḥyā sent him a contribution of thirteen hundred pounds. The year after that Prince Aḥmad gathered contributions and sent them to him. Prince Ḥusayn kept in contact with the mufti and sent him donations until his death in 1948.[54] In a poem, a sayyid who briefly ruled Radāʿ and who Jews considered fair in his dealings asked the Muslims of the world the question: "Is there succor for our brothers in faith [Palestinians] when they are harmed by a humiliated and abased people?"[55] Jamal and Manṣūrah say that Yemen's de facto prime minister, ʿAbdallāh al-ʿAmrī, was both highly supportive of the mufti and greatly troubled by the Nazi persecution of the Jews of Europe. In 1944 he asked Manṣūrah whether he knew what was happening to European Jewry and advised local Jews to pray for them.[56]

In a 1938 telegram on Palestine to Adolf Hitler, Benito Mussolini, Edouard Daladier, and Neville Chamberlain, later published in the state newspaper, *Al-Īmān,* Imām Yaḥyā asked the European leaders "to set up a fine, sufficient, verdant place appropriate for the Jews other than Islamic Palestine, which is eternally holy to Muslims."[57] Imām Yaḥyā's son Ḥusayn represented Yemen at the 1939 St. James Conference on Palestine in London. There he warned that events in Palestine were radicalizing the Yemeni masses and that his father's attempts to calm the situation and dissuade Jews from leaving Yemen were not enough to protect the large Jewish community from reactionary violence.[58] In a speech that was sharply critical of Zionism, he called upon the gathered Muslim leaders:

> Let us feel genuine compassion for what the Jews have suffered, mourn for them, and undertake all legal means that may reduce their suffering and enable them to achieve their share of simple happiness in life. However, I cannot

> deny that sympathy for the Jews in all of the Arab countries is diminished and becomes lax on account of the events in Palestine.[59]

One historian claims that one of Imām Yaḥyā's aides, 'Abd al-Karīm Muṭahhar, although a functionary in the xenophobic government of the supposed backwater that is Yemen, showed a keen eye to developments in 1920s Palestine that most of his Arab contemporaries in Palestine and elsewhere did not possess. He saw that Jewish immigration was being used to found a Jewish state and that Palestinian opposition to Zionism was not limited to rioting among Muslims but included (nonviolent) protests to the British by both Muslims and Christians.[60]

In Yemen by the late 1940s, contradictory disinformation about events in Palestine abounded. Ṣāliḥ al-Ẓāhirī, who had left Yemen, sent Hebrew newspapers to his son Mordecai, who was in prison. The Jew translated *Haarets, Davar,* and *Ma'ariv,* along with several lesser-known newspapers, for Muslim inmates.[61] One of Mordecai al-Ẓāhirī's fellow prisoners asked him to remember their friendship, get him out of prison, and spare his family "if, at some point, the Israeli army attacks and conquers Yemen."[62] His father heard the same thing from Muslim friends of his.[63] Ẓāhirī heard rumors ranging from exaggerated pronouncements of Arab military victories to the idea that the Zionist army possessed atomic weapons from "fanatical Muslims and simpletons." "Nevertheless," he writes, "most or all of them used to declare in public that there was nothing connecting what happened in the Land of Israel to the way of life in Yemen insofar as [the rumors] dealt with Jews in Palestine, who were Zionists, and not with Jewish 'People of the Pact' in Yemen."[64] In contrast, "some simple people in the lower echelon of the Yemeni government used abusive language in regard to Jews: 'you are already fooling the head [of state], having learned from the Zionists.'"[65]

While it is unlikely that the Yemeni elite sympathized with Israel, their interests occasionally clashed with those of Arab nationalists outside of Yemen. During World War II Yemen suffered from long periods of drought and epidemics. A general deterioration in economic life brought about by high prices and the scarcity of goods harmed the community as well. Against this backdrop, Imām Yaḥyā may have done an about-face on his position on Jewish emigration from Yemen to Palestine. (Avraham Madhalah attributes the imām's change of heart to a disturbing dream he had in which his father ordered him to release the rooster from the chicken coop. The rooster represented the Jews and the chicken coop represented Yemen.[66]) In a letter by Yitsḥaq Ben-Tsvi to David Ben-Gurion, Ben-Tsvi said a visiting Arab delegation had warned Imām Yaḥyā that Yemen's Jews would become foot soldiers in a war against Islam. The imām silenced them by saying if they or their countries agreed to support the Jews, he would return to his old policy of strictly enforcing laws against leaving.[67] Imām Aḥmad, for his part, distrusted the Arab League and the Muslim Brotherhood for their support of the coup following his father's assassination.[68] In 1967, during the civil war that gripped Yemen after Aḥmad's death in 1962, Zaydī tribes cheered the Egyptian defeat at the hands of the Israelis.[69] Since Egypt backed the overthrow of the imāmate, they must have reasoned that Israel was the lesser of the two evils. In addition the Palestine question served as a foil for debates concerning only Yemen. An opponent of Imām Yaḥyā, Ḥusayn Muḥammad al-Maqbalī, recalls his strategy when he wrote a sharply worded article attacking Zionism. "The aggression (*ʿunf*) found in the article was not actually directed at the Zionists. Instead Imām Yaḥyā, his family, and his system of government were the targets."[70]

Jewish intermediaries like Ẓāhirī, Jamal, and Manṣūrah describe individual Muslims as "Jew haters," "fanatical Muslims," or "foes of the Jews." Yet such accounts of dyed-in-the-wool anti-Semites contradict one another. For example, Jamal identifies Imām Yaḥyā's son Aḥmad (later imām himself) as a Jew hater, while Sālim Manṣūrah saw him as fair and compassionate in his dealings with Jews. Manṣūrah identifies Aḥmad al-Jīrāfī as an Arab nationalist who squeezed Jewish emigrants for cash.[71] Jamal and Aharon Ḥamdi describe him as a righteous man. Jamal singles out the chief judge Zayd al-Daylamī as a Jew hater. Ṣāliḥ al-Ẓāhirī describes his close friendship with the chief judge, who ate with his family on Fridays. Although Ẓāhirī does not name the man (having already discussed his appetite for bribes), there is a good chance that he was the same person. Ẓāhirī visited his son Ḥasan, a wealthy landowner who lived in a rural area south of Dhamār, and asked about the elder Daylamī's well-being.[72]

To Beat a Qadi

In his study of interreligious relations in medieval Aragon, Nirenberg outlined several overlapping spheres of social violence, including both the institutional and the systemic, or ritual. According to him, ritualized violence against minorities could simultaneously integrate them into the larger society and "make brutally clear the sharp boundaries . . . that separated [them]."[73] Nirenberg also pointed out the extent to which violence against minorities could represent a type of communication between different factions within the majority.[74] Yet what does minority violence against members of the majority mean? This is a situation he does not analyze.

One of Ṣāliḥ al-Ẓāhirī's anecdotes, a complicated story of spiraling violence, illustrates well the interconnectedness of the various factors motivating interreligious violence in Yemen. Each of two Muslims in Radāʿ sold the same parcel of land to two prominent families, the Daylamīs and the Ghālibs. Each seller claimed to have inherited the land from his father. The two families pursued legal action, and a qadi from Sanaa, Ḥamūd al-Jandārī, was appointed as an arbitrator.[75] Ẓāhirī, who held a very low opinion of Jandārī, writes:

> When he stood in court [al-Jandārī] not dare denounce the Jews or say that he was not prepared to adjudicate because the prosecutor or the defender was a

Ṣāliḥ al-Ẓāhirī soon after emigrating to Israel in 1949, from Mordecai Yitshari, *Ḥayyim so'arim.*

Jew. This is because the law gave no special status to either [Muslim or Jewish] party in a litigation except in matters of evidence, where the testimony of a Jew or a woman against a Muslim was not accepted.[76]

Two contradictory wills were presented at the arbitration between the Daylamīs and the Ghālibs. In one of them, the father left his land to the son who had sold it to the Daylamīs. In the other will, the father left the land to his other son, who had sold it to the Ghālibs. Ḥamūd al-Jandārī judged that second will had been written more recently and thus during the father's descent into senility, a point he supported with reference to the newness of the paper and ink.

The Ghālibs asked the Jew Ṣāliḥ al-Ẓāhirī to appeal the decision to Sanaa. Ẓāhirī plied the Daylamī family attorney, ʿAbdallāh b. ʿAbbās, with lunch and a gift of perfume for his wife. The attorney, who was an "extroverted person," comfortable in the Jew's company, and unhappy with the low fee he had received from the Daylamīs, revealed to Ẓāhirī that the family had bribed Jandārī to receive a positive outcome by giving him a large plot of land that they owned next to his house. They had underpaid the lawyer because he was superfluous.[77]

Ẓāhirī's story relies upon an additional subplot. A Jewish widow from Sanaa married a Jew from Radāʿ and moved there with her daughter from her previous marriage. Both women were beautiful, Ẓāhirī adds (and this detail will become relevant). Five years later the new husband pressured his wife to marry her daughter to a Jew from eastern Yemen with whom he had lived for a time, rejecting many other potential suitors. Mother and daughter disliked this man intensely. "[He] grew up in a primitive environment and lacked the natural attributes and cultural habits of an urban environment," the daughter is reputed to have said. The women called him "the Bedouin."

One Sabbath in the fall of 1939, "the Bedouin" returned home and made a drunken pass at his wife. He did not see his mother-in-law standing nearby. The older woman berated him and punched him in the face. He threatened her, which only made her angrier. She took off her shoe and proceeded to beat him. Her husband appeared and, seeing his wife beating the man, slapped her, kicked her, and dragged her into the next room with the expectation that she would calm down. The two men left the house to defuse the situation. When they returned several hours later the women were missing. The two men went looking for them and heard from a Jew who lived at the edge of the Jewish Quarter of Radāʿ that he had seen them heading west, probably to Qadi Ḥamūd al-Jandārī's house.

The two men told Ṣaliḥ al-Ẓāhirī, who was entertaining with friends and students, what had happened. The group debated the proper course of action. One faction was of the opinion that while the presence of beautiful married Jewish women in the qadi's house was galling, it was understandable insofar as the women were Sanaani through and through "in their idioms and accent" (and presumably in their aristocratic bearing) and thus sought the protection of another Sanaani, albeit a Muslim man. Moreover, since Ḥamūd al-Jandārī hated Jews, there was no practical way for the two men to retrieve their wives. Finally, the women were rebellious and did not merit risking danger.

Ẓāhirī, in contrast, planned to save the women's honor (which, it seems, was an extension of that of their husbands). One of his students, Shim'on Cohen, from a family of potters in a village northeast of Radāʿ, agreed to help Ẓāhirī.[78] The two of them recruited a Jewish merchant woman who sold to the Jandārī family, Mrs. Ṣubārī, to help them. Ẓāhirī carried a walking stick, "in the manner of the important Muslims of status from among the notables of the city." Mrs. Ṣubārī knocked on the door of the Jandārī house and announced that Ẓāhirī wanted the two women released so that they would return to their husbands. Ḥamūd al-Jandārī threatened Ẓāhirī with violence, first from the fourth-story window, then from the door.

Ẓāhirī made a gesture of handing Jandārī his staff, then warned of the damage to the qadi's reputation were he to publicize his being alone with married Jewish women. Jandārī began beating him with the stick. Shim'on Cohen found a tree branch and struck Jandārī on the forehead. At the end of the ensuing free-for-all Cohen had received a superficial but bloody chest wound from the qadi's *janbiyyah*. In addition, Jandārī's twenty-something son and his brother-in-law had been beaten by Cohen, and Jandārī sustained two additional heavy blows to the head.

The local courthouse was only ten minutes away and the authorities swiftly intervened. A qadi took a statement from Jandārī, then advised him to attend to his head wounds while the damage assessor was consulted. The qadi ordered soldiers to arrest and imprison Cohen.

Ẓāhirī went to the assessor's house with a soldier. It was nighttime by now, and the assessor, who was a friend of Ẓāhirī's, used a brush by lamplight to find the bruises under the hair on his scalp. He had already seen Jandārī's wounds. When the assessor touched Ẓāhirī's head, the Jew cried out in pain, grabbed the assessor's hand, and slipped him five riyāls that he had readied on the way there. Every time the damage assessor "found" a new bruise with the aid of the Jew's histrionic exclamations, he recorded the magnitude of the injury. He dropped his report on the way out and Ẓāhirī pocketed it. (Perhaps he hadn't dropped it at all.) The Jew then wrote a telegram to Imām Yaḥyā telling him of the disappearance of the Jewish women and the altercation at Jandārī's house. Unspecified Muslims telegraphed the imām as well, alerting him to the assault on Jandārī. A local qadi who was a friend of Cohen's, Muḥammad al-ʿIzzānī, attempted to elicit Cohen's version of events.[79]

Cohen was apprehended and bound with four shackles, which was unusual.[80] Ẓāhirī was arrested as well. Soldiers went to Jandārī's house, retrieved the Jewish women, and returned them to their husbands. The local governor, the sayyid Yaḥyā al-Dhārī (d. 1945), interviewed Ẓāhirī, intending to relay the details to the imām.[81] Ẓāhirī claimed that Jandārī's own son-in-law, disoriented by the darkness, had inflicted his head wounds.

Shimʿon Cohen also misled investigators. When a judge asked him to remove his clothes and then inquired about the blood on his chest, Cohen claimed that it came from a slaughtered animal whose lungs he was checking for ritual impurity. When the judge retorted that only a rabbi (*ʿaylum*) could certify ritual purity, Cohen replied, "I am a priest (*cohen*)—above a rabbi!"

According to Ẓāhirī, Ḥamūd al-Jandārī, stung by the shame of having been beaten up by "the son of a Jewish potter woman," changed his story on the night of the incident after having spoken to the investigating qadi. Henceforth he accused Ẓāhirī of having struck him. In his court testimony Jandārī insisted upon calling Ẓāhirī a *ḥarbī* (a non-Muslim who is not protected by the state), even after the judge interjected that "dhimmī" (Person of the Pact) was the appropriate term. His stated intention was to brand Ẓāhirī "a rebel and a man who fought against the Yemeni monarchy and its citizens so that his penalty would be death."[82]

Ẓāhirī rushed to visit Shimʿon Cohen and convinced him to read his testimony from a prepared statement that the older man had written in complex literary language. He included short vowels so that Cohen would pronounce the Arabic words properly. (Written Arabic normally contains vowels only in texts intended for children and in copies of the Qur'an.) Cohen read this speech, which included a denial of Jandārī's charges, in court. The judge and his scribe could barely keep from smiling and the audience erupted in laughter when they heard a language "whose proper place was the Friday prayers in the mosque" emanating from a low-status man like Cohen.[83] The judge announced that witnesses' testimony would be heard in three months' time.

Ẓāhirī signed a "bail bond" and paid fifty riyāls for Cohen's release from prison, and Cohen returned to his work as a builder. Jandārī's relatives attempted to get revenge. "All who ambushed him and tried to harm him earned Cohen's fisticuffs," writes Ẓāhirī. He explains that they then hid the shame of having been beaten up by him, "for if it was known that a Muslim was struck by a Jew the matter would have been considered a great shame for him and his entire family."[84]

Ẓāhirī details with particular relish his fight with one of Jandārī's relatives outside of the public latrine adjoining a mosque. After turning the tables on his assailant, Cohen is said to have said, "The Torah enjoins the priest to lash you this way," as he counted out the blows he rained on the man with a stick. When it became clear to the man that Cohen intended to put him in the toilet, he begged to be released. "Don't worry," Cohen said. "I won't dip you in Jewish excrement—only the feces of pious Muslims like you." When the man promised never to attack Cohen again, he was allowed to leave.[85]

Rumors that Jandārī had hired men to kill Cohen soon circulated. In response to the fear in his extended family, Ẓāhirī advised Cohen to travel to Aden. He cut off his sidelocks, wore "Muslim clothes," "impersonated a Muslim before those he happened upon on the way," and traveled south using back roads. When he feared that Jandārī's men might find him in Aden, he traveled to Asmara in Eritrea. (Many merchants from Radāʿ worked in Asmara.[86]) From Asmara he traveled to Sudan.

Not long after Cohen's departure, Jandārī asked the local judge to allow two witnesses to testify prior to their upcoming court date, as they had pressing business in Asmara. The judge denied his request, saying the court had to attend to other pressing matters, but suggested that the men might testify before any authorized notary and introduce the testimony later. The witnesses appeared before the notary Qadi Muḥammad al-ʿIzzānī (Shimʿon Cohen's friend). They testified that shortly after the incident they had run into Ṣāliḥ al-Ẓāhirī in a jewelry shop and that he had told them that both he and Cohen had hit Qadi al-Jandārī in the head. They said Ẓāhirī had asked them what they would have done if a man were alone with their wives. They replied that they would not have been satisfied with a beating but would have killed the man responsible. They also testified that they knew Ẓāhirī well, since he had worked as an attorney for one of their relatives.[87]

Ṣāliḥ al-Ẓāhirī says that he encountered Jandārī by chance soon after this and asked him how he could justify flouting the Islamic prohibition against false witnessing. He said that Jandārī explained that the punishment only applied to Muslims who bore false testimony against other Muslims. "However, a Muslim's oath against a Jew will earn him an additional reward in paradise," the qadi is reported to have replied.[88]

Ẓāhirī then organized a "sting operation" against Jandārī's witnesses. First he bribed their shaykh with "a reasonable sum" and the shaykh convinced them to tell the Jew the truth. Ẓāhirī invited them to his home and acted hospitably toward them. The witnesses told him that before they had testified against him, they had been brought to Jandārī's house. He had paid them "a reasonable sum" and returned a parcel of land that he had seized two years earlier for nonpayment of rent from a tenant farmer who was their relative. They further admitted that their testimony had been scripted by Jandārī.

Unbeknownst to the two men, the mayor of Radāʿ and his secretary were sitting in an adjacent room whose door was concealed with a curtain. After the men confessed, these two onlookers appeared and cursed the men. The false witnesses fell at their feet, pleading for forgiveness and kissing their shoes. Ẓāhirī asked the mayor and his aide to keep what they had heard a secret unless these witnesses neglected to follow a new plan that he then outlined. Ẓāhirī advised them to go to the courthouse and testify anew that the "Ṣāliḥ al-Ẓāhirī" they had seen in the jewelry shop was an old man.

In court Ẓāhirī contested the men's earlier testimony by arguing, in essence, that a defendant must have the right to confront his accusers. Jandārī countered that no such right applied to Jews, much less a "warlike Jew" like Ẓāhirī. "The testimony of Muslims against Jews is accepted in every circumstance, even if it is not in [their] presence," Jandārī argued. Furthermore, even if the point that the witnesses ought to testify in the defendant's presence were conceded, they were in Asmara and could not appear in court, he added. The judge ruled that their prior testimony would be legally admissible only if Ẓāhirī agreed to their not appearing.

Present in court was ʿAbdallāh Ghālib, a scion of the patrician Radāʿ family who had sought Ẓāhirī's intervention in the land dispute that revolved around Jandārī at the beginning of this story. He stood up and said, "Excuse me, your honor. I heard the names of the witnesses and I know them personally. They are here. This morning they were in my shop and bought goods from me."

The judge sent two soldiers to fetch the men, and in half an hour they returned and brought the men in one at a time. The first witness repeated his testimony about the fighting words they had heard from "Ṣāliḥ al-Ẓāhirī." Ẓāhirī asked him, "Did you see me?" and he replied that he was not the man they had seen. "Ṣāliḥ al-Ẓāhirī is another man, who does not resemble you at all," the witness said, trembling, his face pallid. "He was an older man with a white beard and wrinkled cheeks." Jandārī protested and the judge prodded, but the witness insisted he had seen someone else, adding that "a man's neck depends upon his testimony and I cannot change the truth."

The second witness corroborated the new story. (The first witness was still present.) The judge evidently found the story dubious and, with his face contorted in anger, warned the witness to tell the truth. The second witness relented. "What is to be done, sir? Sometimes Satan causes man to stray. I swear to God I do not want to go to hell. Ḥamūd al-Jandārī's son-in-law controlled us like Satan, enticing us to undertake this error," he said. The judge delivered a sentence against the two men for false witnessing: (nonlethal) crucifixion in the market in the sunlight, ten lashes during each of the first three days, then prison and two chains. Jandārī's son-in-law was given prison with two chains.

Ẓāhirī then introduced a new argument. Even if the witnesses were telling the truth the first time and Ẓāhirī was the one who struck Jandārī, this would contradict Jandārī's testimony given on the night of the incident that Shimʿon Cohen had done it. The judge announced a postponement of the proceedings for an additional two weeks. Ẓāhirī was asked to either go to jail in Cohen's stead or pay five hundred riyāls for his bond. The Ghālibs advised him to pay the bond rather than risking the potential damage to his honor of people thinking he had been jailed at Jandārī's behest and not as surety for Cohen. They offered to pay all or part of the fee themselves and with the assistance of other unnamed people, presumably Muslims, who wanted to maximize the damage to Jandārī's reputation that the incident was causing him.

Jandārī met with the assessor again to retrieve the report on his wounds that he had written on the night of the incident. Ẓāhirī spoke with the assessor afterward. The assessor asked Ẓāhirī where the report he had written on him had gone. The Jew feigned ignorance to its location but promised to look for it. He met the assessor the next day, report in hand. However, this was not the report that the assessor had written on the night of the incident but a document of Ẓāhirī's own devising. He entered the assessor's house, copied the forged report, signed it, and gave both copies to the assessor. The assessor said he did not need the copy, since the Jew had found the original. (In his original report the assessor's exaggeration of Ẓāhirī's injuries had been facilitated by a small bribe and Ẓāhirī's cries of pain during the examination. This second report must have exaggerated them even further.)

Two days before the appointed court date, while Cohen was in the Sudan, Ẓāhirī asked the judge for a continuance, claiming that Cohen had disappeared. Cohen had told his family that he was going to Ṣaʿdah, north of Radāʿ, and Ẓāhirī introduced a receipt for a telegram as evidence for his having sent Cohen a message in Ṣaʿdah several days earlier asking him to return for his court appearance. The judge reminded Ẓāhirī that he would have to either pay Cohen's bond or be jailed in his place as surety. He also postponed the trial an additional three weeks. When the new date arrived, Ẓāhirī paid the five hundred riyāls and the judge suggested that he and Jandārī submit to arbitration.

Jandārī evidently concluded that after having suborned perjury, the best he could hope for was to receive monetary damages from Ẓāhirī. Jandārī chose Qadi Muḥammad al-ʿIzzānī's son, Qadi ʿAbdallāh al-ʿIzzānī, as arbitrator. The Jew selected the mayor, Qadi Muḥammad ʿAbd al-ʿAzīz, as the arbitrator. Jandārī's damage assessment report indicated he had sustained 620 riyāls in damages. Ẓāhirī's (forged) damages amounted to 390 riyāls. The younger al-ʿIzzānī, judging by the superficiality (even invisibility) of Ẓāhirī's wounds, accused him of having cast a spell on the assessor, who was known for his integrity. "I would not have thought that a wise and learned man like you would occupy himself with belief in follies in which only the hoi polloi believe," Ẓāhirī replied. Jandārī protested as well, but the arbitrator reminded him of the fragility of his position given his contradictory testimony about who had hit him and his involvement in tampering with witnesses.

Qadi ʿAbdallāh al-ʿIzzānī suggested as a settlement that Ẓāhirī, while not admitting culpability for the assault on Jandārī, pay half of the 230 riyāl difference between the damages sustained by the two men, buy a bull or a cow, accompany the arbitrators and others unnamed to Jandārī's house on a day of his choosing, and present the animal there for slaughter. Three of the Ghālib men went to the market to buy a bull, loudly informing all passers-by that its slaughter would appease Ḥamūd al-Jandārī for the blows he had received from a Jew. In order to gainsay an audience for this event, Jandārī waived the custom of slaughtering a bull as a sign of subservience and contrition, and the matter came to an end.[89]

On the face of it, Ẓāhirī's story possesses the cumulative and violent qualities of folk songs like "The House That Jack Built." It also resembles the familiar wish-fulfillment folktale in which the weak defeats the powerful. Like the amoral Br'er Rabbit of the *Uncle Remus Tales,* the Jew uses every means at his disposal, including deceit, forgery, and blackmail, to humiliate and defeat his enemy. He arranges for his Muslim foe to receive a beating and gets away with it. In terms of the sharīʿa, whose courts serve as the stage for much of the story's action, the central salient point is that the testimony of Jews is of such low value that it is practically impossible for them to offer testimony against Muslims. Thus Ẓāhirī beats his powerful foe, as it were, with one hand tied behind his back.

The case calls to mind as well political theorist Wendy Brown's analysis of a "politics of injury," rooted in Nietzschean "*ressentiment,*" which claims minority rights through the legal system while strengthening the hegemonic power of that system in doing so. In his unapologetic pursuit of power (and his unconcern with violence), Ṣāliḥ al-Ẓāhirī appears to be less Nietzsche's cringing mouthpiece for ressentiment and more his leonine "magnificent blond beast roaming lecherously in search of booty and victory," characteristic of the noble races (including the Arabs) when released in the wilderness outside of conventional morality.[90]

Yet the dynamics of the story are still more complex and involve a series of violent reversals of the social hierarchy. The story shows the multifaceted and interconnected nature of the social hierarchy itself. Individual Yemenis are beholden to status-driven systems based on religion, tribe, gender, profession, and geography, which at times conflict with one another and at times offer their own distinctive methods to resolve these conflicts. The Jew Ṣāliḥ al-Ẓāhirī's violent confrontation with Qadi al-Jandārī challenges the social boundaries between Muslims and non-Muslims, a fact that enables the qadi to attempt to brand him a rebel against the state (a ḥarbī). However, the Muslim attorney, who, unhappy with his pay, reveals the plotting of the sayyid Daylamī family to the Jew, thereby transgresses such boundaries himself. So too the Jewish woman who beats her bumpkin son-in-law, claiming to deserve better as a cosmopolitan woman of Sanaa, challenges men's putative monopoly on violence.

Shimʿon Cohen's physical assaults on the men of the Jandārī clan shames them not only because of his Jewishness but also because he is the son of a potter woman. When he addresses the court in elegant language, Cohen's doubly low status occasions laughter. Ironically it also allows him to assault a number of Muslim men, since they are too embarrassed to report it. Qadi al-Jandārī is among them, and his unsuccessful attempt to take retribution for his beating without admitting it was Cohen who had beaten him ultimately allows the potter's son to go unpunished. His low status also heightens the sardonic humor of his threat to use one of Jandārī's relatives as a tool for latrine work.

The plot hinges upon gradations of power and the attendant ability to inflict violence. At the top rest the imām, his soldiers, and the judicial apparatus. Yet influential tribal shaykhs wield considerable power, which the imām ignores at his peril. In Yemeni society even sayyids and qadis, high-status Muslims, were understood to live under the protection of the tribes. In this story, when the false witnesses have to choose between crossing a sayyid (al-Jandārī) and crossing their shaykh, they choose the former.

The dispute between the two wealthy sayyid families, the Daylamīs and the Ghālibs, forms the outermost ring in the story's concentric circles of conflict. They put the Jew up to assaulting the qadi who has cheated them, and then they shoulder at least some of the costs of the trial and its settlement. Ẓāhirī's desire to remove the two Jewish women from Jandārī's house represents an attempt to preserve the status of their husbands who, as Jewish men, share his own rung in the hierarchy. (Ẓāhirī's second wife considers him a bully. He will not give her a divorce, so she leaves him and converts to Islam along with their daughter. She later emigrates to Israel and reconverts to Judaism, but her daughter, who is married to a Muslim, remains in Yemen.[91])

Most of the individuals involved in this case possess conflicted loyalties. Recurring throughout the story are instances in which one person is forced to choose between their status-driven affinity to a second person and their social familiarity or friendship with a third person. In the instance discussed above, a Jew sides with his friend over his wife. The two Jewish women choose their geographical affinity with Qadi al-Jandārī over their affinity to their religious community. The Jew Mrs. Ṣubārī, who does business with the Jandārī family, is enlisted as an agent in the defense of Jewish manhood when she acts as the "lookout" for Ẓāhirī and Cohen in their quest to recover the errant women. The Muslim lawyer sides with his friend, the Jew Ẓāhirī, over his peer, Qadi al-Jandārī. Ẓāhirī chooses the Jews over his friendship with the assessor. Qadi ʿAbdallāh al-ʿIzzānī disregards his father's friendship with Shimʿon Cohen when he agrees to serve as Qadi al-Jandārī's arbitrator. The mayor of Radāʿ and the Ghālib family side with Ẓāhirī against Qadi al-Jandārī. As a tale of the triumph of the weak over the strong, in this case a Jew against a Muslim judge, one is struck by the fact that the Muslims involved never close ranks against the Jew, resulting in the judge's losing despite the legal disadvantages to which the Jew was subject.

The loyalties of the two false witnesses, who are cousins, are the most thoroughly tangled, and they play their hand poorly. Their loyalty to a kinsman who has lost his land to Qadi al-Jandārī outweighs their personal relationship with Ẓāhirī, leading them to commit perjury. Their loyalty to their shaykh outweighs that loyalty. Their claim of not knowing Ẓāhirī disintegrates under scrutiny. They are finally undone by their mercantile relationship with ʿAbdallāh Ghālib, who knows they were not in Eritrea and chooses the Jew Ẓāhirī over them.

Punctuating the narrative are consultative interludes involving interreligious eating in private homes, during which actors cement their bonds, thereby strengthening their positions for the ensuing conflicts. Ẓāhirī eats with the Muslim lawyer, announces his intention of confronting Qadi al-Jandārī while entertaining other Jews on the Sabbath, and hosts the false witnesses. Qadi Muḥammad al-ʿIzzānī visits Shimʿon Cohen at home in the hopes of hearing his side of the story. The various outbreaks of violence reverse the home's proper role as a place of mediation and an extension of the honor of its owner and his group. Thus the intrusion into Qadi al-Jandārī's home calls for the ritual slaughter of a bull therein, a tribal custom that recalibrated relationships that had gone sour and as restitution for transgressions. The fact that invoking this right would have forced the qadi to publicize his shame constitutes the final moving part in Ẓāhirī's elaborate scheme.

Structurally, the instances of violence seem neither ritualized nor cathartic. Instead they represent bids to radically redistribute honor and shame, power and weakness, with these qualities understood as being zero-sum in nature. The Jewish woman from Sanaa wants her "Bedouin" son-in-law to be subservient to her. Ẓāhirī and Shimʿon Cohen want power over Qadi al-Jandārī. The sharīʿa court's violent public humiliation of the false witnesses is retribution for their affront to religion and the imām.

Each violent act is, in turn, manipulated by others who occupy a higher rung of the hierarchy. Qadi al-Jandārī likely seeks to derive benefit from the domestic violence in the Jewish home, and the Ghālib family benefits from Ẓāhirī's and Cohen's humiliation of Jandārī. Finally, in punishing the false witnesses, the imām perhaps sends a message of deterrence to unruly tribesmen.

Ṣāliḥ al-Ẓāhirī, while similar to Sālim Saʿīd al-Jamal in profession, status, and intimate knowledge of the Islamic legal system, portrayed the law in a markedly different manner than did Jamal. Jamal presents himself as a principled advocate for individual rights and the rule of law in their most universalistic iterations. The climax of the Jew's sting operation, when the mayor rebukes the false witnesses, thereby demonstrating the falsehood of Qadi al-Jandārī's contention that Islam not only permits swearing falsely against Jews but also encourages it, becomes, for Ẓāhirī, simply another means by which he may maximize his honor and humiliate his enemy. In Jamal's self-presentation, this triumph of the sharīʿa's universality over its hierarchical nature would have been the key moment of the entire story.

In terms of the actual operation of the sharīʿa court system, in this story one finds a seemingly paradoxical combination of scrupulousness and dishonesty, severity and leniency. A judicial bureaucracy springs to action to gather information, render judgment, apprehend and jail suspects, and punish those who are judged guilty. But people who are widely regarded as honest and fair accept bribes or show partiality (almost always toward Ẓāhirī). Yet the public crucifixion and beating of the false witnesses demonstrates that there were ethical boundaries that could be contravened only at great risk.

Qadi al-Jandārī's putative hatred for the Jews plays a role in the events insofar as it gives him the motive and opportunity to exploit the sharīʿa's handicap against non-Muslims in the realm of testimony. (Although when he pays witnesses and is caught, he overplays his hand.) Nevertheless, the central salient point to be gleaned from the story is that the dividing line between Muslim and Jew operated within a much larger hierarchically organized network of conflicting loyalties and that the most powerful Muslim did not always win.

As a final note to the issue of Jewish violence against Muslims, it is worth bearing in mind that Jews shared in the nonlegal tribal ethos of Yemen that placed great value upon a person's honor. Occasional violence presumably lent credibility to a person's self-presentation as one capable of dealing out violence. While Jews may have possessed less of it than did Muslims, neither group would deny that some Jews and Muslims were more honorable (and thus more worthy of business partnerships and other beneficial social ties) than others. The prospect of what amounted to stealing honor from a Muslim likely justified the expenditures in legal fees that some Jews made. Even if the beating took place "behind the scenes," at least other Jews would get wind of such symbolic victories. Muslims who had exceeded a level of humiliation that Jews could tolerate could be chastened through such attacks (through both the violence itself and the mediation by elders that followed).

The 1948 Sanaa "Blood Libel"

The possibility that Jewish violence against Muslims could exceed even the beating of an important Muslim man arose a number of times in Yemen during the early twentieth century. Jewish sources describe several instances when Muslims accused Jews of murder. For years a Muslim alcoholic from a prominent family in the Muslim neighborhood that adjoined the Jewish Quarter of Sanaa, "al-Balaqah," frequented festive occasions and houses in mourning in the Jewish Quarter with the knowledge that ʿaraq would be served in those places. He collapsed on a Jewish street and died. His family accused the Jews of having murdered him. A judge rounded up Jewish workers and demanded a 1,600-riyāl payment for their release.[92] In general, tensions ran high between the Muslims of Balaqah, who were mainly laborers, and the Jews in the neighboring Jewish Quarter, who referred to them as "the people of Balaq (the king of Moab)."[93]

A Jewish shoemaker who was the only Jew living in a certain small village was accused of murdering its shaykh when the shaykh's corpse was discovered near the Jew's shop. Witnesses testified that the Jew killed the man. Imām Yaḥyā's representative had the Jew and the witnesses brought to Sanaa. Under the imām's questioning, the shoemaker is said to have asked, in turn, "What motive would I have had to kill him? Would I be allowed to assume his post and become the shaykh of the village?" Following his investigation, the imām discovered that the shaykh's rivals had had him killed and arranged for false testimony. They were severely punished and the Jew received 700 riyāls as compensation.[94]

The fact that Jews were sometimes wrongfully accused of killing Muslims does not mean that individual Jews were always innocent of such crimes. The Jews of a small village in the south decided to have a troublesome tribesman killed, probably in the 1920s. They hired a Muslim who dabbled as a peddler, cattle rustler, and contract killer to commit the murder. During the attempted murder the man was only wounded, so the Jews of the village scattered in fear of vengeance. In a nearby village the sudden influx of Jews taxed the local synagogue, which lacked a rabbi. In a strange coincidence, a learned Jew from Sanaa who happened to have been fleeing after having killed a Muslim himself, arrived in the village and agreed to serve.[95]

In Dhamār, probably in the mid-1920s, a robber dubbed "the Climbing Cat" terrorized the Jewish community (whether he burglarized Muslim homes as well is unclear). He began by breaking in to a house and frightening the women by appearing suddenly with his dagger drawn. His break-ins became increasingly brazen. He moved on to demanding food, then demanding alcohol (of which he was especially fond), and finally demanding the women give him their valuables. "Woe to her who hid something from him," writes Yosef ʿAtsṭah. Since the robber came from a wealthy and well-connected family, Jewish leaders despaired of a legal solution and three of them decided to kill him. They began to invite him to their homes to drink. On one occasion he drank until he passed out. The three Jewish leaders killed him and buried his corpse in the town dump.

Three months after the disappearance of the Climbing Cat, his family hired a shaykh known as an expert in missing persons cases, but the investigation led nowhere. Not long afterward the family figured out what must have happened. Two of the three Jews who killed the robber had died, so the family took the remaining man hostage. They held him for six months, but he did not confess under torture. The Jew's family paid a ransom for him, but the robber's family still wanted vengeance. One of the other killers, now deceased, had a five-year-old son. His widow worked as a domestic servant in a Muslim house. When her mistress began asking pointed questions about her little boy, she suspected a plot and she and the boy fled Yemen for Palestine.[96]

If the "norm" of murder represented the apogee of public antagonism between male rivals, such a murder, serving the interests of the weak and carried out through subterfuge, must have disturbed Muslims. The idea that Jews, in their social marginality, might see themselves as having no recourse other than murder may itself have led Muslims to suspect them of various unsolved killings.

One Sabbath in December 1948 two girls from al-Balaqah were found dead in a well in the courtyard of a three-story house just inside the Quarter called "the Kisār Storehouse." The owners of the house had emigrated to Israel. When their bodies were discovered, residents of the Muslim neighborhood accused the Jews of their murder and called for revenge. The governor sent soldiers to arrest the Jews who lived close to the house. According to Mordecai al-Ẓāhirī, the soldiers cast a much wider net than this mandate enjoined and rounded up the leaders of the community. The mob abused them, throwing stones, plucking their beards and sidelocks, and striking them. Forty-one men were imprisoned.

The Jewish men were shackled and crammed within two small rooms. At night they had difficulties lying down and were frequently awoken by cellmates' flatulence and the younger men's jokes about it. They passed the daylight hours chewing qāt, smoking water pipes, studying religious literature, and praying. (During prayer times the adherents of the Dor De'ah movement used one of the rooms and the kabbalists used the other.) Some of the wealthier Jews bribed the warden in order to go home for a few hours.

A Muslim inmate offered Mordecai al-Ẓāhirī his own theory of the girls' demise. He had spoken to a family friend, a resident of al-Balaqah whose business was selling firewood and animal fodder to Jews. He worked for the 'Aṭiyya clan, who ran this business.[97] The firewood seller said that a married woman of the 'Aṭiyya clan, the only Muslim family that operated shops in the Jews' market, lived in a house across from the Kisār Storehouse with several other families. She had arranged to meet her lover in the abandoned Jewish house but, unbeknownst to her, had been followed and observed by three girls from a neighbor's family. (Ẓāhirī speculated that the firewood salesman was the woman's lover.) She drowned two of the girls in the well. The third witnessed the murders and escaped. When Qadi 'Alī al-'Amrī learned of the girl's account, he discounted its evidentiary value by comparing her testimony to that of the insane. He convinced the girl that she had not seen anything untoward.[98]

Hārūn Ḥamdī offers a slightly different account of the crime. A sixteen-year-old orphan girl who lived with the 'Aṭiyya family dashed the girls against a tree and threw them in the well. (No motive is provided.) A ten-year-old girl and two of her friends had witnessed the murders. She told her mother, who, after suffering from insomnia for days, told this to a Jewish umbrella repairman. Qadi 'Alī al-'Amrī, who Ḥamdī describes as a "hoodlum," kept the 'Aṭiyya girl at his house for the duration of the investigation. Ḥamdī suggests that the roundup of Jews was the brainchild of two influential Muslim men of al-Balaqah. They were getting revenge for their embarrassment at having supported the coup against Imām Yaḥyā and the looting of their neighborhood by tribesmen.[99] (A third source on the events in question, an anonymous letter to Ṣāliḥ al-Ẓāhirī from Sanaa, includes the details of Qadi al-'Amrī's both discounting the young eyewitness' testimony and hosting the 'Aṭiyya girl at his house.[100])

There is reason to suspect that a desire on the part of the imām and his aides to take advantage of the deaths to "shake down" the Jewish community lay behind the mass arrests. On such harassment, which usually took place on a much smaller scale, Shlomo Dov Goitein "gathers that the Muslim villagers fared no better than the Jews."[101] Nevertheless, there is more to the situation than simple extortion. According to Ḥamdī, Imām Aḥmad appointed a three-judge commission of inquiry after the Jews were arrested. It consisted of sayyid Zayd Zabārah, "an avowed hater of Jews"; Qadi Aḥmad al-Jirāfī, "one of the righteous among the nations" and a member of the court of appeals; and Qadi ʿAlī al-ʿAmrī, a "hooligan."[102] Whether or not these characterizations are accurate, this description of the composition of the commission implies that the authorities sought to placate a number of Muslim constituencies by designating the participants.

Some of the Jews protested to Zabārah and Jirāfī that the subservient status of the Jews in Yemen rendered the perpetration of this brazen crime impossible, insisting further that their cooperation with the commission of inquiry ought not to imply their acceptance of the idea that the perpetrator must be a Jew. This offended Zabārah, who rejected the possibility that a Muslim could have committed so grievous a crime against another Muslim. In a subsequent meeting with Jirāfī, the Jews raised the multiplicity of suspects, the lack of discernible motive, and the long imprisonment without trial.[103] Jirāfī replied that the charges against the Jews had been concocted but that the powerful Zabārah stood behind them and needed to be outmaneuvered with caution.

After interviewing the sixteen-year-old suspect and the mother of one of the girls who had witnessed the murders, Zabārah and Jirāfī, embarrassed, found themselves in a difficult situation. They had to choose between handing out baseless convictions and releasing the Jews, which would have shamed them and aggrieved the parents of the murdered girls. Only at this point were most of the prisoners released. Since Prince Ḥasan, the governor of Sanaa, was, according to Ḥamdī, a "Jew hater," Jews bribed a worker in the telegraph office in order to have petitions concerning the imprisoned men sent to Imām Aḥmad in Taʿizz. Sālim Manṣūrah holds Ḥasan, the son of Imām Yaḥyā who served as the governor of Sanaa under his brother Imām Aḥmad, responsible for a general deterioration of the status of the Jews of Yemen.[104] Qadi Jirāfī confided in Ḥamdī: "A decision has been reached that the [remaining] prisoners will be released in exchange for bail money pending trial." Zabārah and Jirāfī debated the proper charge, with Zabārah demanding 15,000 riyāls and Jirāfī demanding 1,000. Imām Aḥmad arrived at an intermediate figure of 3,000, arguing that the harm caused to the Jews' reputations did not outweigh the danger posed by the girls' families if they were not appeased. The money would be presented by a shaykh or other important Muslim man as if he were putting up the Jews' bail.[105] Imām Aḥmad agreed to release all but four of the Jewish prisoners after the payment was made. These remained in prison for another nine months and then were sent directly by truck to

Aden and on to Israel.[106] In response to these events, the World Jewish Congress pressured the British Foreign Office to accelerate the pace of Jewish emigration from Yemen.[107]

Ṣāliḥ al-Ẓāhirī, who was in Aden at the time, tells of concocting at least some of this foreign influence in a telegram he and an English-speaking friend wrote in Arabic and in English. He signed it, "Y. Berkowitz, M. Goldstein, and another fifteen names like this," explaining that he "used European Jewish names as if they were ministers in the Israeli government." With characteristic lack of modesty, he claims that this telegram led the imām to release most of the Jews from prison.[108]

By describing the incident as a "blood libel," Jewish sources obscure the local dynamics of this episode, instead contextualizing it within the sweep of (European) Jewish history. Needless to say, the Christianity essential to the blood libel legend was represented in this incident only by the British government. In addition, had the imām or his brother genuinely wanted simply to extort from the Jewish community, surely they could have gotten more money with less effort. Instead, the sloppy denouement to the affair suggests that the Muslim judges found themselves in a tricky situation where ersatz damages and a secret one-way trip to Israel for the accused provided the most efficacious solution in a high-profile murder investigation.

If the Yemeni Muslim cultural imagination considered Jewish men to be weak, effeminate, socially marginalized, and resentful of this fact, the idea that one or more may have been responsible for the murder of female children becomes plausible, as Zabārah implied. However, in this case this popular suspicion trumped the patronage system through which Jews enjoyed the protection of powerful Muslims. By creating the fiction that the cash payment came from a shaykh or other notable, the judges dramatized the reestablishment of the Jews' protected status. Nevertheless, the circumscription of Imām Aḥmad's actions would be difficult to imagine under his father's reign. This suggests that the ground rules of Jewish-Muslim interaction shifted measurably after the assassination of Imām Yaḥyā and the establishment of the State of Israel in 1948.[109]

Conclusion

DESPITE THE VARIED provocations to the sharīʿa system that they had in common, the Jewish intermediaries Ṣāliḥ al-Ẓāhirī, Sālim Manṣūrah, and Sālim Saʿīd al-Jamal articulated strikingly distinctive political personae. Ṣāliḥ al-Ẓāhirī's grim yet amusing anecdotes of confrontation (often violent), disguise, imprisonment, and escape demonstrate the great lengths to which he went in affirming his manifold and contradictory passions. He was at once royalist, revolutionary, and Zionist, but above all he was worthy of the respect due "one of the Zaydīs." His fight to have his eccentric flag, incorporating symbols of both Shiʿite legitimacy and Zionism, flown before Imām Yaḥyā's retinue in Radāʿ sums up this lack of apprehension about being himself. He reveled in a protean character that encompassed Jewish observance, Jewish nationalism, and an Islamic learning that was good enough to allow him to lead Friday prayers in a mosque and draft a fatwa. Cases in which he antagonized a qadi who objected to his riding a luxurious donkey or his engineering of the beating of an influential qadi demonstrate his knack for manipulating the machinery of power, including the legal system, to his advantage.

Ẓāhirī's shape-shifting and power-hungry persona extends as well to other Jews who appear in his violent trickster tales, becoming virtual extensions of himself: his son Mordecai, who realized, however briefly, his father's dream of inclusion among the Muslim elite when he told Jewish jokes and read Israeli newspapers to sayyids and qadis who had been imprisoned after the assassination of Imām Yaḥyā; a cousin who beat a bigoted sayyid until he soiled himself; and construction worker and "potter's son" Shimʿon Cohen, who physically assaulted a number of Muslims, played the part of a learned man in court, fled to Africa, and ultimately avoided punishment.

Sālim Manṣūrah's monarchism must have also possessed a self-contradictory character. What justification for the rule of the Muslim Commander of the Faithful could a Jew proffer? Here one should bear in mind the idea, widespread among Muslims and Jews in Yemen, that irrespective of the sharp disparity in social status, the ongoing practice of Islam, in the form of its uncompromising monotheism, enables Judaism to flourish, and the ongoing practice of Judaism affects such basic elements of life as rainfall. Yemen could serve as the mountainous redoubt of Abrahamic religion in a world falling to secularism. Thus in Manṣūrah's account, Imām Aḥmad attempts to convince him (and, by extension, all of the Jews) not to leave the country by saying, "Islam and Judaism remain only in Yemen." Similarly, in Jamal's account of an imaginary conversation between Imām Yaḥyā, Hajj Amīn al-Husseini, and himself, the Jew and the imām agree that the relationship between Islam and Judaism in Yemen is qualitatively different from that relationship elsewhere in the world.[1]

Sālim Saʿīd al-Jamal depicted himself as the proponent of an audacious and wide-ranging civil rights agenda in Islamic law. The fatwa on the Zohar, which was written almost two decades before Jamal's career in the service of the imām, established the idea that a non-Muslim may practice his religion as he chooses, even when it is objectionable to both Muslims and other non-Muslims. It became a fundamental point of reference for Jamal in subsequent intra-Jewish battles.

In Jamal's struggle to ride his bicycle legally and his quest for non-Muslim abutters' rights, he sought freedom of mobility both within Yemen and abroad (provided no horses or mules were involved). In asking for abutters' rights, he also sought to normalize a non-Muslim's ability to consolidate wealth. In his objection to the wine decree, he sought freedom from collective punishment. While lacking the subtlety of his other provocations, Jamal's verbal confrontations with his Muslim opponents aimed to set in motion the resolution of the tension in Islamic law between universal human dignity and the abasement of non-Muslims. While on one level such struggles may have represented self-interested attempts to maximize Jamal's own power, they simultaneously aimed, as Karl N. Llewellyn and E. Adamson Hoebel put it, "to persuade relevant persons that such capture [of power] will serve the commonweal," creating new legal norms in the process.[2] Needless to say, none of this would have been necessary or even comprehensible if Islamic law were a priori humanistic and tolerant of non-Muslims.

Jamal included the phrase "one who swears fealty to Islam" (*muṭīʿ al-islām*) in his signature on petitions addressed to Imām Yaḥyā and other Muslim jurists. The equivocal character of this phrase encapsulates his stance toward Islamic law. He sought to ingratiate himself by seeming to accept his subservience in Islamic social hierarchies while at the same time appealing to a transcendent equalitarian ideal that he identified as representing Islam. He swore fealty to his ideal of egalitarian Islam rather than hierarchical Islam.

Yet Jamal's efforts offer a catalog of defeat. His bike riding occasioned constant harassment; his interventions on behalf of Jewish dung collectors, vintners, and property owners all failed. What are the reasons for this failure? The personal risks he took were rationalized by an exceedingly rare combination of imāmic patronage, connections, wealth, and a keen sense of fairness (or, for those who disliked him, an exaggerated sense of his own importance). Most Jews did not share all of these qualities, and thus his efforts never became a mass movement. What support he had seems to have come mainly from the Dor De'ah movement, which represented at most a third of the deeply divided Jewish community of Sanaa.

If Jamal had few allies in the Jewish community, he had even less support among the Muslims. Moreover, his most important ally, Imām Yaḥyā, supported his actions for reasons that were quite different from those that Jamal retrospectively attributed to him. The imām did not oppose discrimination against non-Muslims. In fact, he renewed the hated "Latrines Decree," the "Orphans Decree," and the mandatory grinding of flour as among the first steps in establishing his rule. He was, however, deeply concerned with ensuring the stability and tranquility of his realm. He supported Jews' right to study the Zohar despite a deep hostility toward mysticism. Banning it would have destabilized the Jewish community.

Jamal was valuable to the imām for his proven ability to mediate between the worlds of Muslim officialdom and the Jewish community. Jamal assiduously collected the poll tax from the anti-kabbalist Jews. The imām consulted him in matters having nothing to do with Jews as well. He may have reasoned that allowing Jamal to ride a bicycle, which was not explicitly banned in Islamic law, was an acceptable cost for the benefits the imām received.

The imām viewed public challenges to the Jews of Sanaa in general and Jamal in particular as veiled threats to his rule. While Imām Yaḥyā did not support Jamal's civil rights struggle, he may have rescued him when he got into trouble for another reason. Jamal's enemies among the Muslim learned class were also the imām's rivals. When the Jew provoked them into acting, the imām was able to gather intelligence about their motives, tactics, and membership.

In 1946 Zayd al-Daylamī openly challenged the Imām's rule. He demanded an end to arbitrary tax collection and exploitation by public officials. He is also said to have stopped attending Friday prayers, implicitly challenging Yaḥyā's status as imām.[3] At one point the imām placed him under house arrest.[4] Nevertheless, Qadi 'Abdallāh al-Shamāḥī insists that while his own father, Daylamī, Qāsim al-'Izzī, and some other ulama were critical of the imām (and, apparently, Jamal), they did not join one of the opposition groups.[5]

Shamāḥī also writes of the strategy mounted by the nascent opposition to the imām's rule, which included his father, to inflame existing rivalries between the imām's sons on one hand and chief minister 'Abdallāh al-'Amrī and the Wazīr clan ('Alī and 'Abdallāh) on the other.[6] The powerful al-'Amrī would have been a key member of a new government. The Sacred National Pact drawn up by the revolutionaries in 1948 included an appendix listing the members of a future government. There al-'Amrī retained his post of chief minister.[7] Indeed, the revolutionaries considered him essential to their success, and thus the plan to kill Imām Yaḥyā was nearly scrapped when it became clear that ʿAmrī would be accompanying him.[8] (The two rivals were shot to death in the same car.) Jamal's impression of the divisions within Yemen's leadership was thus confirmed.

The rivalry between the imām and the ulama also possessed a structural character that transcended the individual personalities in question. The term "judicial crisis" is perhaps cliché and ordinarily refers to an oppressive backlog of cases. Nevertheless the term is appropriate to the sharīʿa courts before the Jewish intermediaries launched their provocations. The Islamic judiciary had become sharply divided. An imām whose decisions bound all Zaydī Shiʿi Muslims (and, in theory, all other Muslims too) by virtue of his office counterbalanced a cadre of judges who regarded themselves as strict constructionists who anchored every opinion in Muslim scripture. While an imām needed judges in order to rule, the fact that these judges espoused a judicial philosophy that contradicted his own, even denying his legal authority altogether, ensured perpetual conflict.

These judges were Salafis (from the Arabic *salaf*, meaning "pious ancestors"). In their constructionism they sought to hearken back to the earliest phase in Islamic history, skirting centuries of legal interpretation in the process. The story of how the Salafi movement emerged from within Zaydī Shiʿism is told by Bernard Haykel in his *Revival and Reform in Islam*. Yemeni Salafism constituted one branch in a much larger Salafist tree, whose branches included the Wahhabis of Saudi Arabia, the Egyptian Muslim Brotherhood, and the Indian Deoband school. The conflict between Imām Yaḥyā and the Salafi judges is a virtual archetype in contemporary Islamic thought. Clashes between traditional authority figures and the Islamic orthodoxies that legitimized them on one side and reformist Salafi movements on the other are a recurrent theme in modern Islamic intellectual history.

The Jewish intermediaries' struggle calls into question the idea put forward by scholars of Islam and progressive Muslims (not mutually exclusive categories) that Salafist thought offers a liberal third way between secular democracy and Islamic reaction by virtue of its reformist character. In 1920s–1930s Yemen those jurists advocating a return to the original sources of Islam did so in order to restrict the activities of non-Muslims. Moreover, appeals to interpretive principles of legal theory such as "broader interest" (*maṣlaḥah*) did not automatically result in the application of the more humane of several possible legal interpretations. Indeed, in the eighteenth-century debate over the collection of excrement, the opposite was the case.

In responding to such criticisms, legal formalists ask of realists: if laws cannot predict judicial outcomes, what predictive value inheres in underscoring the nonlegal factors in decision making? In the "trouble cases" analyzed in this book, these nonlegal factors are legion: "fireside equities" or personal relationships between a qadi (or an imām) and litigants (or, more broadly, the rung in the social hierarchy to which they belonged); implicit analyses of the economic impact of a given decision (for example, of the impact of dung collecting on the bathhouses); idiosyncratic personality traits; the importance of two ideological profiles—orthodox Zaydī imāmic loyalist or strict constructionist Salafi Zaydī; and, finally, a tension between ubiquitous judicial bribery and principled Muslim moral outrage against corruption. While the fragmentary nature of the available documentation may excuse the lack of a general *predictive* theory that would account for the formulation of law in early twentieth-century Yemen's sharī'a court system (much less the inevitable hard cases that result from non-Muslim interactions with this system), fleshing out these nonlegal factors itself represents progress.

Two further observations: First, idiosyncratic personality factors are extremely difficult to pin down in light of each writer's differing perception of a given judge, most notable in the inverse relationship between a qadi's putative malevolence and the strength of his friendship with the writer in question. Second, just as a vital stream of legal realist scholarship in the United States focuses upon the predictive value in a judge's political party, the constructionist-Salafist wing of the judiciary in Yemen seems to have been more reliably negative in their reaction to the Jewish intermediaries' provocations than that of the orthodox Zaydīs.

The fact that the Jewish intermediaries enlisted Islamic sources in their quest for expanded rights proves that one can construct a strong prima facie case for the equality of Muslims and non-Muslims in Islam. However, the only people making such cases were Jews. Moreover, such visions depended upon a sovereign imām like Yaḥyā who either supported this agenda (as Jamal thought Yaḥyā did) or simply allowed considerable leeway to influential Jews (as Yaḥyā certainly did). After Imām Yaḥyā's assassination in 1948, the brief triumph of his enemies, the short reign of Yaḥyā's son Aḥmad, and the Revolution of 1962, the environment in which this vision of coexistence between Muslims and dhimmīs under sharī'a could be realized no longer existed.

The fact that the Jewish intermediaries knew Islamic law by living under it underscores the importance of nonlegal codes in their activities. Just by learning formal Arabic and comporting themselves in confrontational ways they challenged the impermeability of the boundaries separating Muslim and Jew. In their demands for respect, equal treatment, and business opportunities, they represented the interests of the new Jewish mercantile elite in Yemen.

Although the Jewish intermediaries did not succeed, they put before us a fascinating "what if?" scenario of modern Middle Eastern and Jewish history. As interpreters of Islamic law, they hoped to find a solution to the lowly status of the Jews in the world within the arena of the sharī'a courts. It is worth recalling that the Dor De'ah movement, to which Jamal, Ẓāhirī, and Manṣūrah belonged, stressed a return to the Judaism of medieval thinkers like Se'adya Gaon and Maimonides. Theirs was the Maimonides of the *Mishneh Torah,* not the more subversive Aristotelian of the *Guide of the Perplexed.* The importance of Arabic and Islam to their project, as when Ḥayyim Ḥibshūsh defended his reading Muslim religious texts during the synagogue service, bears remembering as well.

In his *Epistle to Yemen,* Maimonides shows apprehension at Muslims' capacity to oppress Jews, but in other epistles he judges that the presence of Islamic monotheism in the world is a good thing. There is a debate as to whether Maimonides saw Islamic law as positive, and even inspired by Judaism. Did he, in keeping with rabbinic consensus, disapprove of Gentiles observing precepts other than the so-called Noahide laws?[9] Dor De'ah in Yemen seems to have had a more positive view of Islamic law. In implementing their theological platform on the political level, Jamal, Ẓāhirī, and Manṣūrah, along with Dor De'ah, may have envisioned a situation in which pious Jews were able to observe their law among Muslims who observe their own law as a social system functioning as God intended. Secular nationalism, whether offered by an Arab state or a Jewish state, did not play a role in their imagination. Thus the three intermediaries' provocative Yemeni campaign, neither liberal nor revolutionary, might be described as the quest for Maimonidean citizenship.

Notes

Introduction

1. Yohanan Friedmann, *Tolerance and Coercion in Islam: Interfaith Relations in the Muslim Tradition* (Cambridge, UK: Cambridge University Press, 2003), 2–6.

2. The tolerant statements in Yemeni legal sources "are admittedly not representative," remarks Ahmad Dallal, "but, taken together, illustrate the manifold potentials for reforming the Islamic legal tradition." He argues further that "European models for dealing with minorities were far less open than Islamic ones." Ahmad Dallal, "Yemeni Debates on the Status of Non-Muslims in Islamic Law," *Islam and Christian-Muslim Relations* 7, no. 2 (1996): 190.

3. Friedmann, *Tolerance and Coercion*, 6.

4. Ibid., 194–195; Matthias B. Lehmann, "Islamic Legal Consultation and the Jewish-Muslim *Convivencia:* al-Wansharīsī's *Fatwā* Collection as a Source for Jewish Social History in Al-Andalus and the Maghrib," *Jewish Studies Quarterly* 6 (1999): 40; Bernard Lewis, *The Jews of Islam* (Princeton, NJ: Princeton University Press, 1984), 14–16; Gideon Libson, "Otonomiyah shipuṭit u-peniyah la-ʿarkha'ot mi-tsad bene he-ḥasut ʿal pi meqorot muslimiyim bitqufat ha-ge'onim," in *Ha-Islam ve-ʿolamot ha-shezurim bo: Qovets ma'amarim le-zikhrah shel Ḥava Latsarus-Yafah* (Jerusalem: Hebrew University Institute of Asian and African Studies, 2002), 348–349; Norman Stillman, "The Judeo-Islamic Historical Encounter: Visions and Revisions," in *Israel and Ishmael: Studies in Muslim-Jewish Relations*, ed. Tudor Parfitt (Richmond, Surrey: Curzon Press, 2000), 6–7.

5. Friedmann, *Tolerance and Coercion*, 199: "In the field of interfaith relations, it is therefore not possible to suggest a consistent evolution from leniency to rigor, which Schacht posited for the development of Muslim law in general."

6. Khaled Abou El-Fadl, Joshua Cohen, and Ian League, *The Place of Tolerance in Islam* (Boston: Beacon Press, 2002), 13.

7. Ze'ev Maghen, "The Interaction between Islamic Law and Non-Muslims: *Lakum Dīnukum wa-lī Dīni*," *Islamic Law and Society* 10, no. 3 (2003): 268, 272.

8. See Jesse Ferris, *Nasser's Gamble: How Intervention in Yemen Caused the Six-Day War and the Decline of Egyptian Power* (Princeton, NJ: Princeton University Press, 2012).

9. Shalom Seʿadyah Gamliel, *Bate hakneset be-tsanʿa' birat teman* (Jerusalem: Makhon shalom le-shivṭe yeshurun, 1996/1997), 1:124n1.

10. Muḥammad Qā'id al-Ṣā'idī, *Ḥarakat al-muʿāraḍah al-yamaniyyah fī ʿahd al-imām yaḥyā b. muḥammad ḥamīd al-dīn (1322–1367h./1904–1948m.)* (Sanaa, Yemen: Markaz al-dirāsāt wa l-buḥūth al-yamanī, 1983), 188.

11. Dallal, "Yemeni Debates," 182.

12. Muḥammad Rashīd Riḍā, *al-Khilāfah* (1922; repr. Cairo: al-Zahrā li l-iʿlām al-ʿarabī, 1988), 77–81; Paul Dresch, *A History of Modern Yemen* (Cambridge, UK: Cambridge University Press, 2000), 51.

13. Muḥammad b. ʿAlī al-Akwaʿ, *Ḥayāt ʿālim wa-amīr* (Sanaa, Yemen: Maktabat al-jīl al-jadīd, 1987), 1:335–338; J. Leigh Douglas, *The Free Yemeni Movement, 1935–1962* (Beirut: American University of Beirut, 1987), 32, 48–49.

14. Bernard Haykel, *Revival and Reform in Islam: The Legacy of Muḥammad al-Shawkānī* (Cambridge, UK: Cambridge University Press, 2003), 207.

15. ʿAbd al-Wāsiʿ b. Yaḥyā al-Wāsiʿī, *Taʾrīkh al-yaman al-musammā furjat al-humūm wa l-ḥuzn fī ḥawādith wa-taʾrīkh al-yaman* (Cairo: al-Maktabah al-salafiyyah, 1927/1928), 265–272; A. Z. al-Abdin, "The Role of Islam in the State: The Yemen Arab Republic (1940–1972)" (PhD diss., University of Cambridge, 1975), 52 (Abdin's citation is incorrect).

16. ʿAbdallāh b. ʿAbd al-Wahhāb al-Shamāḥī, *al-Yaman: al-Insān wa l-ḥaḍārah* (Beirut: Manshūrāt al-madīnah, 1985), 221; Abdualaziz K. al-Msaodi, "The Yemeni Opposition Movement, 1918–1948" (PhD diss., Georgetown University, 1987), 212–213.

17. Gerald J. Obermeyer, "Ṭāghūt, Manʿ, and Šarīʿa: The Realms of Law in Tribal Arabia," in *Studia Arabica et Islamica: Festschrift for Ihsan Abbas on His Sixtieth Birthday*, ed. Wadad al-Qadi (Beirut: American University of Beirut, 1981), 370–371; Karl Rathjens, "Ṭāghūt gegen scherīʿa: Gewohnheitsrecht und islamisches Recht bei den Gabilen des jemenitischen Hochlandes," *Tribus: Jahrbuch des Lindenmuseums* 1 (1951): 173.

18. Shelagh Weir, *A Tribal Order: Politics and Law in the Mountains of Yemen* (Austin: University of Texas Press, 2007), 162–164, 210–211; Ettore Rossi, "Il diritto consuetudinario delle tribù arabe del Yemen," *Revista degli Studi Orientali* 23 (1948): 11; Rathjens, "Ṭāghūt gegen scherīʿa," 181; Obermeyer, "Ṭāghūt, Manʿ, and Šarīʿa," 368–369; ʿAbd al-Karīm b. Aḥmad Muṭahhar, *Sīrat al-imām yaḥyā b. muḥammad ḥamīd al-dīn al-musammāh katībat al-ḥikmah min sīrat imam al-ummah*, ed. Muḥammad b. ʿĪsā al-Ṣāliḥiyyah (Amman: Dār al-Bashīr, 1998), 1:58, 258; Yaḥyā b. Muḥammad al-Hāshimī, *al-Qaḍāʾ fī l-yaman fī l-qarn al-rābiʿ ʿashar al-hijrī wa-mā baʿduhu* (Sanaa, Yemen: Maktabat Khālid b. al-Walīd, 2003), 178.

19. This is Rossi's conjectural translation; it is not clear from the text. Rossi, "Il diritto consuetudinario," 15.

20. Rossi, "Il diritto consuetudinario," 10, 11; Obermeyer, "Ṭāghūt, Manʿ, and Šarīʿa," 369. On the various "dodges" that could "prevent the alienation of property by out-marrying females," see David S. Powers, "Law and Custom in the Maghrib, 1475–1500: On the Disinheritance of Women," in *Law, Custom, and Statute in the Muslim World: Studies in Honor of Aharon Layish*, ed. Ron Shaham (Leiden: E. J. Brill, 2006), 17–40.

21. Rossi, "Il diritto consuetudinario," 11.

22. Muṭahhar b. Muḥammad al-Jarmūzī, *al-Jawharah al-munīrah*, quoted in ibid., 9–10.

23. Walter Dostal, "'Sexual Hospitality' and the Problem of Matrilinearity in South Arabia," *Proceedings of the Seminar for Arabian Studies* 20 (1990): 21; Dostal, *Eduard Glaser: Forschungen im Yemen* (Vienna: Verlag der Österreichischen Akademie der Wissenschaften, 1990), 137–151.

24. Rathjens, "Ṭāghūt gegen scherīʿa," 184. Dostal makes three additional important points about this practice: (1) the women involved were unmarried blood relatives of the host (sisters, daughters), (2) their consent was required, and (3) children resulting from such unions were raised by the host's family and took their mothers' names. "'Sexual Hospitality,'" 19.

25. Rathjens, "Ṭāghūt gegen scherīʿa," 184.

26. Ḥayyim Tsadoq, *Be-Ohole teman* (Tel Aviv: Defus D. Ben Nun, 1980), 53–54; Shalom Medinah, *Masaʿot r. moshe medinah u-vanav* (Tel Aviv: Ha-Agudah la-ṭipuaḥ ḥevrah ve-tarbut, 1994), 157–158.

27. Hāshimī, *al-Qaḍāʾ fī l-yaman*, 135, 179–181, 186.

28. Yehudah Ratshaby, "Yehudim u-muslimim bi-sifrut ha-meshalim," in *Be-Meʿaglot teman: Mivḥar meḥqarim be-tarbut yehude teman* (Tel Aviv: the author, 1987), 231–232.

29. Yosef Riḍā, *Temana: Mavo le-erets al-ḥugariyah*, ed. Efrayim Yaʿaqov (Nahariyah, Jerusalem: Ḥadre teman, 1995), 99n5.

30. Nissim Binyamin Gamlieli, *Taḥat kanfeha shel ima: Roman Otobiyografi mi-ḥayyav shel yeled yehudi be-teman* (Tel Aviv: Afiqim, 2002), 45–46.

31. Lawrence Rosen, *Law as Culture: An Invitation* (Princeton, NJ: Princeton University Press, 2006), 51.

32. Sālim Manṣūrah, *'Aliyat mirbad haqsamim: Tiy'ur ha-'aliyah ha-gedolah shel yehude teman*, ed. Moshe Gavra (Bene Beraq, Israel: Ha-Makhon le-ḥeqer ḥakhme teman, 2003), 36; Shalom Se'adyah Gamliel (Sālim Sa'īd al-Jamal), *Ha-Yehudim ve-ha-melekh bi-teman* (Jerusalem: Makhon shalom le-shivṭe yeshurun, 1986), 1:146.

33. Msaodi, "Yemeni Opposition Movement," 171–172; Ismā'īl al-Akwa', *Hijar al-'ilm wa-ma'āqiluhā fī l-yaman* (Damascus: Dār al-fikr, 1995), 871; Aḥmad Jābir 'Afīf, *Shāhid 'alā l-yaman: Ashyā' min al-dhākirah* (Sanaa, Yemen: Mu'assasat 'afīf al-thaqafiyyah, 2000), 49; 'Abdallāh Juzaylān, *Lamaḥāt min dhikrayāt al-ṭufūlah* (Cairo: Maktabat madbūlī, 1984), 81–82; Dresch, *History of Modern Yemen*, 49; Douglas, *Free Yemeni Movement*, 61–62; Gabriele vom Bruck, *Islam, Memory, and Morality in Yemen: Ruling Families in Transition* (New York: Palgrave Macmillan, 2005), 51.

34. Shalom Gamliel, *Ha-Yehudim*, 2:90–91, 127–131; Bat-Zion Eraqi Klorman, *Yehude teman: Historyah ḥevrah, tarbut* (Tel Aviv: Open University, 2008), 3:256; Muḥammad Ḥasan, *Qalb al-yaman* (Baghdād: Maṭba'at al-ma'ārif, 1947), 84; 'Alī Muḥammad 'Abduh, *Lamaḥāt min ta'rīkh ḥarakat al-aḥrār al-yamaniyīn* (Sanaa, Yemen: al-Ma'had al-firansī li l-āthār wa l-'ulūm al-ijtimā'iyyah, Muntadā nu'mān al-thaqāfī li l-shabāb, 2003), 1:84–85.

35. Nissim Binyamin Gamlieli, "Solele-ha-derekh le-''aliyat "al kanfe nesharim' be-re'i te'udot u-mikhtavim," in Shalom b. Se'adyah Gamliel, Mishael Maswari Caspi, and Shim'on Avizemer, eds., *Orḥot teman* (Jerusalem: Makhon shalom le-shivṭe yeshurun, 1984), 143.

36. Ismā'īl al-Akwa', *Hijar*, 1753–1754; Muḥammad al-Akwa', *Ḥayāt 'ālim wa-amīr*, 2:101.

37. Shalom Se'adyah Gamliel, *Pe'ame ha-'aliyah mi-teman* (Jerusalem: Makhon shalom le-shivṭe yeshurun, 1987), 254.

38. Shalom Gamliel, *Ha-Yehudim*, 1:150–151.

39. Ibid., 1:162–163. In 1941 the qadi who did this was upbraided by a more powerful qadi who was conducting such a surprise inspection of the house of a Muslim, thereby threatening the modesty of his womenfolk and contravening a Qur'anic (33:53) admonition against such behavior. Aḥmad b. Muḥammad al-Wazīr, *Ḥayāt al-amīr 'alī b. 'abdallāh al-wazīr* (n.p.: Manshūrāt al-'aṣr al-ḥadīth, 1987), 389.

40. Yeḥiel Ḥibshūsh, *Mishpaḥat ḥibshush* (n.p.: Shlomo Davidovitch, 1985), 1:466.

41. Nissim Binyamin Gamlieli, *Teman be-te'udot: Yehude damt ve-ha-maḥoz* (Jerusalem: Makhon shalom le-shivṭe yeshurun, 1997), 50n4. However, Shalom Bene Moshe describes the childless wife of a Jew as converting to Islam to marry an influential Muslim. *Sefer Bamsilah na'aleh* (Reḥovot, Israel: the author, 1988), 100–101.

42. Ismā'īl al-Akwa', *Hijar*, 673. The imām's dark complexion is also discussed in 'Abdallāh Juzaylān, *Lamaḥāt min dhikrayāt al-ṭufūlah*, 24–25, 31.

43. Bene Moshe, *Sefer Bamsilah*, 59–61.

44. Ibid., 51–52 (quotation at 52).

45. Lawrence Rosen, *The Justice of Islam: Comparative Perspectives on Islamic Law and Society* (Oxford: Oxford University Press, 2000), 41.

46. Bene Moshe, *Sefer Bamsilah*, 55–57.

47. Mordecai Yitshari (al-Ẓāhirī), *Hayiti ben 'arubah be-teman* (Rosh Ha-'Ayin, Israel: A.M.B. Admor, 1989), 136–137; Nissim Binyamin Gamlieli, *Ḥadre teman: Sippurim ve-aggadot* (Tel Aviv: Afiqim, 1978), 163–165.

48. Ẓāhirī was from Radā', a hotbed of resistance to Imām Yaḥyā and support for 'Abdallāh al-Wazīr. Shamāḥī, *al-Yaman*, 266, 269. He had close relationships with many Muslims in the Bedouin tribes east of the city, who had risen against the imām and were in turn branded Khawārij by the government. Msaodi, "Yemeni Opposition Movement," 136–139. His son notes that he had corresponded with al-Wazīr, owned revolutionary material like the *Voice of Yemen*

newspaper, and had high hopes for the revolutionary regime that took power in 1948. Tsadoq Yitshari (Ṣāliḥ al-Ẓāhirī), *Kakh baraḥti mi-teman* (Rosh Ha-ʿAyin, Israel: Mordecai Yitshari, 1988), 13–14, 29, 87. Moreover, Manṣūrah says that he "supported and aided the rebels who killed Imām Yaḥyā." *ʿAliyat mirbad haqsamim*, 243. These facts render suspect his claim of having been pursued by Imām Aḥmad's troops for his Zionist activities.

49. Mordecai Yitshari, *Hayiti*, 215, 223–224 (quotation at 215).

50. Tsadoq Yitshari, *Kakh baraḥti*, 109–114.

51. Mordecai Yitshari, *Hayiti*, 264.

52. Manṣūrah, *ʿAliyat mirbad haqsamim*, 205.

53. Ibid., 58–59.

54. Tudor Parfitt, *The Road to Redemption: The Jews of the Yemen, 1900–1950* (Leiden: E. J. Brill, 1996), 83; Tudor Parfitt, *Israel and Ishmael: Studies in Muslim-Jewish Relations* (Richmond, Surrey: Curzon Press, 2000), 220.

55. Gilʿad Tsadoq, *Sefer Zikhron teman: Sippure nifla'ot, demuyot hod, u-minhagim mi-yahadut teman* (Bene Beraq, Israel: the author, 2005).

56. See Mordecai Yitshari, *ʿAlilot ve-naftulim mi-teman* (Rosh Ha-ʿAyin, Israel: the author, 1990), 6–7 (quotation at 6).

57. Stefan Leder, "Conventions of Fictional Narration in Learned Literature," in *Story-telling in the Framework of Non-fictional Arabic Literature*, ed. Stefan Leder (Wiesbaden: Harrassowitz, 1998), 59–60.

58. Mordecai Yitshari, *Ḥayyim soʿarim* (Netanyah, Israel: Ha-Agudah la-ṭipuaḥ ḥevrah ve-tarbut, 1996), 147, 172.

59. Kerstin Hünefeld, *Imām Yaḥyā Ḥamīd al-Dīn und die Juden in Ṣanʿāʾ (1904–1948): Die Dimension von Schutz (*dhimma*) in den Dokumenten der Sammlung des Rabbi Sālim b. Saʿīd al-Ǧamal* (Berlin: Klaus Schwarz Verlag, 2010), 109.

60. Ṭuviah Sulami, "'Megillat ha-yeshuʿah' le-rav shalom gamli'el bein metsiyut ve-dimyon," *Tehudah* 23 (2008): 51–61.

61. Parfitt makes the case that economic factors were paramount in individual Jews' decisions to leave Yemen for Israel. *Road to Redemption*, 122, 180.

62. Nissim Gamlieli, *Ḥevyon teman: Zikhronot, sippurim, aggadot ḥayyim mi-ʿolam aḥer* (Ramlah, Israel: the author, 1983), 14.

63. Ratson Halevi, *ʿAlilot me-ʿolam le-ʿolam* (Tel Aviv: Afiqim, 2005), 69.

64. Alain Rouaud, "L'Émigration Yéménite," in *L'Arabie du Sud*, ed. Joseph Chelhod (Paris: Maisonneuve et Larose, 1984), 2:231, 233, 241.

65. Lawrence Rosen, *The Anthropology of Justice: Law as Culture in Islamic Society* (Cambridge, UK: Cambridge University Press, 1989), 11.

1. The Islamic Judicial System and the Jews

1. Nazīh Mu'ayyad al-ʿAẓm, *Riḥlah fī bilād al-ʿarabiyyah al-saʿīdah: Min miṣr ilā ṣanʿāʾ* (Beirut: Manshūrāt al-madīnah, 1986), 186; Ameen Rihani, *Arabian Peak and Desert: Travels in al-Yaman* (London: Constable & Co. Ltd., 1930), 104; Brinkley Messick, *The Calligraphic State: Textual Domination and History in a Muslim Society* (Berkeley: University of California Press, 1993), 169; Haykel, *Revival and Reform*, 202.

2. *Terminiello v. Chicago* 337 U.S. 1 (1949); Rosen, *Anthropology of Justice*, 58.

3. Before he became imām, one of his teachers is said to have judged him to be a suitable candidate for the imāmate "but for his miserliness." Ismāʿīl al-Akwaʿ, *Hijar*, 1700. On the imām's miserliness, see Aḥmad Muḥammad Nuʿmān, *al-Atrāf al-maʿniyyah fī l-yaman* (Aden, Yemen:

Mu'assasat al-Sabbān, 1965), 46–47; Ismāʿīl al-Akwaʿ, *Hijar,* 603, 671, 1461, 1976; Muḥammad al-Akwaʿ, *Ḥayāt ʿālim,* 1:233, 289; Shamāḥī, *al-Yaman,* 188; Ṣā'idī, *Ḥarakat al-muʿāraḍah,* 40, 107; Ibrāhīm b. ʿAlī al-Wazīr, *Zahrā' al-yaman: Umm fī ghimār al-thawrah* (Bethesda, MD: Kitab, 1997), 38; al-ʿIzzī Ṣāliḥ al-Sunaydār, *al-Ṭarīq ilā l-ḥurriyyah: Mudhakkirāt al-ʿizzī Ṣāliḥ al-sunaydār* (Sanaa, Yemen: Iṣdārāt wizārat al-thaqāfah wa l-siyāḥah, 2004), 29; ʿAfīf, *Shāhid ʿalā l-yaman,* 48–51.

4. Yeḥiel Ḥibshūsh, *Riḥlah fī riḥāb al-yaman* (n.d, n.p.), 44; Yeḥiel Ḥibshūsh, *She'erit ha-pleṭah be-teman: Yehude teman she-be-teman ve-ha-mishṭar he-ḥadash* (Bene Beraq, Israel: Ḥibshūsh family, 1990), 39.

5. Yosef Qāfiḥ, *Halikhot teman,* ed. Yisrael Yeshayahu (1961; repr., Jerusalem: Makhon Ben-Zvi, 2007), 369.

6. On "trouble cases," see Karl N. Llewellyn and E. Adamson Hoebel, *The Cheyenne Way: Conflict and Case Law in Primitive Jurisprudence* (Norman: University of Oklahoma Press, 1941), 28–29.

7. Thomas Kühn, "Shaping and Reshaping Colonial Ottomanism: Contesting Boundaries of Difference and Integration in Ottoman Yemen, 1872–1919," *Comparative Studies of South Asia, Africa, and the Middle East* 27, no. 2 (2007): 315–331.

8. Isa Blumi, *Chaos in Yemen: Societal Collapse and the New Authoritarianism* (London: Routledge, 2011), 84–90.

9. Avraham ʿOvadiah, *Netivot teman ve-tsiyon: Zikhronot,* ed. Yosef Tobi (Tel Aviv: Afiq-im, 1985), 28.

10. Eraqi Klorman, *Yehude teman,* 3:15, 80, 207.

11. Jewish National and University Library, MS Ar. 120, "*Niẓām al-yahūd*"; Kerstin Hüne-feld, "*Niẓām al-Yahūd* ('The Statute of the Jews'): Imām Yaḥyā's Writing to the Jews of Ṣanʿā' from 1323/1905," *Chronique du Manuscrit au Yémen* 16 (2013): 26–76.

12. On the dating and historical context of the Pact of ʿUmar, see Milka Levy-Rubin, *Non-Muslims in the Early Islamic Empire* (Cambridge, UK: Cambridge University Press, 2011).

13. R. B. Serjeant and Ronald Lewcock, *Ṣanʿā': An Arabian Islamic City* (London: World of Islam Festival Trust, 1983), 421.

14. Menashe ʿAnzi, "Hashpaʿat ha-tmurot ha-mediniyot ʿal yehude tsanʿa' be-reshit ha-me'ah ha-ʿesrim," in *Miṭṭuv Yosef: Sefer ha-yovel li-khvod yosef ṭobi,* ed. Ayelet Ettinger and Dani Bar Maʿoz (Haifa, Israel: Haifa University, 2011), 2:115, 117.

15. Gamliel, *Ha-Yehudim,* 2:32.

16. Ibid., 2:8–25.

17. Gamliel, *Peʿame ha-ʿaliyah,* 249.

18. Mark R. Cohen, *Under Crescent and Cross: The Jews in the Middle Ages* (Princeton, NJ: Princeton University Press, 1994), 63.

19. Aharon Ben David, *Bet ha-even: Halikhot yehude tsfon teman* (Qiryat ʿEqron, Israel: Ahavat teman, 2008), 20. See also Pinḥas Qafarah, *Mini teman u-ve-shaʿarayim-reḥovot: Shivʿim shanah (1907–1977),* ed. Shimʿon Graydi (Reḥovot, Israel: the author, 1978), 23–24.

20. Yosef Tobi, *Yehudi be-sheruṭ ha-imām: Ish ha-ʿasaqim ve-soḥer ha-nesheq yisra'el tsub-ayri* (Tel Aviv: Afiqim, 2002), 15–16; Muḥammad ʿAlī al-Shahārī, *Ṭarīq al-thawrah al-yamani-yyah* (Cairo: Dār al-hilāl, 1966), 78.

21. Yosef ʿAtsṭah, *Ḥayye yosef,* ed. Simḥah Zarmaṭi-ʿAtsṭah (Tel Aviv: Afiqim, 1987), 22–23.

22. Paul Dresch, *Tribes, Government, and History in Yemen* (Oxford: Oxford University Press, 1989), 137; vom Bruck, *Islam, Memory, and Morality,* 283n9.

23. Msaodi, "Yemeni Opposition Movement," 66–67.

24. Ṣā'idī, *Ḥarakat al-muʿāraḍah,* 40, 88, 101; Shalom Gamliel, *Ha-Yehudim,* 1:52.

25. Nissim Binyamin Gamlieli, *Teman u-maḥaneh ge'ulah* (Tel Aviv: the author, 1966), 90; Gamlieli, *Teman be-teʿudot,* 30, 207; ʿOvadiah, *Netivot Teman,* 25–33; Yosef Riḍā, *Temanah,*

27n; Ḥayyim Tsadoq, *Be-Ohole teman,* 313. The imām also employed a number of Turkish officials, physicians, and hundreds of Turkish officers and soldiers, as well as Yemenis who had spent time in Istanbul, knew Turkish, and had served under the previous administration. (Muṭahhar, *Sīrat al-imām yaḥyā,* 1:183, 193–194, 207–208; Ismāʿīl al-Akwaʿ, *Hijar*). On the continuity between Ottoman and imāmic administration, see Haykel, *Revival and Reform,* 199–200; Messick, *Calligraphic State,* 107–108.

26. Aḥmad Muḥammad Nuʿmān, *al-Aṭrāf,* 38–47. See also vom Bruck, *Islam, Memory, and Morality,* 47.

27. Msaodi, "Yemeni Opposition Movement," 206.

28. Ismāʿīl al-Akwaʿ, *Hijar,* 1461; Dresch, *History of Modern Yemen,* 48. See also Sayf al-Dīn Saʿīd Āl Yaḥyā, *al-Yaman fī ʿuyūn al-baʿthah al-ʿaskariyyah al-ʿirāqiyyah, 1940–1943m.* (al-Ḥāzimiyyah, Lebanon: al-Dār al-ʿarabiyyah li l-mawsūʿāt, 2006), 142; Douglas, *Free Yemeni Movement,* 12.

29. Haykel, *Revival and Reform,* 196, 210–212; Dresch, *History of Modern Yemen,* 43–45; vom Bruck, *Islam, Memory, and Morality,* 51; Ṣāʾidī, *Ḥarakat al-muʿāraḍah,* 199; Muḥammad ʿĪsā al-Ṣāliḥiyyah, *al-ʿAllāmah al-amīr sayf al-islām, zayn al-ʿābidīn, al-ḥusayn b. yaḥyā ḥamīd al-dīn, 1327–1367 h./1909–1948 m.* (Irbid, Jordan: Yarmuk University, 2009), 193–195; Aḥmad ʿUbayd b. Daghr, *al-Yaman taḥta ḥukmi l-imām aḥmad, 1948–1962* (Cairo: Maktabat Madbūlī, 2005), 283; Aḥmad b. Muḥammad al-Wazīr, *Ḥayāt al-amīr,* 240, 298–299, 313n1, 314; Aḥmad al-Shāmī, *Riyāḥ al-taghyīr fī l-yaman* (n.p., 1984), 218, 228–229, 237; ʿAbduh, *Lamaḥāt,* 1:43; Douglas, *Free Yemeni Movement,* 14–15, 118; Msaodi, "Yemeni Opposition Movement," 208–209.

30. Muṭahhar, *Sīrat al-imām yaḥyā,* 1:101, 107–108; Msaodi, "Yemeni Opposition Movement," 70–71.

31. Āl Yaḥyā, *al-Yaman,* 118.

32. Ibid., 124, 150.

33. Muḥammad al-Akwaʿ, *Ḥayāt ʿālim,* 1:330–333.

34. Moshe Tsadoq, "Ha-Yaḥasim bein ha-yehudim ve-ha-ʿaravim be-teman," in *Yahadut teman: Pirqe meḥqar ve-ʿiyyun,* ed. Yosef Tobi and Yisrael Yeshayahu (Jerusalem: Ben Zvi Institute, 1975), 160.

35. Shalom Gamliel, *Bate hakneset,* 1:38–41. On the legal system under Imām Yaḥyā, see also Anna Würth, *Aš-Šarīʿa fī Bāb al-Yaman* (Berlin: Duncker & Humblot, 2000), 37–43.

36. Yosef Qāfiḥ, *Halikhot teman,* 373n1.

37. Ismāʿīl al-Akwaʿ, *Hijar,* 1733; Muḥammad al-Akwaʿ, *Ḥayāt ʿālim,* 1:330.

38. Reuven Sharʿabi, *Yeḥi re'uven ve-al yamot: Zikhronot re'uven sharʿabi* (Reḥovot, Israel: Afiqim, 2004), 71.

39. Abdin, "Role of Islam," 192.

40. Yosef Qāfiḥ, *Halikhot teman,* 369–370.

41. Abdin, "Role of Islam," 195–196.

42. Yosef Qāfiḥ, *Halikhot teman,* 369.

43. Ben David, *Bet ha-even,* 306.

44. Dani Bar Maʿoz, *Yiqov ha-din et ha-har: Maḥaloqot u-falganut biqhilat yehude teman* (Reḥovot, Israel: ʿAmutat Eʿeleh ve-tamar, 2005), 256.

45. Yeḥiel Naḥshon, *Hanhagat ha-qehilah ha-yehudit be-teman (Meʿot 17–18)* (Tel Aviv: Ha-Agudah la-ṭipuah ḥevrah ve-tarbut, 2002), 156–158. It seems that in the town of Ḥujariyyah, the rabbinic authorities succeeded in their demand that appeals by Jews to Muslim courts be made with their prior consent. Violators of this rule were fined and Muslim judges asked for referrals from the rabbinic court (ibid., 137n254; Yosef Riḍā, *Temanah,* 149). See also Isaac Hollander, "Halakha, Sharīʿa, and Custom: A Legal Saga from Highland Yemen, 1990–1940," in *Islamic Law: Theory and Practice,* ed. Robert Gleave and Eugenia Kermeli (London: I. B. Tauris,1997), 157; Gamlieli, *Teman be-teʿudot,* 27; Medinah, *Masaʿot r. moshe medinah,* 128.

46. Gamlieli, *Teman be-te'udot,* 246. See also Yosef Tobi, "Ha-Qehilah ha-yehudit be-teman," in *Moreshet yehude teman: 'Iyyunim u-meḥqarim,* ed. Yosef Tobi (Jerusalem: Bo'i teman, 1977), 111–112.

47. Yehudah Ratshaby, "'Inyane yehudim ba-arkha'ot shel goyim," in *Ḥiqre 'ever ve-'arav mugashim le-yehoshu'ah blau 'al yade ḥaverav ba-melot lo shiv'im,* ed. Ḥaggai Ben Shammai (Tel Aviv: Tel Aviv University, 1993), 515f.; Naḥshon, *Hanhagat ha-qehilah,* 138.

48. Gamlieli, *Teman be-te'udot,* 250.

49. Yosef Tobi, "Yerushat nashim ba-ḥevrah ha-yehudit ve-ha-muslimit," in *Bat Teman: 'Olamah shel ha-ishah ha-yehudiyah,* ed. Shalom Serri (Tel Aviv: E'eleh be-tamar, n.d.), 35–50; Naḥshon, *Hanhagat ha-qehilah,* 144, 149–150.

50. Gamlieli, *Teman be-te'udot,* 232.

51. Ibid., 230–235.

52. Naḥshon, *Hanhagat ha-qehilah,* 141–144; Isaac Hollander, "*Ibra* in Highland Yemen: Two Jewish Divorce Settlements," *Islamic Law and Society* 2, no. 1 (1995): 1–23; Amnon Ḥever, "Ha-Shipuṭ ha-rabani be-teman 'al pi ha-'musawwadah', sefer ha-proṭoqolim shel bet din tsan'ā' (me'ot 18–20)" (PhD diss., Tel Aviv University, 2000), 155–161.

53. Bene Moshe, *Sefer Bamsilah,* 61–64.

54. Gamlieli, *Taḥat kanfeha,* 124. On *taḥlīl* marriage, see Yosef Rappoport, *Marriage, Money, and Divorce in Medieval Islamic Society* (Cambridge, UK: Cambridge University Press, 2005), 98–100; Barbara Freyer Stowasser and Zeinab Abul-Magd, "Tahlil Marriage in Sharī'a, Legal Codes, and the Contemporary *Fatwa* Literature," in *Islamic Law and the Challenges of Modernity,* ed. Yvonne Yazbeck Haddad and Barbara Freyer Stowasser (Walnut Creek, CA: Altamira Press, 2004), 161–182; Encyclopedia of Islam, 3rd edition, *sub* "Ḥiyal."

55. Shalom Gamliel, *Ha-Yehudim,* 1:50–63. This "governor," sayyid Hāshim b. 'Alī al-Murtaḍā, may, in fact, have been a high-ranking qadi. Muḥammad Zabārah, *Nuzhat al-naẓar fī rijāl al-qarn al-rābi' 'ashar* (Sanaa, Yemen: Markaz al-dirāsāt wa l-abḥāth al-yamaniyyah, 1979), 620.

56. Yosef Riḍā, *Temanah,* 72n22.

57. Ḥever, "Ha-Shipuṭ ha-rabani be-teman," 164.

58. Gamlieli, *Teman be-te'udot,* 24–25.

59. Gamlieli, "Solele-ha-derekh," 133.

60. Amnon Cohen, Elisheva Simon-Pikali, Eyal Ginio, *Yehudim be-vet ha-mishpaṭ ha-muslimi: Ḥevrah, kalkalah, ve-irgun qehilati bīrushalayim ha-'othmanit* (Jerusalem: Ben Zvi Institute, 2003), 1. For a more recent challenge to the "paradigm of autonomy" with regard to Jewish and Islamic law, see Uriel Simonsohn, *A Common Justice: The Legal Allegiances of Christians and Jews under Early Islam* (Philadelphia: University of Pennsylvania Press, 2011), introduction, chapter 6.

61. Gamlieli, *Teman be-te'udot,* 250–256. Shalom Medinah says Muslims also lived in the Jewish Quarter of Ibb. *Masa'ot r. moshe medinah,* 141.

62. Medinah, *Masa'ot r. moshe medinah,* 142.

63. Nissim Ṭayri, *Bitla'ot ha-galut ve-ha-ge'ulah: Harpatqa'ot ve-nissim bayn radā' le-'aden,* ed. Mordecai Yitshari (Ramat Gan, Israel: the author, 1998), 48–50.

64. Boaz Cohen, *Jewish and Roman Law: A Comparative Study* (New York: Jewish Theological Seminary of America, 1966), 2:728.

65. Shalom Gamliel, *Bate hakneset,* 3:164.

66. Ibid., 1:416–417; Shalom Gamliel, *Ha-Yehudim,* 1:355–361.

67. Shalom Gamliel, *Bate hakneset,* 3:164–165.

68. Yeḥiel Ḥibshūsh, *Mishpaḥat ḥibshūsh,* 1:306.

69. Ibid., 1:307. See Serjeant and Lewcock, *Ṣan'ā',* 316–317.

70. Ben David, *Bet ha-even*, 404–405.
71. Nissim Gamlieli, *Ha-Qami'ah: Sippurim mi-ḥayye ha-yehudim be-teman* (Ramlah, Israel: the author and his sons, 1980), 176–177.
72. Mordecai Yitshari, *Ḥayyim so'arim*, 70.
73. Gamlieli, *Ḥadre teman*, 85–86.
74. Ṭayri, *Bitla'ot ha-galut ve-ha-ge'ulah*, 56; Shalom Bene Moshe, *Sefer dor le-dor yesaperu*, ed. Shim'on Graydi (Reḥovot, Israel: the author, 1985), 83.
75. Mordecai Yitshari, *Hayiti*, 104; Yosef Ḥubārah, *Bitla'ot teman virushalayim*, ed. Shim'on Graydi (Jerusalem: the author, 1970), 94–95; Shāmī, *Riyāḥ*, 355; Yosef Qāfiḥ, *Halikhot teman*, 373.
76. Mordecai Yitshari, *Hayiti*, 178.
77. Ibid., 187.
78. Tsadoq Yitshari, *Kakh baraḥti*, 69.
79. Mordecai Yitshari, *Hayiti*, 164.
80. Gamlieli, *Taḥat kanfeha*, 216; Shalom Se'adyah Gamliel, *Pirsum yeshu'ot hashem la-yehudim be-teman* (Jerusalem: Makhon shalom le-shivṭe yeshurun, 1997), 91–92.
81. 'Afīf, *Shāhid 'alā l-yaman*, 62; Shalom Gamliel, *Ha-Yehudim*, 1:196.
82. Gamlieli, *Taḥat kanfeha*, 216.
83. Sunaydār, *al-Ṭarīq ilā l-ḥurriyyah*,184.
84. Aḥmad 'Abd al-Raḥmān al-Mu'allimī, *Madhābiḥ wa-aghlāl: Mudhakkirāt min sujūn ḥajjah* (Damascus: the author, 1998), 330.
85. Shalom Bene Moshe, *Sefer 'al kanfe dor*, ed. Nissim Binyamin Gamlieli (Reḥovot, Israel: the author, 1995), 50.
86. Yosef Qāfiḥ, *Halikhot teman*, 373.
87. Mu'allimī, *Madhābiḥ wa-aghlāl*, 30, 45–47, 49–50, 89, 97–98, 99–100, 106, 110, 137, 184, 278, 328–330.
88. Yosef Qāfiḥ, *Halikhot teman*, 374.
89. Muḥammad al-Akwa', *Ḥayāt 'ālim*, 1:353–354; Weir, *Tribal Order*, 188, 276–277 (see index under *tanfīdh*); Douglas, *Free Yemeni Movement*, 13–14; Msaodi, "Yemeni Opposition Movement," 100.
90. Shalom Gamliel, *Ha-Yehudim*, 1:82–83.
91. Bene Moshe, *Sefer Bamsilah*, 51–52.
92. Aḥmad b. Muḥammad al-Wazīr, *Ḥayāt al-amīr*, 206.
93. Hallaq, *Sharī'a*, 162–163, 343 (quotation at 343).
94. Ibid., 170.
95. Ibid., 172, 343.
96. Abdin, "Role of Islam," 85, 177, 198; 'Abd al-Raḥmān al-Bayḍānī, *Asrār al-yaman* (Cairo: al-Dār al-qawmiyyah li l-ṭibā'ah wa l-nashr, 1962), 110.
97. Yosef Qāfiḥ, *Halikhot teman*, 370.
98. Tsuriel Ḥatukah, *Zikhronot u-temunot mi-teman ve-'ad matan* (n.p.: the author, 2003), 20.
99. 'Abdallāh b. Miftāḥ, *al-Muntaza' al-mukhtār min al-ghayth al-midrār al-ma'rūf bi-sharḥ al-azhār* (Ṣa'dah, Yemen: al-Jumhuriyyah al-yamaniyyah, Wizārat al-'adl, 2003), 10:56–59 (henceforth *Sharḥ al-azhār*); Aḥmad b. al-Qāsim al-'Ansī, *al-Tāj al-mudhhab li-aḥkām al-madhhab* (Sanaa, Yemen: Maktabat al-yaman al-kubrā, 1947), 4:205–206.
100. Rosen observed this trait as well. Rosen, *The Culture of Islam: Changing Aspects of Contemporary Muslim Life* (Chicago: University of Chicago Press, 2002), 13.
101. Gamlieli, *Ḥevyon*, 30. See also Tobi, "Ha-Qehilah," 97.
102. The narrator of this anecdote, Nissim Gamlieli, says that 'Abdallāh al-Wazīr was the governor of Dhamār and served from 1914/1915 to 1918/1919. Zabārah, *Nuzhat al-naẓar*, 369. His

brother Muḥammad also served as governor of Dhamār (*Nuzhat*, 514), and it is possible that Gamlieli confused the two men.

103. Nissim Binyamin Gamlieli, "Shne sippurim mi-ḥayye ha-yehudim be-ʿir damār," *Tehudah* 19 (1999): 12–14.

104. Mordecai Yitshari, *Ḥayyim soʿarim*, 261.

105. Quoted in Hāshimī, *al-Qaḍāʾ fī l-yaman*, 229.

106. Ibid., 182n1.

107. Shalom Gamliel, *Ha-Yehudim*, 2:169. Messick writes of Ottoman attempts at brevity in legal writing in Yemen. *Calligraphic State*, 191–192.

108. Gamlieli, *Teman be-teʿudot*, 23.

109. Sunaydār, *al-Ṭarīq ilā l-ḥurriyyah*, 163–64; Ismāʿīl al-Akwaʿ, *Hijar*, 1498, 1502.

110. Muḥammad b. ʿAlī al-Akwaʿ, *Ṣafḥah min taʾrīkh al-yaman al-ijtimāʿī wa-qiṣṣat ḥayātī*, (n.p., n.d.), 3:33–34.

111. Mordecai Yitshari, *Ḥayyim soʿarim*, 58–59.

112. Mordecai Yitshari, *Hayiti*, 216.

113. Ismāʿīl al-Akwaʿ, *Hijar*, 85.

114. Ibid., 652–656.

115. Haykel, *Revival and Reform*, 203.

116. Shamāḥī, *al-Yaman*, 205.

117. Ismāʿīl al-Akwaʿ, *Hijar*, 591.

118. Quoted in Ṣāʾidī, *Ḥarakat al-muʿāraḍah*, 245.

119. Ḥayyim Tsadoq, *Be-Ohole teman*, 42.

120. Yitsḥaq Tsubayri, *Mi-Tsanʿāʾ ve-ʿad tsiyon* (Qiryat Ono, Israel: Mekhon Mosheh le-ḥeqer mishnat ha-rambam, 1992), 90–96.

121. Ṣāʾidī, *Ḥarakat al-muʿāraḍah*, 40, 71–72, 80–81, 101; Abdin, "Role of Islam," 198; Aḥmad b. Muḥammad al-Wazīr, *Ḥayāt al-amīr*, 436.

122. The riyāl was a locally minted copy of the 1780 Maria Theresa thaler. Sālim Saʿīd al-Jamal judged the value of a riyāl in Yemen in the 1930s to be equivalent to twelve dollars in 1996. Shalom Gamliel, *Bate hakneset*, 3:262n5. This is corroborated by an incident in which a man lost his temper after being charged one-half riyāl for three cups of coffee and "a meal with butter and eggs" at a roadside rest stop in Yemen in 1949, insisting that he owed only one-quarter riyāl (three dollars according to al-Jamal's exchange rate). Mordecai Yitshari, *Hayiti*, 228. In a 1938 Yemeni-Italian arms contract, one British pound was deemed equal to 13 Yemeni riyāls. Ṣāliḥiyyah, *al-ʿAllāmah*, 129. Aḥmad Jābir ʿAfīf estimates that the fortunes of Sanaa's wealthy merchants in the 1940s ranged from 50,000 to 100,000 riyāls. Afīf, *Shāhid ʿalā l-yaman*, 264.

123. Hāshimī, *al-Qaḍāʾ fī l-yaman*, 232–233. See also Āl Yaḥyā, *al-Yaman*, 180–181, 250–251.

124. Gamlieli, *Teman be-teʿudot*, 24–25.

125. Aharon Ḥamdi, *Zeh sefer ḥokhmah u-musar* (n.p.: Ha-Agudah la-ṭipuaḥ ḥevrah ve-tarbut, 1996), 36.

126. Gamlieli, *Teman u-maḥaneh geʾulah*, 84.

127. The version of the poem in qadi Ismāʿīl al-Akwaʿ, *Hijar al-ʿilm*, 74–75, 1731–1732, differs slightly from that in Abdin, "Role of Islam," 294, which is quoted here. The attribution of the poem to Iryānī is Akwa's and its dating to 1918 is Abdin's.

128. Muṭahhar, *Sīrat al-imām yaḥyā*, 1:260–261, 264, 266 (quotation at 264).

129. Hāshimī, *al-Qaḍāʾ fī l-yaman*, 225–229.

130. Muḥammad al-Akwaʿ, *Ḥayāt ʿālim*, 1:318–319; Hāshimī, *al-Qaḍāʾ fī l-yama,n* 227.

131. Gamlieli, *Ḥadre teman*, 86–91. See also 158–163.

132. Shalom Gamliel, *Bate hakneset*, 3:202.

133. Sunaydār, *al-Ṭarīq ilā l-ḥurriyyah*, 117, 126.

134. Aḥmad b. Muḥammad al-Wazīr, *Ḥayāt al-amīr*, 209–210.

135. Muṭahhar, *Sīrat al-imām yaḥyā,* 1:193.
136. Sunaydār, *al-Ṭarīq ilā l-ḥurriyyah,* 24–25.
137. Aḥmad b. Muḥammad al-Wazīr, *Ḥayāt al-amīr,* 387–391; Aḥmad b. Muḥammad al-Shāmī, *Min al-adab al-yamanī: Naqd wa-ta'rīkh* (n.p.: Dār al-shurūq, 1974), 81, 83.

2. Changing God's Law

1. S. D. Goitein, "Portrait of a Yemenite Weavers' Village," *Jewish Social Studies* 17, no. 1 (1955): 14–15n34.
2. 'Aẓm, *Riḥlah fī bilād,* 144. In contrast, a French woman who stayed in Sanaa in 1947–1948 commented on the cleanliness of the streets of the Jewish Quarter. Markaz li l-dirāsāt wa l-buḥūth al-yamanī, *Thawrat 1948: al-Mīlād wa l-masīrah wa l-mu'aththirāt* (Beirut: Dār al-'awdah, 1982), 512.
3. Gamlieli, *Ha-Qami'ah,* 104.
4. Yosef Qāfiḥ, *Halikhot teman,* 377.
5. Cited in Serjeant and Lewcock, *Ṣan'ā',* 421.
6. Shalom Gamliel, *Ha-Yehudim,* 2:46–48.
7. Ibid., 2:150–154.
8. He may have done this after he left Yemen in 1944.
9. Eraqi Klorman, *Yehude Teman,* 3:15; Yehudah Nini, *The Jews of the Yemen, 1800–1914* (Philadelphia: Harwood Academic Publishers, 1991), 24–26; Parfitt, *Road to Redemption,* 86–88; Āl Yaḥyā, *al-Yaman,* 213, 254–255, 270, 302.
10. Shalom Se'adyah Gamliel, *Pequde teman: Mas he-ḥasut be-teman* (Jerusalem: Makhon shalom le-shivṭe yeshurun, 1982), 65.
11. 'Anzi, "Hashpa'at ha-tmurot," 114.
12. Ben-David, *Bet ha-even,* 465–466.
13. Eraqi Klorman, *Yehude Teman,* 3:17; Serjeant and Lewcock, *Ṣan'ā',* 394–395.
14. Yehudah Ratshaby, "Yehude teman taḥat shilṭon ha-turkim," *Sinai* 64 (1963): 59–60; Ḥubārah, *Bitla'ot teman virushalayim,* 42; Parfitt, *Road to Redemption,* 35.
15. 'Anzi, "Hashpa'at ha-tmurot," 104, 111.
16. 'Amram Qoraḥ, *Se'arat teman,* ed. Shim'on Graydi (Jerusalem: Yaḥyā 'Amram Qoraḥ, 1954), 48–49; Ḥubārah, *Bitla'ot teman virushalayim,* 39; Yosef Riḍā, *Temanah,* 48; Eraqi Klorman, *Yehude Teman,* 3:20.
17. Tobi, "Ha-Qehilah," 71. See also 80, 87, 96–97.
18. Ismā'īl al-Akwa', *Hijar,* 1748; Muḥammad al-Akwa', *Ḥayāt 'ālim,* 2:86.
19. Ṭayri, *Bitla'ot ha-galut ve-ha-ge'ulah,* 50–52. Even though Ṭayri read Ṣāliḥ al-Ẓāhirī's account and Ẓāhirī's son Mordecai edited Ṭayri's book, the two accounts of the same events differ slightly.
20. Mordecai Yitshari, *Hayiti,* 128.
21. Mordecai Yitshari, *Ḥayyim so'arim,* 450–52; Ṭayri, *Bitla'ot ha-galut ve-ha-ge'ulah,* 50–52 (quotation at 52).
22. Manṣūrah, *'Aliyat mirbad haqsamim,* 113, 120, 124.
23. On *corvee* labor, see Msaodi, "Yemeni Opposition Movement," 84, 98–103; Muṭahhar, *Sīrat al-imām yaḥyā,* 1:265; Goitein, "Portrait," 15; 'Afīf, *Shāhid 'alā l-yaman,* 48.
24. Gamlieli, *Taḥat kanfeha,* 253–255.
25. Bene Moshe, *Sefer Bamsilah,* 77–78. Other sources describe government campaigns to kill—and not capture—baboons. Ismā'īl Akwa', *Hijar,* 1747; Muḥammad al-Akwa', *Ḥayāt 'ālim,* 2:89–95; Carmela Abdar, "Ha-Mivneh ha-miqtso'i shel toshve tsurm al-'ūd ke-biṭui le-

ma'amado ve-ha-tahalikhim she-'avru 'alav," in *Le-Rosh yosef: Meḥqarim be-ḥokhmat yisra'el*, ed. Yosef Tobi (Jerusalem: Afiqim, 1995), 487.

26. Halevi, *'Alilot*, 184; Ratson Halevi, *Mi-'olam le-'olam* (Bene Beraq, Israel: Hotsa'at Afiqim, 2002), 208.

27. Gamlieli, *Taḥat kanfeha*, 185.

28. *Sharḥ al-azhār*, 10:495.

29. Sherman Jackson, "Fiction and Formalism: Toward a Functional Analysis of *Uṣūl al-fiqh*," in *Studies in Islamic Legal Theory*, ed. Bernard G. Weiss (Leiden: E. J. Brill, 2002), 195.

30. Muḥammad 'Alī al-Shawkānī, *al-Badr al-ṭāli'*, ed. Ḥusayn al-'Amrī (Beirut: Dār al-fikr, 1998), 397.

31. The three scholars are the emir's son 'Abdallāh b. 'Īsā (1762–1809), 'Alī b. 'Abdallāh al-Jalāl (1756–1810 or 1825), and 'Abdallāh b. Mubārak al-Mālikī. Joseph Sadan has written two articles on this controversy: "Bein hagzerot 'al yahadut teman ba-sof ha-me'ah ha-17 le-'gezerat ha-meqamtsim' be-me'ot ha-18 ve-ha-19," in *Mas'at Moshe: meḥqarim be-tarbut yisra'el ve-'arav mugashim le-moshe gil*, ed. E. Fleischer, Mordecai Akiva Friedman, Joel L. Kraemer (Jerusalem: Mossad Bialik, 1998), 202–236; and "The 'Latrines Decree' in the Yemen versus the *Dhimma* Principles," in *Pluralism and the Other: Studies in Religious Behaviour*, ed. Jan Platvoet and Karel van der Toorn (Leiden: E. J. Brill, 1995), 167–185. I disagree with Sadan's conclusions about the causes of the debate, the development of the major arguments, and its chronology.

32. Ḥayyim Ḥibshūsh, "Qorot yisra'el be-teman le-r. Ḥayyim Ḥibshūsh," ed. Yosef Qāfiḥ, *Sefunot* 2 (1958): 274.

33. Ronald Lewcock, *The Old Walled City of Ṣan'ā'* (Ghent: UNESCO, 1986), 72, 97.

34. Ḥubārah, *Bitla'ot teman virushalayim*, 48.

35. 'Ovadiah, *Netivot teman ve-tsiyon*, 47; 'Atsṭah, *Ḥayye yosef*, 18–19; Ben David, *Bet ha-even*, 9.

36. Thomas B. Stevenson, *Social Change in a Yemeni Highlands Town* (Salt Lake City: University of Utah Press, 1985), 45.

37. Sadan, "'Latrines Decree,'" 177.

38. Yosef Tobi, *Toldot yehude teman mi-kitvehem* (Jerusalem: Merkaz zalman shazar u-merkaz dinur, 1980), 29–30. The Jewish chronicler who adds this detail, Sulaymān Ḥibshūsh, says this happened in 1846, which cannot be correct, because Saḥūlī died in 1795.

39. 'Amram Qoraḥ, the last chief rabbi of Yemen, speculated that bathhouse owners and jurists colluded to force the Jews to collect excrement for these reasons. Qoraḥ, *Se'arat teman*, 26–27.

40. Haykel, *Revival and Reform*, 20.

41. Even Saḥūlī's enemies praised him for his "struggle against the Jews." Muḥammad Zabārah, *Nayl al-waṭar min tarājim rijāl al-yaman fī l-qarn al-thālith 'ashar* (Beirut: Dār al-'awdah, n.d.), 2:386–387.

42. Haykel, *Revival and Reform*, 114–115.

43. On this issue, see Bat-Zion Eraqi Klorman, "The Forced Conversion of Jewish Orphans in Yemen," *International Journal of Middle East Studies* 33, no. 1 (2001): 23–47, and Ari Ariel, "A Reconsideration of Imam Yahya's Attitude toward Forced Conversion of Jewish Orphans in Yemen," *Shofar* 29, no. 1 (2010): 95–111.

44. Serjeant and Lewcock, *Ṣan'ā'*, 422–423; Moshe Tsadoq, "Ha-Yaḥasim," 162; Shalom Gamliel, *Pequde teman*, 48 (he does not specify a year).

45. ' Ovadiah, *Netivot teman ve-tsiyon*, 39–40.

46. Muḥammad 'Alī al-Shawkānī, *Kitāb al-fatḥ al-rabbānī min fatāwā al-imām al-shawkānī*, ed. Abū Muṣ'ab Muḥammad Ṣubḥī b. Ḥasan Ḥallālah (Sanaa, Yemen: Maktabat al-jīl al-jadīd, 2002), 10:5124.

47. This translation is based upon Uri Rubin, "Qur'ān and Poetry: More Data Concerning the Qur'ānic *Jizya* Verse (*'an yadin*)," *Jerusalem Studies in Arabic and Islam* 31 (2006): 139–146.
48. Shawkānī, *Kitāb al-fatḥ*, 10:5048.
49. Ibid., 10:5019.
50. "Munāsib mulā'im mursal." Ibid., 10:5019.
51. Ibid., 10:5032.
52. Ibid., 10:5033.
53. He writes: "You know that it is proper to inform the worker of his wage before the work begins and to pay him before the sweat on his brow dries." Ibid., 10:5096–5097.
54. Ibid., 10:5094.
55. Ibid., 10:5071.
56. Ibid.
57. Ibid., 10:5085–5086: "awwaluka nuṭfatun madhiratun wa-ākhiruka jīfatun qadhiratun wa-ḥashwuka fīmā bayna dhālika bawlun wa-'adhirah." My thanks to Christopher Melchert for information on this figure.
58. Abdin, "Role of Islam," 38–39. The high alert for impurity among Zaydīs seems to have rubbed off on the Jews as well. In Damt a widow who was summoned to take an oath on Torah scroll in an inheritance dispute had to remove her pants (she wore a long dress as well) before entering the synagogue lest she bring in a stain. Women, especially young mothers, were not allowed to approach Shabazi's tomb, because their pants might contain a blood stain. Gamlieli, *Taḥat kanfeha*, 55–56, 269, 404–406.
59. Ze'ev Maghen, "Strangers and Brothers: The Ritual Status of Unbelievers in Islamic Jurisprudence," *Medieval Encounters* 12, no. 2 (2006): 220.
60. "Fa-lā naqūlu lakum ujbirū l-yahūda 'alā hādhihi l-khaṣlati ma'a karāhatihim wa-'adm riḍāhum wa-lakinnā naqūlu murūhum bi-dhālika fa-in qabalū wa-raḍū."
61. Shawkānī, *Kitāb al-fatḥ*, 10:5049.
62. Muṭahhar, *Sīrat al-imām yaḥyā*, 1:40–44; Muḥammad al-Akwa', *Ḥayāt 'ālim*, 1:318.
63. Muṭahhar, *Sīrat al-imām yaḥyā*, 1:32–36, 47–48, 50–57; Ṣāliḥiyyah, *al-'Allāmah*, 8n2.
64. Parfitt, *Road to Redemption*, 120, 206; Manṣūrah, *'Aliyat mirbad haqsamim*, 287–288, 293, 295. Shalom Gamliel describes an attempt by Prince 'Alī to build a soap factory staffed by Jews. *Ha-Yehudim*, 2:54; *Pirsum*, 36.
65. Letter from Qoraḥ to Manṣūrah, reproduced in Manṣūrah, *'Aliyat mirbad haqsamim*, 293. Parfitt is mistaken when he says: "[The Jews'] street cleaning and refuse collecting role must have seemed a little anachronistic by 1949 even in the Yemen." *Road to Redemption*, 204. On the idea that Jews had to teach Muslim trades before they left, see Parfitt, "The Jewish Image of the Imam: Paradox or Paradigm," in *Israel and Ishmael*, 217.
66. Wael B. Hallaq, "Was the Gate of *Ijtihad* Closed?" *International Journal of Middle East Studies* 16, no.1 (1984): 3–41; Aḥmad Dallal, "Appropriating the Past: Twentieth-Century Reconstruction of Pre-Modern Islamic Thought," *Islamic Law and Society* 7, no. 3 (2000): 325–358.
67. Dallal, "Appropriating the Past," 356.
68. *Sharḥ al-azhār*, 10:498.
69. Ibid., 10:496n4.
70. Parfitt, *Road to Redemption*, 107–108.
71. Yosef Riḍā, *Temanah*, 150–151.
72. Ḥamdi, *Zeh sefer ḥokhmah u-musar*, 19.
73. Mordecai Yitshari, *Hayiti*, 225–226.
74. Shalom Gamliel, *Ha-Yehudim*, 2:95.
75. Mordecai Yitshari, *Hayiti*, 144–153.
76. Tsadoq Yitshari, *Kakh baraḥti*, 100–101 (quotation at 100).

77. Bene Moshe, *Sefer Bamsilah,* 47–49.
78. Halevi, *'Alilot,* 37–38.
79. Ibid., 66–72.
80. Halevi, *Mi-'olam,* 64–65.
81. Ṭayri, *Bitla'ot ha-galut ve-ha-ge'ulah,* 56.
82. Yeḥiel Ḥibshūsh, *Ḥayye ha-yeled be-teman* (n.p.: Ḥibshūsh family, 1991), 53, 76–78, 171.
83. Gamlieli, *Teman be-teudot,* 252–253. See also Bene Moshe, *Sefer Bamsilah,* 80.
84. Halevi, *'Alilot,* 118–120, 127.
85. Shalom Lahav, *Qehilat yehude bayḥān* (Netanyah, Israel: Ha-Agudah la-ṭipuaḥ ḥevrah ve-tarbut, 1996), 46.
86. Ben David, *Bet ha-even,* 18–19, 181; Gamlieli, "Solele ha-derekh," 136; Bat-Zion Eraqi Klorman, "Aharon 'afjin ve-ha-'aliyah mi-tsfon teman: Diyyun histoṛiyografi," *Pe'amim* 84 (2000): 96.
87. Shalom Gamliel, *Ha-Yehudim,* 1:41. On the Ḍubyānī donkey, see Halevi, *'Alilot,* 32–33, 66; Gamlieli, *Ḥevyon,* 124, 126n3; Ben David, *Bet ha-even,* 16; Bene Moshe, *Sefer dor le-dor,* 152.
88. Medinah, *Masa'ot r. moshe medinah,* 32–33 (quotation at 33).
89. Shalom Gamliel, *Ha-Yehudim,* 1:42.
90. Ibid., 1:42.
91. Ibid., 1:42–45.
92. Ibid., 1:47.
93. Ibid., 1:43.
94. *Sharḥ al-azhār,* 10:115, 117n5; 'Ansī, *al-Tāj al-mudhhab,* 4:234.
95. Shalom Gamliel, *Ha-Yehudim,* 1:48.
96. Ibid., 1:48.
97. Ibid., 1:43.
98. *Sharḥ al-azhār,* 1:202–203; 'Ansī, *al-Tāj al-mudhhab,* 1:20. On the issue of the ritual (im) purity of nonbelievers in Islamic law, see Maghen, "Strangers and Brothers," and Leor Halevi, "Christian Impurity versus Economic Necessity: A Fifteenth-Century Fatwa on European Paper," *Speculum* 83 (2008), 917–945.
99. Yeḥiel Ḥibshūsh, *Riḥlah,* 46.
100. Stevenson, *Social Change,* 45.
101. Ḥayyim Tsadoq, *Be-Ohole teman,* 315.
102. Gamlieli, *Ḥevyon,* 18–19; 'Ovadiah, *Netivot teman ve-tsiyon,* section on his flight to Aden; Yeḥiel Ḥibshūsh, *Ḥayye ha-yeled,* 100.
103. Sunaydār, *al-Ṭarīq ilā l-ḥurriyyah,* 93.
104. Gamlieli, *Taḥat kanfeha,* 22, 309–311.
105. Ibid., 119–120.
106. Ibid.; Ben-David, *Bet ha-even,* 406, 413–414.
107. Gamlieli, *Ḥevyon,* 31n4.
108. Shalom Gamliel, *Ha-Yehudim,* 1:48–49.
109. Ibid., 1:44; Yosef Qāfiḥ, *Halikhot teman,* 374.
110. Shalom Gamliel, *Ha-Yehudim,* 1:48n18.
111. *Sharḥ al-azhār,* 10:118–119.
112. 'Ansī, *al-Tāj al-mudhhab,* 4:235.
113. Shalom Gamliel, *Ha-Yehudim,* 2:50.
114. Serjeant and Lewcock, *Ṣan'ā',* 114. Juzaylān also reports that the sons of the governor of Ta'izz, Muḥammad b. Muḥammad al-Bāshā, had bicycles (57–58).
115. Mordecai Yitshari, *Hayiti,* 146.
116. vom Bruck, *Islam, Memory, and Morality,* 93.

117. Shalom Gamliel, *Pirsum,* 30–31 (quotation at 31).
118. Ibid., 31, 33–34.
119. Ibid., 35–36 (quotation at 35).
120. Ibid., 37, 41.
121. Ibid., 36.
122. Ibid., 39–40.
123. Ibid., 41. On the ways adults encouraged or discouraged such assaults, see Moshe Tsadoq, "Ha-Yaḥasim," 153–154. On the role of children in policing interreligious boundaries, see David Nirenberg's thought-provoking discussion in *Communities of Violence: Persecution of Minorities in the Middle Ages* (Princeton, NJ: Princeton University Press, 1996), 224–227.
124. Shalom Gamliel, *Pirsum,* 43–44.
125. Shalom Gamliel, *Ha-Yehudim,* 2:148–50.
126. Shalom Gamliel, *Pirsum,* 47–50 (quotation at 47).
127. Sunaydār, *al-Ṭarīq ilā l-ḥurriyyah,* 51, 75, 115. See also Ismāʿīl al-Akwaʿ, *Hijar,* 1906; Muḥammad al-Akwaʿ, *Ḥayāt ʿālim,* 2:142n1.
128. Mordecai Yitshari, *Hayiti,* 165.
129. Shalom Gamliel, *Pirsum,* 51–54. The idea that some opponents of Imām Yaḥyā would consult his son should not be surprising. Muḥammad ʿĪsā Ṣāliḥiyyah makes the important point that the opposition to imāmic rule was not monolithic, and an influential segment of it supported Aḥmad. *al-ʿAllāmah,* 194.
130. Shalom Gamliel, *Pirsum,* 58.
131. Ibid., 59–62.
132. See Christopher S. Thompson, *The Tour de France: A Cultural History* (Berkeley: University of California Press, 2008).

3. Muslim Jews and Jewish Muslims

1. Shalom Gamliel, *Pirsum,* 89–91; Halevi, *Mi-ʿolam,* 294.
2. Mordecai Yitshari, *Hayiti,* 161.
3. Ratshaby, "Yehudim u-muslimim," 232.
4. William M. O'Barr, *Linguistic Evidence: Language, Power, and Strategy in the Courtroom* (New York: Academic Press, 1982).
5. Tsadoq Yitshari, *Ḥayyim soʿarim,* 71–72; Gamlieli, *Ḥevyon,* 97–98.
6. Avraham Madhalah, *Ein li erets aḥeret* (Tel Aviv: Eʿeleh ve-tamar, 1997), 31–33.
7. Abdin, "Role of Islam," 235. The report is cited by Parfitt, *Road to Redemption,* 45. Ḥasan, *Qalb,* 116.
8. Shalom Gamliel, *Bate hakneset,* 1:402.
9. Yeḥiel Ḥibshūsh, *Ḥayye ha-yeled,* 104.
10. Gamlieli, *Taḥat kanfeha,* 385.
11. Ibid., 154.
12. Halevi, *Mi-ʿolam,* 169, 177–178.
13. Yeḥiel Ḥibshūsh, *Ḥayye ha-yeled,* 104.
14. Shalom Gamliel, *Bate hakneset,* 3:244–245.
15. Yeḥiel Ḥibshūsh, *Mishpaḥat ḥibshush,* 1:483.
16. Ibid., 1:442–443.
17. Yehudah Levi Naḥum and Yosef Tobi, "Quntres 'Ḥayye ha-temanim' le-rav yosef shemen," in *Yahadut teman: Pirqe meḥqar ve-ʿiyyun,* ed. Yosef Tobi and Yisrael Yeshayahu (Jerusalem: Ben Zvi Institute, 1975), 28.

18. Tsubayri, *Mi-Tsan'ā' ve-'ad tsiyon,* 69–74. Tsubayri is not sure if the Muslim in question is Rājib or Muḥammad Ghamṣān [*sic*]. Muḥammad b. Muḥammad Ghamḍān, a sayyid and prominent merchant who died in 1939, seems the most likely possibility. Zabārah, *Nuzhat,* 578.

19. Mordecai Yitshari, *Hayiti,* 122–123.

20. Ismā'īl al-Akwa', *Hijar,* 1544.

21. Shalom Gamliel, *Ha-Yehudim,* 1:72–73. On Jewish conspiracy theories concerning the origins of the Qur'an, see also Shalom Gamliel, *Bate hakneset,* 2:250–251n3, 279n8; Nissim Gamlieli, *Teman be-te'udot,* 47.

22. Medinah, *Masa'ot r. moshe medinah,* 150.

23. Yosef Tobi, "*Histoire de la Communauté Juive du Yémen aux XIXe et XXe Siècles,*" in *L'Arabie du Sud,* ed. Joseph Chelhod (Paris: Maisonneuve et Larose, 1984), 124n28; Yosef Riḍā, *Temanah,* 66n13; H. St. J. B. Philby, *Arabian Highlands* (Ithaca, NY: Cornell University Press, 1952), 278.

24. 'Ovadiah Zandani, *Yalquṭ 'ovadiah: Mi-hare baraṭ le-moshav yinon,* ed. Nissim Binyamin Gamlieli (Tel Aviv: Afiqim, 1986), 110; 'Ezra Qehati, *Yeqiray be-teman u-be-tsiyon: Pirqe ḥayyav ve-zikhronot* (Tel Aviv: Afiqim, 1999), 57n40.

25. Aharon Ben David, "'Al 'aliyatam shel yehude tsa'dah ve-ha-svivah bi-shnat ha-tash'a (1951)," *Tehudah* 19 (1999): 77.

26. Manṣūrah, *'Aliyat mirbad haqsamim,* 170; Ḥamdi, *Zeh sefer ḥokhmah u-musar,* 39–42.

27. Ḥubārah, *Bitla'ot teman virushalayim,* 75.

28. Yeḥiel Ḥibshūsh, *Mishpaḥat ḥibshush,* 1:51; Eraqi Klorman, *Yehude teman,* 3:36–37.

29. Yeḥiel Ḥibshūsh, *Mishpaḥat ḥibshush,* 1:135.

30. Serjeant and Lewcock, *Ṣan'ā',* 396; Ḥayyim Gamliel, *Pirqe ḥayyim* (Ramat Gan, Israel: Gamliel family, 1998), 48.

31. Mordecai Yitshari, *Ḥayyim so'arim,* 107–109, 111.

32. Shalom Qoraḥ, *Iggeret bokhim* (Bet Shemesh, Israel: Ha-Va'ad le-hadpasat ḥibure MaHarShaQ, 1962), 18.

33. Shāmī, *Riyāḥ,* 347.

34. Ṭayil, *Bitla'ot ha-galut,* 18

35. Mordecai Yitshari, *Ḥayyim so'arim,* 40–42.

36. Gamlieli, *Teman u-maḥaneh ge'ulah,* 88–91, 94, 97–99; Gamlieli, *Ha-Qami'ah,* 52.

37. Ismā'īl al-Akwa', *Hijar,* 632.

38. Mordecai Yitshari, *Ḥayyim so'arim,* 44–45.

39. Ibid., 252–253.

40. On the tradition of *ḥumaynī* poetry in Yemen, see my *Like Joseph in Beauty: Yemeni Vernacular Poetry and Arab-Jewish Symbiosis* (Leiden: E. J. Brill, 2009).

41. Mordecai Yitshari, *Hayiti,* 156–157 (quotation at 157).

42. Erich Brauer, *Ethnologie der Jemenitischen Juden* (Heidelberg: Carl Winters Universitätsbuchandlung, 1934), 79.

43. Shmuel Yavnieli, *Masa' le-teman* (Tel Aviv: Hotsa'at mifleget po'ale erets yisra'el, 1952), 21.

44. Muḥammad b. Muḥammad Zabārah, *Ā'immat al-yaman bi l-qarn al-rābi' 'ashar li l-hijrah* (Cairo: al-Maṭba'ah al-salafiyyah, 1955), 178, 181, 373 (quotation at 181).

45. Sunaydār, *al-Ṭarīq ilā l-ḥurriyyah,* 24.

46. Yosef Riḍā, *Temunah,* 146n.

47. Gamlieli, *Teman u-maḥaneh ge'ulah,* 95–96.

48. 'Anzi, "Hashpa'at ha-tmurot," 112; Eraqi Klorman, *Yehude teman,* 3:89–90.

49. Yosef Tobi, *The Jews of Yemen: Studies in Their History and Culture* (Leiden: E. J. Brill, 1999), 185.

50. Mordecai Yitshari, *Ḥayyim so'arim,* 60–67.

51. Tsadoq Yitshari, *Kakh baraḥti,* 50; Mordecai Yitshari, *Hayiti,* 133.

52. Zandani, *Yalquṭ,* 107–108; Ben David, "'Al 'aliyatam," 74; Parfitt, *Road to Redemption,* 147.

53. Bene Moshe, *Sefer dor le-dor,* 149, 155–156.

54. Medinah, *Masa'ot r. moshe medinah,* 204.

55. Yeḥiel Ḥibshūsh, *Mishpaḥat ḥibshush,* 1:469. This source does not clarify the logistics of wearing what were presumably "clip-on" sidelocks.

56. Ismā'īl al-Akwā', *al-Amthāl al-yamāniyyah* (Sanaa, Yemen: Maktabat al-jīl al-jadīd, Mu'assasat al-risālah, 1984), 1:371–372.

57. Ben David, *Bet ha-even,* 144.

58. Reuven Shar'abi, *Yeḥi re'uven ve-al yamot,* 70.

59. See Weir, *Tribal Order,* 174–177.

60. Shlomo Dov Goitein, *Jews and Arabs: Their Contacts through the Ages* (New York: Schocken, 1955), 74.

61. Shim'on Ballas, *Outcast,* trans. Ammiel Alcalay and Oz Shelach (San Francisco: City Lights Books, 2007), 33–35, 58.

62. Gamlieli, *Ha-Qami'ah,* 13, 17.

63. Gamlieli, *Ḥadre teman,* 181.

64. Tsadoq Yitshari, *Kakh baraḥti,* 101.

65. Ibid., 110–112; Bat-Zion Eraqi Klorman, "Yemen: Religion, Magic, and Jews," *Proceedings of the Seminar for Arabian Studies* 39 (2009): 127; Medinah, *Masa'ot r. moshe medinah,* 36.

66. Bene Moshe, *Sefer dor le-dor,* 91–92, 95, 131; Medinah, *Masa'ot r. moshe medinah,* 43, 121; Qehati, *Yeqiray,* 53.

67. Yosef Riḍā, *Temanah,* 32n1.

68. Ḥayyim Ḥibshūsh, *Masa'ot ḥibshūsh,* ed. Shlomo Dov Goitein (Jerusalem: Ben Zvi Institute, Hebrew University of Jerusalem, 1983), 131–132n7.

69. Halevi, *Mi-'olam,* 24–25.

70. Zayd Muḥammad Ḥajar, "Awḍā' yahūd ṣan'ā' al-ijtimā'iyyah," *Dirāsāt yamaniyyah* 46 (1992): 171.

71. Halevi, *Mi-'olam,* 46, 278, 288 (quotation at 46).

72. Ratshaby, "Yehudim u-muslimim," 231; Moshe Tsadoq, "Ha-Yaḥasim," 156. Another version of this proverb defines the things that separate Jew from Muslim as "religion, the knife, and marriage." Gamlieli, *Taḥat kanfeha,* 170.

73. Gamlieli, *Teman u-maḥaneh ge'ulah,* 119–121; Zandani, *Yalquṭ,* 109.

74. Bene Moshe, *Sefer Bamsilah,* 90.

75. Gamlieli, *Taḥat kanfeha,* 18–19.

76. Ibid, 21, 23.

77. Ibid., 24.

78. Ibid., 24–26.

79. Ibid., 52.

80. Ratshaby, "Yehudim u-muslimim," 235; Gamlieli, *Teman be-te'udot,* 48n3.

81. Gamlieli, *Teman be-te'udot,* 48n3.

82. Bat-Zion Eraqi Klorman, "Muslim Society as an Alternative: Jews Converting to Islam," *Jewish Social Studies* 14 (2007): 101–102.

83. Halevi, *'Alilot,* 173.

84. Ibid., 189.

85. Ṭayri, *Bitla'ot ha-galut,* 31–32.

86. Gamlieli, *Teman u-maḥaneh ge'ulah,* 42; Gamlieli, *Ha-Qami'ah,* 130–131.

87. 'Ovadiah, *Netivot,* 41–42.

88. Rihani, *Arabian Peak and Desert,* 182–183.

89. Ḥusayn Muḥammad al-Maqbalī, *Mudhakkirāt al-maqbalī* (Damascus: Dār al-fikr, 1986), 118–120.

90. Ben David, *Bet ha-even,* 402–404.

91. Ratshaby, "Yehudim u-muslimim," 234; Yeḥiel Ḥibshūsh, *Mishpaḥat ḥibshush,* 1:472; Mordecai Yitshari, *Hayiti,* 96; Eraqi Klorman, "Muslim Society," 104; Gamlieli, *Teman be-te'udot,* 49; Gamlieli, *Ḥadre teman,* 154–156; Bene Moshe, *Sefer Bamsilah,* 90; Ben David, *Bet ha-even,* 476.

92. Gamlieli, *Ḥevyon,* 85–86; Gil'ad Tsadoq, *Sefer Zikhron teman,* 47–48; Moshe Piamenta, *Dictionary of Post-Classical Yemeni Arabic* (Leiden: E. J. Brill, 1990–1991), 161.

93. Sunaydār, *al-Ṭarīq ilā l-ḥurriyyah,* 61.

94. Shlomo Dov Goitein and Menaḥem Ben Sasson, *Ha-Temanim: Historiyah, Sidre ḥevrah, ḥayye ha-ruaḥ: Mivḥar meḥqarim* (Jerusalem: Ben Zvi Institute, 1983), 288ff; Norman Stillman, trans., *The Jews of Arab Lands: A History and Source Book* (Philadelphia: Jewish Publication Society, 1979), 257.

95. The following Arabic text is so solecistic that I mildly classicized it here: "anta 'ārif anna fī filasṭīn al-ḥukm fīhā zayy amrīkah, lā 'ād yahūdī 'alā yahūdiyyatihi wa-lā 'ād al-islām wa l-yahūdiyyah illā 'indinā fī l-yaman. Lā takhāf, iḥnā nitāqīkum." Manṣūrah, *'Aliyat mirbad haqsamim,* 67–68.

96. Yeḥiel Ḥibshūsh, *Mishpaḥat ḥibshush,* 1:471.

97. Shalom Qoraḥ, *Iggeret bokhim,* 96.

98. Each of the three intermediaries decried the secularism of the Israeli state. Shalom Gamliel, *Pe'ame ha-'aliyah,* 169; Tsadoq Yitshari, *Kakh baraḥti,* 197–199; Manṣūrah, *'Aliyat mirbad haqsamim,* 255.

99. 'Ovadiah, *Netivot,* 37–38, 40–41.

100. 'Atsṭah, *Ḥayye yosef,* 37.

101. Reuven Shar'abi, *Yeḥi re'uven,* 67–68.

102. Mordecai Yitshari, *Ḥayyim so'arim,* 94–95.

103. Ibid., 302–305.

104. Yosef Riḍā, *Temanah,* 117–119.

105. Gamlieli, *Ha-Qami'ah,* 50–63. See also Gamlieli, *Teman u-maḥaneh ge'ulah,* 65–68; Moshe Tsadoq, "Ha-Yaḥasim," 147.

106. Ḥayyim Ḥibshūsh, *Masa'ot ḥibshūsh,* 262.

107. Reuven Shar'abi, *Yeḥi re'uven,* 43–44. Nissim Gamlieli describes the situation in nearly identical terms (*Teman be-te'udot,* 28).

108. Yosef Riḍā, *Temanah,* 124, 126.

109. Lahav, *Qehilat yehude bayḥān,* 85–87.

110. On the role of Imām Yaḥyā's *madrasah al-'ilmiyyah* in training this new cadre of bureaucrats, see Messick, *Calligraphic State,* 108–114; vom Bruck, *Islam, Memory, and Morality,* 51.

111. Nazīh Mu'ayyad al-'Aẓm, *Riḥlah fī bilād al-'arabiyyah al-sa'īdah: Min miṣr ilā ṣan'ā'* (Beirut: Manshūrāt al-madīnah, 1986), 301–302.

112. 'Atsṭah, *Ḥayye yosef,* 31; Reuven Shar'abi, *Yeḥi re'uven,* 25; Bene Moshe, *Sefer 'al kanfe dor,* 25.

113. Yosef Riḍā, *Temanah,* 93.

114. Ibid., 52–53, 69n8.

115. Madhalah, *Ein li erets aḥeret,* 43.

116. Ibid., 45.

117. Dresch, *History of Modern Yemen,* 28–29; Muṭahhar, *Sīrat al-imām yaḥyā,* 1:276–281; 'Abduh, *Lamaḥāt,* 39–101; Yaḥyā Manṣūr Naṣr, *Shi'r wa-dhikrayāt* (Beirut: Manshūrāt al-'aṣr al-ḥadīth, 1986), 51–52.

118. Aḥmad b. Muḥammad al-Wazīr, *Ḥayāt al-amīr,* 176; Aḥmad al-Shāmī, *Riyāḥ al-taghyīr,* 210–212; Muḥammad al-Akwaʿ, *Ḥayāt ʿālim,* 1:273–276, 346, 407–415. This story is disputed by ʿAbduh, who claims that the various conspiracies uncovered by the governor of Taʿizz, ʿAlī al-Wazīr, merely served as pretexts for his violent crackdowns. ʿAbduh, *Lamaḥāt,* 39–101.

119. Parfitt, *Road to Redemption,* 49–50.

120. Mordecai Yitshari, *Hayiti,* 122.

121. Eraqi Klorman, "Yemen: Religion, Magic," 128.

122. Yosef Riḍā, *Temanah,* 52n24, 58n17.

123. Mordecai Yitshari, *Hayiti,* 120–121.

124. Paul Fenton, "Pulmus muslimi mi-teman neged ha-rambam: Ha-Imam al-shawkani ve-sifro ba-ʿinyan ḥayye ʿolam ha-ba," in *Le-Rosh yosef: Meḥqarim be-ḥokhmat yisra'el,* ed. Yosef Tobi (Jerusalem: Afiqim, 1995), 409–434.

125. See my "*Halakhah* through the Lens of *Sharīʿah:* The Case of the Kuhlani Synagogue in Sanʿa', 1933–1944," in *The Convergence of Judaism and Islam: Religious, Scientific and Cultural Dimensions,* ed. Michael Laskier and Yaacov Lev (Gainesville: University Press of Florida, 2011), 126–146.

126. Mordecai Yitshari, *Ḥayyim soʿarim,* 263.

127. Mordecai Yitshari, *Hayiti,* 175.

128. Ibid, 206.

129. Muḥammad al-Akwaʿ, *Ṣafḥah,* 2:99.

130. Gamlieli, *Ha-Qamiʿah,* 38–39. On "donkeying," see chapter 4.

131. Mordecai Yitshari, *Hayiti,* 213–237.

132. Halevi, *ʿAlilot,* 167–210.

133. Ibid., 151–163; Halevi, *Mi-ʿolam,* 70.

134. Lahav, *Qehilat yehude bayḥān,* 132–137.

135. Robert L. Playfair describes a double-bladed saber on a red background in *A History of Arabia Felix or Yemen from the Commencement of the Christian Era until the Present Time* (Bombay: Education Society's Press, 1859), 29. Twentieth-century images of the last imāms' flag depict a single-bladed sword. On the image of Dhū l-fiqar and its association with the imāms of Yemen, see Jane Hathaway, *A Tale of Two Factions: Myth, Memory, and Identity in Ottoman Egypt and Yemen* (Albany: SUNY Press, 2003), 177–180.

136. Mordecai Yitshari, *Hayiti,* 259–264.

137. Shlomo Dov Goitein, *A Mediterranean Society: The Jewish Communities of the Arab World as Portrayed in the Documents of the Cairo Genizah* (Berkeley: University of California Press, 1967), 2:406f.

138. Ḥayyim Gamliel, *Pirqe ḥayyim,* 29.

139. Eraqi Klorman, *Yehude teman,* 3:44, 46, citing Sālim al-Jahrāzī, title: "Le-matsav ha-yehudim be-teman," newspaper: *Ha-Ḥerut,* March 20, 1914 and Yehudah Ratshaby, "Le-Toldot ha-maḥloqet ʿal ha-qabalah biqhilat tsanʿa bi-shnot 1913–1914," *Peʿamim* 88 (2001): 103.

140. Shalom Gamliel, "Ḥakhme ha-yehudim bi-tsanʿa': Maḥloqet ve-ha-shalom she-naʿaseh beinehem," appended to his *Ḥakhme ha-yehudim be-teman be-dorenu ve-ʿad samukh litqufat ha-tana'im* (Jerusalem: Makhon shalom le-shivṭe yeshurun, 1992), 201–209.

141. Eraqi Klorman, *Yehude teman,* 3:42–46.

142. Shalom ʿUzayri, *Gale or: Pirqe hisṭoriyah* (Tel Aviv, 1985), 20; Ḥubārah, *Bitla'ot teman virushalayim,* 71; Eraqi Klorman, *Yehude teman,* 3:63–64.

143. Yoḥai ʿEden, "Pulmus ha-qabalah bi-tsanʿā: Ha-Reqaʿ ha-ruḥani ve-ha-ḥevrati le-pulmus ha-qabalah be-shanim (1912–1944)" (master's thesis, Touro College, 1998), 127n86; 40–41. Mordecai Yitshari's *Ḥayyim soʿarim* contains another 1934 fatwa by a Muslim judge on this issue of Jewish practice (494).

144. Eraqi Klorman, *Yehude teman,* 3:42–43.
145. ‘Anzi, “Hashpa‘at hatmurot,” 2:95, 110, 118.
146. Eraqi Klorman, *Yehude teman,* 3:63.
147. Y. Klingler and Tsiporah Friedman-Maqov, “Maḥaneh hapliṭim ha-yehudim ha-temanim be-‘aden bi-shnat tashad (1944),” *Tehudah* 19 (1999): 34; Eraqi Klorman, *Yehude teman,* 3:69.
148. Shalom Gamliel, “Ḥakhme ha-yehudim bi-tsan‘a’”; Mordecai Yitshari, *Ḥayyim so‘arim,* 114–129.
149. Yosef Tobi, “Challenges to Tradition: Jewish Cultures in Yemen, Iraq, Iran, Afghanistan, and Bukhara,” in *Cultures of the Jews: A New History,* ed. David Biale (New York: Schocken, 2002), 942–945; Moshe Tsadoq, “Nitsane ‘haskalah’ be-teman,” *Davar,* July 30, 1954, 6; ‘Amram Gamliel, “A Spark of Enlightenment among the Jews of Yemen,” *Hebrew Studies* 25 (1984): 82–89; Yehudah Nini, “Pulmus Mi-‘inyan vikuaḥ ‘aqar ‘al ḥokhmat ha-qabalah bein ḥakhme teman be-reshit ha-me’ah,” *Mikha’el* 14 (1997): 215–243.
150. S. D. Goitein, “Mi hayah Eduard Glazer,” in *Shvut Teman,* ed. Yisrael Yeshayahu and Aharon Tsadoq (Tel Aviv: Hots’at “mi-teman le-tsiyon,” 1945), 149–154; Nini, “Pulmus,” 227, 243; Anonymous, *Quntres magen ve-tsinah ha-ḥosef et ha-emet ‘al kat ha-kofrim ha-niqra’im “darda‘im” umegaleh et partsufo ha-amiti shel ha-‘omed bi-roshah* (Brooklyn: n.p., 1993), 46; Eraqi Klorman, *Yehude teman,* 3:34.
151. Wagner, *Like Joseph,* 220–221.
152. Serjeant and Lewcock, *Ṣan‘ā’,* 396.
153. Camīlia Abū Jabal, *Yahūd al-yaman* (Damascus: Dār al-namīr, 1999), 40.
154. Yeshayahu and Tsadoq, *Shvut Teman,* 223–226.
155. Mark S. Wagner, “Jewish Mysticism on Trial in a Muslim Court: A *Fatwā* on the *Zohar*—Yemen 1914,” *Die Welt des Islams* 47, no. 2 (2007): 207–231.
156. See Tobi, *Jews of Yemen,* chapter 10.
157. Eraqi Klorman, *Yehude teman,* 3:27, citing Sālim Jahrāzī.
158. Ibid., 3:49–58.
159. In Ratzhaby, “Le-Toldot ha-maḥloqet,” 104, and Anonymous, *Quntres,* 75, the Qāfiḥ faction went to the Muslim court. In Yosef Tobi, “Mi ḥiber et sefer emunat ha-shem?” *Da‘at* 49 (2002): 88, and Nini, “Pulmus,” 233, the Isḥāq faction brought the issue to the imām’s attention.
160. ‘Uzayri, *Gale or,* 16.
161. Ibid.
162. Shamāḥī, *al-Yaman,* 188.
163. Ismā‘īl al-Akwa‘, *Hijar,* 696, 702 (quotation at 696).
164. Muḥammad Aḥmad Nu‘mān, *Azmat al-muthaqqaf al-yamanī* (n.p.: Dār al-naṣr li l-ṭibā‘ah wa l-nashr wa l-i‘lān, 1964), 17. See also Aḥmad b. Muḥammad al-Wazīr, *Ḥayāt al-amīr,* 276, ‘Abduh, *Lamaḥāt,* 1:118–121, 122–123, 125–126.
165. ‘Afīf, *Shāhid,* 258.
166. Zandani, *Yalquṭ,* 116.
167. Yaḥyā Qāfiḥ, *Milḥamot ha-shem* (Jerusalem: Defus P. ‘Enav, 1931), 129; Nini, “Pulmus,” 242; Ḥayyim Shar‘abi, “Peraqim mi-farashat ‘dor-de‘ah’ be-teman,” in *Shvut Teman,* 206; Yosef Tobi, “Hedim la-vikuaḥ ‘al ha-qabalah bi-sefer ‘‘ets ḥayyim’ le-rabbi se‘adyah naddaf (tsan‘a 1926),” in *Meḥqarim be-lashon ha-‘ivrit uvimad‘e hayahadut,* ed. Aharon Ben-David and Yitsḥaq Gluska (Jerusalem: Ha-Agudah la-ṭipuaḥ ḥevrah ve-tarbut, 2001), 109; Tobi, “Mi ḥiber,” 88f.
168. Eraqi Klorman, *Yehude teman,* 3:61n154.
169. Wagner, *Like Joseph,* 222; Eraqi Klorman, *Yehude teman,* 3:88.
170. Shalom Gamliel, *Ḥakhme ha-yehudim,* 218; Shalom Gamliel, *Bate hakneset,* 2:130–131.

171. Wagner, *Like Joseph*, 227–228.
172. Yosef Tsurieli, *Kalkalah ve-ḥinukh moderni be-teman ba-ʿet ha-ḥadashah* (Jerusalem: the author, 2005), 240, 241.
173. Wagner, "Jewish Mysticism," 214.
174. Ibid.
175. Ismāʿīl al-Akwaʿ, *Hijar*, 222–225, 750f, 2089; Aḥmad Muḥammad al-Shāmī, *Imām al-yaman aḥmad ḥamīd al-dīn* (n.p.: Dār al-kitāb al-jadīd, 1965), 90–97; Juzaylān, *Lamaḥāt*, 85–86; Abdin, "Role of Islam," 44; Yosef Riḍā, *Temanah*, 47–48n, 64–67.
176. Yosef Riḍā, *Temanah*, 66–67. The veneration of Shabazi and his family on the part of Muslims is described in Yosef Riḍā, *Temanah*, 63n2, 67n17, and in ʿOvadiah, *Netivot*, 63. On Shabazi and his poetry, see my *Like Joseph*, chapters 5–8.
177. Yosef Tobi already drew attention to the fact that the imām's rationalistic view of Islam did not translate into his support for Qāfiḥ's rationalistic view of Judaism. Tobi, *Jews of Yemen*, 190.
178. Qadi Ismāʿīl al-Akwaʿ writes that the imām accepted the correctness of both Zaydī and Sunni prayer rites (*Hijar*, 1698), but only Shalom Gamliel dates this to 1919 (*Ḥakhme ha-yehudim*, 214f).
179. Ḥasan, *Qalb*, 205–206; Āl Yaḥyā, *al-Yaman fī ʿuyūn*, 102–103.
180. vom Bruck, *Islam, Memory, and Morality*, 294n15.
181. ʿAnsī, *al-Tāj al-mudhhab*, 4:467f.
182. Sunaydār, *al-Ṭarīq ilā l-ḥurriyyah*, 17–18. On the pro-Sunni faction among the Aḥrār, see ibid., *zay-waw*, 21, 28, 30–31, 60–61, 85–86.
183. Ismāʿīl al-Akwaʿ, *Hijar*, 1708–1710.
184. Muḥammad al-Akwaʿ, *Ḥayāt ʿālim*, 1:379–380, 382–386.
185. ʿAbduh, *Lamaḥāt*, 1:82–84 (quotation at 84).
186. Shalom Gamliel, *Bate hakneset*, 2:93–94.
187. Yosef Tobi, *ʿIyyunim bimgillat teman* (Jerusalem: Magnes Press, 1986), chapter 6; Naḥshon, *Hanhagat ha-qehilah*, 310; Ismar Elbogen, *Jewish Liturgy: A Comprehensive History*, trans. Raymond P. Scheindlin (Philadelphia: Jewish Publication Society, 1993), 293.
188. Shalom Gamliel, *Pequde teman*, 167.
189. Shalom Gamliel, *Bate hakneset*, 1:438.
190. Ibid., 3:154.
191. Ibid., 1:431; 2:117f.
192. Ibid., 2:111.
193. Ibid., 2:282n15.
194. Ratshaby, "Le-Toldot ha-maḥloqet," 120.
195. A similar argument is made in the introduction to the anonymously authored pro-kabbalah work *Emunat hashem* (Jerusalem: Dfus Ḥayyim Tsuqerman, 1937); Nini, "Pulmus," 237.
196. Yeḥiel Ḥibshūsh, *Mishpaḥat ḥibshush*, 1:450; Mordecai Yitshari, *Ḥayyim soʿarim*, 67; Shalom Qoraḥ, *Iggeret bokhim*, 96.
197. Eraqi Klorman, *Yehude teman*, 2:71–73.
198. Aḥmad al-Shāmī, *Riyāḥ al-taghyīr*, 115; Ismāʿīl al-Akwaʿ, *Hijar*, 834, 1119.
199. Ismāʿīl al-Akwaʿ, *Hijar*, 965, 967, 973, 975, 1500; Muḥammad al-Akwaʿ, *Ṣafḥah*, 3:32–33, 159, 169; Sunaydār, *al-Ṭarīq ilā l-ḥurriyyah*, 16, 18, 25, 43; Aḥmad b. Muḥammad al-Wazīr, *Ḥayāt al-amīr*, 605, Aḥmad al-Shāmī, *Riyāḥ al-taghyīr*, 377–378; Aḥmad al-Shāmī, *Min al-adab*, 188–189; Maqbalī, *Mudhakkirāt*, 48–49, 72, 307; ʿAbduh, *Lamaḥāt*, 118; Naṣr, *Shiʿr wa-dhikrayāt*, 46; Dresch, *History of Modern Yemen*, 47; Douglas, *Free Yemeni Movement*, 30–32, 39, 44, 47–48; Msaodi, "Yemeni Opposition," 161.

200. Sunaydār, *al-Ṭarīq ilā l-ḥurriyyah,* 46, 49–50.
201. Ibid., 60–61.
202. Maimonides, *Mishneh Torah, Hilkhot Melakhim,* chapter 11 (Jerusalem: Mosad Ha-Rav Kook, 1962), 416; David Novak, "The Treatment of Islam and Muslims in the Legal Writings of Maimonides," in *Studies in Islamic and Judaic Traditions,* ed. William M. Brinner and Stephen D. Ricks (Atlanta: Scholars Press, 1986), 1:239.
203. Shalom Gamliel, *Bate hakneset,* 2:252n.
204. Ṭayri, *Bitla'ot ha-galut,* 40–42.

4. Concord and Conflict in Economic Life

1. Aharon Ben David says that in north Yemen very few Jews worked in construction. *Bet ha-even,* 7–8. In 1931 Avraham Ṭabīb estimated that half of all builders and plasterers in Yemen were Jews. *Golat teman* (Tel Aviv: Hotsa'at "Omanut," 1931), 46. On cigarettes, which were made for the Turks who remained in Yemen in the imām's service after the transfer of power in 1911, see Medinah, *Masa'ot,* 62–65. The laborious processes of making snuff and cigarettes by hand are also described by Nazīh Mu'ayyad al-'Aẓm, *Riḥlah fī bilād,* 152–153 (Serjeant and Lewcock, *Ṣan'ā',* 177, discuss it as well). Jewish blacksmiths in Sanaa faced a great deal of competition from Muslims, and there were Muslim carpenters as well. Ḥubārah, *Bitla'ot teman,* 29; Bene Moshe, *Sefer 'al kanfe dor,* 29; Lahav, *Qehilat yehude bayḥān,* 74. For a comprehensive list of professions, see Serjeant and Lewcock, *Ṣan'ā',* 167–169. This list, however, does not distinguish between professions that Jews practiced and those that were limited to Muslims. Shahārī details the professions dominated by Jews. *Ṭarīq,* 78.
2. Ṭayri, *Bitla'ot ha-galut,* 37–38; Gamlieli, *Ha-Qami'ah,* 98–101. Today mosques in Yemen generally do not allow entrance to non-Muslims. However, there is evidence that traveling Jews were allowed to sleep in the "tranquil room" (*ghurfat al-haj'ah*) in rural mosques. Goitein, *Ha-Temanim,* 298; Halevi, *Mi-'olam,* 69; Halevi, *'Alilot,* 190, 192, 194.
3. vom Bruck, *Islam, Memory, and Morality,* 163–168.
4. Qafarah, *Mini teman,* 21; Erich Brauer, "He-Ḥaqla'ut ve-ha-mal'akhah etsel yehude teman," in *Shvut teman,* ed. Yisrael Yeshayahu and Aharon Tsadoq (Tel Aviv: Hots'at "mi-teman le-tsiyon," 1945), 77. For the idea that the tribesman actively scorned the trades, see also Zandani, *Yalquṭ,* 66; Bene Moshe, *Sefer 'al kanfe dor,* 29; the works of Gamlieli; Lahav, *Qehilat yehude bayḥān,* 64; Sunaydār, *al-Ṭarīq,* 8; Weir, *Tribal Order,* 58.
5. Gerd-R. Puin, "The Yemeni *Hijrah* Concept of Tribal Protection," in Tarif Khalidi, ed., *Land Tenure and Social Transformation in the Middle East* (Beirut: American University of Beirut, 1984), 488–489.
6. Abdar, "Ha-Mivneh ha-miqtso'i," 493, 495; Halevi, *Mi-'olam,* 123, 218.
7. Halevi, *Mi-'olam,* 43–44. See also Tobi, "Ha-Qehilah," 87, 99–100.
8. Bene Moshe, *Sefer 'al kanfe dor,* 29; Bene Moshe, *Sefer dor le-dor,* 49–50.
9. Ianthe Maclagan, "Food and Gender in a Yemeni Community," in *Culinary Cultures of the Middle East,* ed. Sami Zubaida and Richard Tapper (London: I. B. Tauris, 1994), 169; Serjeant and Lewcock, *Ṣan'ā',* 235.
10. Ṭayri, *Bitla'ot ha-galut,* 44.
11. 'Ovadiah, *Netivot,* 38–39. See also Āl Yaḥyā, *al-Yaman,* 307.
12. Tsubayri, *Mi-Tsan'a,* 50–51.
13. Yosef Riḍā, *Temanah,* 31n1.
14. Ṭayri, *Bitla'ot ha-galut,* 45–46.

15. Gamlieli, *Taḥat kanfeha,* 35, 38; Yeḥiel Ḥibshūsh, *Mishpaḥat ḥibshūsh,* 1:394; Ḥayyim Gamliel, *Pirqe ḥayyim,* 47–48.

16. Serjeant and Lewcock, *Ṣan'ā',* 424; Parfitt, *Road to Redemption,* 120–123, 204, 206.

17. Mordecai Yitshari, *Ḥayyim so'arim,* 65.

18. Ḥasan, *Qalb,* 166.

19. 'Aẓm, *Riḥlah fī bilād,* 265; Muḥammad al-Akwa', *Ṣafḥah,* 3:74.

20. Gamlieli, *Taḥat kanfeha,* 115, 159, 418. See also Bene-Moshe, *Sefer bamsilah,* 31; Bene Moshe, *Sefer dor le-dor,* 48.

21. Parfitt, *Road to Redemption,* 120–123, 204.

22. Esther Muchawsky-Schnapper, *The Jews of Yemen: Highlights of the Israel Museum Collection* (Jerusalem: Israel Museum, 1994), 72; 'Ovadiah, *Netivot,* 79; Manṣūrah, *'Aliyat mirbad haqsamim,* 287–288, 293, 295.

23. Gamlieli, *Taḥat kanfeha,* 83.

24. Serjeant and Lewcock, *Ṣan'ā',* 168.

25. Gamlieli, *Ha-Qami'ah,* 175–176.

26. Yavnieli, *Masa',* 17; Brauer, "He-Ḥaqla'ut," 79, 90–91; Serjeant and Lewcock, *Ṣan'ā',* 168n127, 395n29.

27. Serjeant and Lewcock, *Ṣan'ā',* 167–168.

28. H. Z. Hirschberg, "The Oriental Jewish Communities," in *Religion in the Middle East,* ed. A. J. Arberry (Cambridge, UK: Cambridge University Press, 1969), 1:140–141.

29. Ḥayyim Gamliel, *Pirqe ḥayyim,* 33–34; Shalom Gamliel, *Pe'ame ha-'aliyah,* 255; Serjeant and Lewcock, *Ṣan'ā',* 397.

30. Ḥayyim Ḥibshūsh, *Masa'ot ḥibshūsh,* 250–253; Serjeant and Lewcock, *Ṣan'ā',* 236–237.

31. Ṣāliḥiyyah, *al-'Allāmah,* 190.

32. Ismā'īl al-Akwa', *Hijar,* 590n1.

33. Ḥubārah, *Bitla'ot teman,* 92–96. On the currency, see also Shalom Gamliel, *Ha-Yehudim,* 2:163–164.

34. Ḥayyim Gamliel, *Pirqe ḥayyim,* 39; Ḥayyim Ḥibshūsh, *Masa'ot ḥibshūsh,* 251; Serjeant and Lewcock, *Ṣan'ā',* 237.

35. Ḥayyim Gamliel, *Pirqe ḥayyim,* 30–31.

36. Ben David, *Bet ha-even,* 403; Yael Reshef, "Hitpatḥuyot semanṭiyot she-req'an teqsṭuali balshonot ha-yehudim," in *Leshonot yehude sfarad ve-ha-mizraḥ ve-sifruyotehem,* ed. David M. Bunis (Jerusalem: Mosad Bialik/Misgav Yerushalayim, 2009), 25.

37. Bene Moshe, *Sefer 'al kanfe dor,* 111–116.

38. Aviva Klein-Francke, "Ha-Tsorfut be-qerev yehude teman: Toldoteha, ve-hitpatḥut omanuteha," *Pe'amim* 11 (1982): 69–71.

39. Bene Moshe, *Sefer Bamsilah,* 47.

40. Aḥmad 'Ubayd b. Daghr, *al-Yaman taḥta ḥukmi l-imām aḥmad,* 79–80. There is, however, a disagreement among historians as to whether or not the mercantile class under the Ḥamīd al-Dīn Imāms was predominantly Shafi'i. (Compare Ṣā'idī, *Ḥarakat al-mu'āraḍah,* 112–114.)

41. Eraqi Klorman, *Yehude teman,* 3:197, 200–204; Medinah, *Masa'ot,* 9.

42. Eraqi Klorman, *Yehude teman,* 3:204.

43. Ibid., 3:24, 25.

44. Ḥubārah, *Bitla'ot teman,* 43.

45. Qafarah, *Mini Teman,* 20.

46. Yehudah Ratshaby, "Qehilat Tsan'a bi-shnot 1899–1913," *Sinai* 67 (1970): 213; Eraqi Klorman, *Yehude teman,* 3:78, 80, 91.

47. Eraqi Klorman, *Yehude Teman,* 3:86–87.

48. Avraham al-Mālīḥ, "Masaʿ yom-ṭov tsemaḥ le-teman," in *Shvut teman,* ed. Yisrael Yeshayahu and Aharon Tsadoq (Tel Aviv: Hots'at "mi-teman le-tsiyon," 1945), 290–291, 301.

49. Yeḥiel Ḥibshūsh, *Mishpaḥat ḥibshūsh,* 1:335–336; Menashe ʿAnzi, "Yehude manākhah: Kalkalah, misḥar, u-trumot," *Tema* 11 (2010): 124.

50. Shalom Gamliel, *Ha-Yehudim,* 2:163.

51. Mordecai Yitshari, *Hayiti,* 207.

52. ʿAtsṭah, *Ḥayye yosef,* 26.

53. Shalom Gamliel, *Ha-Yehudim,* 2:46.

54. Serjeant and Lewcock, *Ṣanʿāʾ,* 424; Yeḥiel Ḥibshūsh, *Mishpaḥat ḥibshush,* 1:444, 472.

55. Shalom Gamliel, *Ha-Yehudim,* 2:36, 119–120.

56. Serjeant and Lewcock, *Ṣanʿāʾ,* 420. On the other taxes to which Jewish merchants were subject, see Tobi, *Yehudi be-sheruṭ ha-imām,* 15.

57. Tobi, *Yehudi be-sheruṭ ha-imām,* 18–20. On the traditional industries that the imām took over, see Sulṭān Aḥmad ʿUmar, *Naẓrah fī taṭawwur al-mujtamaʿ al-yamanī* (Beirut: Dār al-ṭalīʿah, 1970), 137–142.

58. Ṣāʾidī, *Ḥarakat al-muʿāraḍah,* 114; Aḥmad b. Muḥammad al-Wazīr, *Ḥayāt al-amīr,* 426–427.

59. Msaodi, "Yemeni Opposition," 73–75.

60. Quoted in Ṣāʾidī, *Ḥarakat al-muʿāraḍah,* 245; Douglas, *Free Yemeni Movement,* 117–118.

61. Shahārī, *Ṭarīq,* 78.

62. Muḥammad ʿAbd al-Karīm ʿUkāshah, *Yahūd al-yaman wa l-hijrah ilā filasṭīn* (ʿAden: the author, 1993), 72. The same idea is repeated in ʿAbd al-ʿAzīz al-Maqāliḥ, *al-Abʿād al-mawḍuʿiyyah wa l-fanniyyah li-ḥarakat al-shiʿr al-muʿāṣir fī l-yaman* (Beirut: Dār al-ʿawdah, 1974), 29. See also Msaodi, "Yemeni Opposition Movement," 77–79.

63. Āl Yaḥyā, *al-Yaman,* 303.

64. Sunaydār, *al-Ṭarīq,* 68–69, 72–73.

65. The facsimile of this long fatwa that Yeḥiel Ḥibshūsh reproduces in his book does not, in fact, deal with this controversy at all. Instead, it treats the land disputes between the Muslim waqf and the Jews of Sanaa over the status of property in the Jewish Quarter

66. Yeḥiel Ḥibshūsh, *Mishpaḥat Ḥibshūsh,* 1:307–311.

67. Ibid., 1:337.

68. Ḥayyim Tsadoq, *Be-Ohole teman,* 40–41.

69. Mordecai Yitshari, *Ḥayyim soʿarim,* 145, 149–150, 153–154, 163. See the complaint against Jamal and his father selling wine to Muslims in Shalom Gamliel, *Ha-Yehudim,* 1:118.

70. Shalom Gamliel, *Ha-Yehudim,* 1:168.

71. There were, however, rural villages where Muslims worked as weavers. Yosef Riḍā, *Temana,* 41n36.

72. ʿAẓm, *Riḥlah fī bilād,* 128–130. On shipping more generally, see Tobi, "He-Qehilah," 71, and on the store, see Tobi, *Yehudi be-sheruṭ ha-imām,* 29–30.

73. Emily Gottreich's characterization of the Jewish Quarter of Marrakesh as a "liminal space" (Victor Turner's term) is germane to the discussion of Sanaa. Emily Gottreich, *The Mellah of Marrakesh: Jewish and Muslim Space in Morocco's Red City* (Bloomington: Indiana University Press, 2007), 76.

74. Yeḥiel Ḥibshūsh, *Mishpaḥat ḥibshush,* 1:488–489.

75. ʿAtsṭah, *Ḥayye yosef,* 40.

76. Tobi, "Ha-Qehilah," 87.

77. Ṭayri, *Bitlaʾot ha-galut,* 36.

78. Gamlieli, *Ḥevyon*, 74.

79. See my "Infidels, Lovers, and Magicians: Portrayals of the Jews in Yemeni Arabic Poetry, 17th-19th Centuries," in *Miṭṭuv Yosef: Sefer ha-yovel li-khvod yosef ṭobi*, ed. Dani Bar Ma'oz and Ayelet Ettinger (Haifa, Israel: Haifa University, 2011), 2:xlvi–lix; Eraqi Klorman, "Yemen: Religion, Magic"; Naḥum and Tobi, "Quntres 'Ḥayye ha-temanim'," 15n20.

80. Mordecai Yitshari, *Hayiti*, 99.

81. Shamāḥī, *al-Yaman*, 245; Abdin, "Role of Islam," 74.

82. Mordecai Yitshari, *Hayiti*, 97–100. Compare Gamlieli, *Ḥevyon*, 48–52.

83. vom Bruck, *Islam, Memory, and Morality*, 38.

84. Gamlieli, *Taḥat kanfeha*, 131–134.

85. Yeḥiel Ḥibshūsh, *Mishpaḥat ḥibshush*, 1:265.

86. Yavnieli, *Masa'*, 20–21.

87. 'Uzayri, *Gale or*, 9.

88. Ḥamdi, *Zeh sefer*, 13, 20.

89. Serjeant and Lewcock, *Ṣan'ā'*, 150; Piamenta, *Dictionary*, 115–116; 'Anzi, "Hashpa'at ha-tmurot," 96, 112–113; Ratshaby, "Yehude teman," 57; Sulaymān b. Yaḥyā Ḥibshūsh, "Sefer eshkolot merorot," ed. S. D. Goitein, *Qovets 'al yad* 2, no. 12 (1938): 25; Yosef Qāfiḥ, *Halikhot*, 373; Reuven Shar'abi, *Yeḥi re'uven*, 69; Gil'ad Tsadoq, *Sefer Zikhron teman*, 54–55; Aḥmad b. Muḥammad al-Wazīr, *Ḥayāt al-amīr*, 479–480; Ḥasan, *Qalb*, 170; Āl Yaḥyā, *al-Yaman*, 310; 'Aẓm, *Riḥlah fī bilād*, 33.

90. Yosef Riḍā, *Temanah*,112–113n; Halevi, *'Alilot*, 124.

91. Tsubayri, *Mi-Tsan'a*, 77–78.

92. Serjeant and Lewcock, *Ṣan'ā'*, 400, 417; Wagner, *Like Joseph*, 91–92; Tsubayri, *Mi-Tsan'a*, 48–50.

93. Halevi, *'Alilot*, 202.

94. Halevi, *Mi-'olam*, 240; Halevi, *'Alilot*, 127.

95. Gamlieli, *Teman be-te'udot*, 80.

96. Goitein, *Ha-Temanim*, 299, Brauer, *Ethnologie*, 112.

97. Shalom Gamliel, *Ha-Yehudim*, 1:189–190.

98. Reproduced in Jamīlah Hādī Rajawī, *Yahūd ṣan'ā': Dirāsah 'an al-awḍā' al-iqtiṣādiyyah wa l-ijtimā'iyyah fatrat al-imām yaḥyā ḥamīd al-dīn* (Sanaa, Yemen: Markaz 'abbādī li l-dirāsāt wa l-nashr, 2006), 129. (This author's reconstruction of the text on pages 63–65 is faulty.) A Judeo-Arabic version of the twelve rules of wine making, dated to 1932, can be found in Shalom Gamliel, *Ha-Yehudim*, 1:129–131.

99. Āl Yaḥyā, *al-Yaman*, 310.

100. Mordecai Yitshari, *Ḥayyim so'arim*, 127–128.

101. Shalom Gamliel, *Bate hakneset*, 1:303.

102. Shalom Gamliel, *Ha-Yehudim*, 1:131n15.

103. Ibid., 1:131n12.

104. Ibid., 1:129; Rajawī, *Yahūd ṣan'ā'*, 130.

105. Medinah, *Masa'ot*, 150–151.

106. Markaz li l-dirāsāt, *Thawrat 1948*, 512.

107. Bene Moshe, *Sefer 'al kanfe dor*, 105–110.

108. Yosef Riḍā, *Temanah*, 152–154.

109. Shalom Gamliel, *Ha-Yehudim*, 1:115, 147.

110. Ismā'īl al-Akwa', *Hijar*, 1760.

111. Yeḥiel Ḥibshūsh, *Mishpaḥat ḥibshush*, 1:490.

112. Mordecai Yitshari, *Hayiti*, 180, 238. On the princes' alleged drinking, see Ḥamūd b. Muḥammad al-Dawlah, *Zawraq al-ḥalwā fī sīrat qā'id al-jaysh wa-amīr al-liwā'*, ed. Zayd b.

ʿAlī al-Wazīr (Sanaa, Yemen: Manshūrāt al-ʿaṣr al-ḥadīth, 1988), 575; Dresch, *History of Modern Yemen,* 69; ʿAfīf, *Shāhid ʿalā l-yaman,* 50; Bayḍānī, *Asrār al-yaman,* 235.

113. Bene Moshe, *Sefer dor le-dor,* 74–78, 117–120.
114. Bayḍānī, *Asrār al-yaman,* 116.
115. Mordecai Yitshari, *Hayiti,* 207.
116. Shalom Gamliel, *Ha-Yehudim,* 1:116; Hāshimī, *al-Qaḍāʾ,* 228, 234.
117. Shalom Gamliel, *Ha-Yehudim,* 1:150–152.
118. Ibid., 1:172–173.
119. Ibid., 1:184–185.
120. Ibid., 1:190–191, 302–305; 2:155–159.
121. Ibid., 1:196.
122. Bene Moshe, *Sefer ʿal kanfe dor,* 51–53.
123. Parfitt, *Road to Redemption,* 173–174.
124. Manṣūrah, *ʿAliyat mirbad haqsamim,* 64, 68, 74–75.
125. ʿAbd al-Karīm al-Rāziḥī, *Ḥunjurat al-shaʿb* (n.p., n.d.), 120.
126. Gamlieli, *Taḥat kanfeha,* 87–90; Gamlieli, *Teman be-teʿudot,* 95.
127. Reuben Sharʿabi, *Yeḥi reʾuven,* 71–73.
128. Gamlieli, *Ḥevyon,* 109–111. See also Bene Moshe, *Sefer ʿal kanfe dor,* 31.
129. On the social divisions in Yemen, see Tomas Gerholm, *Market, Mosque, and Mafraj: Social Inequality in a Yemeni Town* (Stockholm: University of Stockholm, 1977), chapter 4. On these prejudices among Jews, see, for example, Halevi, *Mi-ʿolam,* 42, 245.
130. Gamlieli, *Ḥevyon,* 126–132, 147–151.
131. Manṣūrah, *ʿAliyat mirbad haqsamim,* 134–135, 151; Ḥayyim Tsadoq, *Be-Ohole teman,* 318; Serjeant and Lewcock, *Ṣanʿāʾ,* 419.
132. Manṣūrah, *ʿAliyat mirbad haqsamim,* 138–140, 277, 290, 299–304; Ṭayri, *Bitlaʾot ha-galut,* 105–108; Gamlieli, "Solele ha-derekh," 141.
133. David David, *Derekh geʾulim: Mi-hare gades le-hare yerushalayim* (n.p.: Eʿeleh ve-tamar, 1990), 70.
134. Ibid., 65.
135. Gamlieli, *Teman u-maḥaneh geʾulah,* 293–295; Ṭayri, *Bitlaʾot ha-galut,* 106–108.
136. Lahav, *Qehilat yehude bayḥān,* 120–131.
137. Esther Meir-Glitzenstein, *Zionism in an Arab Country: Jews in Iraq in the 1940s* (London: Routledge, 2004), 204, 240, 245–246, 254; Moshe Gat, *The Jewish Exodus from Iraq, 1948–1951* (London: Frank Cass & Co., 1997), 149.
138. Meir-Glitzenstein, *Zionism in an Arab Country,* 251.
139. Gat, *Jewish Exodus,* 94–95, 146–147.
140. Abbas Shiblak, *Iraqi Jews: A History of the Mass Exodus* (London: Saqi Books, 1995), 115–116.
141. Eraqi Klorman, *Yehude teman,* 3:393.
142. Ibid., 3:390–395.
143. Ibid., 2:32, 35; see also 1:222, Hünefeld, *Imām Yaḥyā,* 118.
144. Such rulings, called "*ikhtiyārāt,*" are discussed in Haykel, *Revival and Reform,* 202, 204–206.
145. Muḥammad Ismāʿīl al-ʿAmrānī, *Niẓām al-qaḍāʾ fī l-islām* (Sanaa, Yemen: Maktabat dār al-jīl, 1984), 232; Hāshimī, *al-Qaḍāʾ fī l-yaman,* 245n1.
146. Yehudah Ratshaby, ed., *Boʿi teman* (Tel Aviv: Afiqim, 1967), 193–228; Serjeant and Lewcock, *Ṣanʿāʾ,* 427–431; Piamenta, *Dictionary,* 418.
147. Manṣūrah, *ʿAliyat mirbad haqsamim,* 168, 200.

148. Eraqi Klorman, *Yehude teman,* 3:234; ʿAmram Qoraḥ, *Seʿarat teman,* 72–73; Parfitt, *Road to Redemption,* 76.

149. Shalom Gamliel, *Peʿame ha-ʿaliyah,* 192.

150. Ibid., 49.

151. ʿUkāshah, *Yahūd al-yaman,* 189–190. ʿUkāshah says the document itself can be found in an appendix to his book, but it is not there. Thus, it is unclear whether the tone of relative evenhandedness toward Muslims and Jews on the issue of foreign travel can be found in the communiqué itself or whether it is the historian's characterization.

152. Shalom Gamliel, *Ha-Yehudim,* 2:97–101.

153. Eraqi Klorman, *Yehude Teman,* 3:390–395; Manṣūrah, *ʿAliyat mirbad haqsamim,* 138–140, 277, 290, 299–304.

154. Manṣūrah, *ʿAliyat mirbad haqsamim,* 152, 190, 207, 222, 271, 274.

155. Parfitt, *Road to Redemption,* 256–257. A Muslim source remarks on the fluctuating rent his family was charged on a house in Sanaa that had been owned by Jews but had been acquired by Imām Aḥmad's agent. Ibrāhīm al-Wazīr, *Zahrāʾ al-yaman,* 131–132.

156. Tsadoq Yitshari, *Kakh baraḥti,* 176, 179.

157. Ṭayri, *Bitlaʾot ha-galut,* 106.

158. Manṣūrah, *ʿAliyat mirbad haqsamim,* 339.

159. Ibid., 188.

160. Ibid., 166–167, 182, 188, 197, 339.

161. The curious expression "the interior lands" (*al-diyār al-dākhiliyyah*) refers to places outside Yemen in Yemeni colloquial Arabic. Piamenta, *Dictionary,* 145–146; Shalom Gamliel, *Peʿame ha-ʿaliyah,* 38n1; Ḥayyim Tsadoq, *Be-Ohole teman,* 304.

162. Shalom Gamliel, *Peʿame ha-ʿaliyah,* 37.

163. Ibid., 35.

164. Goitein, "Portrait," 14.

165. Shalom Gamliel, *Peʿame ha-ʿaliyah,* 55.

166. Ibid., 54.

167. Ibid., 50; Piamenta, *Dictionary,* 174.

168. Shalom Gamliel, *Peʿame ha-ʿaliyah,* 50.

169. Mordecai Yitshari, *Hayiti,* 244.

170. Shalom Gamliel, *Ha-Yehudim,* 1: 308–309.

171. Saleh A. al-Hathloul, "Tradition, Continuity and Change in the Physical Environment: The Arab-Muslim City" (PhD dissertation, M.I.T., 1981), 54. See also Ṣaleḥ Aḥmad El-ʿAlī, "The Foundation of Baghdad," in *The Islamic City,* ed. Albert Hourani and S. M. Stern (Oxford: Cassirer, 1970), 88–89; Jamel Malik, *Crisis in the Built Environment: The Case of the Muslim City* (Singapore: Mimar Book/Concept Media, 1988), 131–132.

172. Alexander David Russell and Abdullah al-Maʿmun Suhrawardy, *Muslim Law: An Historical Introduction to the Law of Inheritance* (1925; repr. London: Kegan Paul, 2008), 67.

173. Menachem Elon, *Jewish Law: History, Sources, Principles,* trans. Bernard Auerbach and Melvin J. Sykes (Philadelphia: Jewish Publication Society, 1994), 2:625–626; Menachem Elon, *Jewish Law (Mishpaṭ ʿivri): Cases and Materials,* trans. Bernard Auerbach, Daniel D. Chazin, and Melvin J. Sykes (New York: Matthew Bender, 1999), 338–344.

174. Gamlieli, *Teman be-teʿudot,* 279–283.

175. Neil B. E. Baillie, *A Digest of Moohummudan Law* (Lahore, Pakistan: Premier Book House, 1965), 1:512.

176. Muḥammad b. ʿAlī al-Shawkānī, *Kitāb al-Sayl al-jarrār al-mutadaffiq ʿalā ḥadāʾiq al-azhār,* ed. Maḥmūd Ibrāhīm Zāyid (Beirut: Dār al-kutub al-ʿilmiyyah, n.d.), 3:171–172; Ḥusayn b. ʿAbdullāh al-ʿAmrī, *The Yemen in the 18th and 19th Centuries: A Political and Intellectual*

History (Durham, UK: University of Durham, Centre for Middle Eastern and Islamic Studies, 1985), 158.

177. ʿAmrānī, *Niẓām al-qaḍāʾ*, 235.

178. Muṭahhar, *Sīrat al-imām yaḥyā*, 1:66–67; ʿAmrānī, *Niẓām al-qaḍāʾ*, 230; Abdin, "Role of Islam," 180; Brinkley Messick, "Property and the Private in a Sharia System," *Social Research* 70, no. 3 (2003): 723.

179. Hāshimī, *al-Qaḍāʾ fī l-yaman*, 244.

180. Ismāʿīl al-Akwaʿ, *Hijar*, 1:367; Brinkley Messick, "Provincial Judges: The *Sharīʿa* Judiciary of Mid-Twentieth-Century Yemen," in *Law, Custom, and Statute in the Muslim World*, ed. Ron Shaham (Leiden: E. J. Brill, 2007), 161.

181. Shalom Gamliel, *Ha-Yehudim*, 1:306.

182. Walter Dostal, "Sozio-ökonomische Aspekte der Stammesdemokratie in Nordost-Yemen," *Sociologus* 24 (1974): 9–10.

183. Gamlieli, *Teman be-teʿudot*, 152.

184. Abdar, "Ha-Mivneh ha-miqtsoʾi," 85–89; Brauer, "He-Ḥaqlaʾut," 76–77; Tobi, "Ha-Qehilah," 69, 80, 89, 91, 96, 98, 102; David, *Derekh geʾulim*, 38; Shahārī, *Ṭarīq al-thawrah*, 78. On the landless tribesmen who worked as sharecroppers and the abuses to which they were subject, see Msaodi, "Yemeni Opposition Movement," 98–103.

185. Halevi, *Mi-ʿolam*, 218.

186. Abdar, "Ha-Mivneh ha-miqtsoʾi," 487, 488; Halevi, *Mi-ʿolam*, 10, 218–220 (quotation at 10).

187. Gamlieli, *Teman be-teʿudot*, 291; Abdar, "Ha-Mivneh ha-miqtsoʾi," 488, 489–490; Tobi, *Yehudi be-sheruṭ ha-imām*, 15.

188. Juzaylān, *Lamaḥāt*, 99–100.

189. See *Encyclopedia of Islam*, 2nd ed., *sub* "Ikāla." See also Tobi, "Ha-Qehilah," 98.

190. See *Encyclopedia of Islam*, 2nd ed., *sub* "Khiyār."

191. Gamlieli, *Teman be-teʿudot*, 125, 139.

192. Ibid., 102, 113

193. Shalom Gamliel, *Bate hakneset*, 1:29, 2:367

194. *Sharḥ al-azhār*, 7:26n2.

195. Quoted in Shawkānī, *al-Sayl*, 3:169.

196. Ibid., 3:169.

197. François-Auguste de Montequin, "*Sharia* and Urban Design: Effects and Reflection of Canon Law on the City of Islam," *Search* 3, no. 2 (1982): 32. On dead-end streets, see Malik, *Crisis in the Built Environment*, 25–128.

198. *Sharḥ al-azhār*, 7:26.

199. Ibid., 7:26.

200. Ibid., 7:26 n3.

201. ʿAnsī, *al-Tāj al-mudhhab*, 3:11.

202. *Sharḥ al-azhār*, 7:26.

203. Ibid., 7:27.

204. Shawkānī, *al-Sayl*, 3:173.

205. Wael B. Hallaq, *The Origins and Evolution of Islamic Law* (Cambridge, UK: Cambridge University Press, 2005), 44n46.

206. Clinton J. Andrews, "Security and the Built Environment: An Interview with John Habraken," *IEEE Technology and Society Magazine* (Fall 2004): 9–11.

207. N. John Habraken, "Design for Adaptability, Change, and User Participation," in *Housing: Processes and Physical Form*, ed. Linda Safran (Philadelphia: Aga Khan Award for Architecture, 1980), 25.

208. Ibid., 23; Andrews, "Security and the Built Environment," 11.
209. Andrews, "Security and the Built Environment," 12.
210. Shalom Gamliel, *Ha-Yehudim,* 1:308–309.
211. Shalom Gamliel, *Pe'ame ha-'aliyah,* 143–159.
212. Yeḥiel Ḥibshūsh, *Riḥlah,* 39.

5. Intercommunal Violence and the Sharīʿa

1. The Syrian traveler Nazīh Mu'ayyad al-ʿAẓm places the robbery and looting of caravans in tribal areas in the south within the context of tensions between the tribes and the British government. *Riḥlah fī bilād,* 130–131. See also Msaodi, "Yemeni Opposition Movement," 46.

2. Manṣūrah, *'Aliyat mirbad haqsamim,* 139–140.

3. Halevi, *'Alilot,* 100–103.

4. Avraham Ṭabīb, *Shave teman* (Tel Aviv: Hotsa'at "Omanut," 1932), 27–28. See also Eraqi Klorman, "Aharon 'afjin," 91, 95.

5. Tobi, "Ha-Qehilah," 79.

6. Ben David, "'Al 'aliyatam," 77.

7. Tobi, "Ha-Qehilah," 93.

8. Zandani, *Yalquṭ,* 46–47. See also 'Ovadiah, *Netivot,* 35.

9. Ḥubārah, *Bitla'ot teman,* 94.

10. Mordecai Yitshari, *Ḥayyim so'arim,* 281.

11. Abdin, "Role of Islam," 202–203; Bene Moshe, *Sefer dor le-dor,* 91, 97; Yosef Riḍā, *Temanah,* 78–81; Zandani, *Yalquṭ,* 44–49; Āl Yaḥyā, *al-Yaman,* 306–307.

12. See, for example, Ḥamdi, *Zeh sefer,* 18; Gamlieli, *Ḥevyon,* 13.

13. Ḥayyim Ḥibshūsh, *Masa'ot ḥibshūsh,* 51–52. See also 48.

14. Gamlieli, *Taḥat kanfeha,* 50–51; Gamlieli, *Teman be-te'udot,* 274.

15. Ratshaby, "Yehudim u-muslimim," 232. Compare with Lahav, *Qehilat yehude bayḥān,* 108.

16. Lahav, *Qehilat yehude bayḥān,* 42.

17. On this multiplication by eleven (*muḥadd'ash*), see Dresch, *Tribes,* 60–62; Weir, *Tribal Order,* 156; Obermeyer, "Ṭāghūt, Manʿ, and Šarīʿa," 368–369; Zandani, *Yalquṭ,* 46; Naṣr, *Shi'r wa-dhikrayāt,* 50–52.

18. Bene Moshe, *Sefer 'al kanfe dor,* 55. See also Gamlieli, *Teman u-maḥaneh ge'ulah,* 92; Moshe Tsadoq, "Ha-Yaḥasim," 154–155. In another instance, the Muslim murderer's property was confiscated by a shaykh. Yosef Riḍā, *Temanah,* 75n30.

19. Moshe Tsadoq, "Ha-Yaḥasim," 154–155.

20. Bene Moshe, *Sefer Bamsilah,* 49–50 (quotation at 50). On the theme of overzealous (and false) Muslim witnesses to Jewish crimes, see Gamlieli, *Ḥadre teman,* 175–176.

21. An example of such an assessment report, conducted on a Jewish woman as part of a divorce proceeding, can be found among the Yemeni material in the Ben Zvi Institute (middle of BZF 357—water damaged, without paper clips). Nissim Gamlieli describes this post as belonging to "a learned *faqīh* knowledgeable in the law of damages." *Ḥevyon teman,* 32n8. See also Shalom Gamliel, *Ha-Yehudim,* 1:368; Gamlieli, "Shne sippurim," 13; Messick, *Calligraphic State,* 136–137.

22. Gamlieli, "Shne sippurim," 10–12.

23. Bene Moshe, *Sefer Bamsilah,* 50–51.

24. Lahav, *Qehilat yehude bayḥān,* 44–45.

25. Zandani, *Yalquṭ*, 67.
26. Yosef Riḍā, *Temanah*, 94–96.
27. Muṭahhar, *Sīrat al-imām yaḥyā*, 1:275–276.
28. Dresch, *History of Modern Yemen*, 65–66.
29. Nirenberg, *Communities of Violence*, 13.
30. Manṣūrah, *'Aliyat mirbad haqsamim*, 42–46. These events are described in a number of Jewish sources. A French writer says that the Jews were well-prepared for the tribal rampage and had carefully hidden their valuables beforehand. Markaz li l-dirāsāt, *Thawrat 1948*, 516.
31. Shamāḥī, *al-Yaman*, 270. See also 278–281.
32. Ḥamdi, *Zeh sefer*, 38.
33. Mordecai Yitshari, *Ḥayyim so'arim*, 276.
34. Ṭabīb, *Shave teman*, 17. Nissim Gamlieli makes virtually the same argument in "Solele ha-derekh," 136.
35. Eraqi Klorman, "Aharon 'Afjīn," 91.
36. Ḥamdi, *Zeh sefer*, 18–19. On poor sayyids, see vom Bruck, *Islam, Memory, and Morality*, 45, 59; Msaodi, "Yemeni Opposition Movement," 205.
37. Gamlieli, *Taḥat kanfeha*, 115–119.
38. Ṣā'idī, *Ḥarakat al-mu'āraḍah*, 84.
39. Muḥammad Aḥmad Nu'mān, *al-Aṭrāf*, 36.
40. Gamlieli, *Taḥat kanfeha*, 229–230.
41. Ibid., 202–203; Gamlieli, "Solele ha-derekh," 136. See also Ṭayri, *Bitla'ot ha-galut*, 53.
42. Halevi, *Mi-'olam*, 176.
43. Zandani, *Yalquṭ*, 70–74.
44. Gamlieli, *Teman be-te'udot*, 78–80; Gamlieli, *Teman u-maḥaneh ge'ulah*, 92.
45. Yeḥiel Ḥibshūsh, *Mishpaḥat ḥibshush*, 1:478. See also Halevi, *'Alilot*, 81–82.
46. Tsadoq Yitshari, *Kakh baraḥti*, 153, 176, 179.
47. Bene Moshe, *Sefer dor le-dor*, 129–130.
48. Parfitt, *Road to Redemption*, 74–75; Yisrael Yeshayahu, "Shvile ha-'aliyah mi-teman le-tsiyon," in *Shvut teman*, ed. Yisrael Yeshayahu and Aharon Tsadoq (Tel Aviv: Hots'at "mi-teman le-tsiyon," 1945), 42.
49. Ismā'īl al-Akwa', *Hijar*, 591.
50. Ibid., 198, 830; Halevi, *'Alilot*, 69–70. The Yemeni newspaper *al-Īmān* described the itinerary of the Islamic Conference delegation in Yemen in June 1934, including their meeting with the imām and stay in Sanaa. See also Philip Mattar, *The Mufti of Jerusalem: al-Ḥajj Amīn al-Ḥusaynī and the Palestinian National Movement* (New York: Columbia University Press, 1988), 63. Ernest Maine judged the mufti's journey to Yemen to be an unsuccessful "bid to extend his influence." Ernest Maine, *Palestine at the Crossroads* (London: George Allen & Unwin, Ltd., 1937), 56.
51. Manṣūrah, *'Aliyat mirbad haqsamim*, 28–29.
52. Parfitt, *Road to Redemption*, 166.
53. Lahav, *Qehilat yehude bayḥān*, 108.
54. Ismā'īl al-Akwa', *Hijar*, 1758; Muṭahhar, *Sīrat al-imām yaḥyā*, 1:386–387; Ṣāliḥiyyah, *al-'Allāmah*, 28, 57.
55. Ismā'īl al-Akwa', *Hijar*, 665.
56. Manṣurah, *'Aliyat mirbad haqsamim*, 33.
57. *al-Īmān* 146 (October 1938), quoted in Ṣāliḥiyyah, *al-'Allāmah*, 31.
58. Ṣāliḥiyyah, *al-'Allāmah*, 39; Ismā'īl al-Akwa', *Hijar*, 1757.
59. Ṣāliḥiyyah, *al-'Allāmah*, 49.
60. Muṭahhar, *Sīrat al-imām yaḥyā*, 1:389.

61. The most prominent rabbi of the same large group of Jewish men that was jailed was shocked at his audacity in possessing such material, but he insisted he had not broken any law. Mordecai Yitshari, *Hayiti,* 157–158, 164.

62. Ibid., 76.

63. Tsadoq Yitshari, *Kakh baraḥti,* 160.

64. Mordecai Yitshari, *Ḥayyim so'arim,* 377.

65. Ibid., 376.

66. Madhalah, *Ein li erets aḥeret,* 17.

67. Eraqi Klorman, *Yehude teman,* 3:255–256.

68. Ibid., 3:380; Shamāḥī, *al-Yaman,* 267.

69. vom Bruck, *Islam, Memory, and Morality,* 286n36.

70. Maqbalī, *Mudhakkirāt al-maqbalī,* 106.

71. Manṣūrah, *'Aliyat mirbad haqsamim,* 151–152.

72. Mordecai Yitshari, *Hayiti,* 235.

73. Nirenberg, *Communities of Violence,* 215–217.

74. Ibid., 11, 68.

75. Mordecai Yitshari, *Ḥayyim so'arim,* 261–262, 269, 284. Ḥamūd al-Jandārī crops up in 1913 as the lawyer for the pro-kabbalah faction ('Eden, "Pulmus ha-qabalah bi-tsan'ā," 134, 136) and in al-'Izzī al-Sunaydār's memoir as a "thinker" (i.e., one who is inclined toward Sunnism) (78).

76. Mordecai Yitshari, *Ḥayyim so'arim,* 269.

77. Ibid., 263.

78. Ibid., 271–272.

79. Ibid., 278. Qadi Ismā'īl al-Akwa' mentions "the qadis of the 'Izzānī family" of Radā' but says he was not able to find useful information about them. *Hijar,* 2059. See also Muḥammad al-Akwa', *Ṣafḥah,* 3:27.

80. On shackling as punishment, see Mordecai Yitshari, *Hayiti,* 72, 178, 187; Gamlieli, *Taḥat kanfeha,* 212–213, 216.

81. Mordecai Yitshari, *Ḥayyim so'arim,* 272–277. Ismā'īl al-Akwa' says that Yaḥyā al-Dhārī governed Radā' temporarily while its usual governor was on a trip to London to attend the coronation of King George VI in 1937. *Hijar,* 663, 1910. This poses a problem insofar as Ẓāhirī says these events occurred in 1939.

82. Mordecai Yitshari, *Ḥayyim so'arim,* 278–279 (quotation at 278). Another Jew recalls being called a "*ḥarbī*" after having struck two Muslims. Ṭayri, *Bitla'ot ha-galut,* 16.

83. Mordecai Yitshari, *Ḥayyim so'arim,* 280–281.

84. Ibid., 281.

85. Ibid., 282.

86. Ibid., 287. "The 1920s and mainly the 1930s and 1940s witnessed increasing numbers of Yemeni Jewish craftsmen travelling regularly to Ethiopia, working for several months and then returning home," writes Bat-Zion Eraqi Klorman. "Yemen, Aden, and Ethiopia: Jewish Emigration and Italian Colonialism," *Journal of the Royal Asiatic Society,* Series 3, 19, no. 4 (2009): 420; Parfitt, *Road to Redemption,* 135n60.

87. Mordecai Yitshari, *Ḥayyim so'arim,* 283.

88. Ibid., 283–284.

89. Ibid., 284–290.

90. Friedrich Nietzsche, *On the Genealogy of Morals,* trans. Douglas Smith (Oxford: Oxford University Press, 1996), 25–26.

91. Eraqi Klorman, "Muslim Society as an Alternative," 98–99, 113n46.

92. Yeḥiel Ḥibshūsh, *Mishpaḥat ḥibshush,* 1:441. Shalom Gamliel also describes tensions between the Muslim residents of Balaqah and the neighboring Jewish Quarter. *Ha-Yehudim,* 1:102–103.
93. Shalom Gamliel, *Ha-Yehudim,* 1:102.
94. Yeḥiel Ḥibshūsh, *Mishpaḥat ḥibshush,* 2:473.
95. Reuven Shar'abi, *Yeḥi re'uven,* 47–48.
96. 'Atsṭah, *Ḥayye yosef,* 38–39.
97. Shalom Gamliel, *Ha-Yehudim,* 1:102.
98. Mordecai Yitshari, *Hayiti,* 159–178. Yitshari says this man was named Yaḥyā al-'Amrī, and Ḥamdī says he was 'Alī al-'Amrī. Ḥamdī's version makes more sense.
99. Ḥamdi, *Zeh sefer,* 43–46, 54; Eraqi Klorman, *Yehude teman,* 3:381.
100. Tsadoq Yitshari, *Kakh baraḥti,* 176, 178.
101. Goitein, "Portrait," 16. See also Halevi, *'Alilot,* 135–138.
102. Ismā'īl al-Akwa', *Hijar,* 1:367.
103. Ḥamdi, *Zeh sefer,* 47–48.
104. Manṣūrah, *'Aliyat mirbad haqsamim,* 57–58. Arab historians do not have kind things to say about Ḥasan either. Shamāḥī, *al-Yaman,* 293, 295, 298; Aḥmad b. Muḥammad al-Wazīr, *Ḥayāt al-amīr,* 241–242; Naṣr, *Shi'r wa-dhikrayāt,* 32.
105. Ḥamdī, *Zeh sefer,* 49–53.
106. Ibid., 53.
107. Parfitt, *Road to Redemption,* 188–192; Manṣūrah, *'Aliyat mirbad haqsamim,* 57.
108. Tsadoq Yitshari, *Kakh baraḥti,* 160–161.
109. Bat-Zion Eraqi Klorman also interprets this incident as a reflection of the deterioration in the relationship between Jews and Arabs in Yemen against the background of the Palestine conflict. *Yehude teman,* 3:383.

Conclusion

1. Shalom Gamliel, *Pirsum,* 72.
2. Karl N. Llewellyn and E. Adamson Hoebel, "The Normative, the Legal, and the Law-Jobs: The Problem of Juristic Method," *Yale Law Journal,* 49, no. 8 (1940): 1382n83.
3. Dresch, *History of Modern Yemen,* 49; Douglas, *Free Yemeni Movement,* 118.
4. Sunaydār, *al-Ṭarīq,* 76.
5. Shamāḥī, *al-Yaman,* 216.
6. Ibid., 200–202.
7. Ibid., 238.
8. Ibid., 243.
9. Novak, "Treatment of Islam and Muslims," 240–243; Marc B. Shapiro, "Islam and the Halakhah," *Judaism* (Summer 1993): 336, 341n36.

Bibliography

Sources in Arabic, Hebrew, and Judeo-Arabic

Abdar, Carmela. "Ha-Mivneh ha-miqtso'i shel toshve tsurm al-'ūd ke-biṭui le-ma'amado ve-ha-tahalikhim she-'avru 'alav." In *Le-Rosh yosef: Meḥqarim be-ḥokhmat yisra'el*, edited by Yosef Tobi, 481–502. Jerusalem: Afiqim, 1995.

'Abduh, 'Alī Muḥammad. *Lamaḥāt min ta'rīkh ḥarakat al-aḥrār al-yamaniyīn*. Sanaa, Yemen: al-Ma'had al-firansī li l-āthār wa l-'ulūm al-ijtimā'iyyah, Muntadā nu'mān al-thaqāfī li l-shabāb, 2003.

Abū Jabal, Camīlia. *Yahūd al-yaman*. Damascus: Dār al-namīr, 1999.

'Afīf, Aḥmad Jābir. *Shāhid 'alā l-yaman: Ashyā' min al-dhākirah*. Sanaa, Yemen: Mu'assasat 'afīf al-thaqafiyyah, 2000.

Akwa', Ismā'īl al-. *Al-Amthāl al-yamāniyyah*. Sanaa, Yemen: Maktabat al-jīl al-jadīd, Mu'assasat al-risālah, 1984 (revised edition).

———. *Hijar al-'ilm wa-ma'āqiluhā fī l-yaman*. Damascus: Dār al-fikr, 1995.

Akwa', Muḥammad b. 'Alī al-. *Ḥayāt 'ālim wa-amīr*. Sanaa, Yemen: Maktabat al-jīl al-jadīd, 1987.

———. *Ṣafḥah min ta'rīkh al-yaman al-ijtimā'ī wa-qiṣṣat ḥayātī*. N.p., n.d.

Āl Yaḥyā, Sayf al-Dīn Sa'īd. *Al-Yaman fī 'uyūn al-ba'thah al-'askariyyah al-'irāqiyyah, 1940–1943m*. al-Ḥāzimiyyah, Lebanon: al-Dār al-'arabiyyah li l-mawsū'āt, 2006.

'Amrānī, Muḥammad Ismā'īl al-. *Niẓām al-qaḍā' fī l-islām*. Sanaa, Yemen: Maktabat dār al-jīl, 1984.

Anonymous. *Emunat hashem*. Jerusalem: Dfus Ḥayyim Tsuqerman, 1937.

———. *Quntres magen ve-tsinah ha-ḥosef et ha-emet 'al kat ha-kofrim ha-niqra'im "darda'im" u-megaleh et partsufo ha-amiti shel ha-'omed bi-roshah*. Brooklyn: no publisher information, 1993.

'Ansī, Aḥmad b. al-Qāsim al-. *Al-Tāj al-mudhhab li-aḥkām al-madhhab*. Sanaa, Yemen: Maktabat al-yaman al-kubrā, 1947.

'Anzi, Menashe. "Hashpa'at ha-tmurot ha-mediniyot 'al yehude tsan'a' be-reshit ha-me'ah ha-'esrim." In *Miṭṭuv Yosef: Sefer ha-yovel li-khvod yosef ṭobi*, edited by Ayelet Ettinger and Dani Bar Ma'oz, 2:95–124. Haifa, Israel: Haifa University, 2011.

———. "Yehude manākhah: Kalkalah, misḥar, u-trumot." *Tema* 11 (2010): 123–155.

'Atsṭah, Yosef. *Ḥayye yosef*. Edited by Simḥah Zarmaṭi-'Atsṭah. Tel Aviv: Afiqim, 1987.

'Aẓm, Nazīh Mu'ayyad al-. *Riḥlah fī bilād al-'arabiyyah al-sa'īdah: Min miṣr ilā ṣan'ā'*. Beirut: Manshūrāt al-madīnah, 1986.

Bar Ma'oz, Dani. *Yiqov ha-din et ha-har: Maḥaloqot u-falganut biqhilat yehude teman*. Reḥovot, Israel: 'Amutat e'eleh ve-tamar, 2005.

Bayḍānī, 'Abd al-Raḥmān al-. *Asrār al-yaman*. Cairo: al-Dār al-qawmiyyah li l-ṭibā'ah wa l-nashr, 1962.

Ben David, Aharon. "'Al 'aliyatam shel yehude tsa'dah ve-ha-svivah bi-shnat ha-tash'a (1951)." *Tehudah* 19 (1999): 74–81.

——. *Bet ha-even: Halikhot yehude tsfon teman.* Qiryat ʻEqron, Israel: Ahavat teman, 2008.

Bene Moshe, Shalom. *Sefer ʻal kanfe dor.* Edited by Nissim Binyamin Gamlieli. Reḥovot, Israel: the author, 1995.

——. *Sefer Bamsilah naʻaleh.* Reḥovot, Israel: the author, 1988.

——. *Sefer dor le-dor yesaperu.* Edited by Shimʻon Graydi. Reḥovot, Israel: the author, 1985.

Brauer, Erich. "He-Ḥaqla'ut ve-ha-mal'akhah etsel yehude teman." In *Shvut teman,* edited by Yisrael Yeshayahu and Aharon Tsadoq, 75–91. Tel Aviv: Hots'at "mi-teman le-tsiyon," 1945.

BZF (Ben Zvi Folder), Goitein Collection, 357.

Cohen, Amnon, Elisheva Simon-Pikali, and Eyal Ginio. *Yehudim be-vet ha-mishpaṭ ha-muslimi: Ḥevrah, kalkalah, ve-irgun kehilati bīrushalayim ha-ʻothmanit.* Jerusalem: Ben Zvi Institute, 2003.

David, David. *Derekh ge'ulim: Mi-hare gades le-hare yerushalayim.* N.p.: Eʻeleh ve-tamar, 1998.

Dawlah, Ḥamūd b. Muḥammad al-. *Zawraq al-ḥalwā fī sīrat qā'id al-jaysh wa-amīr al-liwā'.* Sanaa, Yemen: Manshūrāt al-ʻaṣr al-ḥadīth, 1988.

ʻEden, Yoḥai. "Pulmus ha-qabalah bi-tsanʻā: Ha-Reqaʻ ha-ruḥani ve-ha-ḥevrati le-pulmus ha-qabalah be-shanim (1912–1944)." Master's thesis, Touro College, 1998.

Eraqi Klorman, Bat Zion. "Aharon ʻafjin ve-ha-ʻaliyah mi-tsfon teman: Diyyun hisṭoriyografi." *Peʻamim* 84 (2000): 88–103.

——. *Yehude Teman: Historyah, ḥevrah, tarbut.* Tel Aviv: Open University, 2008.

Fenton, Paul. "Pulmus muslimi mi-teman neged ha-rambam: Ha-Imam al-shawkani ve-sifro ba-ʻinyan ḥayye ʻolam ha-ba." In *Le-Rosh yosef: Meḥqarim be-ḥokhmat yisra'el,* edited by Yosef Tobi, 409–434. Jerusalem: Afiqim, 1995.

Gamliel, Ḥayyim. *Pirqe ḥayyim.* Ramat Gan, Israel: Gamliel family, 1998.

Gamliel, Shalom b. Seʻadyah (Sālim Saʻīd al-Jamal). *Bate hakneset be-tsanʻa' birat teman.* Jerusalem: Makhon shalom le-shivṭe yeshurun, 1996/1997.

——. "Ḥakhme ha-yehudim bi-tsanʻa': maḥloqet ve-ha-shalom she-naʻaseh beinehem." In Shalom Gamliel, *Ḥakhme ha-yehudim be-teman be-dorenu ve-ʻad samukh litqufat ha-Tana'im.* Jerusalem: Makhon shalom le-shivṭe yeshurun, 1992.

——. *Ha-Yehudim ve-ha-melekh be-teman.* Jerusalem: Makhon shalom le-shivṭe yeshurun, 1986.

——. *Peʻame ha-ʻaliyah mi-teman.* Jerusalem: Makhon shalom le-shivṭe yeshurun, 1987.

——. *Pequde teman: Mas he-ḥasut be-teman.* Jerusalem: Makhon shalom le-shivṭe yeshurun, 1982.

——. *Pirsum yeshuʻot hashem la-yehudim be-teman.* Jerusalem: Makhon shalom le-shivṭe yeshurun, 1997.

Gamlieli, Nissim Binyamin. *Ḥadre teman: Sippurim ve-aggadot.* Tel Aviv: Afiqim, 1978.

——. *Ha-Qamiʻah: Sippurim mi-ḥayye ha-yehudim be-teman.* Ramlah, Israel: the author and his sons, 1980.

——. *Ḥevyon teman: Zikhronot, sippurim, aggadot ḥayyim mi-ʻolam aḥer.* Ramlah, Israel: the author, 1983.

——. "Shne sippurim mi-ḥayye ha-yehudim be-ʻir damar." *Tehudah* 19 (1999): 10–14.

——. "Solele-ha-derekh le-ʻaliyat "al kanfe nesharim' be-re'i te'udot u-mikhtavim." In *Orḥot teman,* edited by Shalom Gamliel, Mishael Maswari Caspi, and Shimʻon Avizemer, 132–187. Jerusalem: Makhon shalom le-shivṭe yeshurun, 1984.

——. *Taḥat kanfeha shel ima: Roman otobiyografi mi-ḥayyav shel yeled yehudi be-teman.* Tel Aviv: Afiqim, 2002.
——. *Teman be-te'udot: Yehude damt ve-ha-maḥoz.* Jerusalem: Makhon shalom le-shivṭe yeshurun, 1997.
——. *Teman u-maḥaneh ge'ulah.* Tel Aviv: the author, 1966.
Goitein, Shlomo Dov, and Menaḥem Ben Sasson. *Ha-Temanim: Historiyah, sidre ḥevrah, ḥayye ha-ruaḥ: Mivḥar meḥqarim.* Jerusalem: Ben Zvi Institute, 1983.
——. "Mi hayah Eduard Glazer." In *Shvut Teman,* edited by Yisrael Yeshayahu and Aharon Tsadoq, 149–154. Tel Aviv: Hots'at "mi-teman le-tsiyon," 1945.
Ḥajar, Zayd Muḥammad. "Awḍā' yahūd ṣan'ā' al-ijtimā'iyyah." *Dirāsāt yamaniyyah* 46 (1992): 154–184.
Halevi, Ratson. *'Alilot me-'olam le-'olam.* Tel Aviv: Afiqim, 2005.
——. *Mi-'olam le-'olam.* Bene Beraq, Israel: Hotsa'at "Afiqim," 2002.
Ḥamdi, Aharon. *Zeh sefer ḥokhmah u-musar.* Netanyah, Israel: Ha-Agudah la-ṭipuaḥ ḥevrah ve-tarbut, 1996.
Ḥasan, Muḥammad. *Qalb al-yaman.* Baghdād: Maṭba'at al-ma'ārif, 1947.
Hāshimī, Yaḥyā b. Muḥammad al-. *Al-Qaḍā' fī l-yaman fī l-qarn al-rābi' 'ashar al-hijrī wa-mā ba'duhu.* Sanaa, Yemen: Maktabat Khālid b. al-Walīd, 2003.
Ḥatukah, Tsuriel. *Zikhronot u-temunot mi-teman ve-'ad matan.* N.p.: the author, 2003.
Ḥever, Amnon. "Ha-Shipuṭ ha-rabani be-teman 'al pi 'ha-'musawwadah,' sefer ha-proṭoqolim shel bet din tsan'ā' (me'ot 18–20)." PhD diss., Tel Aviv University, 2000.
Ḥibshūsh, Ḥayyim b. Yaḥyā. "Qorot yisra'el be-teman le-r. Ḥayyim Ḥibshūsh." Edited by Yosef Qāfiḥ, *Sefunot* 2 (1958): 246–286.
——. *Masa'ot ḥibshūsh.* Edited by Shlomo Dov Goitein. Jerusalem: Yad Yitsḥaq Ben-Zvi and the Hebrew University of Jerusalem, 1983.
Ḥibshūsh, Sulaymān b. Yaḥyā. "Sefer eshkolot merorot." Edited by Shlomo Dov Goitein. In *Ha-Temanim: Historiyah, sidre ḥevrah, ḥayye ruaḥ: Mivḥar meḥqarim,* edited by Shlomo Dov Goitein and Menaḥem Ben Sasson, 171–196. Jerusalem: Ben Zvi Institute, 1983.
Ḥibshūsh, Yeḥiel. *Ḥayye ha-yeled be-teman.* N.p.: Ḥibshūsh family, 1991.
——. *Mishpaḥat ḥibshush.* N.p.: Shlomo Davidovitch, 1985.
——. *Riḥlah fī riḥāb al-yaman.* N.p., n.d.
——. *She'erit ha-pleṭah be-teman: Yehude teman she-be-teman ve-ha-mishṭar he-ḥadash.* Bene Beraq, Israel: Ḥibshūsh family, 1990.
——. *Shne ha-me'orot.* N.p.: Ḥibshūsh family, 1987.
Ḥubarah, Yosef. *Bitla'ot teman vīrushalayim.* Jerusalem: the author, 1970.
Ibn Daghr, Aḥmad 'Ubayd. *Al-Yaman taḥta ḥukmi l-imām aḥmad, 1948–1962.* Cairo: Maktabat Madbūlī, 2005.
Ibn Miftāḥ, 'Abdallāh. *Al-Muntaza' al-mukhtār min al-ghayth al-midrār al-ma'rūf bi-sharḥ al-azhār.* (*Commentary [on the Book of] Flowers.*) Ṣa'dah, Yemen: al-Jumhuriyyah al-yamaniyyah, Wizārat al-'adl, 2003.
Jewish National and University Library, MS Ar. 120: "*Niẓām al-yahūd.*"
Juzaylān, 'Abdallāh. *Lamaḥāt min dhikrayāt al-ṭufūlah.* Cairo: Maktabat madbūlī, 1984.
Klein-Francke, Aviva. "Ha-Tsorfut be-qerev yehude teman: Toldoteha, ve-hitpatḥut omanuteha." *Pe'amim* 11 (1982): 62–88.
Klingler, Y., and Tsiporah Friedman-Maqov. "Maḥaneh hapliṭim ha-yehudim ha-temanim be-'aden bi-shnat tashad (1944)." *Tehudah* 19 (1999): 32–43.

Lahav, Shalom. *Qehilat yehude bayḥān*. Netanyah, Israel: Ha-Agudah la-ṭipuaḥ ḥevrah ve-tarbut, 1996.

Libson, Gideon. "Otonomiyah shipuṭit u-peniyah la-'arkha'ot mi-tsad bene he-ḥasut 'al pi meqorot muslimiyim bitqufat ha-ge'onim." In *Ha-Islam ve-'olamot ha-shezurim bo: Qovets ma'amarim le-zikhrah shel Ḥava Latsarus-Yafah*, 334–392. Jerusalem: Hebrew University Institute of Asian and African Studies, Ben-Zvi Institute, and Bialik Institute, 2002.

Madhalah, Avraham. *Ein li erets aḥeret*. Tel Aviv: E'eleh ve-tamar, 1997.

Maimonides. *Mishneh Torah*. Jerusalem: Mosad Ha-Rav Kook, 1962.

Mālīḥ, Avraham al-. "Masa' yom-ṭov tsemaḥ le-teman." In *Shvut teman*, edited by Yisrael Yeshayahu and Aharon Tsadoq, 259–317. Tel Aviv: Hots'at "mi-teman le-tsiyon," 1945.

Manṣūrah, Sālim. *'Aliyat mirbad haqsamim: Tiy'ur ha-'aliyah ha-gedolah shel yehude teman*. Edited by Moshe Gavra. Bene Beraq, Israel: Ha-Makhon le-ḥeqer ḥakhme teman, 2003.

Maqāliḥ, 'Abd al-'Azīz al-. *Al-Ab'ād al-mawḍu'iyyah wa l-fanniyyah li-ḥarakat al-shi'r al-mu'āṣir fī l-yaman*. Beirut: Dār al-'awdah, 1974.

Maqbalī, Ḥusayn Muḥammad. *Mudhakkirāt al-maqbalī*. Damascus: Dār al-fikr, 1986.

Markaz li l-dirāsāt wa l-Buḥūth al-Yamanī. *Thawrat 1948: al-Mīlād wa l-masīrah wa l-Mu'aththirāt*. Beirut: Dār al-'awdah, 1982.

Medinah, Shalom. *Masa'ot r. moshe medinah u-vanav*. Tel Aviv: Ha-Agudah la-ṭipuaḥ ḥevrah ve-tarbut, 1994.

Mu'allimī, Aḥmad 'Abd al-Raḥmān al-. *Madhābiḥ wa-aghlāl: Mudhakkirāt min sujūn ḥajjah*. Damascus: the author, 1998.

Muṭahhar, 'Abd al-Karīm b. Aḥmad. *Sīrat al-imām yaḥyā b. muḥammad ḥamīd al-dīn al-musammāh katībat al-ḥikmah min sīrat imam al-ummah*. Edited by Muḥammad b. 'Īsā al-Ṣāliḥiyyah. Amman, Jordan: Dār al-Bashīr, 1998.

Naḥshon, Yeḥiel. *Hanhagat ha-qehilah ha-yehudit be-teman (Me'ot 17–18)*. Tel Aviv: Ha-Agudah la-ṭipuaḥ ḥevrah ve-tarbut, 2002.

Naḥum, Yehudah Levi, and Yosef Tobi. "Quntres 'Ḥayye ha-temanim' le-rav yosef shemen." In *Yahadut teman: Pirqe meḥqar ve-'iyyun*, edited by Yosef Tobi and Yisrael Yeshayahu, 115–143. Jerusalem: Ben Zvi Institute, 1975.

Naṣr, Yaḥyā Manṣūr. *Shi'r wa-dhikrayāt*. Beirut: Manshūrāt al-'aṣr al-ḥadīth, 1986.

Nini, Yehudah. "Pulmus mi-'inyan vikuaḥ 'aqar 'al ḥokhmat ha-qabalah bein ḥakhme teman be-reshit ha-me'ah." *Mikha'el* 14 (1997): 215–243.

Nu'mān, Aḥmad Muḥammad. *Al-Aṭrāf al-ma'niyyah fī l-yaman*. Aden, Yemen: Mu'assasat al-Sabbān, 1965.

Nu'mān, Muḥammad Aḥmad. *Azmat al-muthaqqaf al-yamanī*. N.p.: Dār al-naṣr li l-ṭibā'ah wa l-nashr wa l-i'lān, 1964.

'Ovadiah, Avraham. *Netivot teman ve-tsiyon: Zikhronot*. Edited by Yosef Tobi. Tel Aviv: Afiqim, 1985.

Qafarah, Pinḥas. *Mini teman u-ve-sha'arayim-reḥovot: Shiv'im shanah (1907–1977)*. Edited by Shim'on Graydi. Reḥovot, Israel: the author, 1978.

Qāfiḥ, Yaḥyā. *Milḥamot ha-shem*. Jerusalem: Defus P. 'Enav, 1931.

Qāfiḥ, Yosef. *Halikhot teman*. Edited by Yisrael Yeshayahu. 1961. Reprint, Jerusalem: Makhon Ben-Zvi, 2007.

Qehati, Ezra. *Yeqiray be-teman u-ve-tsiyon: Pirqe ḥayyav ve-zikhronot*. Tel Aviv: Afiqim, 1999.

Qoraḥ, ʻAmram. *Seʻarat teman*. Edited by Shimʻon Graydi. Jerusalem: Yaḥyā ʻAmram Qoraḥ, 1954.

Qoraḥ, Shalom. *Iggeret bokhim*. Bet Shemesh, Israel: Ha-vaʻad le-hadpasat ḥibure MaHarShaQ, 1962.

Rajawī, Jamīlah Hādī. *Yahūd ṣanʻā': Dirāsah ʻan al-awḍāʻ al-iqtiṣādiyyah wa l-ijtimāʻiyyah fatrat al-imām yaḥyā ḥamīd al-dīn*. Sanaa, Yemen: Markaz ʻabbādī li l-dirāsāt wa l-nashr, 2006.

Ratshaby, Yehudah. "Yehudim u-muslimim bi-sifrut ha-meshalim." In *Be-Meʻaglot teman: Mivḥar meḥqarim be-tarbut yehude teman*, 230–236. Tel Aviv: the author, 1987.

———. ed., *Boʻi teman*. Tel Aviv: Afiqim, 1967.

———. "ʻInyane yehudim be-teman ba-ʻarkha'ot shel goyim." In *Ḥiqre ʻever ve-ʻarav mugashim le-yehoshuʻah blau ʻal yede ḥaverav ba-melot lo shivʻim*, edited by Ḥaggai Ben-Shammai, 515–535. Tel Aviv: Tel Aviv University, 1993.

———. "Le-Toldot ha-maḥloqet ʻal ha-qabalah biqhilat tsanʻa bi-shnot 1913–1914." *Peʻamim* 88 (2001): 98–123.

———. "Qehilat tsanʻa bi-shnot 1899–1913." *Sinai* 67 (1970): 202–218.

———. "Yehude teman taḥat shilṭon ha-turkim." *Sinai* 64 (1963): 53–77.

Rāziḥī, ʻAbd al-Karīm al-. *Ḥunjurat al-shaʻb*. N.p., n.d.

Reshef, Yael. "Hitpatḥuyot semanṭiyot she-reqʻan teqsṭuali balshonot ha-yehudim." In *Leshonot yehude sfarad ve-ha-mizraḥ ve-sifruyotehem*, edited by David M. Bunis, 21–41. Jerusalem: Mosad Bialik/Misgav Yerushalayim, 2009.

Riḍā, Muḥammad Rashīd. *Al-Khilāfah*. 1922. Reprint, Cairo: al-Zahrā li l-iʻlām al-ʻarabī, 1988.

Riḍā, Yosef. *Temanah: Mavo le-erets al-ḥugariyah*. Edited by Efrayim Yaʻaqov. Nahariyah, Jerusalem: Ḥadre teman, 1995.

Sadan, Joseph. "Bein hagzerot ʻal yahadut teman ba-sof ha-me'ah ha-17 le-ʻgezerat ha-meqamtsim' be-me'ot ha-18 ve-ha-19." In *Ma'ot Moshe: Meḥqarim be-tarbut yisra'el ve-ʻarav mugashim le-moshe gil*, edited by E. Fleischer, Mordecai Akiva Friedman, Joel L. Kraemer, 202–236. Jerusalem: Mossad Bialik, 1998.

Ṣā'idī, Muḥammad Qā'id al-. *Ḥarakat al-muʻāraḍah al-yamaniyyah fī ʻahd al-imām yaḥyā b. muḥammad ḥamīd al-dīn (1322–1367h./1904–1948m.)*. Sanaa, Yemen: Markaz al-dirāsāt wa l-buḥūth al-yamanī, 1983.

Ṣāliḥiyyah, Muḥammad ʻĪsā al-. *Al-ʻAllāmah al-amīr sayf al-islām, zayn al-ʻābidīn, al-ḥusayn b. yaḥyā ḥamīd al-dīn, 1327–1367 h./1909–1948 m*. Irbid, Jordan: Yarmuk University, 2009.

Shahārī, Muḥammad ʻAlī al-. *Ṭarīq al-thawrah al-yamaniyyah*. Cairo: Dār al-hilāl, 1966.

Shamāḥī, ʻAbdallāh b. ʻAbd al-Wahhāb al-. *Al-Yaman: al-Insān wa l-ḥaḍārah*. Beirut: Manshūrāt al-madīnah, 1985 (third printing).

Shāmī, Aḥmad b. Muḥammad al-. *Imām al-yaman aḥmad ḥamīd al-dīn*. N.p.: Dār al-kitāb al-jadīd, 1965.

———. *Riyāḥ al-taghyīr fī l-yaman*. N.p., 1984.

———. *Min al-adab al-yamanī: Naqd wa-tu'rīkh*. N.p.: Dār al-shurūq, 1974.

Sharʻabi, Ḥayyim. "Peraqim mi-farashat ʻdor-deʻah' be-teman." In *Shvut Teman*, edited by Yisrael Yeshayahu and Aharon Tsadoq, 198–211. Tel Aviv: Hots'at "mi-teman le-tsiyon," 1945.

Sharʻabi, Reuven. *Yeḥi re'uven ve-al yamot: Zikhronot re'uven sharʻabi*. Reḥovot, Israel: Afiqim, 2004.

Shawkānī, Muḥammad b. 'Alī al-. *Al-Badr al-ṭāli'*. Edited by Ḥusayn al-'Amrī. Beirut: Dār al-fikr, 1998.

——. *Kitāb al-fatḥ al-rabbānī min fatāwā al-imām al-shawkānī*. Edited by Abū Muṣ'ab Muḥammad Ṣubḥī b. Ḥasan Ḥallālah. Sanaa, Yemen: Maktabat al-jīl al-jadīd, 2002.

——. *Kitāb al-Sayl al-jarrār al-mutadaffiq 'alā ḥadā'iq al-azhār*. Edited by Maḥmūd Ibrāhīm Zāyid. Beirut: Dār al-kitāb al-'ilmiyyah, 1985.

Sulami, Ṭuviah. "'Megillat ha-yeshu'ah' le-rav shalom gamli'el bein metsiyut ve-dimyon." *Tehudah* 23 (2008): 51–61.

Sunaydār, Sāliḥ al-. *Al-Ṭarīq ilā l-ḥurriyyah: Mudhakkirāt al-'izzī Ṣāliḥ al-sunaydār*. Edited by 'Alī b. Abdallāh al-Wāsi'ī. Sanaa, Yemen: Iṣdārāt wizārat al-thaqāfah wa l-siyāḥah, 2004.

Ṭabīb, Avraham. *Golat teman*. Tel Aviv: Hotsa'at "Omanut," 1931.

——. *Shave teman*. Tel Aviv: Hotsa'at "Omanut," 1932.

Ṭayri, Nissim. *Bitla'ot ha-galut ve-ha-ge'ulah: Harpatqa'ot ve-nisim bein Radā' le-'aden*. Edited by Mordecai Yitshari. Ramat Gan, Israel: the author, 1998.

Tobi, Yosef. "Hedim la-vikuaḥ 'al ha-qabalah bi-sefer "ets ḥayyim' le-rabbi se'adyah naddaf (tsan'a 1926)." In *Meḥqarim be-lashon ha-'ivrit uvimad'e ha-yahadut*, edited by Aharon Ben-David and Yitsḥaq Gluska, 105–118. Jerusalem: Ha-Agudah la-ṭipuaḥ ḥevrah ve-tarbut, 2001.

——. *'Iyyunim bimgillat teman*. Jerusalem: Magnes Press, 1986.

——. "Mi ḥiber et sefer emunat ha-shem?" *Da'at* 49 (2002): 87–98.

——. "Ha-Qehilah ha-yehudit be-teman." In *Moreshet yehude teman: 'Iyyunim u-meḥqarim*, edited by Yosef Tobi, 68–117. Jerusalem: Bo'i teman, 1977.

——. ed., *Toldot yehude teman mi-kitvehem*. Jerusalem: Merkaz Zalman shazar u-merkaz dinur, 1980.

——. *Yehudi be-sheruṭ ha-imām: Ish ha-'asaqim ve-soḥer ha-nesheq yisra'el tsubayri*. Tel Aviv: Afiqim, 2002.

——. "Yerushat nashim ba-ḥevrah ha-yehudit ve-ha-muslimit." In *Bat Teman: 'Olamah shel ha-ishah ha-yehudiyah*, edited by Shalom Serri, 35–50. Tel Aviv: E'eleh ve-tamar, n.d.

Tsadoq, Gil'ad. *Sefer Zikhron teman: Sippure nifla'ot, demuyot hod, u-minhagim mi-yahadut teman*. Bene Beraq, Israel: the author, 2005.

Tsadoq, Ḥayyim. *Be-Ohole teman*. Tel Aviv: Defus D. Ben Nun, 1980.

Tsadoq, Moshe. "Nitsane 'haskalah' be-teman." *Davar*, July 30, 1954, 6.

——. "Ha-Yaḥasim bein ha-yehudim ve-ha-'aravim be-teman." In *Yahadut teman: Pirqe meḥqar ve-'iyyun*, edited by Yosef Tobi and Yisrael Yeshayahu, 147–163. Jerusalem: Ben Zvi Institute, 1975.

Tsubayri, Yitsḥaq. *Mi-Tsan'a ve-'ad tsiyon*. Qiryat Ono, Israel: Mekhon Mosheh le-ḥeqer mishnat ha-rambam, 1992.

Tsurieli, Yosef. *Kalkalah ve-ḥinukh moderni be-teman be-'et ha-ḥadashah*. Jerusalem: the author, 2005.

'Ukāshah, Muḥammad 'Abd al-Karīm. *Yahūd al-yaman wa l-hijrah ilā filasṭīn*. 'Aden, Yemen: the author, 1993.

'Umar, Sulṭān Aḥmad. *Naẓrah fī taṭawwur al-mujtama' al-yamanī*. Beirut: Dār al-ṭalī'ah, 1970.

'Uzayrī, Shalom. *Gale or: Pirqe historyah*. Tel Aviv: the author, 1985.

Wāsiʿī, ʿAbd al-Wāsiʿ b. Yaḥyā al-. *Taʾrīkh al-yaman al-musammā furjat al-humūm wa l-ḥuzn fī ḥawādith wa-taʾrīkh al-yaman.* Cairo: al-Maktabah al-salafiyyah, 1927/1928.
Wazīr, Aḥmad b. Muḥammad al-. *Ḥayāt al-amīr ʿalī b. ʿabdallāh al-wazīr.* N.p.: Manshūrāt al-ʿaṣr al-ḥadīth, 1987.
Wazīr, Ibrāhīm b. ʿAlī al-. *Zahrāʾ al-yaman: Umm fī ghimār al-thawrah.* Bethesda, MD: Kitab, 1997.
Yavnieli, Shmuel. *Masaʾ le-teman.* Tel Aviv: Hotsaʾat mifleget poʿale erets yisraʾel, 1952.
Yeshayahu, Yisrael. "Shvile ha-ʿaliyah mi-teman le-tsiyon." In *Shvut teman,* edited by Yisrael Yeshayahu and Aharon Tsadoq, 37–54. Tel Aviv: Hotsʾat "mi-teman le-tsiyon," 1945.
Yitshari, Mordecai. *ʿAlilot ve-naftulim mi-teman.* Rosh Ha-ʿAyin, Israel: the author, 1990.
——. *Hayiti ben ʿarubah be-teman.* Rosh Ha-ʿAyin, Israel: A.M.B. Admor, 1989.
——. *Ḥayyim soʿarim.* Netanyah, Israel: Ha-Agudah la-ṭipuaḥ ḥevrah ve-tarbut, 1996.
Yitshari, Tsadoq (Ṣāliḥ al-Ẓāhirī), *Kakh baraḥti mi-teman.* Rosh Ha-ʿAyin, Israel: Mordecai Yitshari, 1988.
Zabārah, Muḥammad b. Muḥammad. *Āʾimmat al-yaman bi l-qarn al-rābiʿ ʿashar li l-hijrah.* Cairo: al-Maṭbaʿah al-salafiyyah, 1955.
——. *Nayl al-waṭar min tarājim rijāl al-yaman fī l-qarn al-thālith ʿashar.* Beirut: Dār al-ʿawdah, n.d.
——. *Nuzhat al-naẓar fī rijāl al-qarn al-rābiʿ ʿashar.* Sanaa, Yemen: Markaz al-dirāsāt wa l-abḥāth al-yamaniyyah, 1979.
Zandani, ʿOvadiah. *Yalquṭ ʿovadiah: Mi-hare baraṭ le-moshav yinon.* Edited by Nissim Binyamin Gamlieli. Tel Aviv: Afiqim, 1986.

Secondary Sources in European Languages

Abdin, A. Z. al-. "The Role of Islam in the State: The Yemen Arab Republic (1940–1972)." PhD diss., University of Cambridge, 1975.
Abou El-Fadl, Khaled, Joshua Cohen, and Ian League. *The Place of Tolerance in Islam.* Boston: Beacon Press, 2002.
ʿAlī, Ṣāleḥ Aḥmad El-. "The Foundation of Baghdad." In *The Islamic City,* edited by Albert Hourani and S. M. Stern, 87–101. Oxford: Cassirer, 1970.
ʿAmrī, Ḥusayn b. ʿAbdullah al-. *The Yemen in the 18th and 19th Centuries: A Political and Intellectual History.* Durham, UK: University of Durham, Centre for Middle Eastern and Islamic Studies, 1985.
Andrews, Clinton J. "Security and the Built Environment: An Interview with John Habraken." *IEEE Technology and Society* (Fall 2004): 7–12.
Ariel, Ari. "A Reconsideration of Imam Yahya's Attitude toward Forced Conversion of Jewish Orphans in Yemen." *Shofar* 29, no. 1 (2010): 95–111.
Baillie, Neil B. E. *A Digest of Moohummudan Law.* Lahore, Pakistan: Premier Book House, 1965.
Ballas, Shimʿon. *Outcast.* Translated by Ammiel Alcalay and Oz Shelach. San Francisco: City Lights Books, 2007.
Blumi, Isa. *Chaos in Yemen: Societal Collapse and the New Authoritarianism.* London: Routledge, 2011.
Brauer, Erich. *Ethnologie der Jemenitischen Juden.* Heidelberg: Carl Winters Universitätsbuchandlung, 1934.

Bruck, Gabriele vom. *Islam, Memory, and Morality in Yemen: Ruling Families in Transition.* New York: Palgrave Macmillan, 2005.
Cohen, Boaz. *Jewish and Roman Law: A Comparative Study.* New York: Jewish Theological Seminary of America, 1966.
Cohen, Mark R. *Under Crescent and Cross: The Jews in the Middle Ages.* Princeton, NJ: Princeton University Press, 1994.
Dallal, Ahmad. "Appropriating the Past: Twentieth-Century Reconstruction of Pre-Modern Islamic Thought." *Islamic Law and Society* 7, no. 3 (2000): 325–358.
——. "Yemeni Debates on the Status of Non-Muslims in Islamic Law." *Islam and Christian-Muslim Relations* 7, no. 2 (1996): 181–192.
Dostal, Walter. *Eduard Glaser: Forschungen im Yemen.* Vienna: Verlag der Österreichischen Akademie der Wissenschaften, 1990.
——. "Sexual Hospitality' and the Problem of Matrilinearity in South Arabia." *Proceedings of the Seminar for Arabian Studies* 20 (1990): 17–30.
——. "Sozio-ökonomische Aspekte der Stammesdemokratie in Nordost-Yemen." *Sociologus* 24 (1974):1–15.
Douglas, J. Leigh. *The Free Yemeni Movement, 1935–1962.* Beirut: American University of Beirut, 1987.
Dresch, Paul. *A History of Modern Yemen.* Cambridge, UK: Cambridge University Press, 2000.
——. *Tribes, Government, and History in Yemen.* Oxford: Oxford University Press, 1989.
Elbogen, Ismar. *Jewish Liturgy: A Comprehensive History.* Translated by Raymond P. Scheindlin. Philadelphia: Jewish Publication Society, 1993.
Elon, Menachem. *Jewish Law: History, Sources, Principles.* Translated by Bernard Auerbach and Melvin J. Sykes. Philadelphia: Jewish Publication Society, 1994.
——. *Jewish Law (Mishpaṭ 'ivri): Cases and Materials.* Translated by Bernard Auerbach, Daniel D. Chazin, and Melvin J. Sykes. New York: Matthew Bender, 1999.
Eraqi Klorman, Bat-Zion. "The Forced Conversion of Jewish Orphans in Yemen." *International Journal of Middle East Studies* 33, no. 1 (2001): 23–47.
——. "Muslim Society as an Alternative: Jews Converting to Islam." *Jewish Social Studies* 14 (2007): 88–117.
——. "Yemen, Aden, and Ethiopia: Jewish Emigration and Italian Colonialism." *Journal of the Royal Asiatic Society,* Series 3, 19, no. 4 (2009): 415–426.
——. "Yemen: Religion, Magic, and Jews." *Proceedings of the Seminar for Arabian Studies* 39 (2009): 125–34.
Ferris, Jesse. *Nasser's Gamble: How Intervention in Yemen Caused the Six-Day War and the Decline of Egyptian Power.* Princeton, NJ: Princeton University Press, 2012.
Friedmann, Yohanan. *Tolerance and Coercion in Islam: Interfaith Relations in the Muslim Tradition.* Cambridge, UK: Cambridge University Press, 2003.
Gamliel, 'Amram. "A Spark of Enlightenment among the Jews of Yemen." *Hebrew Studies* 25 (1984): 82–89.
Gat, Moshe. *The Jewish Exodus from Iraq, 1948–1951.* London: Frank Cass & Co., 1997.
Gerholm, Tomas. *Market, Mosque, and Mafraj: Social Inequality in a Yemeni Town.* Stockholm: University of Stockholm, 1977.
Goitein, Shlomo Dov. *Jews and Arabs: Their Contacts through the Ages.* New York: Schocken Books, 1955.

———. *A Mediterranean Society: The Jewish Communities of the Arab World as Portrayed in the Documents of the Cairo Genizah.* Berkeley: University of California Press, 1967.

———. "Portrait of a Yemenite Weavers' Village." *Jewish Social Studies* 17, no. 1 (1955): 3–26.

Gottreich, Emily. *The Mellah of Marrakesh: Jewish and Muslim Space in Morocco's Red City.* Bloomington: Indiana University Press, 2007.

Habraken, N. John. "Design for Adaptability, Change, and User Participation." In *Housing: Processes and Physical Form,* edited by Linda Safran, 23–29. Philadelphia: Aga Khan Award for Architecture, 1980.

Halevi, Leor. "Christian Impurity versus Economic Necessity: A Fifteenth-Century Fatwa on European Paper." *Speculum* 83 (2008): 917–945.

Hallaq, Wael. *Authority, Continuity, and Change in Islamic Law.* Cambridge, UK: Cambridge University Press, 2001.

———. *The Origins and Evolution of Islamic Law.* Cambridge, UK: Cambridge University Press, 2005.

Hathaway, Jane. *A Tale of Two Factions: Myth, Memory, and Identity in Ottoman Egypt and Yemen.* Albany: SUNY Press, 2003.

Hathloul, Saleh A. al-. "Tradition, Continuity, and Change in the Physical Environment: The Arab-Muslim City." PhD diss., M.I.T., 1981.

Haykel, Bernard. *Revival and Reform in Islam: The Legacy of Muḥammad al-Shawkānī.* Cambridge, UK: Cambridge University Press, 2003.

Hilfskomitee für die Juden in Jemen. *Von den Juden des Jemens.* Berlin: Orient Verlag, 1913.

Hirschberg, H. Z. "The Oriental Jewish Communities." In *Religion in the Middle East,* edited by A. J. Arberry, 1:119–225. Cambridge, UK: Cambridge University Press, 1969.

Hollander, Isaac. "Halakha, Sharīʿa, and Custom: A Legal Saga from Highland Yemen, 1990–1940." In *Islamic Law: Theory and Practice,* edited by Robert Gleave and Eugenia Kermeli, 157–184. London: I. B. Tauris, 1997.

———. "*Ibra* in Highland Yemen: Two Jewish Divorce Settlements." *Islamic Law and Society* 2, no. 1 (1995): 1–23.

Hünefeld, Kerstin. *Imām Yaḥyā Ḥamīd al-Dīn und die Juden in Sanaa (1904–1948): Die Dimension von Schutz (dhimma) in den Dokumenten der Sammlung des Rabbi Sālim b. Saʿīd al-Ğamal.* Berlin: Klaus Schwarz Verlag, 2010.

———. "*Niẓām al-Yahūd* ("The Statute of the Jews"): Imām Yaḥyā's Writing to the Jews of Ṣanʿāʾ from 1323/1905." *Chronique du Manuscrit au Yémen* 16 (2013): 26–76.

Jackson, Sherman. "Fiction and Formalism: Toward a Functional Analysis of *Uṣūl al-fiqh.*" In *Studies in Islamic Legal Theory,* edited by Bernard G. Weiss, 177–202. Leiden: E. J. Brill, 2002.

Kühn, Thomas. "Shaping and Reshaping Colonial Ottomanism: Contesting Boundaries of Difference and Integration in Ottoman Yemen, 1872–1919." *Comparative Studies of South Asia, Africa, and the Middle East* 27.2 (2007): 315–31.

Leder, Stefan. "Conventions of Fictional Narration in Learned Literature." In *Story telling in the Framework of Non-fictional Arabic Literature,* edited by Stefan Leder, 34–60. Wiesbaden: Harrassowitz, 1998.

Lehmann, Matthias B. "Islamic Legal Consultation and the Jewish-Muslim *Convivencia:* al-Wansharīsī's *Fatwā* Collection as a Source for Jewish Social History in al-Andalus and the Maghrib." *Jewish Studies Quarterly* 6 (1999): 25–54.
Levy-Rubin, Milka. *Non-Muslims in the Early Islamic Empire.* Cambridge, UK: Cambridge University Press, 2011.
Lewcock, Ronald. *The Old Walled City of San'a'.* Ghent, Belgium: UNESCO, 1986.
Lewis, Bernard. *The Jews of Islam.* Princeton, NJ: Princeton University Press, 1984.
Llewellyn, Karl N., and E. Adamson Hoebel. *The Cheyenne Way: Conflict and Case Law in Primitive Jurisprudence.* Norman: University of Oklahoma Press, 1941.
Maclagan, Ianthe. "Food and Gender in a Yemeni Community." In *Culinary Cultures of the Middle East,* edited by Sami Zubaida and Richard Tapper, 159–172. London: I. B. Tauris, 1994.
Maghen, Ze'ev. "The Interaction between Islamic Law and Non-Muslims: *Lakum Dīnukum wa-lī Dīni.*" *Islamic Law and Society* 10, no. 3 (2003): 267–275.
———. "Strangers and Brothers: The Ritual Status of Unbelievers in Islamic Jurisprudence." *Medieval Encounters* 12, no. 2 (2006): 173–223.
Maine, Ernest. *Palestine at the Crossroads.* London: George Allen & Unwin, Ltd., 1937.
Malik, Jamel. *Crisis in the Built Environment: The Case of the Muslim City.* Singapore: Mimar Book/Concept Media, 1988.
Mattar, Philip. *The Mufti of Jerusalem: al-Ḥajj Amīn al-Ḥusaynī and the Palestinian National Movement.* New York: Columbia University Press, 1988.
Meir-Glitzenstein, Esther. *Zionism in an Arab Country: Jews in Iraq in the 1940s.* London: Routledge, 2004.
Messick, Brinkley. *The Calligraphic State: Textual Domination and History in a Muslim Society.* Berkeley: University of California Press, 1993.
———. "Property and the Private in a Sharia System." *Social Research* 70, no. 3 (2003): 711–34.
Msaodi, Abdualaziz K. al-. "The Yemeni Opposition Movement, 1918–1948." PhD diss., Georgetown University, 1987.
Montequin, Francois-Auguste de. "*Sharia* and Urban Design: Effects and Reflection of Canon Law on the City of Islam." *Search* 3, no. 2 (1982): 22–41.
Muchawsky-Schnapper, Esther. *The Jews of Yemen: Highlights of the Israel Museum Collection.* Jerusalem: Israel Museum, 1994.
Nietzsche, Friedrich. *On the Genealogy of Morals.* Translated by Douglas Smith. Oxford: Oxford University Press, 1996.
Nini, Yehuda. *The Jews of the Yemen, 1800–1914.* Philadelphia: Harwood Academic Publishers, 1991.
Nirenberg, David. *Communities of Violence: Persecution of Minorities in the Middle Ages.* Princeton, NJ: Princeton University Press, 1996.
Novak, David. "The Treatment of Islam and Muslims in the Legal Writings of Maimonides." In *Studies in Islamic and Judaic Traditions,* edited by William M. Brinner and Stephen D. Ricks, 1:233–50. Atlanta: Scholars Press, 1986.
O'Barr, William M. *Linguistic Evidence: Language, Power, and Strategy in the Courtroom.* New York: Academic Press, 1982.
Obermeyer, Gerald J. "Ṭāghūt, Man', and Šarī'a: The Realms of Law in Tribal Arabia." In *Studia Arabica et Islamica: Festschrift for Ihsan Abbas on His Sixtieth Birthday,* edited by Wadad al-Qadi, 365–371. Beirut: American University of Beirut, 1981.

Parfitt, Tudor. "The Jewish Image of the Imam: Paradox or Paradigm." In *Israel and Ishmael: Studies in Muslim-Jewish Relations,* edited by Tudor Parfitt, 207–225. Richmond, Surrey: Curzon Press, 2000.

———. *The Road to Redemption: The Jews of the Yemen, 1900–1950.* Leiden: E. J. Brill, 1996.

Philby, H. St. J. B. *Arabian Highlands.* Ithaca, NY: Cornell University Press, 1952.

Piamenta, Moshe. *Dictionary of Post-Classical Yemeni Arabic.* Leiden: E. J. Brill, 1990–1991.

Playfair, Robert L. *A History of Arabia Felix or Yemen from the Commencement of the Christian Era until the Present Time.* Bombay: Education Society's Press, 1859.

Powers, David S. "Law and Custom in the Maghrib, 1475–1500: On the Disinheritance of Women." In *Law, Custom, and Statute in the Muslim World: Studies in Honor of Aharon Layish,* edited by Ron Shaham, 17–40. Leiden: E. J. Brill, 2006.

Puin, Gerd-R. "The Yemeni *Hijrah* Concept of Tribal Protection." In *Land Tenure and Social Transformation in the Middle East,* edited by Tarif Khalidi, 483–494. Beirut: American University of Beirut, 1984.

Rappoport, Yosef. *Marriage, Money, and Divorce in Medieval Islamic Society.* Cambridge, UK: Cambridge University Press, 2005.

Rathjens, Karl. "Tāghūt gegen scherīʻa: Gewohnheitsrecht und islamisches Recht bei den Gabilen des jemenitischen Hochlandes." *Tribus: Jahrbuch des Lindenmuseums,* 1 (1951): 172–187.

Rihani, Ameen. *Arabian Peak and Desert: Travels in al-Yaman.* London: Constable & Co. Ltd., 1930.

Rosen, Lawrence. *The Anthropology of Justice: Law as Culture in Islamic Society.* Cambridge, UK: Cambridge University Press, 1989.

———, *The Culture of Islam: Changing Aspects of Contemporary Muslim Life.* Chicago: University of Chicago Press, 2002.

———. *The Justice of Islam: Comparative Perspectives on Islamic Law and Society.* Oxford: Oxford University Press, 2000.

———. *Law as Culture: An Invitation.* Princeton, NJ: Princeton University Press, 2006.

Rossi, Ettore. "Il diritto consuetudinario delle tribù arabe del Yemen." *Revista degli Studi Orientali* 23 (1948):1–36.

Rouaud, Alain. "L'Émigration Yéménite." In *L'Arabie du Sud,* edited by Joseph Chelhod, 2:227–250. Paris: Maisonneuve et Larose, 1984.

Rubin, Uri. "Qur'ān and Poetry: More Data Concerning the Qur'ānic *Jizya* Verse (*ʻan yadin*)." *Jerusalem Studies in Arabic and Islam* 31 (2006): 139–146.

Russell, Alexander David, and Abdullah al-Maʻmun Suhrawardy. *Muslim Law: An Historical Introduction to the Law of Inheritance.* 1925. Reprint, London: Kegan Paul, 2008.

Sadan, Joseph. "The 'Latrines Decree' in the Yemen versus the *Dhimma* Principles." In *Pluralism and the Other: Studies in Religious Behaviour,* edited by Jan Platvoet and Karel van der Toorn, 167–185. Leiden: E. J. Brill, 1995.

Serjeant R. B., and Ronald Lewcock. *Ṣanʻāʼ: An Arabian Islamic City.* London: World of Islam Festival Trust, 1983.

Shapiro, Marc B. "Islam and the Halakhah." *Judaism* (Summer 1993): 332–343.

Shiblak, Abbas. *Iraqi Jews: A History of the Mass Exodus.* London: Saqi Books, 1995.

Simonsohn, Uriel. *A Common Justice: The Legal Allegiances of Christians and Jews under Early Islam*. Philadelphia: University of Pennsylvania Press, 2011.
Stevenson, Thomas B. *Social Change in a Yemeni Highlands Town*. Salt Lake City: University of Utah Press, 1985.
Stillman, Norman, trans. *The Jews of Arab Lands: A History and Source Book*. Philadelphia: Jewish Publication Society, 1979.
———. "The Judeo-Islamic Historical Encounter: Visions and Revisions." In *Israel and Ishmael: Studies in Muslim-Jewish Relations*, edited by Tudor Parfitt, 1–12. Richmond, Surrey: Curzon Press, 2000.
Stowasser, Barbara Freyer, and Zeinab Abul-Magd. "Tahlil Marriage in Shari'a, Legal Codes, and the Contemporary *Fatwa* Literature." In *Islamic Law and the Challenges of Modernity*, edited by Yvonne Yazbeck Haddad and Barbara Freyer Stowasser, 161–182. Walnut Creek, CA: Altamira Press, 2004.
Ṭabīb, Avraham. *Golat teman*. Tel Aviv: Hotsa'at "Omanut," 1931.
Thompson, Christopher S. *The Tour de France: A Cultural History*. Berkeley: University of California Press, 2008.
Tobi, Yosef. "Challenges to Tradition: Jewish Cultures in Yemen, Iraq, Iran, Afghanistan, and Bukhara." In *Cultures of the Jews: A New History*, edited by David Biale, 933–974. New York: Schocken Books, 2002.
———. "*Histoire de la Communauté Juive du Yémen aux XIXe et XXe Siècles*." In *L'Arabie du Sud*, edited by Joseph Chelhod, 2:119–37. Paris: Maisonneuve et Larose, 1984.
———. *The Jews of Yemen: Studies in Their History and Culture*. Leiden: E. J. Brill, 1999.
Wagner, Mark S. "*Halakhah* through the Lens of *Shari'ah*: The Case of the Kuḥlānī Synagogue in Ṣan'a', 1933–1944." In *The Convergence of Judaism and Islam: The Religious, Scientific, and Cultural Dimensions*, edited by Michael Laskier and Yaacov Lev, 126–146. Gainesville: University Press of Florida, 2011.
———. "Infidels, Lovers, and Magicians: Portrayals of the Jews in Yemeni Arabic Poetry, 17th-19th centuries." In *Miṭṭuv Yosef: Sefer ha-yovel li-khvod yosef ṭobi*, edited by Dani Bar Ma'oz and Ayelet Ettinger, 2:xlvi-lix. Haifa, Israel: Haifa University, 2011.
———. "Jewish Mysticism on Trial in a Muslim Court: A *Fatwā* on the *Zohar*—Yemen 1914." *Die Welt des Islams* 47, no. 2 (2007): 207–31.
———. *Like Joseph in Beauty: Yemeni Vernacular Poetry and Arab-Jewish Symbiosis*. Leiden: E. J. Brill, 2009.
Weir, Shelagh. *A Tribal Order: Politics and Law in the Mountains of Yemen*. Austin: University of Texas Press, 2007.
Würth, Anna. *Aš-Šarī'a fī Bāb al-Yaman*. Berlin: Duncker & Humblot, 2000.

Index

'Abbās, 'Abdallāh b., 137
'Abbās, Yaḥyā b. Muḥammad, 88, 91
'Abd al-Ḥamīd II, Sultan, 99
Abdin, A. Z. al-, 21, 125
'Abduh, Muḥammad, 94, 174n118
Abū Jabal, Camīlia, 85
abutters' rights (*shuf'ah*), 117–122, 152
Abyaḍ, Rabbi Yaḥyā al-: blasphemy defense, 65–66; converts to Islam, status of, 77; Husseini visit and letter, 132–133; Jamal liquor raid, 108; liquor industry supervision document, 106–107; royal mint, 98
Aden, 70–71, 80, 85, 133, 150
Afghānī, Jamāl al-Dīn, al-, 94
'Afīf, Aḥmad Jābir, 88
Aḥmad, Imām, 2, 3–4, 6, 11–12, 128, 160n3; Arab League and Muslim Brotherhood, 134; documentary evidence ruling, 113–114; emigration property sales, 114–115; forced Jewish observance, 78; and Husseini, 133; Islamic mysticism, 89–90; Israel, 77–78; Jewish veneration, 12; kabbalah trial, 86; "Kisār Storehouse" murders, 149; and opposition to Imām Yaḥyā, 170n129; and Nu'mān clan, 129; tomb demolitions, 89–90
Aḥrār al-yaminiyūn, al-. See Free Yemenis Party
akhdām. See black people in Yemen
Akwa', Qadi Ismā'īl al-, 34–35, 176n178
Akwa', Qadi Muḥammad al-, 35–36
alcohol, 18, 53, 96, 105–109. *See also* bootlegging; wine; *'araq*
'Alī, Prince (Imām Yaḥyā's son), 60
"'Alī the Weeder," 111
Alliance Israelite Universelle, 100
'Amrī, Ḥusayn al-, 36
'Amrī, Qadi 'Abdallāh al-, 19–20, 133, 153, 154; bicycle riding, 58; kabbalah trial, 87; store decorum ruling, 103–104; usefulness to Imām Yaḥyā, 36
'Amrī, Qadi 'Alī al-, 148
amulets and spells, 68, 80, 84, 104–105
'Ansī, Qadi Aḥmad b. al-Qāsim al-, 121
anthropomorphism: by Jews, 89, 92–94; by Muslims, 89, 90
anti-Kabbalism, 94, 94–95. See also *Dor De'ah*
anti-Semitism, 130
'Anzi, Menashe, 84
"ape man," 74, 82
Arabic: formal, 12, 64, 67–68, 69, 78, 86, 89; Jewish, 25, 64, 65, 67, 69–70, 74–75
'araq, 36, 52, 53, 105, 107, 108, 146
arbitration, 28, 29–30, 87, 137, 142, 142–143
arms bearing. *See* weapons
arrests, 6, 28, 39, 50, 55, 65, 86, 109, 138, 153; mass arrests, 94, 148, 149
Arslān, Shakīb, 3
Asmara. *See* Eritrea
Aṣwār, Ṣāliḥ al-, 128
'Aṭiya clan, 148
'Atsṭah, Yosef, 18, 100, 104
'Azīz, Qadi Muḥammad 'Abd al-, 142

baboon trapping, 41–42
Baḥr al-zakhkhār, 38
Balaqah, 146, 148, 187n92
Ballas, Shim'on, 71
Bannā, Ḥasan al-, 4
bathhouses, 41, 46, 56, 155
Bayḥān, 53, 79, 82, 126, 128
beatings, 63–64, 126–127, 128. *See also* violence
Bedouin, 17, 72, 125, 126, 159n48
Ben David, Aharon, 18, 21, 26, 71, 99
Ben Gurion, David, 78, 134
Bene Moshe, Shalom, 99, 107, 108, 126–127, 159n39
bicycle riding, 2, 5–6, 13, 57–59, 108–109
black people in Yemen, 8, 48, 5–53, 77, 111
blasphemy, 65, 66, 67
"blood libel," 1948, 146, 150
blood money, 126, 184n18
bootlegging, 36, 102, 108, 109, 179n69. *See also* alcohol; wine
boundaries, interreligious, 8, 15, 69, 81–82, 124, 131, 135, 143, 155
bribery, 24, 50–51, 59, 108, 137, 149; among Muslims, 11; arbitration, 29–30, 137; court system, 29, 35; Daylamī, Qadi Zayd al-, 32–33, 135; for exit visas, 33; judicial, 17, 23, 24, 29–33, 50, 60, 155; political dimensions, 33–34; in

prison, 23, 27–28, 109, 148; "prolongation" of cases, 30; shaykhs, 32; witnesses, 67, 140, 142; wound assessment, 142
British Empire, 67, 72, 80, 106, 114, 133, 134, 150, 184n1, 186n81
Brown, Wendy, 143
building projects, 96–97
burial. *See* funerals
butchers. *See* meat
butter, 55, 56, 72, 116

caliphate, 3–4
camels, 49, 52
cemeteries. *See* funerals
cheese, 72
Christianity, 88, 94
"Climbing Cat" murder, 147
clothing, 38, 69–70, 71, 88
coercion, religious, 47, 88–89
coffee, 71, 100, 102, 110–111
Cohen, Amnon, 24–25
Cohen, Blackjack, 52
Cohen, Mark, 18
Cohen, Shim'on, 138, 139–142, 143–144, 151
collective punishment, 109, 152
Commentary [on the Book of] Flowers, 29, 55, 57, 120, 121
commerce: foreign, 99–100; luxury goods, 6, 100–101, 103; nationalization, 101
conversion to Islam, 24, 43, 49, 66, 72, 73, 74, 77, 81, 82, 159n41
courts: Jewish (*bet din*), 2, 21–22, 24, 25, 79, 87, 117–118, 120; Muslim, *see* sharī'a court system; Ottoman, *see* law: Ottoman

Da''ān, treaty of, 17, 40
Ḍāli', al- (town), 91
Dallal, Ahmad, 3, 48, 157n2
damages, 23, 36, 126, 129, 130, 142–143, 184nn17–18, 184n21; beating, 29; extortion, 150; Imām Aḥmad assessment, 109; Imām order, 129; Jamal raid, 108; murder, 4; riding, 36; tribal law vs. sharī'a, 126
Damt, 22, 25, 41, 52, 82, 105, 132, 168n58; deeds, 34, 119, 120; theft from Jewish merchants, 109–110
Darwīsh, Muḥsin al-, 69, 70
dawāshīn. See black people in Yemen
Ḍawrān (town), 109
Daylamī, Qadi Zayd al-, 33, 36, 101, 135, 153; bribery, 32, 135; Imām Yaḥyā opposition, 32, 153; Jamal, 60, 109; photo of, 31
Daylamī family, 135, 137, 143
dentistry, 98, 99
Dhamār, 26, 78, 104, 107, 147; looting, 115; mediator payments, 29–30; Yosef 'Atsṭah, 18, 78, 104
Dhārī, Yaḥyā al-, 139, 186n81
dhimmi (non-Muslims), 1, 3, 139, 155
Dhubḥān, 87–88
dining, interreligious. *See* kashrut
disguises, 11, 67, 70–71, 79, 151
disputes, intra-Muslim, 80, 132, 174n118
divorce, 22, 23–24, 144, 184n21
documentary evidence, 9, 18, 59, 61, 113–114, 119
documents: divorce, 12, 20, 22, 24; forged, 34, 77, 142; legal, 3, 5, 6, 8, 106–107, 119; payment for, 29, 30
donkeying, 81, 105
donkeys, 48–50, 51–55, 58, 68, 131, 151
Dor De'ah, 156; currency accusations, 98; formal Arabic, 68; Islamic inspirations, 94; Islamic law view, 156; kabbalah and magical, 84; medieval Jewish thinkers, 155; prayer practices, 84; prison prayers, 148; support for Jamal, 153
Dostal, Walter, 4
Dhū l-fiqar (sword), 83
drunkenness, 35, 53, 55, 57, 106, 123, 151
dung collection, 18, 39–40, 42–43, 47, 94–95, 97, 124, 154–155, 167n38, 167n39; authorities on, 44–46; in contemporary Yemen, 48

emigration, 13–15, 67, 71, 112–113, 150; emigrants and emigrant property, 111–117, 122–123
Eritrea, 33, 115, 140
Ethiopia, travel to, 186n86
evidence. *See* testimony; witnesses
equality, Islamic legal sources, 155
excrement collection. *See* dung collection, latrine-connected work
exit visas, 33, 115
extortion, 149, 150. *See also* bribery

Fadl, Khaled Abou el-, 1–2
fatwas, 4, 8, 65, 92, 108; Ẓāhirī, Rabbi Ṣāliḥ al-, 11, 151; Zohar fatwa, 87–92, 152
flag, Ẓāhirī's imāmic-Zionist, 6, 10, 11, 83, 95, 151
flour grinding, 17, 40, 41, 42, 81, 153
folklore and storytelling, 12, 18, 25, 26, 35–36, 51, 77, 105, 111, 143–146
food, kosher. See *kashrut*

"forcible billeting," 28
forgery, 17, 34, 66–67, 88, 110, 142, 143
Frankfurter, Felix, 16
Free Yemenis Party, 4, 32, 68
Friedmann, Yohanan, 1, 157n5
funerals: Jewish, 10; Muslim, 51, 63, 79, 91, 105

Gamliel, Shalom, 165n122, 168n64, 176n177, 187n22
Gamlieli, Nissim, 7, 13, 23, 105, 109, 164n102, 184n21; bribery, 24, 27; intercommunal violence, 131–132; theft from Jewish merchants, 109–110; work smells, 97–98
George VI, King, 186n81
Ghālib family, 135, 137, 141, 144, 145
Ghamḍān, Muḥammad b. Muḥammad, 171n18
Glaser, Eduard, 85
Golden Crown on the Laws of the Rite, The, 90, 121
Gotein, Shlomo Dov, 149
Gottreich, Emily, 179n74

Habraken, John, 121–122
Ḥajjah (town), 28
Halevi, Ratson, 13–14, 42, 65, 72, 74, 82, 119
Halevy, Joseph, 85
Hallaq, Wael, 28–29, 48, 121
Ḥamdī, Aharon, 33, 67, 105, 130, 148, 149
Ḥamīd al-Dīn, Yaḥyā (Imām). *See* Yaḥyā, Imām
Ḥammām Damt. *See* Damt
Hanafīs, 18, 115, 117, 121
harrassment, by *sayyids*, 130–131. See also *sayyids*
ḥarbī, 139, 143
Ḥasan, Prince, 149, 187n104
Hathloul, Saleh al-, 117
Haykel, Bernard, 3, 32, 154
Ḥever, Amnon, 24
Ḥibshūsh, Hārūn, 84, 102
Ḥibshūsh, Ḥayyim, 42, 67–68, 156
Ḥibshūsh, Yeḥi'el, 16, 78, 101–102, 108, 122, 132, 179n65
Ḥibshūsh family, 100, 101–102, 116, 122
Hodeida (port), 17, 40, 100
honor, 64, 72, 125, 146, 176n177; in Islam, 45; Jewish, 6, 8, 138; redistribution of, 145–146; Shim'on Cohen case, 138
horses, 6, 44, 48, 50, 52, 55, 70, 152
Ḥubārah, Yosef, 98, 125
Ḥujariyyah (town), 162n45

humiliation, 38–39, 44, 45–46, 50–51, 87, 145; labor, 41, 42, 45, 47
Ḥusayn, Prince, 133–134
Husseini, Mufti Amīn al-, 132–133, 185n50
Ḥūthī, Yaḥyā b. Muḥammad b. 'Abbās al-, 84–86, 87, 88–89

ijtihād, 3, 48
Imām Aḥmad. *See* Aḥmad, Imām
Imām al-Murtaḍā, 29, 121
Imām Yaḥyā. *See* Yaḥyā, Imām
Imām Yaḥyā b. Ḥamza al-Mu'ayyad, 121
imāmic-Jewish merchant alliances, 101–102
imām-ulama rivalry, 153–154
imports, effects, 100, 116–117
impurity, 47, 51, 56, 57, 168n58
inheritance, 4, 11, 22, 135, 168n58
intermediaries, Jewish, 5–14, 7, 151, 155, 156. *See also names of specific intermediaries*
Iraq, 112–113
Iryānī, Qadi Yaḥyā b. Muḥammad al-, 34
'Īsā, 'Abdallāh b., 46
Isḥāq, Chief Rabbi Yaḥyā, 86, 88, 89, 90, 91–92
Islam, conversion to, 43. *See also* conversion to Islam
Islam, Sunni, 90. *See* Sunnis
Islamic Conference (1931), 132, 185n50
Israel, 7, 13–15, 78, 173n98. *See also* emigration
'Izzānī, Qadi 'Abdallāh al-, 142, 144–145
'Izzī, Qadi Qāsim al-, 32, 36, 60, 153

Jābir, Aḥmad, 60, 108, 116
Jackson, Sherman, 42
"Jahrāzī, Sālim al-," 86
Jalāl, 'Alī b. 'Abdallāh al-, 45–46
Jamal, Rabbi Sālim Sa'īd al-, 2, 5–6, 7, 8, 13, 108–109; abutters' rights (*shuf'ah*), 117, 118, 120, 122; alcohol, 55–56, 103, 109, 179n69; bicycle riding, 6, 7–8, 57–61, 152; blasphemy accusation, 66; defeats, 152–153; Dubyānī donkey, 53–55; enemies, 60; Imām Yaḥyā, 153; Kabbalah controversy, 91–92, 94; non-Muslim rights, 7–8, 152–153; perfume, 100; political agenda, 61–62; poll tax, 153; property nationalization order, 116–117; qadi crimes, 36; raid on, 108–109; royal mint, 98; sectarian policy, 91; self-depictions, 151–152; ulama petition, 117–118, 120; and Ẓāhirī, Rabbi Ṣāliḥ al-, 145; Zaydism, 17, 120
Jandārī, Governor Aḥmad al-, 128–129
Jandārī, Qadi Ḥamūd al-, 135–137, 137–141, 143–144, 146, 186n75

Jerusalem, sharī'a court use, 24–25
Jewish Agency, 102
Jewish courts. *See* courts: Jewish
Jewish factions. *See* kabbalism; *Dor De'ah*
Jewish intermediaries, 156. *See* intermediaries, Jewish
Jewish jobs. *See* trades, Jewish
Jewish roots, of prominent Muslims, 66–67
Jews: patronage of, 77, 78, 125–126, 128; stereotypes, 56, 104
jinn, 82, 105. *See also* magic
Jirāfī, Aḥmad al-, 36, 135, 149
jizya. *See* poll tax *(jizya)*
Joint Distribution Committee, 85
Judaism, Muslim familiarity with, 79, 81
Judeo-Arabic, 25, 78, 95
judges. *See* qadis
judicial documentation and prolongation, 30–32
judicial oath ceremonies, 25–26
judicial outcomes, nonlegal factors, 154–155
judicial philosophies, 154
judicial posts, 30, 35. *See also* qadis
judicial process, 28–29
judiciary: divisions, 154; Jewish folktales, 35–36
Juzaylān, 'Abdallāh al-, 119

kabbalism, 83–85, 91–92, 98, 148; kabbalah trial, 84–95, 175n159, 186n75
kadijustiz, 16
kashrut, 10, 52, 71, 72–74, 77
Katībat al-ḥikmah min sīrat imam al-ummah, 35
Kawākibī, 'Abd al-Raḥmān al-, 3
Khamrī, Shim'on al-, 107
Khārijites/Khawārij, 159n48
"Kisār Storehouse" murders, 148–150
Klein-Francke, Aviva, 99
Klorman, Bat-Zion Eraqi, 94, 99–100, 113
Kühn, Thomas, 17

laḥūḥ (type of bread), 72
land disputes, 9, 18, 21, 114, 118
land sales, 22, 113, 114, 115, 118–120
lashes, 66, 139, 141
latrine-connected work, 98, 144. *See also* dung collection
Latrines Decree, 40, 42, 44, 45–46, 62
law: Ottoman, 16, 17, 18, 24, 115, 117; Yemeni, 18. *See also* Ottoman empire, Ottoman rule
lawyers, sharī'a, 21, 68, 137, 145, 186n75
Leder, Stefan, 12
legal orthodoxy, 48
legal realism, 36, 154, 155
legal systems, 24–25, 120
legal theory, 45, 47, 154
levirate marriage, 24
liquor. *See* alcohol; bootlegging
literacy, 64, 65
locusts, 52
looting, 114, 115, 129–130, 132, 148, 184n1, 185n30
Lot (Biblical figure), 65, 67
luxury goods, 6, 100–101, 103. *See also* perfume

Ma'abar, 49, 58
Madhalah, Avraham, 64, 134
Maghen, Ze'ev, 2
magic, 68, 80, 84, 104, 105
Maḥalwī, Muḥammad b. 'Abdallāh al-, 77, 94
Maḥwīt, 27, 109
Maimonides, Moses, 68, 81, 94, 156
Manākhah (town), 40, 41
Manṣūrah, Rabbi Sālim, 2, 6–7, 11–12, 41; emigration, 111, 115; Husseini meeting, 133; personality, 151–152
Manṣūrah, Ya'īsh, 6, 106
Maqbalī, Ḥusayn Muḥammad al-, 74, 135
maṣlaḥah, 44, 48
meat, 9–10, 71–74, 85, 97
Medinah, Shalom, 25
memoirs, 5, 11, 12–13, 16–17, 43, 81–82, 113
merchants, 41, 100–101, 102–103, 132, 155, 165n122; attacks, 124, 125; Muslim, 19, 87, 101–102
"Messiah, the," 80–81
military supplying, 99, 178n40
minting, 98–99, 165n122
Mishneh Torah. *See* Maimonides, Moses
monopolies, 101, 106, 107
Montequin, Francois-Auguste de, 120
Msaodi, Abdualaziz, 4, 101
Mu'ayyad, Imām Yaḥyā b. Ḥamza al-, 121
muḥallil, 23
muḥtasib, 53, 55, 60, 66
murder, 96–97, 124, 126, 129–130, 184n5, 184n18; accusations, 146–150; damages, 4, 126
Murtaḍā, Imām al-, 29, 121
Muṭahhar, Qadi 'Abd al-Karīm, 34–35, 134
Muṭahhar, Qadi Muḥammad b. 'Abdallāh, 58

Naddāf, Sa'īd al-, 93, 176n195
Naḥshon, Yeḥi'el, 162n45
Naḥum, Rabbi Ḥayyim, 40
nationalization, 101, 113–118, 120, 122

neighbor's rights, 117–122, 152
newspapers, Hebrew, 134
Nietzsche, Friedrich, 143
Nirenberg, David, 129, 135
Noaḥide laws, 53, 156
Nu'mān, Aḥmad Muḥammad, 19
Nu'mān, Muḥammad Aḥmad, 131
Nu'mān clan, 5, 128, 129

oath taking (Jews), 25, 26, 168n58
O'Barr, William M., 63
observance, Jewish, 77
1001 Nights, The, 69
orphans, 18, 43, 47, 66, 82, 143, 148
Orphans Decree, 43, 153
Ottoman empire: abutters' rights (*shuf'ah*), 117, 121; continuation of practices, 19, 161n25; courts, 24–25; and Jews, 17, 40, 99, 104–105; legal reforms, 17; rule, 2, 17, 19, 40, 69–70, 99, 100, 105. *See also* law: Ottoman

Palestine, 132, 133, 134, 135, 187n109. *See also* Israel
Palestinians (Arabs), 13, 80, 113, 122, 123, 133, 134, 185n50
Parfitt, Tudor, 12, 132, 168n65
perfume, 78, 100, 137
phylacteries, 78
poetry, 68, 69, 84
pogroms, 130
"politics of injury," 143
poll tax *(jizya),* 19, 39, 44, 46, 101, 107
polytheism charge, 86, 89, 92–94
prayer rites, 90, 91–92, 176n178
prayer shawls, 21, 78, 84
predictive theory, 155
preemption. *See* abutters' rights (*shuf'ah*)
prison, 26–28, 68–69, 74, 99, 125, 134
prisoner release, 149–150
profanity, Jews' use, 55, 64
prohibitions, Jewish, 38, 44
prolongation, 30–32
property law: Ḥanafī (Sunni), 18, 115, 117, 121; Ottoman, 18
property nationalization order, 114–117, 122
prostitution, 4, 105
protection (patronage) hierarchies, 125, 144

Qādir, Ḥusayn b. 'Abd al-, 60
qadis, 16, 19, 29–30, 32–33, 36, 127. *See also* sharī'a court system; bribery
Qafarah, Pinḥas, 96
Qāfiḥ, Rabbi Yaḥyā al-, 68, 84–86, 88, 89, 176n177
Qāfiḥ, Yosef, 21, 29
Qāsim, Prince al- (Imām Yaḥyā's son), 103, 116
qāt, 6, 26, 28, 50, 68, 71, 97, 106, 148; sales, 127
Qattān, Ṣalība villa, 122–123
Qoraḥ, Rabbi 'Amram, 40, 49, 167n39, 168n65
Qoraḥ, Shalom, 78
Qur'an, 17, 42, 44, 65–68, 91, 94

rabbinical courts. *See* courts: Jewish
rabbis, 9–10, 21, 112, 162n45. *See also individual names*
Radā' (city), 6, 25, 38, 68, 69, 81; flour grinding, 41; prison, 68; Imām Yaḥyā visit, 82–83; qadi bribe request, 32; violence, 135–146; Ẓāhirī flag, 6, 83; Ẓāhirī, Rabbi Ṣāliḥ al-, 159n48
Rathjens, Karl, 4, 158n24
Raydah (town), 109
Rāziḥī, 'Abd al-Karīm al-, 109
real estate, 115–116, 118–120. *See also* property law
realism, legal, 36, 154, 155
Record of Wisdom Concerning the Life of the Imām of the Muslims, The, 35
reform, 94, 154
rescission rights, 119–120
retribution, 125–126
Riḍā, Muḥammad Rashīd, 3
Riḍā, Yosef, 80
riding, 44, 48–49, 52, 124. *See also* donkeys; bicycle riding
Rihani, Ameen, 74
riots, 129–130, 132, 133
riyāl, 33, 98–99, 165n122
robberies, violent, 128–129, 139, 142
Roiling Sea, 38
Rosen, Lawrence, 5, 9, 15
rulings on Jewish affairs, Muslim, 81

Sabbath, 27, 78, 79, 81
Saḥūlī, Qadi, 41, 43, 44, 167n41
Ṣā'idī, Muḥammad Qā'id, 130–131
Salafism, 48, 154–155
Ṣāliḥiyyah, Muḥammad b. 'Īsā al-, 35, 170n129
Sanaa, 20–22, 25–26, 98, 119, 131; Aḥmad constituent property dealings, 115–116; alcohol, 57, 105, 106; "blood libel," 1948, 146; courtyard of justice, 16; dung collecting, 44; emigration, 67, 114; Ḥibshūsh family, 101–102, 122; Imām Yaḥyā, 17, 118; intercommunal tensions, 187n92; internal travel, 5–6, 49,

52, 53–54, 58, 59–61; Jewish Quarter, 18, 19, 38, 103, 106–107, 114, 146–147, 179n74; "Kisār Storehouse" murders, 14; modern school, 65, 86, 87, 89; 1948 riots, 129–130; preparatory and professional school, 100; property issues, 113–115, 182n155; women, 137–138, 145
Ṣanā'i prison, 20, 28
Ṣārūm, Riḍā al-, 87, 93
sayyids, 8, 19, 20, 90, 100, 105; dung collectors, 40; emigré property, 122–123; fights with Jews, 65, 69–70, 151; poor, 130–131; rebellious, 34–35; respect demands, 131; riding issues, 49–53, 58
schools, 86, 87, 100. *See also* Sanaa: modern school
Se'adya Gaon, 65, 68, 78, 155
sectarianism, 83, 91, 92, 93
Serjeant, R. B., 85
servants, Jews as, 96–97
Shabazī, Rabbi Sālim al-, 90
Shāfi'īs, 79–80, 90, 91, 93, 101. *See also* Sunnis
Shahārī, Muḥammad 'Alī al-, 101
Shamāḥī, 'Abdallāh b. 'Abd al-Wahhāb al-, 32, 130, 153
Shāmī, Aḥmad al-, 68
shape-shifting. *See* trickery, Jewish
Shar'abi, Re'uven, 110–111
sharī'a court system, 2, 5, 9, 18, 145, 154; coercive tactics, 26–27; Ḥibshūsh, Yeḥi'el conclusions, 16; Imām Yaḥyā overhaul, 16–17; Jewish use, 2, 21–22, 24, 162n45; market courts and swindling, 110; non-Muslim cases, 3; operations and boundaries, 145–146; outcomes, 155; structure, 20–21; tribesmen status, 20
sharī'a law and "lawyers," 2, 5, 13–15
Sharḥ al-azhār. See *Commentary [on the Book of] Flowers*
Shawkānī, Muḥammad b. 'Alī al-, 47, 48, 91; abutters' rights (*shuf'ah*), 118, 121; intellectual legacy, 48, 81, 167n31; Latrines Decree, 42–43, 44
shaykhs. *See* tribesmen
Shibḥ, Hārūn, 100
Shiblak, Abbas, 113
shuf'ah, 117–122, 152
Shulkhan arukh, 78, 84
sidelocks, 38, 52, 67, 88, 125, 140, 148
silversmithing, 98–99
Six-Day War (1967), 135
social hierarchy, 8–9, 143
soup. *See* meat
status hierarchies, 20, 96–97, 111
status shifts, Jewish, 150
Ṣubayrī, Dāwud, 11
Ṣubayrī brothers, 103–104
sumptuary laws, 19, 62, 63
Ṣumṣām Tawfīq b. 'Abdallāh, 8
Sunaydār family, 101
Sunnis, 56, 89, 90–91, 94, 121; Sunni opposition, 94. *See also* Hanafīs; Shāfi'īs
superstitions, Muslim, 10, 80
synagogue property, 81

ṭāghūt, 4–5, 126
Ta'izz, 48, 52, 78, 80, 111, 128, 129
Tāj al-mudhhab li-aḥkām al-madhhab, 90, 121
Tallit, 21, 78, 84
Talmud, 78, 107, 117
tanfīdh, 28
taqlīd, 48
tarbushes, 69–70, 88
taṭwīl, 30–32
taxation, 19, 101, 119. *See also* poll tax (*jizya*)
Ṭayri, Nissim, 94–95, 104
tefillin, 78
testimony: vs. documentary evidence, 113–114; false, 34, 55, 140, 147; against Jews, 140–141; by Jews, 24, 26, 40, 113–114, 143–144; by Sunnis, 91; women's, 137. *See also* witnesses
Thawr, Qadi Muḥammad al-, 49–51
theft, 63, 98–99, 109–110, 111, 112, 184n1. *See also* robberies, violent
Tobi, Yosef, 101, 176n177
trade, foreign, 99–100
trade school, 100
trades, Jewish, 33, 39–40, 48–49, 55, 71, 96–98, 177n1
transvestitism, 79
travel, 33, 182n151, 186n81, 186n86
tribal lands, 18, 119–120
tribal law and practice, 4–5, 71–74, 126
tribesmen: as clients, 32; and Jewish observance, 79; under Ottoman regime, 70; protection of Jews, 14, 108, 125–126; robberies, 124, 125, 128; Sanaa looting, 114, 130; in sharī'a courts, 20; status, 20, 77, 143; vendettas and feuds, 71, 124, 128, 142; as witnesses, 24
trickery, Jewish, 10, 79, 95, 111, 151
"trouble cases," 17, 154
Tsadoq, Gil'ad, 12

Tsadoq, Moshe, 102–103
Tsemaḥ, Yom Ṭov, 100
Tsubayri, Yitshaq, 171n18

ulama, 2, 4, 32–33, 126, 153–154; query to the, 117–118, 120
ʻUmar, Pact of, 17–18, 70, 116
uṣūl al-fiqh, 45, 47, 154
ʻUzayri, Shalom, 105

vendettas, 124, 128
violence, 111, 127, 130, 145; compensation, 127–128, 129; court choice, 126; intercommunal, 53, 124, 131–132, 135–146, 145; Jewish, 52, 126–127, 146, 147, 151; Jewish quarter, 138; and shame, 139, 143; taboos, 125, 126, 128. *See also* riots
vom Bruck, Gabriele, 58, 90

waqf land, 18, 114, 118, 120, 179n65
Wazīr, ʻAbdallāh al-, 32, 50, 108, 128, 164n102
Wazīr, Aḥmad b. Muḥammad al-, 80
Wazīr, ʻAlī al-, 129, 174n118
Wazīr, Muḥammad b. ʻAlī al-, 34–35
Wazīr clan, 153
weapons, 48, 49, 104, 108, 125, 127; Jewish ownership, 41, 125, 129; Turkish, 129
Weber, Max, 16
Weir, Shelagh, 28
wine, 27, 34, 105–107, 152; intoxication charge, 55–57; rape charge, 109. *See also* alcohol; bootlegging
witnesses, 24, 56, 140–141, 144–145, 148; pro-Muslim bias, 24, 126, 129. *See also* testimony
women, 87, 103–104, 125; Ghazāl al-Tayyis, 9; Jewish, 22, 40, 87, 97, 115; modesty, 8, 87, 97, 108, 159n39; Muslim, 8, 81, 104, 105, 148; Shimʻon Cohen case, 137–144; social hierarchy, 8; testimony, 137; tribal law and practice, 4; violence by, 143
work, 97–98
World Jewish Congress, 150
World War II, 7
wound assessment, 137, 138, 142, 184n21

Yaḥyā, Imām, 2–3, 6, 7, 10, 17–20; alcohol crackdowns, 106; assassination and effects, 11, 113–114, 128, 129, 154, 185n30; bicycle riding, 59; bribery appeals, 33; "Christian" rhetoric, 88; and compromised qadis, 36; court reform, 16–20, 17, 30; family drinking, 108; Ḥammām Damt stay, 82; individual belief, 90; Jewish emigration, 134; Jewish judicial procedures, 25; Jewish studies, 78; and Jews, 18–19; kabbalism, 86, 87, 89, 93–94; opposition, 32–33, 59, 60, 153–154; Ottoman practices, 19; Palestine telegram (1938), 133; Sanaa riots, 129–130; *sayyid* class, 20; sectarian policy, 90–91; Shawkānī interest, 48; travel permission, 33; Wazīr criticism, 35
Yarīm, 9, 25, 58
Yavnieli, Shmuel, 98
Yemen, geography, 2
Yeshayahu, Yisrael, 109, 132
Yitshari, Mordecai. *See* Ẓāhirī, Mordecai al-
Yitshari, Tsadoq. *See* Ẓāhirī, Rabbi Ṣāliḥ al-

Zabārah, Muḥammad, 132, 149
Ẓāhirī, Mordecai al-, 10–11, 13, 82, 117, 125, 151; amulet request, 104; bicycle riding, 58; bootlegging, 108; Hebrew newspapers, 134, 186n61; "Kisār Storehouse" murders and mob, 148; "the Messiah" 80–81; Muslim pogroms, 130; prison learning, 69
Ẓāhirī, Rabbi Ṣāliḥ al-, 2, 6–7, 10–12, 68, 151; amulets, 104; Arabic, 25, 69; *ʻaraq,* 107; blasphemy defense, 65–66; disguise, 11; donkeys (al-Thawr), 50–51; factionalism, 84; family circumstances, 144; fatwas, 11, 25; flour grinding, 41; as fugitive, 51; Hebrew newspapers, 134; imprisonment and observance, 27–28; Jewish flag, 6, 83; "Kisār Storehouse" prisoners, 150; legal education, 69; Muslim judges, 30, 32, 50; oath taking, 26; opposition movement connections, 159n48; photo of, 136; property nationalization, 117; Radāʻ violence, 135–146; *sayyid* beating, 68–69; sharīʻa, view of, 11; *Stormy Life,* 12; teaching of Muslim, 78
Ẓāhirī family, 100
zakāh, 119
Zandānī, ʻOvadiah, 128, 131
Zaydī courts, 40
Zaydism, 2, 3, 18, 89, 120; abutters' rights (shufʻah), 117–118, 120, 121; Dhubḥān modern school, 87–88; documentary evidence, 18, 113–114; dung collection and orphan surrender, 47; Imām's role in, 3, 12; and Jamal, 120; and Jews, 49, 79–80, 94; judges, 155; land definition, 44; law manuals, 120, 121; pan-Islamic jurisprudence, 3; ritual impurity, 47, 51, 56, 168n58; Salafism, 154; Sanaa

Jewish Quarter renegotiation, 18; Sunnism, 89, 90–91; testimony and documentation, 113–114; women's testimony, 137
Zionism, 113, 132–135, 151
Zohar, 81, 86, 87, 89, 93, 176n195; fatwa, 87, 152; sectarian differences, 92; trial, 84–95. *See also* kabbalism
Zubayrī, Qadi Luṭf al-, 26, 36, 106; bicycle document, 59–60; corruption, 59–60; and Jamal, 60, 108; and punishment for alcohol, 106; oath ceremony, 25–26; qadi crimes, 36; Qur'anic idioms, 65; value to Imām Yaḥyā, 36; Ẓāhirī nationalization, 117
zunnār. *See* sidelocks

MARK S. WAGNER is Associate Professor of Arabic at Louisiana State University and author of *Like Joseph in Beauty: Yemeni Vernacular Poetry and Arab-Jewish Symbiosis.*

www.ingramcontent.com/pod-product-compliance
Lightning Source LLC
Chambersburg PA
CBHW071818230426
43670CB00013B/2497
9780253014870